Written by a woman who n
an impact on my life — t
z

MW00606065

Ask ME About
MARY KAY

The true story behind the bumper sticker
on the pink Cadillac

Jackie Brown

 Strategic Book Publishing

Strategic Book Publishing
An imprint of Strategic Book Group
P. O. Box 333
Durham, CT 06422
www.StrategicBookGroup.com

ISBN: 978-1-60860-183-7

Printed in the United States of America

Book Design: Judy Maenle

Dedication

*This book is dedicated to all the salespeople
who were there in the beginning of both companies
and helped build the solid foundations for the giant
corporations they became, and to all direct sales
companies that continue to offer a way
to make dreams come true.*

Acknowledgments

This book could never have been finished without the help of people mentioned on this page.

First, my appreciation goes to my wonderful family, especially Sharon and Shannon, who so graciously accepted my absence from so many events during the year it took to write this book. A special thanks to Steve Hamm for his valuable technical help and, to my son-in-law, Mike, for suggesting the title.

Special acknowledgement goes to the following people who provided important help without asking anything in return: Ramah High for proofreading and editing every chapter; D'Lesli Dave for her expert advice and guidance; Alice and Frances for taking me to the hospital in the middle of the night and caring for me and my dog until we were well; Arthur, who helped me rescue chapters when my computer crashed; Sue, for delivering wonderful food to my door when she knew I was skipping the holidays; Melba, Pat, and my neighbor Wanda, who filled in for whatever I asked them to do.

In addition, my appreciation to my line-dancing friends who provided constant encouragement as did my out-of-town friends who stayed in touch by phone and e-mail.

And last but not least, my publisher, who took a chance on a first-time author, and to all the departments involved in the publishing process, from the art department to the many editors who contributed their help to make the book better. My special appreciation goes to Lynn Eddy and Mark Bredt for going way beyond the call of duty to help with whatever I needed.

Finally, my eternal gratitude to God for allowing me to see a dream I've had for so long, come true. And, for showing me through this endeavor, that the real treasure in life is having friends like those mentioned here.

Table of Contents

Jackie Brown

Prologue

Isaac and Rebekah had twin boys, Esau and Jacob. As the firstborn, Esau was heir to the family fortune upon his father's death.

One day, after Esau came home from hunting all day, he was ravenously hungry. He found Jacob cooking stew, told him he was starving, and asked him for a bowl.

"Of course," Jacob replied, "provided you give me your birthright as the eldest son for it."

"What good is a birthright if a man is dying of starvation?" Esau replied lightheartedly.

"Then vow to God that it is mine."

Esau gave the "vow," and ate the food. Not believing he had really given anything away, he forgot about the incident and went on with his life. Years later, when the father, Isaac, was near death, he was tricked by Rebekah, who favored her youngest son over the oldest, into blessing Jacob instead of Esau. This was the second time Esau had been tricked, and he did not accept the betrayal without a fight. Although Jacob and Esau were eventually reconciled, this deception caused great conflict for years to come.

In spite of the deception, however, God blessed not only Esau, but Jacob too. Jacob and his descendants were given the Promised Land.

Paraphrased from the Living Bible Genesis 26 through 33

The following is another story of trickery, betrayal, and deceit. And as in the story of Jacob and Esau, these same elements are the basis of a battle between two women who were once close, and of the turmoil and tragedy that spread from the conflict.

CHAPTER ONE

Pretty in Pink

As Marjie and I slipped into a pew in the church, the organist was playing, "What a Friend We Have in Jesus." Even though I usually loved everything about flowers, today the sweet, sickening scent of them grabbed me and forced me into full awareness of the sadness that permeated the entire place. The service was about to begin, and the family was seated in the front row. Friends and acquaintances filled the rest of the pews.

Late one night earlier that week, Jean Rochelle, mother of four daughters ages five through ten, had put a gun in her mouth and pulled the trigger. I had spoken to her the morning of that very day and knew that she was overwrought. I had tried to assure her everything would be all right, but even as I hung up the phone, I knew she did not believe me.

I glanced at Jean's little girls sitting side by side and heard their anguished sobs. Their hands were still tiny, and they shook as they wiped the tears streaming down their cheeks. I could barely control my own tears. Leaning over to Marjie, I choked, "In a million years I would never have believed that competition between two cosmetic companies could bring one woman to such a state. What did she ever do to deserve this? She was caught between two factions, and I don't think she knew what hit her."

Marjie nodded silently. Words were superfluous. As the pastor began his eulogy, my mind returned to an icy winter day three years earlier.

* * *

3

I sat behind my desk looking out the window from the top floor of the Southland Life building. From where I sat, I could see the blurred horizon where the colorless sky met the city's edge. Although everything was one color—gray—somehow the scene still lacked harmony. A freezing rain pelted the streets far below me. The few people that were willing to brave the harsh weather walked with their heads bowed against the wind. I glanced at the calendar on my desk: December 13, 1963. It could not have been a worse time to spend Christmas in Dallas. Since Kennedy's assassination weeks earlier, the grief that weighed the city down seemed intolerable. It had become a desolate place. Even the Salvation Army bells sounded hollow and sad, and the festive lights of Neiman Marcus failed to cheer up the scene.

Dallas seemed to mirror the mood of the entire country. The Camelot feeling that the Kennedy family had created was full of magic and glamour. Ordinary people like me missed it and longed for a way to bring it back into our lives. On the other hand, the assassination had also shocked us into realizing that you couldn't really count on anything. It could all change in a fraction of a second, so if you wanted to seize the brass ring and make something of your life, you had to do it now. This was especially true for all of us in the law firm; we had stood on the street below our office and waved and cheered as the president and first lady wove their way through town in the motorcade. And only minutes later, the president was shot.

I was mired down in my own morass. Since first coming to work at the law firm, I had come face-to-face with reality. This firm was considered among the best in town for paying their secretaries. Salaries ranged from $400 to $600 a month. No matter how hard I worked or how ambitious I was at this firm, that salary would never finance the future I had planned for myself. I had a consuming desire to overcome my past in rural Arkansas and make money, a lot of money. It was as simple as that. When I heard how much one of the top secretaries was earning after fifteen years, I said to myself, *That isn't enough. I've got to do better.*

Looking around the law office, I tried to cheer myself up by seeing it again as I had when I had walked in to apply for a job there a year earlier. The place was dark in an old money sort of way, with elegant cherry-wood furniture polished to a high gloss. Persian carpets covered the floors. When clients came in, a butler in a white coat served hot, fresh cinnamon buns from a silver tray. Even the clients, in their designer suits and hand-made shoes, added to the decor. The partners had achieved the success they wanted. I needed to do the same.

I pushed myself away from the desk and left for my lunch break. Somewhere in the break room I knew there was a copy of the Dallas Morning News. I had hoped to use my lunch hour to do some Christmas shopping, but the weather canceled that idea; instead, I decided to peruse the want ads. I did not know what credentials I might possess that would help me land an extra job to bring in more income, but perhaps something would catch my eye. Something did. At the top of the list, an ad read: "New cosmetic company is interviewing for consultants to sell cosmetics and wigs. Position offers opportunity to earn a wig by Fashion Tress by wearing one and showing it to friends."

It was like offering a minnow to a catfish. How could I not take the bait? I had wanted a wig for years, but they were entirely too expensive, especially Fashion Tress Wigs that regularly sold for $300, a small fortune in those days. Until this moment, I had considered a Fashion Tress wig about as out of reach as a diamond-studded tiara. I dialed the number in the ad. "Mary Kay Cosmetics," said a voice at the other end of the line. It was a softly feminine voice, and the words were perfectly enunciated without a trace of the usual Southern accent. I told the woman I was calling about the ad in the paper.

"I'm especially interested in earning a wig," I said, and then did not hesitate to add, "Can you tell me how I can do that?"

A soft laugh preceded her answer. "I can, but it's a little too involved to talk about it on the telephone. Would you be interested in a job where the only limit to the amount of money you earn is the one you place on yourself?"

My mother had raised a hard-working girl, so the answer was an unequivocal yes. "Who wouldn't be?" I laughed. My mother had also raised a scrupulously honest girl, so I continued, "But if you mean in sales as your ad implies, I'm afraid I have almost no experience in that area. I did sell Clover Leaf Salve when I was nine years old, if that counts."

She chuckled. "Experience isn't necessary. What is your name?"

"I'm sorry. My name is Jackie Brown."

"I'm Mary Kay."

Three words that would change my life.

At 4:30 that afternoon, as my friend Doris drove me to Mary Kay's office at Exchange Park, the rain had turned to light snow. My husband and I had only one car, and he usually drove it to work, so I asked Doris, who was a notoriously soft touch, to take me on this errand. Normally it was a fifteen-minute drive to the north of downtown, but today we were mired in traffic, making me concerned that my simple request to Doris would turn into an outright imposition.

"Look at this mess," Doris said. "How did you ever get Ned to agree to let you make this appointment on a day like this?"

"Easy," I said, "I didn't tell him. Listen, I really appreciate your doing this. I was afraid that if I didn't come today, all the positions might be filled."

"The reason I said yes is that I know it's the anniversary of your baby's death, and you're depressed. This is the first enthusiasm I've seen from you in a long time."

I smiled my appreciation. It was, indeed, the anniversary of my baby girl's death (who, upon advice from my doctor, had no name), and the anguish I felt was only just beginning to diminish. I watched Doris negotiate through traffic and I remained silent. She was a brunette with large brown eyes and a ready smile. Such a good woman; such a big heart. Her husband was in the seminary, and they were struggling to survive on Doris's limited income, which made the fact that she took the time to drive me to this interview even more special. She would make a great minister's wife.

Exchange Park consisted mainly of the Exchange Bank on the first floor, plus several other small businesses. The aroma of coffee and freshly baked bread emanating from the restaurant reminded my stomach that I had skipped lunch to read the want ads. I hoped the interview would not keep me long from my dinner. To prevent Mary Kay from prolonging the meeting, I would tell her I had a friend waiting for me.

Suddenly, I found myself standing in front of the display window of a company that obviously sold cosmetics. Everything was pink. Filmy pink curtains were drawn back with a shiny pink silk chord. A flower arrangement in twelve shades of pink stood in the middle of the display. Below it, the products were showcased: white jars with pink labels, bottles of cool green liquid, an open black compact revealing five fashionable shades of lip color on one side and five shades of eye shadow on the other. The colors intoxicated me. Then my eye caught sight of wigs, two of them, off to the side. The sound of footsteps caused me to turn around. Standing in the doorway was a woman who had what today we would call "big hair." She was dressed in a dark blue suit that was proper, but cut low enough to reveal a chest of smooth white skin.

"Jackie?" she asked.

"Yes."

"I'm Mary Kay," she said as she walked toward me, her hand outstretched.

I shook it and told her how much I admired her window display.

"You're a tiny little thing," she said by way of an answer. "I was larger than that when I was born. Come in and let's get started. You said you didn't have a car. How did you get here?"

"I got a friend to drive me."

"You mean you talked a friend into driving you here on a snowy day like this? And you said you had no sales experience."

As I followed her into her office, she reminded me of Ann Southern, a busty blond with star quality and confidence to spare. Even though she was a little on the plump side, I could tell she had worked hard to minimize the extra weight and project the best appearance possible. Although she told me on the phone that she had a grown son who worked with her, her pale skin was virtually flawless, barely a line or wrinkle in sight. Her make-up–pink rouge and matching lipstick, luxurious black eyelashes, and a thin line of blue shadow to accentuate them—made her look glamorous. Those lashes, I wondered, could they be? Yes, they were false. But they had been glued on so perfectly that I could not find the beginning or end of the false lash. Her hair was perfect too. Was that a wig? It was, I decided. This woman was exciting. She was glossy. She radiated money and abundance. She was exactly what I wanted to be.

The entrance to the office was a small reception area that displayed the cosmetics. The desk was, of course, vacant at that time of day. Her entire company took up only 500 square feet, and the personnel consisted of her, her son Richard, and a secretary, Barbara Acker. While the quarters were small, they were decorated in glitzy high style, a sharp contrast to the sedate look of old money in the law offices I was used to. With a rush of adrenaline, I forgot all about Doris who was wandering the hallways waiting for me.

In comparison with the reception area, Mary Kay's office was ordinary, just the usual fare of desk, phone, and file cabinets. The exceptions were the Styrofoam heads propping up wigs in various and sundry colors. After we settled at her desk, she began. "Women want to earn what they are worth, and in most professions, they aren't allowed to do that."

I hated to interrupt but I couldn't help asking a question. "Just how much can you earn at a job like this?"

She looked at me for a moment and answered, "As sales manager in my previous job I earned $25,000 a year." I gasped at the astronomical sum. "But wait," she continued. "A man in that position would be paid twice that." My head was spinning. I had never allowed myself to even dream of making that kind of money. Where I came from it wasn't possible. Yet it was her next statement that pushed the magic button somewhere deep inside of me. "I am an ambitious woman, but as a Christian my priorities are God first, family second, and work third." I sat speechless for what seemed like an eternity. She had expressed my sentiments exactly. While I had a burning desire to make money, I did not want to desert my faith or my family.

As Mary Kay went on to tell me about the company—how they marketed their products through the "party plan," and what the prospects were for the future—I could not take my eyes off the woman. I had the profound feeling that this moment had been predestined. As the feeling intensified I had a mental picture of a door I had never before had access to being unlocked. That door led to a better life. Here was a person I could pattern myself after, someone who could help me accomplish what I wanted in life.

She began going into detail about what the term 'party plan' really meant. I had heard of the term because of the popularity, at the time, of Stanley Home Products and World Gift parties. Stanley manufactured brooms and household cleaners. They also sold mops and a variety of other products. World Gift sold gift items that had been gathered from around the world. Everyone I knew had been to a sales party given by a friend. I had not attended one myself because I was usually too busy at night taking college classes. My need to better myself knew no bounds.

"We call our presentations 'beauty shows,'" she said. "We don't want the guests to think it's all fun and games . . . although it is fun, of course."

How could it not be fun? I was thinking. Helping women put on wigs and make-up seemed like a dream job to me. I put my face on before going to work in the morning and it was the best part of my day.

Finally Mary Kay said, "You really need to try the products."

I hesitated a moment, thinking of Doris, but the moment passed. I was too excited to pass this up. As she proceeded to take the products out of a demonstration case, she told me the story behind the company: "I was giving a Stanley party one evening, and a woman showed up and began handing out samples of her own products to the guests. It was small time, just jars of cream which her father, a hide tanner in Mena, Arkansas, had developed."

9

"Excuse me, "I interjected, "did you say a hide tanner?"

"Yes," she answered and continued. "As he turned those stiff, ugly hides into soft pieces of leather for gloves he began to wonder if he could do something similar with the human skin. His family laughed at his idea so he began experimenting on himself, using a modified form of the process. At each step of the softening process, a new product emerged. He soon noticed that his hands and face looked younger. When he died at seventy he looked like a man of fifty."

Mary Kay paused for breath and I jumped in. "Is this story true?" I asked, hoping it was.

"Absolutely," she answered. I had sat spellbound as she related the story and I sensed that others would also. "Upon his death," she continued, "his daughter put the formulas into cosmetic form and began marketing the skin care line."

I interrupted again. "What was her name and what was the name of her company?" I had lived a short time in Mena and thought I might know of the family. Mary Kay seemed reluctant to give me names, but finally said her name was Ova Spoonemoore and she was the one handing out samples at her Stanley party. "And the name of her company?" I prodded, my legal background kicking in.

"Beauticontrol," she answered. As she went on to tell it, far from being offended that someone was handing out other products at her party, she wanted to try them herself. The results she personally received from them were so startling that they made her want to buy the formulas and go into business for herself with her own line of cosmetics. Although the realization of her dream was not to come about until after her tenure with World Gift, finally Mary Kay Cosmetics had become a reality.

When the story finished, my facial began. As I worked the cleansing cream into my face, it liquefied immediately. There was a tingling sensation and a slight scent of menthol. After removing it with a warm washcloth, my skin felt smooth and immaculately clean. The next product was called Magic Masque, an oatmeal-based powder that was mixed with water and applied all over the face, leaving holes only for the eyes. While it dried, she explained more about how a show worked. The consultant (salesperson) went to a person's (referred to as the hostess) home, where six other women were present to receive the facial I was just then undergoing. For her trouble, the hostess received merchandise credit, which came to 20 percent of the sales of the show, provided that two women who were attending the show scheduled shows of their own.

"You see," Mary Kay said, "that is how you build. From one show, you book two more, and from those two you book four, and on down the line."

"Where do the wigs come in?" I asked, interrupting again.

"They come in after the cosmetics. Actually, we expect a lot of people will use their merchandise credit to help them buy a wig."

The names of people I knew rang in my mind like a bell in a cash register because I realized they would all want to have a show. The masque came off my face, and I felt the improvement in the texture of my skin right away. Then I applied the cool green skin freshener to tighten the pores. To heighten my interest, Mary Kay had me touch my tongue with a drop of it. The sensation reminded me of eating green persimmons when I was a child. Every time she explained what was in the products and why they benefited the skin, it made sense to me. These were products I could believe in, and if I could believe in them, I knew I could sell them. Finally, she handed me the Super Night Cream, which again had an instant softening effect. I picked up the jar and sniffed the contents. The fragrance was softly feminine and slightly sensuous.

After the skin care regimen was over, Mary Kay guided me through the make-up routine. There was an emollient cream foundation, eye shadow, lip color, eyebrow pencils, and mascara. With every product, I looked closely at Mary Kay's face and chose the one she seemed to be wearing. I am not sure how conscious I was of this at the time, but looking back, I see that I wanted to be just like her. I even chose a foundation that matched Mary Kay's fair skin perfectly, but it was far too light for my own. I didn't care. I saw what it did for her and felt it would make me look just as glamorous. The only product I had trouble with was the eyebrow pencil. With its soft lead, I had to brush repeatedly to get my brows to look natural. This was slightly disconcerting because I considered myself to be an eyebrow expert. Since my own brows were pencil thin, I had spent hours in front of the mirror learning how to give myself "Ava Gardner brows." I was to learn, as I advanced in my new career, that knowing how to do brows was an important ingredient for success in the cosmetics business.

When we were all finished, Mary Kay finally asked me the question I had been waiting for. "Would you like to try on a wig?" My own hair was dark brown, but I chose the blond wig, the one that was closest in color to what Mary Kay was wearing. When I looked in the mirror, I didn't recognize the person who was staring back at me. I didn't know her, but I liked the way she looked.

After explaining what I had to do to sign up as a consultant, Mary Kay leaned back and said, "What do you think?"

"Could we stop just a minute?" I said. "I need to call my husband." A frown flickered across her face but eventually she nodded at me to go ahead.

Ned. The idea that I had not told him I would be late, nor where I was going, had dogged me throughout the entire interview. I knew he would not want me to seek an extra job since it would take time away from the family. So, adhering to the principle that it is easier to ask for forgiveness than permission, I had decided to interview for the job and tell him about it afterwards. He answered the phone with a curt hello, and I immediately heard the anxiety in his voice. "Where are you?"

"Doris brought me out to a job interview. It's going to be a while yet, so you and Sharon go ahead and have dinner." I spoke quickly, hoping to head him off at the pass. To his sputtering questions, I answered with, "I'll explain it all when I get home." I knew there was going to be a scene.

As I returned to my interview, I tried to appear calm. "Let me see if I have this straight," I said. "All I have to do tonight is give you a check for twenty-five dollars for this demonstration kit. And the kit has everything in it that I need for a show, correct? And I can use those products myself?"

Again, Mary Kay nodded. She reminded me that the kit even contained mirrors to put out for each guest. Later, I would have to buy my own wig, but she would loan me one for the first show. Also, she pointed out, I would probably want to buy my products ahead of time for shows so I wouldn't waste extra time delivering them individually to the customers. Her final point was about appearance.

"We don't have a lot of rules, but we do require that all our salespeople wear a girdle, white gloves, and hose when representing the company."

I was used to that at the law firm, so it was no problem, but handing over a check for twenty-five dollars was. I decided it was time to go out and see where Doris was. I found her impatiently flipping through a magazine in the reception area. She had called her husband too, and I could tell by her somber look that he wasn't pleased. I asked her to wait one more minute and went over to the display window again. There they were: jars and creams and cakes of eye color and false eyelashes. I knew my friends and what they would like. They would all want to buy these. I handed Mary Kay a check and left.

On the drive home, I couldn't stop gushing about the colors and the texture of the products and about what a great opportunity it was to make a lot of money. Since I would double the price I paid for a product, I would make a gross profit of 50 percent on every single thing I sold. Of course, I didn't tell Doris how much profit I would make. Since I considered her my first customer, I explained, instead, how she could receive the products herself at a huge discount just by having a show at her house.

"Look at my face," I said to seal the deal. "Isn't it great?"

She hesitated, and then said delicately, "Actually, you look a little pale to me."

It didn't faze me. I was exhilarated. "Just feel my face. It's smoother than it's ever been. I cannot wait to use the rest of what's in this kit. And the story behind her business is so interesting."

Enthusiasm is, indeed, contagious, and by the time we reached my neighborhood in Mesquite, a suburb of Dallas, Doris agreed to host my first beauty show and invite the other secretaries from the firm. Since Christmas was only two weeks away and pre-Christmas was the best time of year for sales, we wasted no time and set up the show for the following Monday night.

I did not want Ned to open the door and make a scene before Doris had a chance to pull her car out of the driveway and turn around, so I had her drop me off a block away. All the way to the door, I rehearsed the case I was going to put before him and scolded myself for not getting a head start and doing it in the car. The front lights were all on. My feet crunched loudly on the icy grass, and I moved to the sidewalk hoping to soften the noise. My heart, which had been racing in anxiety, softened as I looked through the window into our warm and gracious living room. The Thomasville furniture—orange and turquoise tweed sofa, two matching Danish modern coffee tables, high-backed dining chairs with seats of black leather—were things we had sacrificed for. They were classic designs and would never go out of style. I still have some of them today. I looked at the vaulted ceilings, the cream-colored carpet, and the red brick wall with Ned's painting on it. We had bought this house of ours for $12,000; I loved every inch of it.

As I stood in front of the door, I thought, *I can't put it off any longer*. Holding the kit in one hand and my purse in the other, I rang the doorbell with my elbow.

The way the door jerked open instantly told me that Ned had been standing right behind it. Sharon stood next to him, and they both stared at me as if I were an escapee from the loony bin. I only applied to sell beauty products, I protested inwardly, not to be a Playboy Bunny. What is all the fuss?

"Where have you been?" Ned bellowed. "I was about to call the police."

"Sh-h-h. The whole neighborhood can hear you. I'll explain everything after I come inside and get warm."

As I passed him, I looked at his face. Those green eyes and chiseled features that all my friends thought made him so handsome now made him appear stern and unrelenting. Before he opened his mouth, I knew what his objections would be. He would not like it that I had accepted a position without first consulting him. He would not want me spending more time away from him and my daughter. He would not approve of me taking a job that operated on commission. Ned had always been a safe and cautious man; money made on commission was not as trustworthy as a regular paycheck.

Indeed, all that I thought he would say, he did say. His mouth was set in a thin, firm line, and his voice was chastising. As the minutes ticked by, I could feel all the enthusiasm that had built up over the past hour dissipating. I apologized for not telling him about the interview first, but covered myself by explaining that it had all happened too quickly. I then tried to convince him that this was the opportunity we had been praying for by assuring him that I was not about to up and quit my job at the law firm like an irresponsible teenager. I was just going to take on something extra that offered me the potential to make far more money than I ever could as a secretary. I tried showing him the products, which he fumbled with and then set down angrily.

Now I was mad. "Just give them back to me," I said, snatching a lip and eye palette from his hand. "This is why I didn't tell you where I was going. I didn't argue with you when you wouldn't let me go back to school after our baby died. You pointed out that Sharon was my daughter, and it was my responsibility to support her. My mother always told me I had to pull my own weight, so I agreed with you, and this extra job is part of my plan. I want her to have a better life than I ever did. I want her to go on to a college education: that takes money. I AM going to do this, Ned." In a fit of frustration, I put everything back in the kit and snapped the case shut. "Right now, I'm exhausted. There's no use saying anything more tonight."

Sharon stood watching the exchange with her large brown eyes opened wide. Like any nine-year-old, she hated to hear a cross word between her parents, let alone an outright confrontation. "It's okay," I whispered. "You get ready for bed. I'll come in and kiss you good night."

Sharon's real father had died when she was three years old. Since he had been away in the military and in college most of her young life, it had always been just the two of us anyway. Ned and I married when she was five, and the one thing I could never criticize about him was how good he was to my daughter. He was a wonderful dad. In the beginning, he struck up a relationship with her to get into my good graces. He wasn't my type, either physically or temperamentally, and when I kept refusing to go out with him, he won my heart through Sharon. Now we were a family, and for all intents and purposes, Ned was her father. The one thing he did that blurred the illusion of being the perfect dad was his constant reminder to me that I was the one financially responsible for her.

I slipped into Sharon's room after the lights went out. We were all proud of that room, of the white organdy curtains and matching bedspread and the pink pillows on the bed surrounded by stuffed animals. She had always been such a tidy child. The clothes she had been wearing minutes before were folded neatly on a chair. I moved them and sat down.

"Stay with me?" she murmured.

We had slept together most of her early life. That changed once Ned and I married, but the inclination still remained within her. "Of course," I whispered, climbing under the covers next to her. The snow had stopped, and the moonlight slipped through the blinds and rested on her golden blond hair. She said her prayers, which resembled more of a personal conversation with God than any formal recitation. They included blessings for everyone, including Sniffles the dog.

"I wouldn't let you go for a dollar," she said to me when she finished.

"And I wouldn't let you go for anything," I said back. She had been saying that to me since she had learned to enunciate her first sentences, although I never knew where the expression came from. If I couldn't convince Ned why it was important to make the sacrifice to take time away from the family, it was important that I convince her. I told her how excited I was and how much it could mean to all of us. If I were enough of a suc-

16

cess at it, I would be able to quit my nine-to-five job and drive her to school in the mornings as I had always wanted to.

"Wouldn't that be perfect?" I asked. But she was already sound asleep, and more beautiful even than when she was awake. People were always telling me how lovely she was, but I was careful to point out to her that "Pretty is as pretty does. It's your spirit and how you treat others that counts."

I considered sleeping with her all night—surely she was a better bedfellow tonight than my husband would be—but I did not want to set him off any further. Over on his side of the bed, Ned was apparently asleep. I wanted to make one last attempt to make him understand that I was doing this for us, not for me. Our family would always come first with me. As I had sat in Mary Kay's office that afternoon, I had the feeling that this was what I was destined to do. I wasn't sure he realized that or how much it meant to me to take success into my own hands. I lay awake for a while, then touched his foot with mine. It was cold, and there was no response. The moment to explain passed, and as I fell asleep, my thoughts drifted into the pink world of Mary Kay where money grew on trees.

CHAPTER TWO

Wigs and White Make-Up

The next morning dawned bright and cold. However, the chill in the air at breakfast wasn't caused by the weather. Ned made an effort to act normal, but I could still feel the frost from the night before. As usual, he scanned the newspaper while he sipped his coffee, but he wouldn't look me in the eye. Sharon filled the void with chatter about the Christmas program at school. She was playing the part of an angel, and I could tell by the look on her face that she considered it to be the star role.

"You and Daddy will be there?" she asked anxiously.

"Wild horses couldn't keep me away," I answered, hugging her close.

"Me either," Ned added, with genuine enthusiasm, and I breathed a little sigh of relief. Maybe we were going to recover the Christmas spirit after all. There was so much we needed to talk about, but I knew we couldn't get involved too deeply since we both had to leave for work.

"Ned," I began cautiously, "Doris is going to host my first show on Monday night. Mary Kay said that Christmas is the best time of year for sales and I'm hoping that I can make a little extra money to help with our gift buying."

He slowly turned to look directly at me and nodded. "I suppose you're telling me you'll need the car that day," he said matter-of-factly. I would have to take the car to the office because I worked downtown and would have to head straight to the Mary Kay show from there. Grateful for his calm acceptance, I nodded and hurried to tell him my plan before I lost my nerve.

"You'll need to get a ride to work that day, but I promise it won't become a habit. I'll limit the nights I work, and you'll know in advance when I'll be away in the evening. Ned, this extra job is to make our lives easier, not harder." Before he could answer, a horn blew loudly, signaling my ride was waiting. I threw them both a kiss, grabbed my coat and purse, and hurried out the door.

At the office, Doris was waiting for me. It was a little before 8:30, so we headed for the coffee room. "Jackie," she began, "I talked with my husband about this and I just might be interested in going into the business myself." She spoke in her usual low-key way and even though she wasn't oozing enthusiasm, I was surprised that she was so interested. Then I remembered Mary Kay's words, "Everybody's a prospect, even the ones you least expect." I couldn't help smiling at how smart my new mentor was; whatever I needed to know I could learn from her.

I told Doris we'd talk more about it once she saw how good the products were, certain that they would sell themselves. As the other secretaries filed into the room we explained that we were having a "beauty show" on Monday night at Doris's house; everyone in attendance would receive a free facial and each one would get to try on a fabulous Fashion Tress wig as well. There was a little gasp of excitement from the group as they waited to hear more. Everyone in the office wore make-up, and although wigs were expensive, almost all of them wanted to wear those as well. (I learned this from coffee room discussions.) They were the quick and easy way to have a good hair day, every day. Unfortunately, only six people, including Doris, could attend. Instantly, five people were on board. Seeing the disappointed looks on the other faces, I added quickly, "Some of you can be standbys; and we'll make sure all of you get to attend the next one.

"I'll bet you get the whole set free with your hostess credit," I whispered to Doris as we hurried to our desks. I was excited that not only were they were interested in attending, they could afford to buy. That night I memorized the thin manual Mary Kay had given me, which contained minimal information. As I used the products myself, I thought of her explanation about each one. I realized suddenly that I knew almost nothing about what

I was expected to do. It was like being thrown into the water and told to swim. I was beginning to feel a little desperate. There was no way I could convince the secretaries at my first show that I was an expert in the field of cosmetics, but at least I knew more about these new products than they did.

On Monday night, six expectant faces looked up at me from Doris's kitchen table. Because Doris's husband was in school, their budget was tight, so the apartment was small and void of frills. Since the entire group was from the law office, most of us were still wearing our office clothes. We were expected to "dress to the teeth" for our jobs (to impress the elite clientele), so no one looked particularly comfortable in this humble setting. And we all were part of the major fad of the early sixties—"big hair." It was quite a chore to rat the hair up high enough to achieve the fashionable look, which was one reason we were eager to wear wigs.

"Where is the wig?" someone demanded straight off, and suddenly everyone was talking at once about it. I knew I had to gather their attention but had no idea how to get it.

Taking a deep breath, I just jumped in. "Ladies," I said in what I hoped was an authoritative voice, "we have to be back at work early in the morning, and if we're going to make you all gorgeous, we'd better get started. We'll talk wigs after your facial." Laughing, they settled into the presentation, and I made a mental note: "When desperate, use humor."

I began with the origin of the products: the story of the hide tanner. They sat without moving, with the same transfixed look I'd had the first time I heard it. We all found it extraordinary that a man could take an old dead hide and turn it into something as soft and beautiful as an expensive glove. And that every step in the process turned into an individual cosmetic product that really worked—not just on an animal hide but on a woman's face. A thrill ran through me, and I knew beyond a doubt that it wasn't just I that felt the power in this story.

I moved as quickly as I could through the skin care, having them feel their faces after using each item just as Mary Kay had done with me. But it was still taking far too long. None of them used skin care regularly, which meant I had to show them how to apply each item. Plus, they couldn't stop talking and laughing and seemed totally unconcerned that hours were ticking by. Was I the only one who knew the alarm was going off tomorrow morning?

Finally, we were ready for the glamour products. Although there were several foundation colors, I chose the one that Mary Kay wore (almost white) for them all because that's what I'd done in my interview with her. They managed to apply this themselves, but needed help with eyebrows, eyeliner, and blush. I glanced at my watch. It was 10:30 p.m. I could visualize Ned tapping his foot.

"Okay, ladies," I said to the group when they were finally finished. I had a feeling they hadn't absorbed anything I said about applying make-up. I'd just have to worry about that later. They were staring at their reflections in the small mirrors in front of them. I had no idea how to close the show so I just blurted out: "I want you to tell the person next to you how you think she has improved." Again, this started a splatter of conversation and I wondered if I would get home by daylight. But it turned out to be worth it, because each woman related specific improvements to the one next to her, which prompted a flurry of writing on sales slips. I breathed a sigh of relief.

Mary Kay had told me to be quiet and still as customers made final decisions and wrote down their orders. The sale should have already been made, and if I started talking again, they might hesitate and do what is called in the business "make me buy it back." That advice alone turned out to be one of the greatest truths I ever learned about successful selling. Since then, I have watched others make the fatal mistake of talking too much and then "buying it back."

The show had not inspired confidence in me. Instead, I was overwhelmed with how much I didn't know, and I wondered if I was up for the task. Just as people were finishing their orders, one of them got up and went to the bathroom. When she returned she was wearing the platinum wig I thought I had discreetly concealed on a side table. Bedlam ensued because all the women wanted to try it on, and by the time I regained control of the group, it was midnight. I was exhausted, but still somewhat determined. All the way home, I thought about how chaotic the show had been. I remembered what Mary Kay had told me: "Every problem has a solution," and with a jolt of new determination, I decided to find the solution to holding their attention by "analyzing and improving." There was nowhere to go but up.

Ned was waiting up for me even though it was 1:00 a.m. Too tired to speak, I just looked at him. "Well?" he asked, raising his black eyebrows, almost defiantly. Then added, "How much did you sell?"

"About $70 in cosmetics. After I paid hostess credit, my profit is $28. I think that's pretty good for my first show," I said, hoping he would agree.

"So," he began, "you only made $28 for five hours of work?" I hesitated before answering, because I could tell he was spoiling for a fight, and I was too tired to go there.

"Ned," I answered calmly, "that's about what I earn at the law firm for a whole day, before deductions. And, they all say they are buying wigs, so I'll make even more, ultimately."

"How much are they?" he asked, in a slightly nicer tone.

"There are three prices: $100, $200, and $300. Even if all of them only buy the $100 wig, it will be a $600 sale, which is an additional $180 profit for me." (The actual total for wigs sold turned out to be about $1,200.) Ned did the math and his face softened. That was much more than he and I both made in a week. From this, I learned one of the most important things of all on how to get Ned's support. I just had to "show him the money."

In spite of the late hour, I decided to take a bath to relax. I toweled dry and on impulse rubbed the Mary Kay pink body lotion all over me. This was the only product that Ned liked. As I got into bed beside him and glanced in his direction, he opened his eyes, reached out, and pulled me close to him. "Smells sexy," he murmured drowsily.

A sense of relief washed over me. Suddenly I knew he was going to be all right with my new job. If he had not given in,

I would have given up, because for the first time in my life I finally had a "normal" family—a mother, a father, and a child at the dinner table. Just like Mary Kay, I believed in, "God first, family second, and job third." With Ned now on board, nothing could shake my enthusiasm.

I couldn't wait to get to the office the next morning and call Mary Kay about my first show. Richard answered the phone, and the energy in his voice heightened my excitement about my news. Before I could report, however, he said, "Did you give a recruiting talk?" The comment caught me off guard, and for a moment, I was speechless.

"Richard," I finally answered, "the show took five hours as it was, and if I'd said one more thing I would have had to spend the night." He laughed and told me to think about adding just a sentence about looking for people who wanted to get in on the ground floor of the new company. I added another mental note to do as he suggested.

When Mary Kay came to the phone, she praised me for the cosmetic sales, but not for the wigs. "Remember Jackie, people will probably only buy one wig. Your bread and butter will be your reorder business from the cosmetics. You can pat yourself on the back when a show is at least $100, you book two more, AND you get a new recruit. Just something for you to keep in mind."

I got the message. The wig craze might come and go, but cosmetic sales would be forever. I had already become dependent on her praise, and I hated to hear a touch of disappointment in her voice. However, I still didn't understand why that many wig sales didn't seem to count for anything.

It was just seven days until Christmas. Everyone had placed their orders and wanted their wig before then, and I worked frantically to get them all out to the office, either during the noon hour or after work. Between that and talking to everyone I knew to set up more shows, I was in a dazed state most of the time. I did manage to get out my sewing machine and make Sharon's angel costume. Luckily, the office was slow during the holidays. Mostly, my boss attended parties with clients, so I had more time than usual to use the phone for personal business.

I talked with Richard and Mary Kay almost daily and felt special to be able to call them. I wondered if the other nine people in the company did, too. Neither mother nor son ever mentioned anyone else. Richard had me so revved up over the marketing plan (even though I didn't yet really understand it) that I had begun to dream of an army of recruits out selling Mary Kay cosmetics. And, of course, I was making money off every sale. I hoped Richard wouldn't ask me about recruiting again until I had something to report, so I decided to get busy. I called a good friend who worked downstairs in my building and asked her to meet me for lunch in the building's coffee shop.

When I arrived, I was surprised to see her husband there. He had recently graduated dental school and worked nearby. I jumped in with both feet, telling them about the products, the marketing plan, and the fact that I was "in on the ground floor." I explained that by selling to six people at a time I could make far more than I did at the law firm. They listened politely without comment. Finally, I stopped talking and waited for their response. My friend said nothing but her husband made a remark that left me stunned. He said, "That's all well and good, but what are you going to do when you run out of friends?"

I had no reply. As soon as I got back to my office, I called Mary Kay because it bothered me that he had caught me off guard. She said calmly, "Why didn't you reply, 'I don't know; you started your practice with only friends. What did you do?'" I knew she was right, since I was one of his first patients. This incident was just the first of many signs that Mary Kay was much more than just a "pretty face." And, years later, this friend became a recruit.

The negative opinion expressed by my friend was just a part of a much larger reaction. This was a time when many people considered salesperson to be a derogatory term. It conjured up the image of someone trying to get his foot in the door while you were trying to keep him out. In analyzing this situation, I realized that my approach had to be just the opposite. I had to learn to talk about my products or business opportunity only when the person I was talking with was anxious to hear about them. I decided to tantalize them with an interesting story about my business and then wait for the questions.

One morning as I was trying to juggle all the things I had going, one of the secretaries who had not been involved in any of our discussions approached me. "Tell me about the wigs," she said. I went through my sales pitch about how great they were to have on "bad hair days." She stopped me short and said, "I want to go out to see them today." I know I looked shocked. Everyone knew this woman had several children to support on her own. How could she afford even the cheapest wig? She listened politely as I explained the finance plan, but then said, "I'm interested in one that I can sleep in."

Shocked again, I asked, "Why in the world would you want to sleep in it?"

"Because I entertain clients," she answered nonchalantly. I was so naïve that at first I didn't even know what she meant. We fitted her with the $300 hand-tied platinum wig, very much like Mary Kay's. Instead of the finance plan, she shelled out three $100 bills. (This sale was part of the $1200 total in wig sales.) Several years later I ran into this woman at Love Field airport. She was wearing a fur coat and a huge diamond ring on her left hand that looked to be over three carats. She introduced me to her husband, who was also decked out in a diamond tiepin, which was at least as large as hers. She had married one of the clients. I was glad she had bought into an easier lifestyle, and I hoped the wig had helped her close the sale.

As Christmas day drew closer, it became harder to get anyone to take time to have a beauty show. They all promised "after the New Year." Thinking I must be doing something wrong, in one of our daily chats, I voiced my concern to Mary Kay. She reassured me that I was doing great, pointing out the volume of sales I had already generated. But she was still concerned that I didn't yet have a recruit. Recruits were the stepping-stones of her business plan.

After talking with her, I couldn't decide if I felt better or worse. She had sandwiched the criticism for not recruiting in between praise for my sales. I was left with a distinct sense of dissatisfaction. I had to find a way to improve my sales skills and to recruit. If Mary Kay could do it, surely I could, too.

Even though Ned was now more supportive, two of my brothers were not. They were afraid I would quit my job as a secretary (which is exactly what I eventually did) and sell Mary Kay products full time. Since they used the same arguments Ned had used, I knew it had been discussed. Gordon, my older brother, was a surgeon, and Gene, the younger one was next to me in age and was in pharmacy school. They were my role models for success, so their concerns bothered me. As usual, I turned to Mary Kay with my problem. She wasn't nearly as impressed by my brothers' accomplishments as I was. "Just tell them that one day you will make far more money than they do," she said matter-of-factly. I laughed because I thought she must be joking, but it was a nice thought anyway. One year later, I showed them my monthly check and they became among my most staunch supporters.

I spent so much time in the car that I had a lot of time to analyze what I was doing wrong and how to improve. I started thinking how Mary Kay had recruited me. She had tapped into my interests. By getting me to tell her what I wanted most in life, I had revealed my suppressed ambition. Then she showed me that she was paving the way for me to achieve my goals.

But everyone isn't like me, I thought. How will I reach them? Then I realized that they didn't have to be like me. All I had to do was figure out what each person's true goal was and show her how to reach it. The only thing that mattered was that people got what they wanted. It occurred to me to compare people with cups. Some were giant mugs, like me; some were regular size, similar to coffee cups; and some were demitasse, just wanting a little something extra. The secret to being an expert salesperson was to offer each one a chance to fill her cup, whatever size or shape it was.

Finally, it was just three days until Christmas, and Mary Kay was going to have a Christmas party/sales meeting at her house. She lived in a duplex on Northwest Highway. I couldn't wait to see how it was decorated. Just as I anticipated, it had the same ambiance as the office. She used lavender tones with the pink, and the effect was total femininity. I couldn't imagine a man living here. I looked around for signs of her late husband, who had died a few months earlier. I had heard his name was George Hollenbeck, but that was all I knew about him. I became more curious about her personal life every day, but felt it would be rude to ask questions.

Everyone showed up looking her best so it was a fine look-ing group of people. And, of course, Mary Kay was the "star" of the show. As usual, her makeup and hair were flawless and she wore a cocktail type dress that was gray-blue in color. It seemed to shimmer as the light hit it and in fact gave a soft glow to her entire appearance.

Eight of the ten beauty consultants (active salespeople) in the company were present as well as Richard. He was tall and trim, with a pleasant face that made you want to smile at him. His whole manner exuded confidence, which was unusual for someone so young, just twenty-one. He was already married, but his wife wasn't present. Jan Jack was introduced as one of the very first recruits to sign up. She had dark hair and a pleasing smile. I liked her immediately and went to sit next to her. Then I met Dalene Brewer, who had worked in the vitamin business with the late Mr. Hollenbeck. She seemed close to my age and talked very little. All she really revealed was that her husband was a policeman.

I turned to Jan and asked, "Since Dalene was a friend of her husband, is she also a special friend of Mary Kay's?"

Jan hesitated, but finally replied, "I do think they talk almost every day." I thought it was a little unusual that I hadn't heard her name before but that was all. I had no clue of the major role she was to play in the company and in my life.

Computers at that time were like something from the future— totally new and foreign. Mary Kay was already planning on making them a part of the business and presented Richard as "a computer genius." Most of us had never seen one and were prop-erly impressed. This was how the company would keep up with the complex marketing program he was going to present.

For the sales meeting part of the program, Richard brought out a blackboard and drew a circle at the top. "Think of this circle as you," he began. Then he drew five circles underneath, connecting each one with a line to the top circle. "These are your recruits. And in addition to your own sales, you will make an extra 4 percent on everything they buy from the company. When you have to depend on your own efforts, you only have twenty-four hours a day, but when you recruit, you multiply yourself and that's the way you make big money. Then when you step up to management and become a director, after completing the qualifications, you can earn an additional 12 percent on the same people. It doesn't end there, but that's enough for you to absorb tonight."

My head was spinning. Now I knew why they kept emphasizing recruits; they were the key to making money, not just selling the cosmetics yourself. At this point, there were only ten consultants in the company, so the world seemed to hold endless possibility for the people in this room. Anyone in the country could be a recruit, and that was a whole lot of people. When Mary Kay got up to speak, there was total silence as we waited in anticipation.

"Well," she began, "I have a surprise for you. When we meet again the first week in January, the person with the highest sales in December will win an elegant prize. And, I do mean elegant."

My heart skipped a beat. The room began to buzz like a beehive that's just heard about a new patch of flowers. Everyone was talking and laughing excitedly. A prize? An elegant prize? This was the best Christmas ever. The party showed no signs of breaking up, but I had to glance at my watch because husbands hadn't been invited, and I had promised Ned that I'd try to be home by now.

Reluctantly, I retrieved my coat and purse and went to tell Mary Kay good-bye. As she walked me to the door, she surprised me by saying that I was definitely in the running for the "elegant prize." Really? But I had only been there a half a month, and I thought Mary Kay was a little disappointed in me.

This meant I must be doing far better than I expected. She added that Dalene and I were neck and neck. I hadn't realized she was my main competition. My heart fluttered with excitement to be in the running.

She continued, "I know you're going to Arkansas for Christmas; take your demo case along, and maybe you can make some sales and even get a recruit." I hadn't planned on working over the holiday, but I was flying so high I didn't care. But then she frowned, and I braced myself for what was coming. "By the way, why are you leaving the party so early?" For the very first time I saw tiny wrinkles form between her eyes. I could tell she wasn't pleased, but I wasn't worried. She had told me she had strong family priorities, so I didn't mind telling her my reason for leaving. "I promised Ned that I would be home by ten to spend some time with him, and I want to be there to kiss Sharon goodnight before she goes to sleep. You know I haven't been home much lately."

A cloud passed over her face, as she looked me squarely in the eye. She then spoke in the sternest voice that I had ever heard her use, "Doesn't your husband know yet that this is your business?"

CHAPTER THREE

Fanning Out

The parting look on Mary Kay's face and the tone in her voice disturbed me as I drove home. In the short time I'd been with her company, I had become more and more committed to it. However, my family was still near the top on my list of priorities, and I felt guilty that I'd broken my promise to limit the time I spent at my new job. In an effort to shake the conflicting feelings, I said out loud, "I'm just overreacting. She couldn't have meant it like it sounded. Besides, as soon as I get things moving, I can slow down, and then I'll make it up to Sharon and Ned." But even as I said the words, I could hear the faint ringing of a warning bell somewhere in the distance.

I decided to do only two more work-related things until after Christmas. I'd been thinking nonstop about how I could recruit on a big scale, as Mary Kay and Richard kept telling me I had to do. An idea then popped into my head that seemed plausible. I called people I knew in different areas around Dallas and invited them to my house on December 29, reassuring them that they would not be asked to buy anything. It was just to help me practice my presentation, and of course they would get a free facial and would also get to try on a Fashion Tress wig. I didn't think it important to mention that I also planned to give a recruiting talk. I decided not to tell Ned until the day before the show to avoid hearing the negatives from him; I wanted to keep my spirits high.

The second thing I decided to do was to call a friend in Arkansas, where we would be going Christmas afternoon. After explaining the whole concept, I asked if she could get a group of people together for a beauty show (no small task for the day after Christmas). She hesitated, but because she was a good friend, she finally agreed. I told her with as much enthusiasm as I could muster that I would be introducing a revolutionary new product and she would be the first in the state to get to try it. The only other time I devoted to business was "thinking time" about how to improve my sales and recruiting skills.

For the next two days, we concentrated on Christmas. Ned, Sharon and I loved everything about the holiday. We had gotten our tree up a few days earlier—a fresh cedar filled with turquoise and bright tangerine balls that complemented the décor of our living and dining room. Hundreds of tiny, twinkling clear lights were reflected in the balls, and the packages were wrapped in paper of the same color, each one tied with sparkling gold ribbon. It was magical. We drank our morning coffee there, and in the evening turned out all other lights while the three of us sat looking at the tree and listening to Christmas carols.

In spite of the exciting events of the last few weeks, a feeling of sadness returned and hovered over us. A few days later would be the first anniversary of our baby girl's death. The nursery had been maintained, and even though the door stayed closed, I knew every inch of the room. It was decorated in white with accents of blue and yellow. A picture of a small boy and girl on their knees praying hung over the crib. I had been able to shut out the constant ache during the past few days, but now it was back again. I knew Ned and Sharon felt the same way, but we seemed to have a silent agreement not to discuss it. I knew I would have to work especially hard to see that Sharon celebrated Christmas as usual. Her Christmas program at school had been a smashing success. She was the perfect angel in the flowing white robe, fluffy wings, and golden blonde hair.

Ned, the first one up on Christmas morning, made coffee and hot chocolate and lit the candles around the room. He sat down by the tree as I went to get Sharon from her room. Unlike other children that rushed in and started opening packages, Sharon always waited for me. As we reached the living room, she stopped and began twisting the ends of her hair. This was what she did when overcome by shyness.

"Sharon," Ned teased, "I know you want to read the Christmas story before we open gifts so you'd better get your Bible."

"Oh, Daddy," she said giggling, "you know that's not how we do it." She plopped down beside him and began handing out gifts, all signs of shyness gone.

In spite of the cloud of sadness, it was a warm, loving Christmas. Our respective families called throughout the morning, as was our tradition. Mine was scattered throughout Arkansas and Texas, whereas Ned's family lived in Florida. Although we both came from Christian backgrounds, we grew up under drastically different financial circumstances.

Ned's family consisted of his parents, his twin brother, Ted, and four other children. When the twins (who were the youngest) were born, his parents hired a full-time maid that stayed with them until the children were almost grown. During the depression years this placed them in the higher echelon. They attended church as a family, and all of them had a sweet Christian spirit.

In comparison, my father died when I was three days old, leaving my mother with ten children to support. She became a maid, a laundress, and anything else that would help her keep her brood together. It was her influence that caused me (as well as most of my brothers and sisters) to choose faith and ambition.

She didn't preach about faith, she lived it. Each night, after twelve hours of hard labor, she soaked her feet in a tub of hot, salty water and read the only book I ever saw her read, the Bible. During the day as she hung clothes out to dry in most kinds of weather, she sang in an off-key voice the hymn "When the Roll is Called Up Yonder, I'll be There." She did preach that hard work and education were the keys to a better life for us all, even though she had only completed the eighth grade herself. That's why she tried so hard to impart the desire for more to us.

By early afternoon, my family was on its four-hour drive to Arkansas. We spent holidays with different ones in our families. This year we would be staying with my first husband's parents, the C. D. Franks (Sharon's real grandparents). When Ned and I married, they simply included him as a member of their own family. We knew that all of his favorite foods would be waiting, and not only for him, but all of our favorites as well. That was what Mrs. Franks did to make us feel special.

The next day I held the beauty show with six friends from high school days. I knew they had gone through all of this for me, not out of any special interest in cosmetics. My presentation had become easier and faster (from thought and practice). After the story about the hide tanner, I said, "I wanted to do this today to primarily ask you to help me find people to sell these fabulous cosmetics and wigs in this area. They're going over like wildfire in Dallas and after your facial you'll see why."

The show went far more smoothly than before, except, when I tried to apply the almost white shade of make-up to a woman with a dark complexion, I learned a valuable lesson: Just because that shade worked for Mary Kay, it definitely did not work for everyone.

I stressed the importance of skin care (and for the first time, my customers bought skin care sets) over glamour make-up, and I was jubilant when sales totaled over $100. Again, I wondered if they were just trying to help me.

Before I had a chance to talk about recruiting, Sue Finley, a special friend from my high school class, brought it up. "How many hours a week do you have to work at this job?" she asked.

"That's up to you, since you're in business for yourself as an independent contractor." I knew she worked with her mother in a flower shop and was probably interested in something part time. Intuitively, I asked, "Do you want to earn extra money for something special?" Instantly, she replied.

"Yes, I do. I want a diamond ring for myself, and a pickup truck for Joe. How long would it take me to earn enough for that?" We figured she would need just a few hundred dollars, since she didn't want a big diamond or a new truck.

"I think if you hold two or three shows a week for a while, it won't take you long at all." Then I thought to myself, *She fits into the demitasse cup category.*

When she said she would do it, I almost fainted. My first recruit on top of a $100 show, mostly from skin care. It couldn't have gotten much better. The wig had been set in front of them the last part of the show, but surprisingly no one asked to try it on, although they had looked it over when they thought I wasn't watching. I wondered about the lack of interest until some time later I realized there was a simple explanation: The two groups had entirely different needs. The secretaries at the law firm had to present a professional look every day, while life in a small town was much more casual.

As I pulled out of the driveway I seriously considered calling Mary Kay long distance about my new recruit, but I decided not to bother her. In retrospect, I would say Sue was the easiest recruit I ever got, and maybe the most unusual because a few months later, she called me and said, "Well, I got my ring and Joe's truck, so I'm quitting." I never dreamed that she wouldn't want something else after she accomplished her first goal.

From that point on I made sure new recruits kept new goals in front of themselves. One unusual occurrence with Sue was that the skin care products she sold to a mutual friend of ours caused an allergic reaction because of the ammoniated mercury, an ingredient in the night cream. From then on I tested the product on the customers' arm before selling it to them. (Our friend still points out that she was the first to be allergic every chance she gets.)

Of course, I did call Mary Kay the minute I got home. The usual praise was magnified. She added that I could be headed for greatness in sales, instead of being stuck in a lowly secretarial job. When I returned to work on December 28, I was restless and couldn't concentrate on the legal document I was typing. But something else was bothering me, too. On an impulse I walked into Henry Baer's office. I had worked for him since joining the firm, and we were on a first name basis. "Henry," I began, "would it be okay if I take a longer lunch hour and stay late this evening?"

"Go ahead," he said, with a look of understanding. He knew it was the anniversary of my baby's death. I hadn't been to Restland Cemetery alone before; shivering from the cold wind,

I drew my coat tightly around me. It took me a while to find the Baby Land section, but when I did, a strange feeling came over me, and I looked down. There was the tiny grave with the smallest of headstones, etched with a rosebud on each corner. The engraving read simply, "Baby girl Brown. Birth and Death: December 28, 1962." I was unprepared for the raw grief that engulfed me. How could a baby that I had never been allowed to even hold have such an impact even today? When I'd heard of Jackie Kennedy losing a baby under similar circumstances, I had thought: *Too bad, but at least she hadn't become attached.* Now I knew, firsthand, that almost at conception, a baby claims part of the mother's heart and never lets go.

I looked around at the vast number of tiny graves in the area, and my tears were for them all. I knelt and kissed my baby's headstone and sat down beside it on the ground. As a Christian, I knew it wasn't my place to question God, but there was one thing I had to ask: "Lord, how can I accept the fact that my baby didn't even have a chance at this life?" Almost immediately an answer filled my head: "Because where she is now is a far better place."

Without warning, the wind stopped blowing, and I got up to leave. As I unlocked the car door I felt something I hadn't in a year: the constant despair was finally lifting. Suddenly, the sunshine felt warm and wonderful on my back. I decided to wait for the right moment to share the experience with Ned.

I knew I would never forget her, but a whole new year lay ahead. I felt that my work with Mary Kay played a part; it showed promise of better things to come. Mary Kay and Richard had recognized a spark of ambition in me and had stoked it into a small bonfire. I was filled with a need to get "the army of recruits" to capture the pot of gold at the end of the rainbow.

When I told Ned my plan to have people come to our house from all around Dallas, he surprised me with a question. "How did you get them to say they would come all the way out here in weather like this? We couldn't even get people out for our Christmas program at church which was in downtown Dallas." Good question. I felt as though cold water had just been thrown on my flame of hope, and I suddenly wondered if anyone would even show up.

I had invited friends from near and far. After taking down Christmas decorations, I cleaned the house from top to bottom, because most of the guests hadn't seen it. When I arrived home from work on the evening of the show, Ned had a nice fire going in the fireplace, coffee was brewing, and hot spiced tea was simmering on the stove. He was trying to be supportive, and I gave him a hug in appreciation.

To protect my Thomasville table, I had purchased pale pink plastic place mats for each guest and washcloths in a deeper pink. The hostess of a previous show had seemed a little embarrassed when she brought out mismatched ones for the guests, so I decided to invest in the Mary Kay colors. In the center of the table, on a beveled glass mirror tray, I arranged the complete set of Mary Kay Cosmetics. I finished the setting by putting the pencils with flowers on one end (that came in the demo kit) in a crystal bud vase in the center of the tray.

I assessed the room and was again filled with wonder at having our own home. Ned was going to stay in the den where he could hear what was going on without actually watching the women remove makeup.

At precisely 7:00 p.m., the doorbell rang, and the first arrivals rushed in, shivering from the cold.

"Come in before you freeze," I said as I hastily closed the door behind them.

Clara said, "Sure feels good in here," and Suzanne added, "Smells good, too," probably referring to the spiced tea. At least two people were excited, and I was instantly ashamed of how easily I'd been discouraged by Ned's weather comment. After other guests arrived, there were introductions and a little chit-chat. Finally, I asked if they would like to see the house before we got started, because one thing I could count on was that women always want to look around whatever house they were in. They paused to say hello to Ned and Sharon, complimented me on everything possible, and—thank goodness—ignored the closed door to the nursery. The show was ready to begin.

After the hide tanner's story, they began to chatter among themselves. Again, I remembered what Mary Kay had said, "Combat obstacles head on." I couldn't think of anything humorous to say so I had to try something new. First I made and held eye contact with each one as I slowly looked around the room. Then I said: "Ladies, I've told you that I'm not planning to sell you anything, and we are going to have fun, but if you listen very carefully, this could be the most important two hours you'll ever spend. You will learn what skin care works best for you and why it works. This knowledge will improve your complexion immediately, but will also ensure that your skin looks good ten years from now."

This caught their attention and they settled down. Again, I made eye contact with each one as we started the skin care program. "Now, pretend I'm your fairy godmother and can change your complexion in any way you want. What would that be?" Simultaneously, each one picked up a mirror and examined her face. "Clara, let's start with you." She was concerned about frown lines and crows-feet. The changes the rest of them wanted ran the gamut from less oily, less dry, less wrinkling, and fewer pimples to smoother texture and lighter freckles.

As they talked, I remembered the before-and-after pictures in the demonstration kit. Mary Kay had said Mrs. Spoonemore herself took the photos that showed visual evidence of vast improvement in almost every problem that had just been mentioned. At that moment I had an epiphany on how to close the sale when the time came.

Massaging the cleansing cream into her face, Suzanne asked, "What causes the tingle?"

"A touch of menthol," I answered, pleased that she'd noticed. As they removed it with warm, wet washcloths, contented sighs of relaxation filled the room. I knew they were thinking how good it would feel to remove makeup this way at the end of a weary day.

"How much does this stuff cost?" Mesquite cooed, caressing her face with her fingertips.

"You'll be surprised how reasonable it is. And of course, there's a way you can get it all free." They all began to ask how that was possible, and I promised to discuss it further at the end of their facial.

Moving to the next step, which was the masque, I showed them how to mix the oatmeal powder with water and apply it to their faces, and suggested they add a little fresh lemon juice to lighten freckles. The guest who had mentioned that problem quickly made a note on the sales slip in front of her.

I cautioned them to keep quiet while the masque was drying so it wouldn't crack and spoil the effect. It also kept them from talking. During this time I applied a small amount of the Super Night Cream to the inside of each lady's elbow to test for a reaction to the ammoniated mercury. The FDA required a special label on a product that contained this ingredient. Looking back, I realize this was probably the first exfoliating product to be marketed, and it produced remarkable results.

The five more minutes it took for the masque to dry gave me time for my recruiting talk. "I know some of you have jobs. I want you to be thinking about what you like about your job and what you dislike, if anything." I could tell from their laughter there would be plenty of that.

"Ask yourself whether it pays you what you feel you are worth. Are you your own boss? Do you get recognition for a job well done?" As the expressions on their faces changed, I realized they were checking off the list. "Finally, do you feel that you are making a difference for other people? In the short time I have been doing this, I've learned that when someone looks better, they feel better. As a result, their self-esteem improves and then all other areas of their lives are better as well."

"Okay," Suzanne mumbled through the masque, "go ahead and tell us more about this dream job of yours."

"We'll get into it more later, but there are a couple of things you can be thinking about. As you know, I've been with the company only since December 13. In that time I've earned a gross profit of a little more than $500." They gasped in disbelief. I'd earned that money in sixteen days. In the mid-1960s, the average weekly wage for all workers was under $100, and women's earnings were far less than men's.

"It's true," I added. "Mary Kay says that $1,000 a month is possible, even on a part-time basis. I'm keeping my full-time job until I'm certain, but by summer I hope to work full time at this." I went on to explain that because they were from different areas around Dallas they could be the first to introduce the products there.

Suzanne raised her hand and asked if she could ask a question. I nodded, and she said, "If you sell the products, can you buy wigs at a discount?"

"Absolutely," I replied, "and of course you buy cosmetics at a large discount, also." In spite of the oatmeal masque on their faces, I could see glimmers of excitement in their eyes. "When you're finished with the facial, you'll know that these products will sell."

After removing the masque and applying the skin freshener, the facial was done. They couldn't stop feeling their faces and looking at themselves in their mirrors. I smiled to myself and hoped Ned was listening to all of this. Mary Kay had said that selling skin care first was the best thing to do, and I was now convinced that she was right. Even though I didn't expect to sell it to them tonight, I did want them to have a show in order to earn it with their hostess credit in the event they decided not to sell it themselves.

We moved as quickly as possible through the glamour products. They applied the Day Radiance, a cream foundation, which made the skin look smooth and flawless, not dry or wrinkled, without the need of a powder to finish it off—another first in the cosmetic business. I had finally learned my lesson about light foundation and chose a shade that closely matched the skin tone of each guest. I helped anyone with a problem applying it and praised them when they did it right. A little praise never hurt, not in sales, and not anywhere. After the skin care, the glamour moved quickly as they seemed more familiar with applying these kinds of products.

Finally it was time to close the sale. I reminded them it was just for practice, but I wanted to finish as I did normally. Then I charged into my close. "First, I want you to test me to see if

I covered the use of the products correctly." As I held up each product, one of them would pipe up and explain how to use it. Correct use of the products was important, and they had remembered it all. They understood what each product did and how they should use it to get results.

Unsurprisingly, they were engrossed with looking at themselves in the mirrors. "When I go home looking this good, my husband is going to insist that I buy the whole thing," the woman from Irving commented. Everyone laughed, but nodded in agreement.

"I'm glad you brought that up because so many people think it's the glamour makeup that makes the difference. And, you're right when you say that's what your husband will notice. But pick up your mirrors and look into them. When you go home tonight that glamour makeup will wash off." I leaned forward and looked them in the eye once again for emphasis. "But remember, that face underneath is going to be there from now on. Taking proper care of your skin today will have a great impact on how it will look many years from now."

The lady from Pleasant Grove, who hadn't said a word, now grinned and said, "You're wrong about one thing."

Surprised, I asked, "Really? What's that?"

Pointing to her face, she quipped, "This makeup is not coming off this face tonight."

"Mine either," echoed the group.

I had to laugh. "Okay, just this once. But please don't make a habit of sleeping in make-up. Deal?"

"Deal," they chorused.

I assured them we would soon be finished and then added, "Remember the things you wanted to improve? Here are some before-and-after pictures of women with problems similar to yours. The 'after' pictures were taken after using the products for only six weeks," I said. They passed the sheet around, eagerly looking for the problem that resembled theirs. Next, I explained that if this were a regular show (and not one for practice) I would suggest that they start by purchasing the skin care set (in case the complete set was too expensive). Then they could book a show of their own and probably get the glamour products free with hostess credit. "I'll stop talking now. Feel free to ask questions if you want."

The silence seemed to go on forever. Then, they all started to talk at once, but Clara held up her hand to signal silence and said: "Can't we just go ahead and buy our skin care tonight? There are plenty of other things that we want to get at our own shows."

They were obviously determined to buy the skin care and it took a moment to catch my breath. "Of course, you can," I said, "but I just didn't want you to think you had to buy something tonight, after I told you that this was primarily for me to practice."

Luckily, I had products there, ready to sell. I had used some of my profits to buy them. I got Ned to help me bring them in. He was grinning from ear to ear and mouthed the word, "Great!" (I knew he meant that you couldn't beat 100 percent sales.)

Six skin care sets at $15.95 each totaled almost $96. Because I didn't have to pay hostess credit, one-half of that amount was clear profit, and I had not expected a sale at all. Suzanne was right. This was a "dream" job.

I finally brought out the wig, and even though they were obviously interested in owning one, they had been far more interested in purchasing cosmetics and the job opportunity. Richard is going to love this, I thought, smiling to myself. He always said the money wasn't in the wigs.

While Ned collected products, we drank coffee and spiced tea, and talked nonstop, as only a group of women can do. They wanted to set up shows in January, naming people they were going to invite. This gave me the opportunity to give them some pointers on how to have the best show possible (at least as much as I had learned about it in two weeks). I explained that the law of averages would probably ensure last minute cancellations by some of the people they invited, so to make sure at least six people showed up, they should always invite nine. Occasionally, more would come, but most of the time it was six. I reminded them that if two people booked shows from theirs, then they would get 20 percent of their sales in merchandise credit. They could easily end up with free glamour make-up.

There was more they needed to know, but the expressions on their faces told me enough had been said for now. Getting customers to show up was the most important thing, so I handed them a pamphlet on "how to have a good show." In addition to what we had discussed, the pamphlet included tips on what to serve, how to dress, and actual words to use when giving invitations.

"It's really important that you read this," I said and each one promised she would.

Every woman there expressed an interest in joining the company; but I knew the law of averages applied here too, so this didn't mean they would all sign up. I felt sure my neighbor would bow out because her husband expected her to be a full-time homemaker. Of course, they all needed to talk with their husbands before making a definite decision. Remembering my decision to sign up and tell Ned later, I said, "Good luck with that."

Ultimately, four out of this group bought demo cases, but one of them never placed a wholesale order. However, this show was definitely the event that launched me onto the road to success with Mary Kay. The shows set up that evening resulted in new ones being booked and new people being recruited not only in their areas, but in Denton, Arlington, Grand Prairie, Fort Worth, and as far away as Jacksonville, Texas (150 miles from Dallas). I was definitely fanning out.

And there was one more benefit from this show. The ones interested in selling insisted I talk with their husbands and explain the marketing plan. Remembering that I hadn't done too well with my own husband, I tried not to show my hesitation and simply agreed. It turned out to be one of the best things I learned to do.

When I sat down with a husband and wife and drew circles on a legal pad (as Richard had done), showing how a consultant could earn money off of a multitude of other people, the husband "got it" immediately. And many times the husband became a partner in the business as well as the best supporter his wife had.

It was almost 11:00 p.m. when Ned and I stood at the door to say good night. On impulse, I asked the group, "Would you please tell me why you agreed to drive all the way out here tonight in this weather?"

After a moment of silence, Clara spoke up and said, "I can only speak for myself, but I decided to come because you were so enthusiastic, and I had to find out what it was all about."

"My reason, exactly," Suzanne said, as the others nodded in agreement. I made a mental note right then and there: "Enthusiasm can be the key to solving all kinds of problems."

As soon as we closed the door, I asked, "Well, what do you think about how it went?"

"I think you batted a thousand, as far as I could tell," he answered. "Let's get a cup of coffee and go sit by the fire."

"Ned," I began as soon as we were settled in front of the dying coals, "I know you take an analytical approach to everything. I want you to tell me why you think they were so receptive, not only to the product, but to the business as well."

As usual, he didn't make a hasty reply. Finally he said, "I think it was because the whole thing was about solving problems—their problems. By showing how the make-up could improve their self-esteem and how the marketing plan could enhance their earning potential, how could they not at least want to learn more about it?" Then he smiled, flashing his white teeth, and added, "Heck, I considered signing up myself."

I stayed up a little while after Ned went to bed. I was so keyed up I knew I couldn't sleep, and I needed to digest what the evening meant for our future. As it turned out, the approach I used on this occasion evolved into the one I used to build a huge sales organization. I condensed the "solving problems" approach into one thing: "Find a need and fill it." I applied this concept to sales and recruiting when training hundreds of new recruits. Ultimately, Mary Kay taped my show presentation and put it into the demo kit of every new recruit. And because the husbands were included from the beginning, Mary Kay actually gained two supporters, instead of only one.

This concept contributed greatly to building a strong foundation for a tiny company that would ultimately grow into a worldwide one, producing sales in excess of one billion dollars a year.

The events of the evening were way too exciting to relate to Mary Kay on the phone. So the next morning I called the law office to say I would be a little late for work. In anticipation of my meeting with Mary Kay, I paid extra attention to my appearance. I wore my new rose wool suit, used only for special occasions, and applied make-up to match: pink lip and cheek color, and I couldn't resist blue eyeliner like the liner Mary Kay wore. I smiled at my reflection in the mirror and contemplated wearing the platinum wig sitting on my dressing table. "No," I decided. It was too obvious.

When I walked in the door to Mary Kay's office, Richard was sitting at the front desk and looked up in surprise. "Is Mary Kay expecting you? There's someone with her right now."

"No, Richard, she's not expecting me," I said, sitting down in a chair beside his desk. "I have some news and I wanted to tell you both in person."

I told him first about selling the six skin care sets without even trying. He stopped me there and said, "Have you thought about what this means?" Not waiting for me to answer, he continued, "According to your orders and counting these, you've sold about twenty sets, right?" I nodded. "When you have 100 customers using the skin care and ordering just $10 a month, do you realize that you will earn an extra $500 profit, free and clear for just answering the phone? And you haven't even been with the company a full month yet."

I hadn't thought of that aspect of the marketing, and suddenly I could actually feel that far more money than I had ever imagined was within my reach. I could tell the excitement in Richard's voice was genuine and I couldn't wait to tell him the rest.

"And, Richard, I have four possible recruits that I am pretty sure will come through."

"From the same show?" He asked, his mouth open in disbelief. "Do you realize that makes five and you could soon be ready to step up to management?" Seeing the blank look on my face, he added, "That means you could possibly make 16 percent on their sales in addition to what you are making on your own. Hold it right there; Mary Kay has to hear this."

After the visitor left her office, Richard and I joined Mary Kay and Richard related the story to her. Hearing him repeat it and seeing the amazed look on Mary Kay's face was the only reward I needed for making the trip to the office. "Has this never been done before?" I asked, still stunned by their reaction.

"No," they said in unison, and we all just sat there for a few seconds, trying to comprehend what all of it could mean. After Richard left to answer the phone, for the next ten minutes I saw Mary Kay at her finest. She started by complimenting my appearance. I had a sudden feeling that she was well aware I was imitating her, and she didn't mind at all. She then repeated what she'd said before about my potential, and added that the sooner I quit my job and joined them full time, the sooner I would encounter "real" success. Then the punch line: "You know, Jackie, I believe you have true executive potential. I can see you as the head of a gigantic group of sales people." And the strange thing was, for the first time, I could see it, too.

As I left her office, I realized there had been a monumental change in how I thought of myself. I came in thinking like a secretary, and by the time I left, it had changed to that of a future executive. I could see the pathway to success clearly in front of me, and I vowed that nothing would stop me now.

CHAPTER FOUR

Prizes and Praise

The New Year rang in new hopes and new dreams for my family. Ned, Sharon, and I thought of nothing but who would win the elegant prize to be given away at Mary Kay's next sales meeting. Their guesses about what the prize might be ranged from wigs to jewelry. But it was when I told them the race between Dalene and me was really tight, that the contest became "us against them," which of course heightened the intensity.

I arrived at work on Monday morning, anxious to talk with Doris about the prize to be given away that evening. She had decided not to become a consultant as I thought she might, but she remained my friend and supporter. When she walked through the door, I hurried up to her and said "Tonight's the night!"

"For what?" she asked in surprise. Since I was consumed with this issue, I found her obliviousness surprising. But I patiently related all the details again. She still had a puzzled look on her face, but finally said, "What is the prize anyway?" I considered just walking away. In the game of carrot and stick, this was the biggest carrot of all, but since Doris wasn't a consultant, none of this held the same meaning for her, so I simply responded that I didn't know what the prize was. That wasn't the point. The point was being special enough to be given the recognition. I asked her if she had, at this place, ever been given anything special for doing a good job—or for that matter, anywhere. A look of understanding crossed her face, and I added, "I rest my case." As a legal secretary, there was no opportunity to excel. At Mary Kay, there was.

I tried to keep my mind on law firm business throughout the day, but at closing time, I rushed to Mary Kay's office, so I could talk privately with Richard before the meeting. Even though the meeting wasn't scheduled until later, Dalene was already there talking with him, so I had to wait. When they finished, Dalene walked slowly toward Mary Kay's office. She stopped just short of entering, and I knew it was because she wanted to listen in on what I was going to say. So I just out waited her.

Richard was looking at me expectantly. I reminded him that I had several prospective recruits who wanted me to show the marketing plan to their husbands. "I want to be sure I'm doing it correctly," I said, as I whipped out my yellow legal pad and started to draw circles in the same way he'd done for me: a large circle at the top, and five smaller ones below, each attached by a line to the big one at the top. This drawing represented a consultant with five recruits.

He said, "That's right so far. But to show the husbands, let's take it further. Men aren't interested in nickel-and-dime stuff. They want to hear about the real money." This statement revealed the status of women in this era. They had almost no prospects for real money, and therefore had low expectations.

Suddenly I knew that if Ned had seen the real money in the beginning, it would have saved a lot of grief. I moved my chair closer so I wouldn't miss a word of what he'd say. He then told me to draw five more circles alongside the five already there, representing a total of ten recruits. "With this many recruits, you could easily become a director." Then he made it personal.

"Let's use you as an example. You did $500 wholesale in just two weeks, right?" I nodded and he continued, "Let's say the ten circles do the same, totaling $5,000." He looked at me, and again I nodded. "As a director, you would make an additional $800, for a total of $1,300." More than three times what I made at the law firm. I knew there was potential, but my head was reeling at the thought of so much money.

"Remember, the director's commissions come to you in a check at the end of every month," he said, knowing I was concerned about not receiving a regular paycheck.

Seeing that I was a little overwhelmed, he quickly told me that wasn't all. He wanted to add one more thing, something that would reel in the husbands. He had me draw two smaller circles under each of the ten, making a total of twenty. "These people were recruited by your recruits. So, using the same guideline, their sales would total $10,000, giving you director commission of an additional $1,200." By now my mouth was hanging open. "And that's added to your $1,300, making a grand total of $2,500." More than six times what I made at the law firm. A huge light flashed in my head.

I jumped to my feet and yelled, "Richard, I get the picture! You're telling me instead of settling for an eight-hour-a-day, low-paying job, I can multiply myself and make money on hundreds, even thousands of other peoples' sales."

Then Richard was on his feet, too, yelling, "That's exactly right," excited I had totally understood the concept. I was to learn very soon that this was not a "get rich quick scheme." Every level of commissions required specific responsibilities.

We'd been so engrossed that we hadn't heard Mary Kay come up behind us.

"What's all the excitement about?" she asked.

Richard winked at me and said, "Nothing special, we were just reviewing the marketing plan."

She then turned to me and said she needed to speak with Richard a minute and asked me to wait in her office, where the meeting would be held. As I entered the door to her office, I heard her say, "Richard, you didn't tell her about what happens when those people under her become directors."

"No, I didn't," he answered and then added, "but I think she'll be ready to hear about it soon." I smiled to myself, still excited about understanding the concept.

I joined the people beginning to stream in for the meeting and soon the room was packed. There were new faces, and I wondered who they were. Then I saw the huge box, wrapped in shiny pink paper and tied with a lavish white bow. The prize. My heart was beating so loudly that I wondered if the others could hear it. Glancing at Dalene, I saw that she was just as tense. We must be very close, I thought, knowing it could go either way.

As usual, Mary Kay presided. And as always, she looked perfect. I wondered idly how she looked without the wig. She welcomed us all and said it was wonderful to have new faces in the group. "Is anybody curious about who's going to win this prize?" she asked, pointing at the gorgeous package as if no one had noticed it.

Some nodded, and some yelled a resounding, yes. Dalene and I could be heard above all the rest. If she's trying to build tension, it's working, I thought.

Mary Kay continued. "Well, I have to say that this was a very close race. Everyone did well in the month of December, but the winner of this prize excelled way beyond just 'doing a good job.'" My heart sank. I knew I could have done better and prepared myself for hearing Dalene's name called. I avoided Mary Kay's eyes.

"The winner has been with the company only one-half the month and she has another full-time job." Stay calm, don't react, I thought. There may be others who fit that description and you don't want to make a fool of yourself.

"The most important thing you need to know about the winner is this: most people would consider what she did impossible. And I have to admit that when I told her December was a great month for sales, I didn't say 'until right before Christmas,' so she continued selling and recruiting throughout the holidays. She didn't know it couldn't be done, so she did it." It sounded more and more like me, and Dalene had a strange look on her face. I shook myself to clear my head and waited. Mary Kay got up from her desk, picked up the box and added, "This prize will go to the person who sold in excess of $1,000 retail during the month, and that total doesn't include wig sales." Suddenly everyone was cheering and clapping as Mary Kay handed me the beautiful package.

Such praise had never before fallen on me. I was overwhelmed with emotion and was afraid I was going to cry. It wouldn't have mattered if the box had been full of cow chips. The praise was the prize; it filled a void inside of me, one I hadn't even known was there. If that was true with me, then I knew it must also be true for countless others.

I hated to mess up the beautiful package by opening it, but everyone was chanting: "We want to see what's inside." It was indeed elegant. Nestled in pink tissue paper was the most exquisite serving dish I had ever seen: a lead crystal, round plate mounted on a silver pedestal. A less grand version might have been called a lazy Susan. Even today, every time I use it, this scene plays again in my mind. Just as important as the gift was the packaging, which I couldn't stop looking at. Mary Kay later explained, "Take a two dollar gift, wrap it in a three dollar package, and give it with a $100 worth of praise." This was to be another important truth that I used from that day on.

Before the program, the visitors told all about themselves. Since they were introduced as simply "visitors," I assumed that they came from the newspaper ad that the company was still running. I stole a glance at Dalene. Her face was motionless, but I thought I saw her chin quiver slightly. My feeling of ecstasy dimmed a little, and I empathized with the disappointment she must have felt.

Then began the main part of the program. Mary Kay held up a brand new 1964 calendar. "Isn't it great?" she asked enthusiastically. "We're entering a New Year that's fresh and clean, just waiting for us to fill it with wonderful, exciting new accomplishments.

Then she explained the new contest for the month. Every one purchasing $500 wholesale cosmetics during the month would win a Fashion Tress wig. After a few seconds when it soaked in, everyone clapped and cheered until Mary Kay had to interrupt to regain control. Everyone could be a winner. How could anyone call this work? I called it fun.

I still remember how Mary Kay instilled a desire to succeed in us. "Success begins right here," she said tapping her head. "If you think you can, you can. If you think you can't, then you can't." There was a lot to learn, but first you had to decide to succeed. After the pep talk, she discussed the specifics of setting up appointments for shows.

She began by asking how many had their appointment books filled to capacity for the week. When not a single hand was raised she said, laughing, "Well, I guess I picked the right subject."

She continued by saying she had taught the method to hundreds of people who used it successfully. Then she added it would work for us if we gave it a try. No one moved as she spoke. "You've probably already had shows with most of your friends. That's good, because the sooner you're with people you don't know, the better. When my friends and family ask to try my products, I say 'sure,' but I'll have to charge you double." We all laughed and she added, "I'm only half joking."

Next she pointed out that salespeople didn't have a very good reputation and were considered "pushy" by lots of people. "So we must use good psychology to change this image." (I smiled to myself because I'd already figured this out.) It was obvious that she knew what she was talking about and the room remained silent. Everyone wanted to catch every word.

Mary Kay got up from her seat and faced the group. "Every business must have people to sell to. Booking appointments is the lifeline of your business. By booking two new shows from each show you hold, you're building a solid foundation for your new career. We're going to discuss using the right words, but the truth is if you ask enough people, no matter how you say it, you will get appointments."

Mary Kay walked over to Jan Jack. She turned to us and said: "I'm at a show, and I've chosen Jan as someone I would like to have a show at her house." She dropped to one knee beside Jan, and began: "I choose two people at each show that I think would be the best hostesses for future shows. Tonight, Jan, I've chosen you. Is there any reason why you couldn't have a show at your house?" She looked her straight in the eye while she talked, and Jan returned her gaze. She had dropped from standing above Jan to below eye level, removing any threat of being pushy.

Jan laughed and said, "If I say 'no,' then I've said 'yes,' right?"

"Right," we all called out. And Mary Kay added that we'd be surprised at how effective it would be.

Winding down, she went on to say there would be much more to be learned about the subject and ended with one of her famous quotes: "Someone has said that 'the mind can't absorb more than the seat can endure,' but there's one more thing we need to do tonight. I want each one of you to tell me how many shows you plan to have this week. Jackie, let's start with you."

She had caught me off guard. I quickly opened my appointment book and checked, then told her I had five booked, which was what I wanted to do as long as I worked at the law firm. "That's good" Mary Kay replied and then added, "However, in order to hold five you need to have at least seven on your book, because according to the law of averages, not all will hold. How about you, Dalene? How many do you plan to have?"

"Six, Mary Kay, and I have eight booked." But I'll bet she doesn't have another full-time job, I thought.

"Good for you, Dalene. Just so all of you know, Dalene has experience in this business. She knows the ropes and I'm predicting you will see great things from her." Mary Kay had just taken the sting out of her losing the elegant prize. And Dalene, relishing the moment, was smiling again. However, I wondered if Mary Kay was playing us against each other. If so, she was doing a pretty smooth job.

After the meeting adjourned, everyone seemed hesitant to leave. They came over to take a closer look at my prize and to congratulate me on winning it. They seemed truly happy for me, and I thought how really nice they were.

As the crowd thinned, I looked over and saw Jan talking with Dalene and a few others. For the first time, I took a good look at Dalene. She was tall and trim and had a pleasant face. Her light brown hair seemed to be naturally curly, and her eyes were gray-blue. There was nothing flashy or glamorous about her; she was just attractive in a natural way.

As I walked up to them, Dalene was saying, "That's not how I book appointments," referring to Mary Kay's demonstration. Jan turned to me and asked me what I thought.

"Well," I answered, stalling for time, "I guess if you have all the appointments you want, then it doesn't matter what method you use for booking them. But for a novice like me, Mary Kay's approach could make getting appointments much easier. I'm definitely going to give it a try." I hoped that was diplomatic enough. We were already rivals, and I didn't want to make an enemy out of her right off the bat.

Although my house was clear across town, because my mind was reviewing the meeting, I seemed to be in my driveway in minutes. Ned and Sharon ran out of the house and jerked the car door open. "Who won?" they cried.

Pointing to the huge box beside me, I answered, "Ta-da," and we all cheered. Sharon grabbed the box, took it inside, and she and Ned had it open in seconds. The look on their faces asked the question: "What is it?" "It's an expensive serving dish," I explained. "Do you think we can get used to eating out of such finery?"

The three of us nestled together on the couch as I related the events of the evening. "There's no doubt that Dalene is my big competition, but tonight our team won." Little did we know this scene would be repeated many times in the years ahead.

I began using Mary Kay's booking technique immediately. At first it seemed a little awkward, and I had to make the system my own. I started by choosing people I felt a connection with, people who returned my smile, who listened intently to the hide tanner story, who obviously enjoyed the presentation, and who mentioned people they knew would like the product. I also asked anyone who showed enthusiasm, because I knew they could get people to attend.

At first, it worked like a charm. My appointment book was filling up rapidly. Then one evening, when I asked someone I had chosen if there was any reason she couldn't have a show at her house, she looked at me as if I had just crawled out from under a rock and answered, "No reason; I just don't want to." I felt as if I had been slapped hard, and I was speechless. The strategy just hadn't worked, and I didn't know how to follow through.

I called Mary Kay the next morning and told her what had happened. I was so crestfallen, I actually wasn't sure I could do this anymore. Calmly, she asked me to come to the office at noon and she'd take me to lunch. She greeted me with a smile and a compliment about my complexion. (I had begun getting other compliments about it, so I felt this was genuine.) Her entire demeanor suggested that everything was fine. I learned later that this was her technique for defusing volatile situations. And, of course, I also learned to use it myself.

We had lunch at the little restaurant near her office, and she asked me to describe what happened in detail. I was worried that she wouldn't understand why this had so disturbed me and hesitated. She assured me that no matter what it was, she had heard it before in her years of experience.

In my usual way, I just blurted it all out.

"She said no, right?" Mary Kay said, cutting to the chase. "Tell me exactly how you felt about her saying no to you." By the hint of a smile on her face, I knew she thought I was over-reacting.

"It wasn't just that she said no, it was the way she said it. It was so dismissive, as if she was totally rejecting me as a person."

"And you're saying that you can't do this anymore because you are afraid there will be more of that kind of rejection."

There was silence for a few seconds, and then I replied, "I guess that's it, and I know you think it's ridiculous."

Again there was a pause but no comment. Finally, she asked, "Is there anything that you can remember being terribly afraid of and then finding one day that the fear had gone away?" I had to think for a minute because there were many things I was afraid of, but I finally answered.

"That's pretty much how I felt about driving in the big city of Dallas when I first joined the company. And when I had to go into strange neighborhoods, I was a nervous wreck by the time I found the right address. I guess it was a fear of the unknown."

"And, you aren't afraid of that anymore?" She asked.

"Not really."

"Why do you think the fear went away?"

I wasn't sure what answer she was looking for. Then I replied, "The only reason I can think of is that I just kept on driving, afraid or not. But Mary Kay, it isn't the same kind of fear."

She looked at me with complete understanding and said, "You're right about that. On a scale from one to ten, fear of rejection and fear of feeling foolish rank right at the top. The kind of fear you mentioned, trying to find your way in a strange place, would probably be about three. However, Jackie, fear of rejection is the number one reason for failure in sales. It seems to be easier to just quit than to face the fear."

"How do you do that? It seems there is always something to be afraid of."

"Of course, there is," she answered. "But you continue doing just what you said about driving. You wanted to get to your destination more than you were afraid of what you had to do to get there. I want you to try something. The next time someone tells you no in a way that makes you feel rejected, here is a response to try. If you are kneeling beside her, stay there, look her in the eye, and say, 'I'm so sorry, I think you would have been wonderful.' Then rise and walk quickly away."

I felt better as I always did after a talk with Mary Kay and thought again what a remarkable woman she was. It was some time before I had the experience again. When I did, I handled it exactly as Mary Kay said. Of course, I called and reported it. "You'll never guess what happened."

She laughed and answered, "I'll bet I could, but go ahead and tell me."

"She came back to me after a while and told me she'd changed her mind and she would have a show after all."

And then Mary Kay and I shared the first of many great laughs together. In closing this conversation Mary Kay said something else that influenced the rest of my life: "You know Jackie, faith is the only real cure for fear of any kind. Don't you think as Christians we should depend on that a little more?"

She'd put the whole experience just where it belonged: where faith was firmly planted, fear might visit, but it would not take control. Sometime there might be a problem big enough to stop me, but I decided then and there that it would not be the tiny two-letter word no.

Because I had shows booked almost every night during the week, I'd begun driving the car to work every day. Ned was riding to his job with a friend who lived near us. Occasionally, a show would be postponed, and then it was a treat to spend the evening with my family.

January was drawing to a close. Ned and I both had birthdays that month; I was thirty and he was thirty-four. He had started saying we should consider having another baby. "If we don't hurry, I'm going to be the oldest dad in the PTA," he said seriously. I just wasn't ready for that step yet, perhaps because sometimes, unexpectedly, the hurt returned, raw and new again. But it's time to tell him about my visit to the cemetery, I thought.

Then I told him about my trip to the Baby Land section of the cemetery on the anniversary of our baby's death, and about the peace I had felt while there. He looked at me and said, "Did you go alone?" I nodded and explained that in spite of the doctor's reassurance that it would be okay the next time, I was still afraid that something could go wrong again. Without saying a word, he took my hand and held it for a long time. I didn't tell him that this fear was a mountain in comparison with the molehills that had to do with work.

As I sat meditating about using faith to overcome the fears in my life, I realized all over again that faith had far more benefits than just overcoming fear. It is the way to a more abundant life; one filled with confidence, joy, and contentment, regardless of the circumstances that weave in and out of our lives.

Suddenly I remembered something that happened when I was ten years old. We had moved into a small Arkansas town not far from our old family farm because my mother wanted us to be near a church so we could attend on a regular basis. She was a Presbyterian but that church only had a service once a month because there was no regular preacher. So I attended the Baptist church the rest of the time, which held services every week. By the time the Presbyterians got a full-time preacher,

I was already a Baptist and would remain one for the rest of my life.

My Sunday school teacher taught us weekly scriptures that stuck with me. One was, "Whatsoever you ask in My name believing, you shall receive." With the blind faith of a child, I stored the scriptures she taught us away in my heart.

It seemed that every kid in town had a bicycle, except me. WWII had just ended, and there weren't many new bikes around. But the dads had assembled some for their children from pieces strewn around. So there was a string of bikes flying down the hill in front of my house every day. Unfortunately, I didn't have a father, so I didn't have a bike. As I watched the other kids, I decided I would one day join them.

In addition to bicycles, comic books—or funny books as we called them—were high on my list of favorite things. Since I didn't have a dime to buy one, when given the opportunity, I was always eager to borrow some. A friend that lived about two miles out of town offered me a stack of them if I'd come out and get them. My friend, Barbara, who was three years younger than me, begged to go along.

I explained that it was a long walk and I didn't think she could do it. But when she cried, I gave in. It would have been much faster without her along, but it turned out fine, because it took both of us to carry the stack back home. We hadn't gone far on the return when Barbara began whining, saying she couldn't walk any farther. It was a hot summer day and I was weary myself. "Okay, Barbara," I said, "how would you like for us to have a bicycle to ride the rest of the way home?"

"Where would we get one?" she asked, perking up. I told her about the scripture verse and explained that faith meant you had to really believe when you asked God for something. "If we get down on our knees and pray and truly believe that God will do it, then we will get what we ask for."

Barbara looked a little skeptical and confused, but we both knelt beside the road and I prayed fervently for a bicycle. When we opened our eyes there was no bicycle. She said immediately, "I knew it wouldn't be there."

"Well, no wonder," I said, irritated. "Didn't you hear me say you had to believe? It's all your fault." There was no doubt in my mind that the only reason a bicycle hadn't materialized was Barbara's lack of faith. We finally made it home on foot with our load of comics.

Several weeks later an uncle I'd never seen before came for a visit. He was my dad's brother and lived in Missouri. My mom worked all day, so he and I spent a lot of time together. We walked to town to get the mail and pick up groceries, and I told him how I hoped that someday I could have a bicycle to make these chores faster. I explained I wanted one with a large basket for groceries and a light for the handle bar, so I could ride at night. He made no comment and I decided he wasn't even listening. A few days later, my uncle returned home.

Several weeks passed, and one day when I was picking up the mail at the post office, the man who ran the hardware store called to me and ushered me into his store as I kept asking why. "You'll see," he replied, smiling. Next to the door sat the most beautiful bicycle I had ever seen—a brand new blue and silver Schwinn, complete with a basket and a light on the handlebars. My uncle had the man order it for me. I was the only kid in town with such a bike. On a hot summer day, I still remember the feeling of flying down the hill on my Schwinn with the wind in my hair.

I laughed to myself at the memory. It was proof that faith did much more than just overcome fear. The hardships over the years had dimmed the blind faith of the child. But I'll get it back again, I promised myself. And one verse I added to the others that I held so dear was "God works in mysterious ways his wonders to perform." This experience was the first of many others that I considered "miracles" in my life.

This new commitment of faith came just in time. I would need it more than ever for what lay ahead.

CHAPTER FIVE

A Step Up the Ladder

The term March Madness took on a whole new meaning for me that month. After working at the law firm all-day, I held shows almost every night. In addition, I interviewed and trained new consultants, so the month seemed to fly by. One morning I walked out the front door and noticed that our dogwood trees were budding, and I felt a pang of regret. My mother always said, "Food feeds the stomach, but flowers feed the soul." I was a true believer, and this was the first year since I'd been married that I hadn't had time to plant spring flowers. Winter was slipping into spring, and I hadn't even noticed. Busy is good, but I didn't want my whole life to slip by while I was selling cosmetics.

I couldn't have held it all together if Ned and Sharon hadn't become my business partners. They took phone calls, mailed orders to customers, and kept up with the inventory, in addition to taking care of home chores like grocery shopping and cooking (although I still baked homemade rolls as often as possible). When I drove into the garage after a late show, they met me at the car, asking about my day as they carried everything inside. It was like having my own welcoming committee.

I had finally picked up the knack of holding onto control of a show, which cut the time in half. When one began at 7:00 p.m., I was usually on my way home by 9:00. My sales actually improved with this change and new shows were easier to book because it didn't take so much time from everyone involved.

When I got home, I would tuck Sharon into bed and talk with her about her day, then listen as she said her prayers. Afterwards, Ned and I settled into our own routine. We talked about his day, and then he would rub my feet, my head, and my back;

59

the tension melted away. I decided that if those perks were added to everyone's marriage vows, the divorce rate would go way down. Our lives were busy, but good.

One of the reasons we didn't mind the extra work was the money was making a difference. We paid bills easily and spontaneously went out to eat; that used to be a luxury. But I still wasn't secure enough to quit my job at the law firm. After my last talk with Richard about the marketing plan, I had decided definitely to one day become a director. However, I had only been with the company three months and there was still so much to learn.

One morning soon after I arrived at the law firm, I got a call from Mary Kay asking me to come to the office on my lunch hour. Since I was the one who usually called her, I was surprised and knew something was up. "If it's important, of course I will," I answered, expecting her to tell me what it was about, but she offered no further explanations.

When I arrived she was alone in her office; the same complimentary, enthusiastic person as always, but I could tell she had something on her mind.

"Is something wrong?" I asked.

"Oh no," she said quickly. "Actually something is very right." She was watching me closely, and I could feel a tension in her that was not ordinarily there. I shifted nervously in my chair, but finally she added, "I think it's time for you to start your qualification for director."

"You know I plan to, but you aren't seriously suggesting that I start right away?"

"Oh, but I am," she replied. "I think you're ready and we have to get some leadership in place in order for the company to grow. This is a fabulous opportunity for you. You have a chance to be the first director in the company."

Instead of being flattered, weariness fell over me like a blanket of dense fog. The thought of adding a single thing to my workload was more than I could stand. She sat silently looking at me, and I remembered her telling me to stop talking when it was time to close the sale, because if you didn't you could lose it altogether. That's what she was doing.

Finally I spoke, "Mary Kay, I know it's a great opportunity and of course I do want to be a director at some point, but it's too much too soon. I'm already on overload and I barely see my family as it is."

She sat silent again for a few seconds, and I suspected she was trying not to be too pushy.

"But as soon as you qualify, then you can quit your job at the law firm. Just think how much more time you will have with your family then." She had taken the reason I gave her for not doing what she wanted and turned it into the exact reason I should. Of course I later used this technique myself.

By pointing out I could quit my other job, she now had my attention. I wanted to be sure I was clear on the details, so I said, "All my recruits and I have to do is to purchase $4,000 retail of cosmetics for three consecutive months. Is that correct?" She nodded, and I continued: "And after qualification my director's check should more than replace my salary?" Again she nodded. "Sounds good. How about if I start qualification some time during the summer months? I need to get a few more recruits to make qualifying easier."

A slight frown crossed her face, which signaled that wasn't the right answer. "I want you to begin the first of April. I don't see any point in delays."

"You're talking about in just a few days?"

She sat looking me in the eye, waiting for what she'd said to completely soak in.

"Why not?" she answered, using the same tactic of asking a prospective hostess why she couldn't have a show, and I wondered if she ever dropped the canned routine. Then she continued.

"Here's the thing: Dalene is going to start her qualification at that time. I thought you'd want the same opportunity." I knew this was really about what was good for the company, but she knew too well what would get my attention.

She's trying to reel me in with the competition, I thought. And I decided to take my time answering.

After what seemed to be a long silence, I said, "I'll talk with Ned about it, but that's all I can promise right now. It's not easy to quit a reliable job." When she opened her mouth as if she were going to object, I rushed on. "I am not going to make the same mistake of not talking with Ned first. He deserves to be in on the decision. There's no way I could, or would, do it without his full support." She now had that vexed look that had become easy to read, and I added: "I know, Mary Kay, if I don't do it, I'll get left behind."

As I was walking out the door, she called out, "Oh, Jackie, did I mention that I'm going to divide up the people in the company now between you and Dalene, if you both qualify?"

As she probably knew I would, I swallowed the bait. Now I considered it far more seriously.

That night Ned, Sharon and I sat down to discuss whether or not I should take this monumental step. I had expected resistance, but surprisingly, Ned and Sharon were excited about it, and began making suggestions on how we could pull it off. Ned suggested that we hire a maid for every Saturday. That would relieve us from most of the house cleaning chores and would give us more family time.

My major concern was that I needed more recruits. We made lists of people who might be interested. Ned listed three women from his work place; Sharon listed two mothers of her friends, and I listed every friend I could think of (who hadn't been contacted already) plus family members. My list included anybody, anywhere. When we finished, I hugged Ned and Sharon and told them how much I appreciated their help. I vowed silently to find something to praise them for every day. Then I told them that if they decided they didn't want me to qualify, all they had to do was tell me. Even though this was their immediate decision, they could reconsider.

"It's going to be fun," Sharon said, and Ned enthusiastically agreed that together, we could do it. It was a brand new adventure. Their willingness to help touched me beyond measure, and I said to Sharon, "And, sweetheart the best thing will be, once I quit my job, I'll be home with you more and we'll get to do the things we've always wanted to do."

"Like going swimming, on picnics, and bike rides," she said with a wide smile.

"All that, and more," I promised.

When I called Mary Kay the next morning to tell her I was in, I could hear relief in her voice. She wasn't sure which way I would turn. From that point on, work took on a whole new meaning. It seemed to claim my life. The only day that remained off-limits was Sunday, and sometimes when I went recruiting out of town, even that day wasn't kept sacred because it usually meant I would leave on Friday night and return on Sunday morning.

Every week I pulled my little band of recruits together. Of course Mary Kay was playing up the competition between Dalene and me, adding more anxiety to the challenge. There was no doubt that it made both groups work harder, but the day would come when I would wonder if the end justified the means.

I was grateful for each one of my recruits, but was frustrated that I still didn't have a "big cup" in the bunch—someone who would see the potential and was willing to work hard for it. Actually, they were all leaning toward the demitasse size, wanting a little money out of it but mostly simply enjoying the fun and excitement. But I felt intense pressure to get more recruits fast, no matter what size cups they were.

As usual when confronted with a problem, I put in a lot of deep "thinking time." I decided, beginning the first of April, to enlist the help of every hostess in gathering prospective recruits. I explained, in front of the group present at a show, that I was having a contest for a free Fashion Tress wig (which I could get wholesale, or give one I had won). Each hostess could give me names of people who might be interested in becoming consultants. After I interviewed each one to determine if she was interested in the opportunity (and if I was interested in her), the hostess's name that recommended the prospect would go into a drawing for the wig. At the end of the month we'd have a luncheon for the hostesses who participated and draw the name of the winner. Each hostess could have her name in several times, increasing her chances of winning.

Because of this idea, I ended up booking more shows, and I knew I couldn't lose. The wig was a great motivator. It worked so well I repeated the offer in May and June. My theory was that once I had the prospects, I could convince a certain number of them to join the company.

I soon had a long list of prospective recruits, but none of them as yet appeared to be a "big cup." No one really had star quality. Nevertheless, I began to visualize the director's plaque on my wall of memorabilia because things were moving so rapidly. And even though my family literally had no free time, the challenge was exhilarating.

Someone in my group mentioned at one of our meetings that they would like to see Mary Kay do a show presentation as the program for one of our sessions. When I called her with the request, she waited so long to answer the question I thought she'd hung up. "Mary Kay?" I asked.

"I'm here," she said, "but I have a confession to make."

Surprised, I waited for the answer. Finally, she spoke, "I tried to hold shows myself, but for some reason I wasn't able to sell my own products, even though I was a sales whiz at Stanley and World Gift. So you see, because of this experience, I'm not comfortable holding a show for all of you. That's one of the reasons I want you and Dalene to hurry up and qualify."

It took two full minutes to recover from this revelation. Mary Kay couldn't sell her own products? That made no sense. I realized she could have made up another reason, but instead had told me the truth, even though it didn't reflect well on her. This experience was one reason that I later couldn't believe she would lie. I had to offer some excuse to my group so I told them that if she did this for us, she would have to do it for everyone else and left it at that.

One of my first out-of-town recruiting trips was to Hot Springs, Arkansas, about a seven-hour drive from Dallas. My sister, Faye, fourth from the oldest in our family, was the hostess. Looking at pictures from her younger days, I could tell she had been a beauty, and she was still very attractive. She also had brains. When she was in high school, we lived on the family farm.

She had to walk two and a half miles to catch the bus for the ten-mile ride on to school. This took a lot of her time, yet she was still valedictorian of her graduating class. She married young, and now had five children and a crystal rock business. But because she was always looking for a way to make life better for her family, she was also interested in the opportunity with Mary Kay.

After the show, she signed up and I talked her into placing her $500 retail order before she had shows of her own scheduled. I later employed this strategy with most new recruits because it turned out that the merchandise sitting in front of them was a motivating factor for them to get to work. And even though I had to classify Faye as a "small cup," I loved having my own sister involved in the business.

We easily made our quota in April. I began to think qualification was going to be a breeze. In addition to getting a lot of new people, my current group had become energized by the competition with Dalene. At least twice a week, Mary Kay reminded us that Dalene's people were in hot pursuit. And we reacted by picking up the pace (as, of course, she intended). But although none of us really knew Dalene, we began to resent her and had the feeling that she was "out to get us."

Years later, a highly successful saleswoman told me that, "People are made to be loved, and things are made to be used. When you mix them up, it turns people against each other." At this point, Mary Kay began to mix them up. Healthy competition had begun to turn into an unhealthy desire to win at all costs. And it would get much worse as the years went by. Ultimately, I learned and taught "compete only with yourself," because I didn't want to pass on the unhealthy aspects of Mary Kay's strategy. You don't have to destroy people to climb to the top. When we do our very best, we end up the winner.

It was a great deal harder to make our quota in May than it had been in April. Mothers weren't as accessible because school was drawing to a close for the summer, and they were busy with their children. Shows had to be postponed more than usual, and recruiting interviews were more difficult to schedule. I knew I had to come up with an answer, quickly. The competition with

Dalene was still on. My other sister, Geneva (there were three girls in the family), lived in Irving, which was in the opposite direction from us (Mesquite). She had never had a show but kept promising she would when school was out. She had a master's degree and taught fourth grade, so the school year, for her, was the work year.

I called her and said, "I've been thinking about your wanting to wait until school is out to have a show, but I thought I should tell you that some of your teacher friends might want to do what I do for a summer job. They would make good money, have fun, and maybe even win a wig." Then I explained about the contest, enticing her with the idea that she might win one as well.

She called me back the next day. She had related the news to her teacher friends, and they wanted to have a show the next Saturday, which was just three days away. Some of them had expressed an interest in the job opportunity, and I had to control myself to keep from yelling "hooray."

Geneva, her husband John (a Baptist minister), and their young son, Michael, lived in one of the choicest areas in Irving. The lots were wooded and all the homes were custom built. When I arrived she had everything in perfect order for the show, complete with coffee and banana and blueberry muffins; even though I had asked her to keep it simple.

I arrived early, yet seven teachers were already present. John and Michael had escaped the group of women by saying they had errands to run. The guests milled around and excitedly picked up the cosmetics and smelled them. We had their interest. Unfortunately for Geneva, the one person that had expressed interest in seeing couldn't come.

However, I was surprised to find that she still wanted to have two shows at her house the following Saturday. Her name was Marjie Slaten, and she had to have two because so many of the teachers wanted to participate. As Geneva related this to me I couldn't shake the feeling that it was just too good to be true; yet I hoped with my entire being that it was.

Geneva's show totaled a little over $150. And since she already had two more shows booked, she received the full

20 percent hostess credit and got the complete set of cosmetics free, plus the false eyelashes as a special gift from me. (In spite of the fact she had a master's degree, she never learned to apply the eyelashes correctly.) She wanted assurance she would still get her name in the drawing for the wig, since Marjie was still a prospective recruit. Geneva had beautiful, naturally curly hair, yet she was still enamored with the idea of having a hairdo that was always ready to go.

All the way home, I kept thinking about teachers as a whole new group of prospects. Even though they were well educated, they were underpaid and underappreciated, like so many of us. To say I was looking forward to Marjie's shows the next week was a major understatement. But there would be only three days left in the month after Marjie's shows, and I still had not met my quota for qualification. There wasn't much time and I needed a strategy. I couldn't just hope for a miracle.

My first strategy was this: Don't panic. I would get Richard to figure out exactly how many more orders I needed to finish my qualification on the Monday after Marjie's shows. Then I would still have Tuesday to finish it off, if necessary.

Once the plan was in place, I relaxed and concentrated on a way to entice teachers into the business. The more I thought about the potential, the more enthusiastic I became. I hadn't even met Marjie Slaten yet, but I had a strong premonition that she was going to play a major role in the business—and I turned out to be very, very right.

I arrived at Marjie's house much earlier than necessary on the next Saturday morning so we could get acquainted before the others arrived. She lived just a few blocks from my sister, so I knew the area. When she opened the door and greeted me enthusiastically (as if she too had been counting the days), I liked her immediately. The weather was warm and the scent of flowers surrounded me as I carried in my supplies. We already have something in common, I thought.

Just like Mary Kay's office, her living room was decorated in shades of pink. I couldn't help interpreting this as a good sign of things to come.

As I set up the cosmetics and place settings for the show, I looked at Marjie closely. She was a tall, slim blonde, with large blue eyes that seemed almost transparent. Her dark lashes and brows told me that she had lightened her hair. She wore a sleeveless sundress with an empire waist, made of small blue checked fabric. She was definitely fashion conscious, which told me she had potential in this business.

As we set up for the show, we chatted. She told me a little about her family, including that she and her husband, Stan, had one young daughter, Sheryl. Stan's mother lived with them also. They were out for the day to make the show easier. I laughed inwardly when I saw that she couldn't keep her hands off the blonde wig.

"Do you want to try it on?" I asked, thinking she reminded me of my own reaction the first time I saw all this.

"Yes, I do," she answered, "but I'll wait until everyone leaves today. I have a hard time keeping my dark roots from showing, and a wig would be a great help with that problem."

All six guests arrived almost at the same time. They taught together in the same grade school. And from the way they talked non-stop, I could tell it was going to be a challenge to keep their attention. Marjie volunteered to wait until the next show for her facial. Instead, she offered to help me with this group and I gratefully accepted.

As I began the hide tanner's story, there was a knock on the door. Marjie returned from answering it with three of the people who had been at Geneva's show. They had come to watch and to hear the product information again. This was the most interested group I'd had, and I was a little overwhelmed. If Marjie weren't helping me, we would never finish in time for the next show at 2:00 p.m.

Even though Marjie and I tried to rush them along, it was 1:00 o'clock when the show finished and they had filled out their orders. Not only did they buy skin care sets and extras, but they kept asking Marjie if she was going to become a consultant and offered to have shows for her if she did. This was a gold mine. Her answer was simply, "I'm thinking about it." School was out for the summer so they had nothing but time, and it was obviously they were reluctant to leave. We had to escort them out the door by announcing that the next group would be arriving in a few minutes.

"Is it always like this?" Marjie asked, as we reset the table for the next group.

"Actually no, Marjie. I have just been priding myself in cutting the time it takes for a show. But I've never had one before where the group was that enthusiastic. You know Marjie, you could have a gold mine here," I said, repeating my own thought.

"How so?" she asked in surprise. I explained the huge potential in specializing in teachers as a group. As recruits, it would be the ideal summer job, where they could be their own boss and set their own hours. Then I told her about how much money she could make at Mary Kay just working part time. In fact, it was the perfect setup.

The doorbell rang, and it was time for the next onslaught. The show took as much time as the first one, and we were both worn out by the time it was over. Yet I was excited because I had never sold so many skin care sets in one day. As we cleaned up, I mentioned that I had made more there today than I did during my last week at the law firm. That caught her interest. While we didn't have time that day to discuss the marketing plan, she did take a moment to try on the blonde wig. I thought she was never going to give it back.

It was a pleasant ride home. I could hardly believe that I had almost sold out my entire inventory, and I had enough money in my pocket from the sales that I could place a pretty large order on Tuesday. I turned on the radio and the perfect song was playing: "I'm into Something Good" by Herman's Hermits.

Ned was waiting outside for me when I drove up. I rolled down the window and said, "What's wrong?" There was a funny look on his face.

"Nothing," he answered, and then he said he had something to tell me after I parked the car. As soon as we were in the house, he began. "Stan Slaten called me. They want us to come over tomorrow after church. He wants to see the marketing plan. I think Marjie may be really interested."

Oh, please God, I thought. Had I finally met "the big cup" I needed so desperately?

Because we went to church in downtown Dallas, the trip afterwards to Marjie's didn't take very long. Marjie, Stan, Sheryl, and Vinita, Stan's mother, were waiting for us. They appeared to "fit together" as a family. Marjie was about five feet nine, and Stan was over a head taller than she was. Sheryl was eight but acted eighteen. She had been trying out her mother's cosmetics and still wore traces of lipstick. Sheryl was standing beside her dad, and I was struck by the resemblance. They both had light brown hair with gold highlights, and their eyes appeared to be almost the same color as their hair.

Stan's mother was quiet in comparison with the rest of her family. But I could tell she was a loving grandmother. She stayed within touching distance of Sheryl the whole time. Marjie finally insisted that they all go watch TV while we talked. Because Sharon (who was a few years older than Sheryl) offered to go with them, Sheryl agreed.

The four of us sat down around the dining table carrying on light conversation. Stan sold life insurance and already knew the potential of being in sales. Ned admitted that sales were not his forte, and he preferred industrial engineering. He was presently working on the design for the Nike Zeus, an antimissile missile.

I knew Ned could talk for hours about his work, so I quickly whipped out my yellow legal pad and got down to business. I had already coached Ned to keep quiet and not interrupt. This was the first time anyone had asked that he come with me, and I was a little concerned about what he might say. Stan completely understood sales and the importance of building a customer base that would continue to order products. So I started with the circles, the top one being Marjie.

After I had drawn the two levels, Stan said, "Can I see that for a minute?" He took the pad and started adding unlimited circles to the sheet. "I gather you're saying that in recruiting these people, you are multiplying yourself, which gives you unlimited earning potential."

In five minutes, Stan had absorbed the concept. "Well, Stan," I said, "that's it, exactly. The only other thing I can add is that teaching school doesn't offer that potential."

"You can say that again," Marjie said, laughing.

We left them to think about it and decided to put it on the back burner. They would do what they would do. Late on Monday afternoon, I got a call from Richard at home. "Are you sitting down?" he asked.

"I am now," I said, perching on the kitchen stool. "What's the bad news?"

"I don't think you're going to call this bad news: Marjie and Stan Slaten just left here. She signed up as a consultant and placed a $1,000 retail order so she could win a wig."

When I told Ned, we sat looking at each other in stunned silence. I had not only made my quota, but had gone way over the requirement. "Ned," I said, as a thought hit me, "I now have a big cup in my group. But it's not Marjie—it's Stan."

Marjie hit the ground running. The people at her shows had shows for her, and she was on her way. Thanks to her, qualifying in June was a piece of cake. Marjie won her first wig, and I added a new one to my collection. Geneva didn't win the hostess contest, but I got her a wig wholesale, so she was happy with the outcome. On July 1, I was full time with Mary Kay.

I had been wondering about how Marjie and Stan's quick trip out to the office had convinced them to sign up right then. So one day I just asked, explaining that most people would have waited at least overnight in making such a huge decision.

"Well," Marjie replied, "Richard made it sound like if I waited there might not be an opening."

Then I told her that was the same reason I had gone out to interview on a snowy day in December. Realizing we had fallen for the same trick, we laughed until we cried, sealing our friendship for life.

CHAPTER SIX

The Summer of '64

I was immeasurably pleased when the summer sun penetrated and lightened the black mood that had engulfed Dallas since last November when Kennedy was assassinated. My spirits, in particular, were on the rise because my fortunes decidedly were. In the middle of June, I decided it was time to tell Henry Baer I was changing professions. I had been his secretary since joining the firm and felt we were friends as well as business associates. I had no previous legal experience, and Henry had always been patient and understanding during my learning process. When I walked into his office and sat down in the chair beside his desk, he said right off the bat, "You're leaving, aren't you?"

Startled I asked, "Are you a mind reader, Henry?"

"Hardly," he replied, "but that's the buzz that's been going around the office for over a month now." I explained that my leaving had nothing to do with him; that it was just an opportunity I couldn't pass up. I laid out the whole concept and how much money I was making just working part time, and I had to see what I could do on a full-time basis. He said he didn't blame me at all, and then we chatted about all we'd been through together. The worst, by far, had been the assassination. Our firm had been one of the sponsors for the luncheon President Kennedy was to attend. A group of us had gone down to the street to watch the motorcade as it wove its way through town. No matter which political party we preferred, we all shared the magical feeling that Jackie and President Kennedy exuded as they smiled and waved when passing by. I had been there during a historical moment, but definitely not one of my own choosing.

It was a cool November day. However, the sun was shining and we were lighthearted and happy. As soon as the motorcade went by, we left and walked two blocks to Cattleman's Restaurant for lunch. About thirty minutes had passed, and we were looking at the menus when an announcement came over the loud speaker: President Kennedy had been shot. Total silence fell over the crowded room and no one moved. Time seemed to stand still as we sat looking at each other. Finally, someone closed a menu with a snap, and people all over the restaurant followed suit. Food was no longer of interest to anyone. As we all stood in line, trying to get out the door at the same time, someone called out, "How badly is he hurt?"

Back at the office, we waited for the answer while huddling around a radio. It finally came when Walter Cronkite announced that President Kennedy was dead. In only a few hours, the lightheartedness turned into feelings of extreme loss and sorrow. Sharing the experience created a lasting bond among all of us in the firm. It would take years for the feelings of horror to subside.

Throughout my whole life, the hardest thing for me to do has been to separate myself from people I care about. The sadness I felt over leaving my friends at the firm now dimmed the excitement of my new career. But I knew it was time to go, so I finally rose from the chair to leave Henry's office.

"Jackie," he called as I reached the door, "I'll probably end up working for you someday." I smiled and waved as I closed the door behind me.

Dalene had also made her quota and qualified as a director. It was a little strange that I hadn't heard the details from Richard or Mary Kay, whether it had been easy or hard or how many new recruits she'd gotten or from where. I had told everyone who would listen about mine, especially, about Marjie Slaten. However, I didn't waste a lot of time on it; there were more exciting things on my mind. Mary Kay had begun hinting that the company might be moving to new offices soon. There was a rumor that a building under construction was being considered because it could soon be ready to move into. There was no doubt that we needed more room. My unit alone was now way too large for Exchange Park.

As soon as I met and passed my quota for qualification, I called all the people in my unit and told them I was having a celebration party at my house. Mary Kay kept her word, and the unattached people in the company were divided between my unit and Dalene's. As far as I could tell there wasn't a big cup in the bunch, but I was thrilled to have the extra people. Jan Jack and Mary Louise Stevens were especially good for my group. They were faithful, supportive, and enthusiastic. Later, Jan became a strong medium cup and qualified as a director. I learned to not judge a cup by the size it appeared to be at the beginning. You never know when sparks will ignite and a cup size will change.

Most of the consultants' husbands came to the party (and some children) so our house was packed. While the consultants knew each other, it was the first time the families had met, so we settled into the living room for introductions and to break the ice. Remembering the importance of praise, I started by praising Ned and Sharon for their help and support. I saw Marjie glance at Sheryl, hoping she would get the hint. Next, I turned the praise to all the others, telling them our success was due primarily to them and the way we'd worked together as a team. On impulse I added, "We're the best, and we'll stay the best." This announcement was followed with cheers and applause, and the mood was set for the rest of the evening.

Ned and I provided roast beef, chicken and dumplings, and hot rolls. The others brought vegetables and desserts. But it was Stan Slaten's contribution that made the meal unforgettable. He brought the ingredients and created a Caesar salad as we watched, explaining each step with the flair of a gourmet chef. The secret was the dressing, and the final step was adding the raw eggs. I flinched at the thought. Raw eggs?

Stan caught the look on my face and announced that everyone had to taste the salad before making a judgment. I wasn't the only one who hesitated before taking a bite. He received a thundering applause from all of us. Since that time, Caesar salad has been one of my favorite foods, but none has ever tasted as good as Stan's did that day.

Now I could see why he did well in sales. He'd convinced me to try something I would never have tried on my own. Intuitively, I knew Stan had far greater potential than I had ever imagined, and one day I would know firsthand that this was true.

We moved into the small den for the rest of the evening, and our guests sat nonchalantly wherever they pleased, now comfortable with each other and totally relaxed.

I talked to the whole group about our beginning with Mary Kay (primarily for the husbands' benefit). Ned joined in saying, "It started out as Jackie's business and then became our business." He admitted he hadn't been fully on board at first, and I could tell by the looks on the husbands' faces that many related to his hesitation. Next, each one took a turn discussing his family and what they hoped to improve in their lives with the Mary Kay money. The answers ranged from paying bills to starting savings accounts for college, but one man's response surprised us all—he wanted to take flying lessons because he'd always wanted to own his own plane. I laughed to myself because I was pretty sure his wife had related Mary Kay's advice. She said the way to handle the ego touchiness of our making more money than our husbands was to let them provide the necessities and for us to provide the niceties. This approach would allow them to maintain their dignity as the providers for the family.

We ended by practicing the song that Mary Kay insisted we sing at our meetings. It was a hymn sung in the Baptist church. "I've got the joy, joy, down in my heart," repeated several times. Mary Kay converted the words to "I've got that Mary Kay enthusiasm down in my heart, and ending with "down in my heart to stay."

Everyone was reluctant at first (especially the men) because it was not considered a regular form of behavior in the professional world; but I looked at Marjie and Jan and we started singing. Since Marjie and I usually had to lead the singing, it would have been nice if one of us could carry a tune, yet we pulled it off anyway. Soon the whole group was singing so loud,

I was sure the neighbors were wondering what was going on at our house. After the first time through, a husband volunteered to accompany us on the piano, so we sang it again even louder. And I had to admit that Mary Kay knew what she was talking about. There is something about music that's contagious; our energy and enthusiasm reached a whole new level.

As we said good night, there were hugs all around. The feeling of awkwardness present in the beginning had been replaced with a feeling of family. Marjie, Stan, and Sheryl stayed behind for a while. We had coffee and discussed what the future might hold for all of us. But none of our speculations even came close to what lay ahead in the years to come.

Dalene and I would begin holding our own sales meetings the first Monday in July, and Mary Kay invited the two of us to lunch to discuss them. My meeting would be at 10:00 a.m., and Dalene's would be in the afternoon. Mary Kay would present our director plaques to us at our first respective meetings. While Mary Kay was talking during lunch, I remembered something I needed to tell her. "I'm taking Sharon to church camp on the same day as our first meeting, but I should be back in plenty of time. I wanted you to know, since Mount Lebanon is a little distance from Dallas and I could always get held up by traffic."

"Jackie, you can't be late. Isn't there someone else who can take her?"

Surprised at the sternness in her voice, I hesitated before answering. "Don't you remember, Mary Kay? This is one of the reasons I quit my job at the law firm. I want to be the one to take her. These are the kinds of things I've never been able to do." She didn't comment further, but the frown stayed on her face.

She reminded us that our meetings were to include education, information, and inspiration, and the rest was pretty much up to us. Other than what we had seen Mary Kay do, we would have to learn by trial and error. Of course we were to begin by singing the "Mary Kay Enthusiasm Song" to raise everyone's spirits, and there was to be no negative talk.

Lunch was over and she pushed her chair back. As we started toward our cars, she called out. "Don't forget, the speed of the leader is the speed of the gang, so you can't slow down on holding shows at this point." Dalene and I looked at each other and quickly looked away. I knew she was smiling, too, which was one of the few times we ever had the chance to react in the same way.

Sharon was out of school for the summer, and just as I had as a child, she loved waking up to the smells of breakfast cooking. It was wonderful to talk and laugh without having to rush out the door at 7:00 a.m. Already I was glad I had made this decision.

Unfortunately, the pace of life did not slow down as much as I had expected or hoped for. Instead, it actually speeded up. Since I no longer worked at the law firm, Mary Kay insisted I book three shows a day, as assurance that at least ten of them a week would hold and not postpone. Since I couldn't possibly hold them all because they were scattered all over town, I passed some of them on to my consultants, which was helpful for our unit.

Nevertheless, handling the logistics took up a lot of time. I'd expected to be home more during the day and Ned would be with Sharon at night. When that didn't happen, I took her with me almost everywhere I went. By the end of summer, she'd been to so many shows I suspected she could give the presentation herself. She was good-natured about being dragged along in my life and never complained. We did get to stop for ice cream or lunch occasionally, and when we did, we left the business of Mary Kay out of the conversation.

One morning Mary Kay called and said a wealthy woman who lived in Inwood Road estates wanted a facial. Mary Kay asked me to go personally. Even though I had another show booked, I called and got Jan Jack to take over for me. We called this dove tailing. Jan would pay me 15 percent of sales and keep the bookings, recruits, and the rest of the sales. So I did lose money by obliging Mary Kay's request, but I agreed because she seemed so impressed that such a wealthy woman was interested in her products. I quickly made arrangements for Sharon to stay with a friend.

When I drove up to the woman's house, I couldn't believe my eyes. I had never been to this elite neighborhood before, let alone invited into such a grand house. For a moment after

I turned off the car engine, I sat looking at the exterior, then took a deep breath to overcome the urge to drive quickly away. I don't think I could have been more nervous if I'd driven up to the Queen of England's palace. I couldn't decide if I should be flattered or angry that Mary Kay had put me in this position.

When I rang the bell, the door opened immediately. The lady of the manor appeared to be about Mary Kay's age and had dark hair, dark eyes, and a dark complexion. "Jackie," she said, "I've been waiting for you."

She drew me inside, chattering constantly. "First of all, I want you to take a look at my statue of Buddha here in the hall." I couldn't help but take a look because it filled up most of the entrance. I had no idea what to say, so I waited. "I want you to put eyelashes on it," she said nonchalantly, as if it were an ordinary request. As I continued to stare, she demanded, "Well, can you do it or not?"

"I guess I can, although I've never before been asked to do anything like this," I replied.

"Okay then, let's get started. I'll have my facial first." As I set up, she quizzed me on my experience and spent the next five minutes impressing me with where she usually had such things done: Neiman-Marcus in Dallas and Elizabeth Arden in New York. Instead of intimidating me, as I suspected was her intention, it gave me a sense of calm, and I decided to treat her exactly like everyone else.

I started with the hide tanner's story as usual, and she interrupted, "Is that true?"

I laughed and told her that was what I asked when I had my first facial. After that she relaxed a little as I looked at her face carefully. She was all the same tone—dark. She needs contrast, I thought; some lighter, brighter colors to compliment her dark tones. After the skin care (which I made her apply herself) was over, she kept feeling her face, and I knew she was impressed. She'd already told me I had to do the make-up for her; that was what she was used to having done. I capitulated, but still pushed for her to do it herself. She would learn so much more. But she waved her hand, indicating refusal, so I asked if she wanted to select the colors. Irritated, she replied, "Absolutely not! I want you to show me just what you can do." I wanted to remind her that I wasn't the hired help and that this facial was free, but I bit my tongue and kept silent.

I made decisions quickly: a mix of light and medium foundations to cover shadows, a lighter shade to highlight her best features, forest green eye liner and shadow for her eyes, and a primary red moist lip and cheek color to add drama to the look. She looked at herself in the mirror after each step without comment. But by the time we added the final step, she couldn't stop looking in the mirror. I could see why. I could hardly believe the transformation myself. "The mascara is the last step, and you have to apply that yourself. It's the safest way." After it was completed, her eyes seemed to sparkle and dance and her lashes appeared long and luxurious.

Finished, I waited for her response and wished for a camera to capture the remarkable transformation. After several minutes, she looked at me, smiled and said, "You did good." I suspected that was one of the most over-the-top compliments she had ever bestowed.

Before tackling the job of putting eyelashes on the Buddha, we had a cup of coffee and she told me about her family. They owned a chain of Mexican food restaurants. I recognized the name; they were known to be the best in town.

After thirty minutes of tedious work while balancing myself on a ladder, I finally got the lashes on the Buddha, hoping this wasn't some sort of religious insult within that tradition. I also hoped it was the only job of this kind I would ever have to do. The price of the lashes was $3.50. It definitely wasn't worth it, but now that it was over, I was grateful to still be in one piece after such a precarious undertaking.

The total sale was about $60, including a complete set, the eyelashes, and one each of almost every other item we used. I didn't have everything with me, so I explained I would pick up the rest at the office and drop it off on my way home (because she insisted she had to have it all that day). Then I picked up my supplies and headed for the door.

"Oh, no," she said, "you can't go yet. I called the restaurant and they have lunch waiting for us." I looked at my watch and decided I could afford the time. But at least that will be the end of it, I thought.

Not so. The following three days, she called the office, complaining that the products were not the same ones I used because she didn't look as good now that she was applying them. Mary Kay tried to tell her it was the application, but she wouldn't agree. Each day I went back for a repeat performance and tried in vain to get her to learn how to put on the make-up herself. Each time, we had to go to lunch afterwards, which was the only bright spot in this experience because the food was excellent. However, this very rich lady was taking up a lot of my time—time I would rather have spent at home.

Ultimately, I asked Mary Kay to call and tell her that I would gladly refund her money. Luckily, I didn't have to, because I'd decided if I did, I wouldn't go calmly into the night. Instead, I would release all my frustrations by snatching the eyelashes right off that statue. I also made another decision. From then on, I would pass on the elite prospects and stick with real people. They're easier.

I am older and wiser now and I've had a lot of time to think about this experience. I have come to this conclusion: My wealthy customer was suffering from a common ailment—loneliness. At that point in my time I didn't dream that a woman in her position would have this problem. Now I know that the condition is no respecter of persons. I regret that I wasn't more perceptive at the time, so that I could have tried harder to help by being friendlier and letting her talk about her life. The experience wasn't wasted however, because I learned another valuable lesson: Money will not always be the answer to life's most painful problems.

Just before the end of June, Sharon and I made a trip to Mary Kay's offices to pick up more supplies. For once I had some free time and we stopped at our favorite store where we bought most of her clothes (now that I had almost no time for sewing). When we walked in the door to the office, Barbara Acker said, "Ned wants you to call him at home."

"Is something wrong?" I asked, surprised at him being home this time of day.

"I don't know," she replied, "but he sounded okay."

She told me to use Richard's phone. I could immediately tell by the sound of Ned's voice that something was wrong, but he would only say to hurry home and we'd talk then. I didn't want to alarm Sharon, so I simply told her we had to skip our plans for lunch because her dad was waiting for us. She looked at me expectantly, and I added, "We'll get to have lunch with him."

He was sitting at the kitchen table drinking coffee when we walked in. His skin was pale and ashen. "Are you sick, Ned?" I asked, hurrying over to him and feeling his forehead. He shook his head and mumbled, "I've lost my job."

"What happened?" As far as I knew there'd been no sign this was coming.

"They shelved the Nike Zeus program, and that was my job." Seeing my expression, he rushed to soften the blow and added that they'd told him there might be an opening in the Greenville plant, which was about fifty miles from where we lived. Then he added, "But I don't honestly know if that's the case."

He sounded dazed, and I asked him quickly if he'd eaten anything. As a diabetic he had to eat on time or he could have an insulin reaction and possibly lose consciousness. He shook his head so I quickly made tuna sandwiches for us all. After we finished eating and Sharon went to her room, I assured him we would be okay. Richard had told me how much my check would be the first of the month (more than twice what I had made at the law firm), and I knew there was no immediate danger of running out of funds.

We decided not to talk about the situation, especially in front of Sharon. She had already experienced far too many problems for her age, and we wanted her to enjoy the summer. We told her simply that Ned would be changing jobs. The next day Ned's former boss called and said he had set up an appointment for Ned with the head of the Industrial Engineering Department in Greenville the following week. This was way beyond the call of duty, and we were touched by his concern. I couldn't help but get my hopes up that the downtime wouldn't last long.

The only person I told about it was Marjie, but I later found out that Ned had mentioned it to Ken Acker (Barbara's husband) at a bridge party we'd attended with them.

Other than that, we tried to keep it to ourselves and act as normal as possible. The gossip mill had a way of distorting the truth, and nothing good ever came of that.

The big day Sharon had been waiting for finally arrived. Jean Hanson and I were taking Sharon and her daughter, Vickie, to the Baptist camp at Mount Lebanon. Everything was packed and ready, with fresh clothes for each day of the week. Since it was also the day of my first sales meeting as a new director, we left earlier than necessary so I would have time to say my good-byes and get back on the road. We made it to camp in record time, then helped the girls settle in and assured them they would receive care packages during the week (a requirement because all their friends would be getting one).

As we prepared to go, they gave us both hugs and Sharon whispered to me, "I wouldn't let you go for a dollar."

I whispered back, "And I love you, too."

Just then their friends came in shouting, "Get your bathing suits on; we're going swimming," and the girls instantly forgot we even existed.

As we began our drive back to town, Jean saw me looking at my watch every so often and said, "Don't worry, you'll be back in plenty of time." I hoped so because I was remembering the look on Mary Kay's face when I told her about the trip. No sooner were the words out of her mouth than we saw a line of traffic just ahead.

"What is it, Jean, can you tell?"

"Looks like a wreck," she answered, stretching her neck out the window for a better view. I sighed and stopped the car. Fortunately, it turned out to be a minor fender bender, and we were soon back on track. It had, however, cost us some time and I arrived for my meeting eight minutes late. Mary Kay was waiting for me with a scowl on her face. You would think I had held up the moon landing. "I'm sorry Mary Kay; there was an accident," I said breathlessly.

She didn't even acknowledge what I said. "They're all waiting for you, so you'd better get right in there" was her only comment. She didn't mention it again. She didn't have to. It was the last time I was ever late.

As I walked into the crowded room, I was welcomed with clapping and cheering, and I knew it was in celebration of the fact that we had reached our goal. I could feel the excitement of the group, and as a rush of adrenaline kicked in, I said, "Let's sing the Mary Kay song." I glanced at Marjie for help and she rolled her eyes, but started to sing anyway. Then I had us do it again, marching. Leaving all inhibitions behind, we sang as loud as we could until we finally fell into our seats laughing and breathless.

Once we were silent, Mary Kay joined us and announced that the company would be moving into a new building soon, even though it wasn't completely finished. "We'll let you know when the meeting rooms will be ready." Then she opened a brown shopping bag and pulled out my director's plaque. I caught my breath at the sight of the gleaming brass plate mounted onto rich walnut wood. I had earned this and I was proud.

The plaque was proof that I had risen from the lowly position of secretary to a prominent one in management. And it still looks great on my wall of memorabilia in the office area of my home. It read: "Mary Kay, Inc. proudly appoints Jackie Brown Unit Director—July 1, 1964." Then Mary Kay sang my praises as never before, telling my story from beginning to end. She closed by dubbing me, "the girl with the golden words." As I pushed back the tears, I wondered if I would ever get passed the sentimentality.

The little ceremony had an effect on the whole group, and I made my first executive decision: I wouldn't keep them much longer. Everyone was tired, including me, and drained from the excitement. There would be plenty of time for training in the weekly meetings from then on. I explained quickly that we would have a regular meeting next week, and it would begin with a "crow time." At the blank looks on their faces, I added, "This is the period when you can tell anything good that has happened to you during the week, and I will expect everyone to have something to crow about." In addition, I added that no one could say anything negative at a meeting. "No matter if your husband ran off with another woman, and your mother-in-law moved in with you, you cannot tell it here."

"I'm half way there," Marjie quipped, laughing (referring to her mother-in-law who had moved in with them). "Uh, oh. Is that a negative?"

Someone in the group answered, "It would be for me."

When the laughter stopped, I continued: "Seriously, we come here to get rejuvenated for the week ahead. In order to do that, we have to leave our problems behind." The thing that would ruin a good sales meeting was for someone to tell about a bad experience, and a game of "I can top that" to begin. Then I explained that if they forgot and said something negative, they had to put a quarter in the dish on the table.

"What happens with the money?" someone asked. I hadn't gotten that far in my plan, so off the top of my head I said they'd find out when the time came. After that, negative talk was never a problem. The word was passed on, and we maintained a constant positive attitude in our meetings, which played a major role in our rapid rise to success.

At this point I left the room and quickly returned with a small gift, beautifully wrapped, and set it in the center of the table. I explained that the person with the top sales for the week would win a prize, and this was it for next week. As I listened to the twitter of excitement, I remembered my own experience with such gifts, and I understood how they felt. A gift as small as this would help to fill a huge need for recognition when a job was well done.

In closing, I told them again how proud I was of all of them, and I knew great things lay ahead for us. I added that we would close each meeting with something inspirational, and they would be asked to participate, but today I would share something of my own. "There is power in believing, not only in God, but in our products and our company. But we also must believe that within our unit, it's all for one and one for all." Which simply meant that we would support each other as we worked together as a team. In quick response, someone started the chant, "We're the best; we'll stay the best," and we did this for years to come.

That night the house was quiet with Sharon away at camp. The day had been hectic, and I was looking forward to an evening alone with Ned. "At least the timing is good," Ned said, referring to Sharon's week at camp. "Maybe by the time she comes home things will look better."

"We'll be fine, Ned. Please don't worry."

"It's that fear thing we talked about. I'm trying to leave it in God's hands and have faith it will be okay. It's just a lot easier to say than do."

"Okay, now it's my turn to help you relax," I said and went to get the body lotion. I rubbed his feet and his back until the tension was gone and he dozed off. As he lay sleeping beside me, I was left alone in the darkness with my thoughts. They darted back and forth, from the positive of my Mary Kay business to the terrible fact that Ned was out of a job. I tried with all my might to hold onto the positive, but just before falling asleep the thought crept back in, Was it all just too good to be true?

CHAPTER SEVEN

Spiking the Punch

Mary Kay called early one morning a few weeks later and asked me to come to the office "as soon as possible." This was slightly unusual; ever since I had become a director and was full time, most of my contact was with Richard. I rarely spent time alone with Mary Kay. As I dressed for the occasion, I felt a little lilt in my mood. This was a special treat.

I made my way to the new office at 1220 Majesty Drive in the Dallas Industrial District. I felt no discomfort from the hot, muggy July day typical for the area. I was filled with anticipation. I had never left Mary Kay's presence without feeling better than when I got there. That was her magic.

A small area for parking in the front of the building meant that, for once, I could park close to the entrance. With my four-inch heels, that was a blessing. Unfortunately, I had to chicken-peck my way across the railroad track to get there, trying hard not to sprain an ankle on the railroad ties. In the lobby I stood still for a moment, filling with pride. It had an ambiance that said, "You're lucky to be in this place." It was so much grander than the old place; Mary Kay was moving up in the world, and she was taking us with her.

The entire front of the building was glass, floor to ceiling. Through it you could see a mirrored wall, where the Mary Kay products had been arranged with great care. Fresh flower arrangements with spring colors had been strategically placed among the products to make them look natural and pretty at the same time. Skillful lighting lent a mystical illusion to the whole setting. Barbara Acker, the secretary, had a desk on the opposite wall, facing the entrance.

She smiled warmly as the door opened. "Come in, Jackie. It's so good to see you. Mary Kay will be with you shortly. Just make yourself at home. You know where everything is."

I took a seat in a comfortable chair across the room from her desk and counted my blessings. The phone rang and while she answered it, I thought about the life that lay before me. I loved almost everything about this business—the spirit, the Christian values, the sense of camaraderie, the incredible confidence that anything was possible.

This was the 1960s, when women had not yet made the inroads into the marketplace that they have today. Back then, women stayed home with the kids or became a nurse, a teacher, or a secretary. Those were jobs that might have provided meaning on one level, but they never let you set big goals for yourself, they never communicated that you had limitless potential and the only thing stopping you was your own resistance. Mary Kay told us we could be whatever we wanted, and it was the message we had been longing for.

I watched Barbara with fondness as she fielded the phone calls. Ned and I had already become friends with her and her husband, Ken. We lived in nearby areas, and when possible we played bridge together on Friday nights. I sank deeper into the leather chair and suddenly felt free, something I had never experienced while working at the law firm. I might have been working more hours here, but I set the schedule myself, and that made all the difference. I felt like a small-business owner, with all the responsibilities, but with all the perks as well.

Dalene and I had been here earlier to discuss the upcoming seminar. Mary Kay had stressed over and over to us that this seminar would determine sales and recruiting for the rest of the year. It would be held in September and would be the first ever for the company. Everyone interested in learning more about it and the opportunity it offered would be invited, along with consultants already involved.

In later years, these events were to become grand affairs, full of pomp and circumstance, with Mary Kay being carried in like a queen dressed in beaded gowns that indeed made her look like

Queen Elizabeth. But this was our first, and humble as it appears looking back, I can still feel the charge of energy I experienced in the days leading up to it.

About 150 people were expected to be coming and the only room large enough for the crowd was the warehouse. We didn't care. We knew that the decorations we had planned would cover up the flaws and make the room festive. The program we had designed was a surefire winner that would send everyone there out into the world fired up for fall sales and recruiting.

When Mary Kay had appointed Dalene and me as key speakers for the event, she made us feel important. The three of us were cooking the entire dinner for everyone by ourselves. Mary Kay was an excellent cook, and she was preparing her specialty, roast turkey, as the main course. Her own unique touch was adding jalapeño peppers to the dressing. She assigned Dalene and me side dishes, using her recipes, of course, to prepare at home and bring to the event. Days earlier she had left the recipe for the carrot-gelatin salad for me. It was written on a sheet from her personal notepad. I glanced at it before folding it and sticking it in my purse. The name at the top of the pad read Mary Kay Weaver. That seemed strange. I knew of only two names that she went by: Rogers (Richard's father) and Hollenbeck, the husband who had died just before she opened the company. "It must be her maiden name," I decided and forgot all about it.

"Mary Kay's ready for you now," Barbara said, bringing me back into the present. As I walked into her office, the first door in the hallway and a stone's throw from Barbara's desk, a strange feeling came over me. I didn't see a single other person around. Richard was nowhere in sight. His office was right next to hers, and I could usually hear him talking on the phone or with one of the other employees. Today there was silence.

Mary Kay looked her usual flawless self. A dark burgundy suit showed off her creamy complexion and provided a perfect contrast for the platinum wig. As always, she wore thick false eyelashes that weren't intended to fool anyone as real. Her lipstick was slightly darker than the usual pale pink, but the indigo blue eyeliner, which she kept trying to get the rest of us to wear, was the same.

Her office had similar décor to the one in Exchange Park, done entirely in shades of pink, white, and gold. It was, however, larger and devoid of the unsightly file cabinets that lined the walls of the previous place. In Richard's office, the black leather couches lent it a modern look, and the dark polished-wood desk made him look like a real executive. The huge blue sailfish that hung behind the desk was perhaps a bit too much.

"What's up, Mary Kay?" I asked, "And where's Dalene?" I expected her to be there simply because we were always dealt with as a pair.

"She couldn't make it today," she said as she took a seat, modestly crossing her legs. She preoccupied herself by scribbling on a piece of paper. "It's fine. I wanted you and me to discuss this matter alone anyway."

"What matter?" I asked. Since her phone call that morning, I had racked my brain, trying to come up with a clue as to what this meeting was about.

"We'll get to it in a minute, but first I want to tell you again how well you're doing. I'm just very proud of you, Jackie. Your new recruits are such high quality. Marjie Slaten especially shows great promise. I understand she has a master's degree." I nodded. "She's considering the idea of not returning to teaching school?"

I nodded again. "But I think her husband is the main reason. Stan really grasps the potential in the marketing plan." I set my purse in my lap. "But the summer isn't over yet, so we'll just have to wait and see. She already has some possible new recruits lined up, too."

My normally attentive boss wasn't paying attention. This was a subject I thought she would care about. After all, the new recruits were her bread and butter. Something else was on her mind.

Suddenly she changed the subject. "Has Ned found a new job yet?"

I blinked rapidly. I didn't know she kept track of us this closely. I kept myself calm as I answered, "He has one that looks promising, but it isn't definite yet. It would be such a godsend though." There was a hint of concern on her face. I rushed in to assure her, "He's only been out of work a few weeks."

She leaned back in her chair. "You're really lucky, you know, that your director's check is more than you made at the law firm. I'm sure that takes a load off your mind."

Just where was this leading? I had never seen her change a subject so fast. It seemed so out of character for her to cut off the praise so quickly. Usually she dwelled on your positive qualities until she had you eating out of her hand. It was the first part of the sandwich: praise first, then the issue, then more praise. Suddenly it was becoming disconcerting that no one else was here; it lent a quality of strangeness to the whole affair, and I wondered if I should be worried. Did everyone know something I didn't and they didn't want to be here?

Still, I let it go. Mary Kay would never deliver bad news herself, not the velvet princess. It couldn't be anything bad because Richard always handled the hatchet jobs. However, it was catching me off guard. But I knew I'd get nowhere by pushing her. I merely nodded and waited.

Mary Kay took a deep breath, and I knew from the look on her face that this was the main course. "It is most important for the seminar to provide strong motivation. We are a relatively new business, and we have to start producing the kind of sales that create lift-off. I want the ripple effects to last the rest of the year." I already knew this, and I was pretty sure that she knew I knew. "In order to accomplish this, everyone in attendance needs to be relaxed, receptive. Do you see?"

Perplexed, I merely mumbled, "Yes."

"I want the whole crowd to get into the spirit and charged up to be tiptop sales people. Don't you agree?"

"Of course," I answered, but now I wanted to be entirely sure of what I was agreeing to. I tried to be helpful. "What do you have in mind? New songs? Marching? Motivational speeches?"

She waved the suggestions away. "Yes, of course. But that's not enough. I want certainty. I don't want to guess if everyone is loosened up and ready to go." Her eyes locked onto mine.

"What . . . would do that?"

She set her pen down emphatically and blurted out, "I want to spike the punch."

I thought I must not have heard her correctly. But when I searched her face for signs that she was joking, I saw only impassivity, waiting. She couldn't possibly mean it. She was a good Baptist, like the rest of us. She knew the church's stand on drinking. I fiddled with the strap of my purse, trying to decide what to do. She kept looking at me for a response. Finally, I tried for the innocent interpretation.

"I don't understand what you mean. Are you saying you want to have two punches, one with alcohol and one without?"

A little sigh of impatience. "No, I'm saying we should have one punch and no one has to know that it contains alcohol." She smiled. "Don't worry. I'm not sending anyone out of here soused. It would just be enough to get them to relax."

I don't know how long I sat there. My mind was replaying all the things I had heard her say. "Faith in God first, family second, hard work," and then success would follow. Everything I had ever heard from her suggested integrity and, nothing underhanded. She was a businesswoman, yes, but I always believed she was cut from a different cloth. Recent memories of her pitting me against Dalene trickled into my mind, but somehow they hadn't bothered me at the time. It wasn't outright trickery, I told myself. It was a way of encouraging competition. Other sales people in my unit seemed to view it that way, and I bought in.

"What do you think?" she asked, without a hint of apology or discomfort.

Finally I found my voice. "Let me get this straight, you want to secretly spike the punch?"

She nodded.

My usual deference to her seemed to fall away. Outrage replaced caution. "I can't believe my ears, Mary Kay. We're both Baptists. Most of my people are dedicated Christians and, believe me, they walk the walk. You know they aren't the ones in the bars on Saturday night and in church on Sunday morning. For heaven's sake, one of the ladies is married to a minister." She began to object but I kept going. "It's not the alcohol that worries me, though."

"Well, then, what is it?"

"It's tricking them."

From the way she looked at me, I was sure she thought I just fell off a turnip truck. I could tell she was thinking, "No tricking people: How simple and childlike can she be?" I didn't care. I was brought up in a house where people were what they seemed to be. If you thought you knew someone, if they presented themselves as honest and above board, then they were. And I was proud of that upbringing. I was attracted to this organization in the first place because I thought I could trust it and the people in it to carry on the same tradition. It never occurred to me that Mary Kay wasn't the highly principled and honorable person she portrayed herself to be.

She stiffened, not just at my words, but at my tone of voice. There was no mistaking the fact that I was appalled. Her eyes turned hard and cold as she continued to look me steadfastly in the eye. "Oh, for heaven's sake, Jackie. Don't be such a prude. I've talked with Dalene about this, and it's fine with her. You'll just have to get used to the idea."

The tension in the room was thick and menacing. This was not what she was expecting, and I could see why. I had never gone up against her before. It was totally contrary to my nature. Without taking my eyes from hers, I got slowly to my feet and said as calmly and quietly as I could, "Mary Kay, that's not going to happen."

I walked out. I did not look back to see how she looked, I just opened the door and left. I passed Barbara's desk and approached the outer door to leave the building. Without looking up from her typewriter, Barbara mumbled, "See you later." I turned then and saw her face; it was unfriendly. My instincts told me that she had heard at least part of the conversation. I had shown up thinking this was going to be an auspicious meeting.

Instead it was dark and vaguely threatening. Barbara's reaction simply sealed it for me.

Outside I breathed in the hot, sticky air. This was affecting me far more than I could have thought it would. I actually felt like I was going to be sick, right there on the steps. I couldn't help taking this thing personally; I felt betrayed. What did it all mean? Everything she said she believed in, every way that she wanted us to believe in her? Was it all a lie? I had to hold onto the railing and pause to catch my breath before walking to my car. Secretly giving alcohol to people who were religiously and morally against it was crossing the line. It revealed the first hint of the dark side of a woman I had come to admire. The more you look up to someone, the harder she falls when you see the true soul. If Mary Kay could do this to people who trusted her, what else was she capable of?

Perhaps it was the heat. Perhaps it was the shock of having a hero fall off her pedestal, but my thoughts wandered. In my hazy state I absentmindedly thought about the railroad track as I crossed it again to reach my car. I hadn't given it much thought on my way in, but now I saw it in a different light. With the veil removed from my eyes, I no longer saw a building that looked splendid and glamorous. Instead I saw an ordinary building, located on the wrong side of the tracks, where if you weren't careful, you'd get hit by a train.

I drove home with the air-conditioning turned up because I couldn't rid myself of the hint of nausea. I tried to ignore it, to tell myself that perhaps I was overreacting. But suddenly I was afraid. When one balloon is popped, others are apt to follow. It occurred to me that Mary Kay could fire me. I had never stood up to her before, and not only that, I had never seen anyone else do so either. For all her sweetness and feminine softness, she was a formidable woman, built of stainless steel. Although it was never mentioned out loud, we all sensed that it was safer to agree with her than to thwart her. And, of course, she made it so easy to cooperate. It always seemed as if it was in our own best interest. Now I had broken the rule. All I could think of was, "Ned doesn't have a job. If I lose mine, we'll have no income at all." It ran through my mind like one of those annoying jingles you hear on the radio and can't get rid of. "What if" began to fill my head.

Then I had a thought that stopped my fearsome thinking in its tracks. "Wait a minute," I said out loud. "My people produce most of the sales in the company."

Mary Kay couldn't afford to get rid of me, not this easily. She had absolutely no one to replace me. She might have wished Dalene could fill in, but we both knew that was idle thinking. This was no unfounded belief in myself; I knew it from the computer printouts that I got each month with my director's check.

As I pulled into my driveway, I decided not to tell Ned about the incident. Until he found a new job, he didn't need the extra worry. In fact, I decided there was no reason to tell anyone. I wasn't sure what Mary Kay would do, but if the information got out, it wouldn't be from me. My resolve was absolute until a few weeks later when I let it leak to Marjie Slaten. She had a degree in psychology, and it would lift a burden from me if I related the event. I told it to her as closely as I could remember and then asked, "What do you think, Marjie?"

She waited a long time before answering and finally said cautiously, "I don't like to make snap judgments. At the very least I can safely say that we haven't yet seen the real Mary Kay. I have a feeling this was only the first glimpse of what lies underneath."

Time would prove her right. When the real Mary Kay emerged over the next couple of years, there was very little resemblance to the sweet, feminine woman that we had known and loved in the beginning.

There was no spiked punch at the seminar. Actually, there was no punch at all. Apparently, Mary Kay didn't want to risk my pitching a fit if I saw a punch bowl there. I never, not then and not later, heard a word mentioned about our meeting. It shouldn't have surprised me. It would have embarrassed her to have people know that she had been put in her place. The first time I went back to the office I dreaded seeing her. I had no idea how she would treat me, but I needn't have worried. There were compliments and praise as usual. No doubt she was as effusive as she ever was, but her words didn't have quite the same effect as before. I saw everything far more clearly now that I had seen the other side of Mary Kay.

Although she never mentioned the incident to me again, I could see in her eyes that she hadn't forgotten.

As the seminar drew closer, the competition became fiercer. Friendliness was in great supply on the surface, but not far below the intense rivalry between Dalene's people and mine was boiling. The ten consultants who had the highest sales for the year were to be honored at a dinner on the closing evening of the seminar. Dalene and I both wanted the top performers to be our own people, a sentiment that was kept going as Mary Kay played us both as the "stars" that everyone should emulate.

At every opportunity she told me how well Dalene was doing, that she was almost overtaking me. She said it with a wink and a smile as if it were all fun and games. But this was no game. Too much money was involved, and there was only room for one at the top. I strongly suspected she did the same with Dalene about me. You never work harder than when you have a worthy rival following closely at your heels.

In the middle of all this, I was hugely and pleasantly surprised: Ned got a new job, and it was much better than the one he had lost. It was in industrial engineering, his major in college. Unfortunately, the company was in Greenville, Texas, almost an hour's drive from our house. His carpool had to leave a little earlier, and it got home a little later, but it was fine. I was independent enough to arrange my schedule so that I could look after Sharon.

As the summer wore on, Sharon and I continued to spend a lot of time together. For a while I got to have it all: career woman and mom. She was an avid reader and had earned a certificate for finishing all the books in her school library. When I took her with me to the office, she brought along a book to read. One of the books was the newly released To Kill a Mockingbird. Sometimes Mary Kay would have Sharon come into her office and read that to her. It was only when she wasn't busy and I was in a sales meeting, but it made Sharon feel extra special.

Even today, it's a story Sharon tells her grandchildren. Not long before Mel Ash, Mary Kay's final husband, died, Sharon and her husband saw them having dinner one night at a Big D restaurant. Mary Kay recognized my daughter and reminded her of those afternoons when, as a child, she had read to her about a lawyer named Atticus Finch, who stood up for his principles.

Final arrangements were being made for the seminar. Marjie, Dalene, and I began to realize that we could all be a lot more successful if we had the full support of the consultants' husbands, so we talked Mary Kay into having a session for them. We wanted to answer questions and explain how they could help us with the business.

It turned out to be a motivating factor for the whole company and a move that let the women conduct their business more efficiently. Husbands were now more willing to stay home with the kids so their wives could hold shows in the evening, the best time. The chores of the day were over and most women were in the mood to socialize and spend money. For Ned and me another good thing came out of this—we became friendly with Dalene's husband. It seemed impossible for me to be close with Dalene because of the enforced rivalry, but I liked her husband. Occasionally he would come by our house to talk. Eventually, he became an interesting source for information about Mary Kay's past.

The big day finally arrived. The company was just one year old, but consultants had spread the word about the new company's booming success to outside areas through friends and relatives. As a result, people streamed into town for the seminar to see what all the hoopla was about. One of the people in this group was my older sister, Faye, whom I had recruited earlier in the summer.

The warehouse, usually full of wares, had been transformed into a meeting room, with all the tables and chairs facing the speakers' podium. Mary Kay had brought in a piano and a pianist to get the excitement going. I suppose she thought she needed the extra help without some spiked punch. Balloons and streamers in every shade of pink hung from the ceiling and lent a festive atmosphere. The crowd of new faces added to the excitement, and everyone present seemed to realize that they were a part of an extraordinary happening that day.

I drove to the seminar alone and arrived an hour early so I could personally greet each new prospective consultant. All were dressed in their Sunday best. I chose my bright yellow boucle knit suit with matching shoes and bag, which contrasted nicely with my dark wig.

The day began with the pianist playing the "Mary Kay Enthusiasm Song". The tune rang throughout the building as people arrived for the seminar. People lined up outside and then filed into the room keeping time with the music. In unison, we marched, clapped, and sang at the top of our lungs. As Mary Kay came to the podium, we spontaneously burst into the song again. A shiver ran down my spine, and for a while I forgot about the punch episode; the wonder of it all returned. Marjie leaned over and whispered to me, "I can't tell the visitors from the consultants." The visitors had joined in the singing and clapping as if they already belonged to the group.

"I can tell who's who," I whispered back.

"How?" she demanded, genuinely curious.

"The visitors are all wearing their own hair."

Marjie looked around the room and suppressed a giggle. She knew exactly what I meant. All the Mary Kay people, taking a cue from her, were wearing wigs and false eyelashes.

The music was ending, and Mary Kay stood at the podium and introduced each speaker. I watched her work her magic again and again by telling in great detail how wonderful the person was. Her introduction was almost as long as the speech itself, but this was her best talent—motivation. She had said to us many times that if a person heard positive things about herself often enough, she would begin to believe them and in turn would live up to the praise. From many years of observing and using this technique myself, I can tell you that it is absolutely true.

One by one, different people stepped up to the podium to give speeches about booking shows, closing the sale, recruiting, and training. Then Mary Kay brought in her accountant,

Bob Hurt, to talk about the tax benefits of being in business for yourself (I was so impressed that I set up an appointment to talk with him about my personal business). Some years later, Bob, a notorious gossip, ended up as another source for startling information about Mary Kay's past.

Mary Kay praised every speaker effusively. However, all that paled compared to the treatment she gave Dalene and me. If you multiply the praise she gave the others by ten, you will have an idea of what it was for us. Mary Kay had dubbed me "the girl with the golden words," and although I knew it was hype, I couldn't help feeling important. Amid thundering applause at the end of the introduction, the feeling was magnified. I felt like a star on Broadway, and it was my time to shine.

After the main presentation, there was a break, during which Dalene and I were to give mock shows in separate meeting rooms so everyone could observe how to do a show of their own and how to best demonstrate the products. Everyone had to choose one to attend. As I waited in the meeting room to begin, I was surprised to see that not only were my consultants and their prospective new recruits present, but also a large group of Dalene's as well. There was hardly space for another single person. A thought fleeted through my head. "If everyone was here, who was at Dalene's?"

Richard was last on the program for the day. Mary Kay found a whole new group of adjectives to describe his brilliance. She was especially proud of her son, and I believe she meant every word. First, she boasted that he was a computer genius, far advanced in the new technology for his twenty-two years. She went on to say he always came into work early and stayed late, and he dealt with almost every aspect of the business.

I saw Ned and Stan exchange a look. It was no secret that they didn't respect Richard; they thought he was merely an upstart who would never have gotten where he was without his mother. I didn't say a word, but I agreed with Mary Kay on this one. This young man had some fine qualities that they didn't recognize, and he most certainly earned his paycheck. After five minutes with him, I was always revived and ready to rush back out to work, no matter how depleted I had felt before. Many times in the years ahead when I had to handle people who dropped the ball, who didn't do their job, who failed to place orders on time, or who mismanaged various other tasks, I wished for a Richard to play his role and get them back on track. I'm not sure he has ever received enough credit for his part in the company's success.

As Mary Kay continued with the introduction, she didn't have to include the fact that he was a master at motivating people. Everyone was about to see that first hand. Richard stepped quickly to the podium, carrying his easel with a blackboard on it. He wore a suit and tie, and every hair on his head was in place. This was unusual because ordinarily bits of hair always seemed to stick up in different areas on his head. He must have engaged in an extra hour of grooming for this first seminar.

As I looked around the room I thought that it was good to see so many men. Men were always hard on him, and I hoped they would give him a chance. "If you have any questions as I present the marketing plan, don't hesitate to speak up. We're talking money here, big money," he began. "Actually, there's probably more money to be made in the cosmetic business than any of us ever dreamed of. You know the saying, 'If a woman has to choose between buying food and cosmetics, she'll take . . .'" He held out his hand to the audience, signaling them to fill in the blank and the crowd roared, "Cosmetics!"

"And," he continued, "if that isn't spectacular enough, the cosmetic business has been found to be recession proof. There is one more thing that also does well in a recession. Does anyone know what that is?" The men chorused, "Alcohol," to the sound of laughter.

Richard whipped out his chalk and began drawing circles on the blackboard. Even though he had done this many times before, he had to repeat it for the new people. And I had learned first hand you had to hear it many times before grasping the full potential. As I looked around the room, I noticed the men taking notes. Stan watched him intently with a fixed stare. First, Richard drew one large circle on the board. He paused and said that this represented each one who joined the company as a consultant. "On this level, the consultant can earn 50 percent gross profits on her sales. By comparison, a grocery store only makes 2 to 3 percent profit on theirs." He explained that I had earned over $500 in December in only two weeks, and on a part-time basis. There was a muffled gasp from the crowd, because $400 a month was considered good pay for a woman at that time. He added that a consultant could recruit immediately and would make a percentage off her recruits even if she chose to remain at the first level.

Next, he quickly drew ten smaller circles underneath, with each one representing a new recruit. When a consultant had this many recruits, she was probably eligible to qualify for directorship. This was the first tier of management. She kept the percentages she had already been making and then made even more off of the whole group. Here, he pointed out that Dalene and I had already passed to that stage and, while making only the same amount of sales ourselves, were earning an additional $1,000 a month or more in director commissions. Again there were whispered exclamations from the audience. That came to $1,500 total. For a woman in those days, this was nothing short of remarkable. "And," he paused for emphasis, "the company is only one year old. Think of how far this will go in a few years."

He waggled his chalk at the audience mischievously. "And now for the second tier," he said as he drew circles underneath the ones already there. "To make this easier to understand, let's use Dalene and Jackie as examples again. When the consultants who are under them become directors, they move up to senior directors. Both of them will soon reach this level, and once again the money goes higher. With five to ten directors under you, you could easily earn four to five thousand dollars a month."

Now you could hear a host of actual gasps. This kind of money was off the charts. "Is this for real?" yelled one of the husbands, and everyone began talking at once. "Absolutely," Richard answered, "but wait, there is an even higher level." He cleared his throat, took a deep breath, and announced with new vigor. "It's the one that will generate more money than you can imagine."

He's referring to the mysterious third tier, I thought to myself and quickly pulled out my legal pad. Ned and Stan did, too. Using the space left on the board, Richard pointed to the circles he had used as recruits and said, "One day, many of these people will also become directors, which means that the top directors will have fifty to one hundred units under them. On this level, you would earn in the neighborhood of ten thousand dollars a month, and maybe even more." This would be equivalent to at least $50,000 today. In the years ahead, the earnings became far greater than the estimates Richard made at that first seminar.

He continued, "But no one is even close to that level right now. I predict that by next seminar it will be a different story. It's something to think about: there IS a pot of gold at the end of this marketing plan."

Now everyone in the room was standing, applauding, and cheering. Every woman present was thinking, At last we'll have an opportunity to make what we're worth.

I stole a glance at Mary Kay. She looked as though she would burst at the seams with pride.

Richard held up his hand to still the applause. "It's about time to dismiss for the afternoon, so that we can all be back at seven o'clock for the awards dinner. But first we have something to give all of you to help you increase your sales and recruiting."

From the back of the room, employees almost ran down the aisles, passing out large bumper stickers that boldly read: "ASK ME ABOUT MARY KAY." Soon the parking lot was flooded with people plastering the stickers onto their bumpers. The rocket to success had been launched and no one there would have believed how far it would go in the future. Seminars in the years ahead were much more extravagant, but no one present at this one would believe any of them was as exciting. And, all of this happened without the spiked punch.

Ned and I hurried to get home and back by 6:30. This wasn't easy since we lived quite a distance away. We had the house to ourselves tonight; Sharon was spending the evening with a friend. We rushed in the door to change into our finest clothes;

then I hit the kitchen and prepared my dish for the dinner. Ned talked nonstop. He had caught the excitement and had begun to visualize the possibilities of where we were headed. We were both looking forward to the awards presentation and were relieved that we didn't have to hurry home to our child. Since Dalene and I were the only directors, we were included in the Top Ten in sales that year. But after that, we, as directors, would be in a separate category of Top Directors because there would be so many more of us. Dalene and I had both worked hard to qualify for directorship during this time. I couldn't wait to see which unit the rest of the winners would come from.

My hair was the easiest part of getting ready for the evening. I whipped off the bouffant wig in the "flip" style and replaced it with a shorter, sleeker one, but still with a bouffant look. I had come to be proficient in makeup during my nine months with Mary Kay. As my complexion improved, I concentrated on perfecting my glamour look. I discovered a wonderful secret about how to create the perfect eyebrow to fit my face shape. The pattern for each person is already on the face; the key is simply learning to spot it. I had also learned how to make my brown eyes look larger with tricks of illusion. My best feature was probably the high cheekbones inherited from my mother, who was 25 percent Cherokee Indian. And of course I was adept at using highlight and shadow on appropriate areas to add drama. A bright coral lip and cheek color finished the paint job, except for the false eyelashes that I had trimmed and applied so that they were not easily detected.

As usual, Ned was dressed and ready to go before me. When I came into the living room, I thought, He is handsome. He wore a black suit, a freshly starched white shirt, and a red, black and gray patterned tie made of silk. His shining black hair, white teeth, and flashing green eyes completed the picture. I thought he belonged on the cover of a movie magazine. To go with his black suit, I chose a black dress. The top was sleeveless and made of a shiny black taffeta. The knee-length full skirt was black lace that swished when I walked. My black silk evening shoes finished it off.

"You look great," he said to me as I entered the room, and I returned the compliment. Perhaps I was reaching, but I was reminded of Jackie and John Kennedy and the feeling of Camelot that they had inspired with their style. As with most people of that era, we thoroughly enjoyed dressing the part.

We were in high spirits as we arrived back at the company. Even though we were early, cars had already taken the front parking. Remembering how Mary Kay felt about being tardy, I was a little anxious by the time we got inside with all the food, but it was apparent that she and Richard were in high spirits, as well. They greeted us at the door, all smiles and warm words. Richard was wearing a tuxedo that fit him so well I wondered if it had been custom tailored. But it was Mary Kay who took our breath away. She was wearing a long, silver evening gown, studded with rhinestones. As the light caught the stones, hundreds of tiny sparkles emanated from her entire body. It was a dazzling effect, as I am sure she had intended it to be. Ned and I stood in the back of the entrance, watching people's expressions when they saw her. We especially wanted to see Marjie and Stan. We weren't disappointed. Marjie was not good at hiding her feelings, and her mouth actually fell open.

Marjie and Stan were a handsome couple. And especially tonight, with Stan in a dark suit, and Marjie in a flowing pink chiffon dress, they were among the "beautiful people." Although Marjie seemed unaware of it, I noticed that men always turned for a second look when she passed by. As people continued to arrive, each one dressed to the nines, Ned commented on what a great looking group it was.

After dinner, the awards began. Although Mary Kay waxed grandly with even more lavish praise for all the winners, it wasn't necessary. We were all so high on the vision we had for what lay ahead that our feet barely touched the floor. Every consultant and potential recruit was hoping that some of the glitter from Mary Kay would rub off on her. As I expected, Marjie did make the Top Ten (even though she had only been in the company since June). Prizes, however, were all equal, so it hardly mattered. This year they were elegant, genuine leather handbags, in different colors and sizes. Each bag appeared to have been chosen to fit each winner.

After hugs and tearful good-byes for the out of town people, Stan, Marjie, Ned, and I met at a nearby coffee shop. We parked side by side, and started for the entrance. A couple stood watching and finally the man said, "Okay, we're asking." Bewildered we just stared at them. "The bumper sticker," he said. By the time we finished our spiel, he looked a little sorry that he'd mentioned it. This was the first of hundreds that asked because of this simple, inexpensive, brilliant marketing tool.

As soon as we were seated in the coffee shop, Stan started rattling off ideas. He wanted calling cards made up immediately with information about Mary Kay Cosmetics. In the center he wanted it to read, "This card entitles you to a complimentary facial." It would bring customers in the door, and that was the key. The idea struck home, and the next week the cards were made and presented to waitresses, beauty operators, salesgirls, and literally to every other woman we came in contact with. One of Mary Kay's favorite sayings was, "If you want to get the word out, don't telephone or telegraph, just tell a woman." She knew that women talk to other women, and although we didn't use the word in those days, this was the best form of networking.

After business, we got around to rehashing the seminar. Stan and Ned did most of the talking. They thought the two of them could do everything better than Richard. Marjie and I just looked at each other and smiled because we knew better. Not only did we understand how complicated the business was, we knew how capable Richard was. Stan urged Marjie to hold more shows and get more recruits. Since his mother would look after their daughter, he couldn't see anything to stop her. "Full steam ahead," he said.

I finally decided to let the two men rave on and asked Marjie if she wanted to join me in a trip to the ladies room.

"Can you believe this?" she asked as soon as we were out of hearing distance. "Pretty soon we'll be working our heads off and they'll be staying home if we let them." She was indignant; they were taking over our area.

"It does sound that way," I admitted, "so we'll have to make sure that doesn't happen. By the way Marjie, I hope you didn't tell Stan about the punch problem." Silence. "Oh no, you already did? He'll tell Ned and I'll be in deep doodoo" (a southern Baptist expression used when someone realized they had gotten themselves into a big mess).

"Well, maybe it'll be okay," she answered without much conviction.

When we returned to the table, Ned seemed a little more subdued, and he did not make eye contact when we sat down. Please let it be my imagination, I prayed, and vowed that I would tell him myself as soon as we got home.

We hadn't been in the car for five minutes when he brought it up. "Why didn't you tell me about the spiking the punch incident?"

"Ned, it happened before you got your new job, and I thought it would be bad timing. I didn't want you to worry."

"Well, when were you going to tell me?"

"Tonight . . . probably."

"So what happens now? Do you think that Mary Kay will let it go without some kind of reprisal?"

I hesitated, choosing my words carefully. "Ned, you know we've always agreed that everything has a price, and this is no exception. Some time, in some way, there will be a price to pay for me going against her on that. Mary Kay has been a little aloof since it happened, but not much. I think at this point she needs me as much as I need her."

He was quiet for the rest of the ride; for now this seemed to satisfy him.

As Ned slept beside me that night, I silently reviewed the day. I felt with absolute certainty that Mary Kay Cosmetics was headed for greatness. But I was uncertain where, or whether, I would fit into that picture. In my final prayer for the evening, I remembered to say, "Not my will, Lord, but Thine."

CHAPTER EIGHT

Season in the Sun

After Mary Kay's first seminar in September, it was as if someone waved a magic wand and expanded the size of my unit exponentially. So many new people attended sales meetings each week that I had to use every trick in the book to remember their names; one of which was repeating the name three times during a conversation.

My unit had not just grown in quantity; we had also grown in quality. Because most of our members came from strong religious backgrounds, we had people of good character as well as good hearts. Marjie added strength to the mix by recruiting people like her, well educated and ambitious.

I could only imagine how challenging the rapid growth was for Mary Kay. One thing she did in order to remain closely connected as the number of consultants increased was to begin a weekly newsletter called The Beauty News and Views. It also helped her feed the flame of competition between Dalene and me by listing our unit totals each week for everyone to see.

At the top of the newsletter's first page was the "Unit Scoreboard." The Brown and the Brewer units were ranked according to which one was top unit for the week, which was obviously to spur on the competition between us. Unfortunately for Dalene, it was usually the Brown Unit. Total sales were listed alongside the unit name and just below this group, consultants' sales were listed in the same manner. This information was stimulating enough, but there was far greater motivation. Beside each name, Mary Kay wrote words of glowing praise for each person. No one understood the power of praise better than I did, and it was magnified when in writing. With a stroke of her pen, Mary Kay recognized a job well done and at the same time created intense competition for the top spots.

Every single one of us wanted to see our name listed in that newsletter each week, and preferably on top. On the day it was due, I ran to the mailbox, but as soon as I opened it, Ned jerked it out of my hand. Marjie said Stan did the same thing, and I suspected everybody in the company was just as eager. It was our little scorecard, right out there in the open for everyone to see.

But Mary Kay began doing something else in the newsletter that was slightly controversial. She quoted scriptures from the Bible in conjunction with sales. She would use verses like, "Knock and it will be opened unto you," and "Seek and you shall find." It bothered me a little, but Ned was furious; he considered it sacrilegious to mix religion and commerce.

"Ned," I pleaded, "this is simply your own opinion. Please don't rock the boat over something like this." Everything was going so well that I was constantly on guard against anything that would spoil the fairy tale we were living. My take on the newsletter was pretty much the same as on almost everything Mary Kay did—it was a brilliant idea. So naturally I started sending one to members of my own unit each month as well.

Marjie had captured the role of "pace setter" for our unit and soon had enough recruits to consider moving up the ladder. Stan was as gung-ho as ever, and together they decided that instead of returning to her teaching job, she would work full time with Mary Kay and begin qualification for directorship. So now, in addition to taking care of my own shows (Mary Kay still insisted I book three a day), recruiting, training, and sales meetings, I had to help Marjie achieve her new goal. I learned the full meaning of the saying, "There ain't no free lunch." Everything had a price, and the higher my paycheck became, the more hours I had to work. Ned figured it up; I now spent a minimum of twelve hours every day on Mary Kay business.

Sharon had started back to school and was chosen for the first of many honors that lay ahead. She was elected as one of the cheerleaders for the grade school football team. I tried constantly to make up for my frantic schedule and the deprivation it caused her by doing for her everything I could. In this case, I made her uniform. Her full circular skirt was white pinwale corduroy that stood straight out when she whirled around, and her blouse and tights were shiny, white cotton satin. A large purple F (for Falcons) was so big it almost covered the front of her blouse. Ned and I went to every game possible to support her and to cheer her on; we relished each moment of the season.

My monthly checks were now over three times what I had made as a secretary, and I decided it was time for me to have my own car. Ned's new job was farther away than the previous one so he needed the one we had. Mary Kay drove a white Cadillac (before the era of the pink ones). Just for the fun of it, I decided to go to the same dealership and fantasize about how it would be to own one of my own. When I told the salesman I was just browsing, that I was sure I couldn't really afford one, he said, "What makes you think that?"

"Because this is my first car, and I don't even have a trade-in," I answered.

Then he asked more questions about what I could afford to pay monthly and whether I could make a down payment. Before I had a chance to answer, he said, "I think I have something here you might be interested in. We have a customer who trades his car in for a new one every two years. He is older, so he puts very few miles on the vehicle. Would you like to take a look at the one he just traded in? It might be used, but it's in mint condition."

"It doesn't cost anything to look, does it?" I asked, excited at the thought. It was a green Fleetwood. The color of money, I thought. It looked almost exactly like the brand new ones in the showroom without a single scratch anywhere. And it had all the latest bells and whistles of a luxury car, which I had never even seen up close before. But what made it irresistible was the ignition key he put in my hand. It was gold-toned and the top part was set with stones, which were replicas of rubies, emeralds, and diamonds. When the sunlight touched it, the colors merged into something like a rainbow, and just holding it in my hand made me feel special.

"Would you like to take it for a drive?" the salesman asked.

By way of an answer I hurried to the driver's side as he rushed to open the door for me. I turned the key and it purred into action. I looked down to check the odometer; it read 12,048 miles. In answer to the shocked look on my face he said, "I told you they didn't drive it very much."

The radio was playing soft music, and the sounds pulsated throughout the interior. As we picked up speed, it seemed to float along with only the touch of a finger to guide it. I was hooked. Smiling as he watched my reaction to the experience, he asked if I had any questions. I shook my head no because I was too embarrassed to ask the one I was thinking. Can I learn to parallel park a car this long?

He told me how much I'd need to put down and the amount of the monthly payment. I quickly totaled the numbers in my head and then told him I was ready to take the plunge; I didn't know you were supposed to negotiate. After a long hesitation he said, "You do realize that your husband will have to be the one to sign the bill of sale."

"Even if I'm buying it with my own money?"

"Yes," he answered. "It's the law."

Now it was my turn to hesitate, but I knew it was the way it had to be. However, I decided to put my two cents in anyway about the "law."

"Mister," I said firmly, so he wouldn't think I was joking, "you can write this down in your little book. One day that law will be changed, and women will stop being penalized just because they're women; and they will be able to buy on their own anything they want and can afford."

We finalized the paper work that evening, and I was the proud owner of my first car: not some junk-heap from the back of someone's garage, but a Fleetwood Cadillac. This purchase kicked off a series of events so perfect that I still think of this time as my season in the sun with Mary Kay.

The next special event of this season was to keep a promise I'd made to myself if I could ever afford it—and it concerned my mother. Her birthday was coming up soon and one day I told

Ned that I wanted (and needed) to visit her. She lived in central Arkansas and it was a long trip, especially for the short time we could stay. Ned's eyes twinkled as he said, "You want to show off that Cadillac, and let people see how you've come up in the world, don't you?"

"No." I exclaimed, and then added, "Well, maybe a little." I went on to explain that I wanted to have someone build a white picket fence around my mother's yard. She had said many times that was her ultimate dream. All of us had helped refurbish her house in some way, but I had never before even come close to being financially able to do something like this. Ned was almost as excited as I was about the trip. We arrived on schedule and when we opened the car door the aroma of food cooking surrounded us. Mama was waiting for us and as we hugged her I asked, "How do you like my new car?"

"Oh, is that new?" she asked and then added, "We'd better eat before the food gets cold." At hearing how unimpressed she was, Ned laughed so hard Mama looked at me for an explanation.

"Don't pay any attention to him, Mama, he just has a warped sense of humor."

After the meal that Ned said was the best he ever ate, I told her what we wanted to do for her birthday. My mother was the silent, stoic type, and the only time I'd ever seen her cry was when my sixteen-year-old brother died. But now her face softened as her chin trembled, and I added quickly, "This is a happy thing. It's what you've always wanted, isn't it?"

She nodded her head, hugged me, and asked, "Are you sure you can afford this?" As I hugged her back I felt the greatest thrill I'd ever had from having extra money and could say to her, "Yes, I can afford it."

After I made arrangements to have the fence finished by her birthday, as always, I made a trip to the grocery store for her. The owner, Jeff Graham, saw me drive up and was standing beside the car by the time I'd turned off the engine. "Is this your car?" he asked in amazement.

"Yes, it is. How do you like it?"

He didn't seem to know what to say, but finally answered, "You sure have come a long way from only owning a bicycle. How did you get a Cadillac?"

While I was enjoying this immensely, I also thought it was distasteful to brag so I said, "Haven't you heard, everyone in Texas has one." Over the years, I heard him repeat this story many times.

The next day, after we'd packed the car and started to leave, I told Mama that after the fence was up I was going to plant bulbs for the yellow daffodils she'd wanted to line the fence. Again, her chin trembled but she quickly controlled it and said, "I have a better idea. I'll go down to the old farm and dig up the ones I planted there. That way I'll have a piece of those days always with me."

The next spring when we visited her again and topped the hill to her house, we paused to take in the lovely sight of the white picket fence lined with yellow daffodils. As I looked around at the neighbors' yards, I realized that the fence and flowers made her place look every bit as good as any in the neighborhood. I was filled with pride and thankfulness that I was able to help make it happen.

After parking, Ned said in a voice hoarse with emotion, "I don't think there could be a better feeling than knowing you helped to make someone's dream come true." Even as he spoke the words, I thought, and it wouldn't have been possible without my earnings from Mary Kay.

Two things happened that cast shadows on this near-perfect time. When Dalene first asked me if some of her people could attend our shows, I tried to graciously bow out of it. I knew she was trying to learn why our sales were higher than hers, and I didn't want to appear secretive or selfish. I explained that because our group had so many new people, sometimes we didn't even have room for our own. I suggested, instead, that she have her people attend the mock shows that were some-times put on at sales meetings because there was more room. Then jokingly, I added, "I know everyone wants to scout out how the competition works, and I can't blame you for that." But

Dalene didn't accept my rejection, and her people kept turning up anyway.

It became such a burden to my people (by taking so much time and energy away from their own duties) that I was getting complaints almost constantly about this problem. They wanted me to find a way to stop it. By now it was obvious that Dalene and her unit were looking for ways to beat us out of the top spot, and they had no qualms about how they did it. I did everything I could think of to solve this problem and nothing had worked.

One day when I was at the office and noticed no one was in with Mary Kay, I decided to mention the problem to her. I tapped on her door and asked if she had a minute to talk. She laid down her paper work and told me to come in, then asked what was wrong. For the first time there was no warm greeting or compliments before beginning a conversation. Her manner caught me off guard, and I hesitated before going in and sitting down across from her. I had thought she'd seemed a little preoccupied lately, but nothing this obvious.

Taking a deep breath, I told her what was going on. I went into specific detail so she could see the seriousness of the situation, not just with me but also with my entire unit. She stared at me as I rattled on, which unnerved me considerably. I finally said, "It doesn't matter what we say or how we say it, they just keep on pushing their way in." Then I stopped talking and waited for her response, but she didn't say a word. She just sat there with a strange look on her face, which I finally realized was boredom. Sitting up straighter in my chair, suddenly the thought hit me. She's not reacting because she already knows all about this. It was her idea. And I knew it was the truth.

She set down the pencil she'd been holding and said, "You know, Jackie, you're making more money than me. Aren't you being a little petty about this?" I blinked and wondered if I'd heard her correctly. When I realized I had, my first reaction was to lash out in retaliation. Instead, I took another deep breath and decided instead to be calm and matter-of-fact. I was not going to give her the satisfaction of rattling me. I returned her steady gaze and waited until she was the one to look uneasy. Two could play this game.

Finally I said, "You know, Mary Kay, I realize that your strategy for building sales is to pit Dalene and me against each other in order to make sales go higher. But now you're saying I'm being petty when I don't want to spend my time helping her become stronger competition? There's something wrong here—I already spend at least twelve hours a day taking care of my business. I would like to spend the little time I have left with my family." (I heard later that Mary Kay had also been helping Dalene get recruits, trying to keep the competition between us strong.)

She looked a little stunned at my rebuttal. But without wavering, I held eye contact, rose to my feet and said, "Sorry I bothered you, Mary Kay. I'll take care of this myself." As I turned the ignition with my jeweled key, I realized it didn't feel quite as special as before. I also knew I hadn't scored any points with Mary Kay that day. I was beginning to get the whole picture: Mary Kay did not tolerate dissent. I had simply dug the hole I'd started with the punch episode a little deeper. After this session, however, the problem with Dalene's people began to slowly decline; I had accomplished my goal after all.

On Sunday afternoons, Sharon and I had started going for a ride in my new car. We soon developed the habit of driving through neighborhoods where we would like to live in case we ever decided to move. Earlier in the summer, thinking we might not have another child, I talked Ned into giving the nursery furniture to a young couple that was expecting a baby. He was reluctant to part with it, but I convinced him that we needed the room to use as an office, which was true. I kept only the pictures of the little boy and girl on their knees praying that had hung over the baby bed. Yet even without the nursery furniture, our house was still too small, largely because there was almost no storage space.

Ned made it perfectly clear that he was not interested in buying another house because he still felt the one we had was just about perfect. So, Sharon and I kept our little excursions to ourselves.

One Sunday afternoon, we drove down Easton Road, which wound through a section of rolling hills in East Dallas. The area was dotted with streams and the streets were lined with large trees. All the houses were custom built. As we drove slowly up Sinclair, Sharon cried, "Look at that house over there," and I glanced quickly to the left. The split-level house was unique in style and had a huge oak tree in front on the slanting lawn, as well as a gurgling stream across the street. A sign in the yard read: FOR SALE BY OWNER.

Sharon begged to look at it, and I was easily convinced because I wanted to see it, too. As we waited at the front door after ringing the bell, we checked out the front of the house even more. The exterior was made of dark brown brick with trim painted a complimentary tan shade. There were huge plate-glass windows in all the rooms, and just below one of them on the ground floor, a planter had been built. It was filled with beautiful plants and flowers that complimented the house perfectly.

Finally the door opened and a lady with a warm smile invited us in. We introduced ourselves and began the tour. After we'd walked through the den, kitchen, and living room, Sharon and I looked at each other and smiled. When we began verbally placing our furniture throughout the house, the owner laughed out loud. She knew we were sold. It was far more prestigious than our current one and more in keeping with our new financial status as well.

The owner could already tell we loved the house, but now I had to tell her about a major obstacle—my husband. We had to bring him over that very night because another couple was interested as well. Time to think fast. Sharon and I laid out our strategy as soon as we were in the car. We decided to ask Ned to join us for a hamburger at Goff's, a well-known place just up the street from the house. The plan was to casually drive past it on the way to eat and then reenact the way we had originally stopped spontaneously.

It was almost dark as we approached the house and Sharon said, like a professional actress, "Oh, look Daddy, isn't that a beautiful house?"

Something about it attracted his attention, so he tapped the brakes to stop while he looked it over in his usual manner, slowly and silently. We already knew he was partial to the split-level style.

"Not bad," he said, finally. Then he turned and looked at me. "What do you think?"

Trying with all my might not to show any reaction at all, I answered, "Looks pretty good, doesn't it. I wonder how much they want for it?"

"Well, I guess it wouldn't hurt to ask."

Slyly, Sharon and I exchanged smiles. As we climbed the steps, I shot a look of warning at Sharon to keep a straight face and reminded myself to do the same. Just as the owner opened the door, I wished we'd called and let her in on the plan so she could play along. As it was, she said the worst possible thing: "Well, I see you managed to get him to come, and I'll bet there's a good story about how that happened." Ned flashed a look of anger when he realized he'd been tricked, but thank goodness, he also saw the humor in the situation and joined in as we all laughed.

We walked through the house, and he looked it over carefully, but it was the built-in workshop in the garage that sold him. The central air-conditioning clinched the deal. I think he was ready to buy right then. He gave her a $500 check for earnest money, with only one stipulation. We needed a month to sell our house before the sale would be final. But after only two weeks, we had a buyer and by the time the month was up, we were ready. Sharon and I kidded him constantly about fooling him, but he insisted he'd known all along that we were up to something.

Two weeks after settling in, I still couldn't believe it was real. I kept expecting to wake up and find it was only a dream. It was late in the fall season and sales continued to climb, which meant my check grew larger each month. But with the growth, I became busier than ever, with little time for enjoying our new life. Ned brought up the fact that now that we were in a larger place, maybe it was time to think of having another baby.

I sent him a look that I hoped said, "You've got to be kidding," but I said nothing out loud. If I didn't have time for my current family, how could I ever work in a new baby? I gingerly suggested that when the time was right for that addition, we would know it. I had learned from my sales experience not to be so confrontational with Ned; it was much easier to communicate without being angry.

One Friday we invited Stan and Marjie over for dinner, and of course to see the house. I knew Marjie was dying to because when we drove by any house with an OPEN HOUSE sign in the yard she insisted we go through it. She had also said that a new house was the first thing she wanted to buy when her check was as big as mine.

Dinner was simple, grilled steaks, baked potatoes, Stan's Caesar salad, and hot rolls. Afterwards we settled in the den and on impulse I said, "Let's christen the fireplace." The night air had turned almost cold and a fire seemed like a good way finish off a nice evening with friends. As we sat drinking coffee and watching the fire, Stan said, "I've been trying to decide all night whether or not I should bring this up."

"What?" the three of us echoed in unison.

He told us about meeting a friend of Dick Kelly's, the president of the company Mary Kay used to work for. When he hesitated, I said "So?"

"There's a lot more to Mary Kay's story than we've heard, and it's not pretty."

"Like what?" Ned demanded.

Suddenly I knew it was going to be bad, so in an effort to head it off at the pass, I interrupted. "Wait a minute Stan. Do we really need to hear anything that might derail us? Marjie is beginning qualification. Ned and I have just bought a new house. Life is good. Mary Kay's company is doing great, and how do we know that anything this man says about her isn't just sour grapes?"

A long silence followed as we sat staring into the fire. "Good point," Stan finally admitted. "Why should we get off the track from achieving our goals?"

I sabotaged his announcement, and we didn't hear about it until much later, although the curiosity about it hung in the air for the rest of the evening. Looking back at the way things turned out, it was probably a good thing that we didn't pursue the rumors at that point. If we had, it could very well have changed the huge success story Mary Kay was to become.

As Ned and I dressed for bed, I couldn't shake the feeling that a volcano was boiling beneath the surface of Mary Kay's growing company. One day it would have to be reckoned with. But not right now, I thought. Not when I was playing the role of Cinderella in the fairy tale we were living, and I wanted desperately to make it to the ball.

CHAPTER NINE

The Show Must Go On

Christmas, 1964, had the earmarks of being the best one our family ever had. From the outside looking in, anyone would think we had it all: a new house, a new car, and more than enough money to buy Christmas gifts without having to check the price tags. And, there was even extra money in the bank.

Ned and Sharon did a great job decorating. They found the perfect large cedar tree to set in front of our huge picture window in the living room. Ned used a new product called "flocking," which was a fake snow, to make the tree look as though it were covered with a heavy snowfall. He trimmed the lowest branches from the tree and used them to line the shelf over the fireplace. The magical setting was even better than the year before. When I walked in the door after a long day of work, the smell of cedar and the sound of Christmas music playing on the stereo greeted me, and the weariness melted away.

I tried to convince myself that it didn't matter that I had no time to be a part of the Christmas preparations. But on Sundays, it hit me. I was forced to remember the true meaning of Christmas then, and I had to struggle to push away the sadness deep inside of me. During one such time, I thought about Mary Kay's verbal commitment to priorities, which were God first, family second, and job third. Instead, it seemed to me that it had become, "Work, work hard, and work even harder." But I knew it was my own fault. I couldn't seem to muster the strength to take a stand and follow my own convictions.

My unit, which was now so large that the meeting room was packed every week, was consumed with the excitement that surrounded the cosmetic business. It was glamorous and fun as well as profitable. In one of our sales meetings, someone suggested we throw ourselves a Christmas party, and after much discussion, we decided to have a formal ball.

In talking about this with Marjie (because she was the only one who knew about the punch fiasco), I mentioned that I wanted to notify everyone exactly what the party would include, so there wouldn't be any surprises. Sometimes the Baptist church took the same stand against dancing as it did alcohol, and I wanted everyone to know that no alcohol would be served, but there would be dancing. They could choose to participate or not. As I talked, Marjie couldn't stop smiling and finally just laughed out loud. "What is it, Marjie?" I demanded, and then before she could answer, I continued, "You're thinking the shoe is now on the other foot, aren't you?" (Referring to the possibility that some people might not believe in dancing, which was similar to the problem with the spiked punch). She just kept laughing and with no other line of defense to offer, I laughed with her.

We reserved a room at a leading North Dallas Country Club, hired a band, and planned the menu. As busy as we were, somehow everyone managed to find time to shop for new evening gowns, long gloves that reached above the elbow, and accessories.

Marjie, deviating from her favorite color of pink, chose a stark white taffeta gown, with a bodice covered in beads. Instead of a wig, she wore her own hair on top of her head in large round curls, with tendrils falling around her face. I chose a soft gold satin gown, also simple, except for the sequins that outlined the scooped neckline. My wig was short, with curls around the face, instead of the pageboy style I usually wore. Like Mary Kay, I felt a wig always looked better than my own hair. We were not afraid to take fashion to its highest level, and we all looked magnificent. As soon as Marjie entered the country club, I went up to her and whispered, "Did you ever dress like this for a PTA party?"

"Oh . . . always," she replied, not cracking a smile. But Stan overheard the remark and laughed loud enough for both of them.

The food was delicious and the presentation of it was perfect in every detail. The band played Christmas songs that were especially good for dancing, and even those that chose not to dance seemed to enjoy listening and watching others as they whirled around the floor in their beautiful clothes.

The evening ended with the band playing traditional Christmas carols. Accustomed to singing at almost every occasion, we spontaneously began to sing along, filling the room with warm feelings as well as great music. And as proof that we'd left business behind for one night, the Mary Kay enthusiasm song was not sung.

Sharon had been begging me for weeks to create a costume for her Christmas program at school. She had a lovely singing voice and was chosen to be one of four carolers. I intended to do it, but there seemed to always be some crisis in my business and then time ran out. Suddenly it was the night of the program and panicked, Sharon asked, "What am I going to do? I don't have a costume." Horrified that I had taken this so lightly, we rushed to her room and started pulling out hats, gloves, and scarves. Everything was old and nothing matched, but it was too late to worry about that now. I assured her she looked just fine and being the good-natured child she was, she gave me a kiss and said "It's okay, don't worry."

Compared with the other singers, Sharon looked wretched on stage, as if her outfit might have been pulled out of a garbage bag. My heart literally ached as I wondered how I could I have let this happen? It looked like nobody cared about her at all. I couldn't stop the tears that rolled down my face throughout the program, as I realized just how far off course my priorities had gotten. Ned felt it, too. He took my hand and held it for the rest of the evening.

As Sharon got ready for bed, I apologized for paying so little attention to her over the past months, and I promised that was going to change. She assured me it was fine and seemed more concerned about me than about her poor costume. But it was the jolt my heart needed to get back to where it belonged.

After Sharon fell asleep, Ned and I talked late into the night. We decided the New Year was the time to start trying for the baby we kept talking about, and the business would have to adjust accordingly.

One morning near the middle of February, when the smell of coffee made me violently ill, I knew our plan had worked. Ned was so excited he wanted to spread the news, but I insisted that it had to be confirmed by a doctor first. I was also wishing there was some way to know the baby would be okay. The doctor I had with our other baby had retired, so I had to shop around and learned about Dr. J. Russell Jordan from a friend. When I thought about it, I realized I had never been completely comfortable with my former doctor, so I was going to be extra careful when choosing one this time.

Ned offered to take off work and go with me on my first visit. I refused, but as I sat in the waiting room, I wished I had said yes. I was apprehensive about what I might hear, and I wanted to be comforted. But after I was seated in Dr. Jordan's office and saw his fatherly manner, the apprehension left and I relaxed.

Before the examination, we talked for a long time. He asked me for specific details about my former pregnancy, including our blood types and the cause of my baby's death. When I told him we didn't have that information, he seemed perplexed and said, "But there's a law that requires an autopsy in such cases. What was the result of that?" When I assured him again that we had been told nothing about an autopsy, he said not to worry; he'd check into it himself. Then he added, "And, I want your husband to come with you on your next visit."

After the examination, he confirmed that indeed I was pregnant. He wrote a prescription for nausea medication and had the technician take more blood than I even knew I had. Afterwards she told me Dr. Jordan would be in touch as soon as he got results from the tests.

When his nurse called to set up the next appointment, she said the doctor wanted it to be "as soon as possible," and she pointedly reminded me that Ned was to come with me. Something about her tone of voice made me uneasy as well as her instructions that it should be "as soon as possible." I hoped my concern was just my over active imagination.

When we arrived for the session with Dr. Jordan, we were ushered into his office immediately. I couldn't shake the feeling that something was wrong and glanced at Ned to see if he sensed it, too. But he seemed calm and relaxed. Dr. Jordan looked somber and tired, and I felt panic rising inside of me. Oh, God, I thought, something is terribly wrong.

For the next hour, the doctor explained just how bad it really was. He had found from the autopsy report that our baby had died because our blood types were incompatible. I was Rh negative, and she was positive. My body had interpreted the presence of positive blood as a threat to my life and had produced huge amounts of antibodies to protect me against the "invasion." The room began to spin around me, and the next thing I knew I was lying on the couch with the nurse holding something over my nose and asking, "Are you okay?" Silently I answered, I'll never be okay again.

Dr. Jordan's voice was compassionate as he continued to explain how seriously all of the information affected my current pregnancy. First, he would take samples of blood from Ned. He explained that it was possible, but not likely, that his type could produce either a positive or negative Rh factor. In the event it was that type, and our baby was negative, then it would have a much better chance of survival.

Since our last baby had died, he warned us not to get our hopes up, and mine were sinking rapidly. He said as a matter of fact, it would actually be best for us to pretend we weren't expecting a baby at all. Ned and I sat as still as cactuses in the desert, trying to comprehend what it all meant. The only sound that could be heard was the ticking of a clock somewhere in the building.

Finally, Ned asked, "Did our former doctor know about this?"

Dr. Jordan hesitated, but said, "I doubt that he knew about the problem with the blood types before the baby was born. I do think he saw the autopsy report as required by law."

The question, "Why didn't he tell us then?" hung in the air. Didn't he think we might try to get pregnant again and this would be helpful to know? However, nothing was mentioned out loud at that time.

The doctor continued, "As bleak as this looks, remember there's a higher power than mine, and we need to hold onto that."

Ned and I sat in the car preparing to leave. He looked at me anxiously and asked, "What are you feeling?"

It was as if his voice came from far away and it took a long time for me to answer, "Nothing, I feel nothing at all. I'm completely numb, and it's like I'm just watching this happen to someone else."

As he pulled into traffic, he said, "That's either shock or God's way of protecting you . . ." He left the sentence unfinished, but I knew what he wanted to say. God was protecting me from the full impact of knowing that my baby, or even both of us, might not survive.

The numbness lasted for the rest of my pregnancy. It was all too monstrous to think about. While it varied in intensity, it had the effect of putting everything in perspective. Now, nothing else bothered me as it had before, which was a good thing, because major challenges waited for me just around the corner.

Ned and I decided not to tell anyone just how serious it was—only to say that the problem we'd had before could possibly crop up again. I knew I had to tell Mary Kay before she heard it through the grapevine. I scheduled an appointment with her, which tipped her off it was something important. As I sat across from her, I was totally calm even though I knew she wasn't going to be thrilled about my news, and probably even downright irritated. She sensed something different in me, and said in a softer voice than usual, "What's wrong, Jackie?"

I told her exactly what Ned and I had decided to say, and nothing more. She waited a long time before answering, and even though I felt no anxiety, I braced myself for her usual reminder that my job came first. I almost laughed at the first thing that came out of her mouth, "You know this is not a good time for this. Your unit has grown so fast it's at a critical stage; you just can't let your guard down now."

I heard a calm voice reply, "Oh, I know, Mary Kay, no matter what happens in our personal lives, 'The Show Must Go On.'" I looked around to see whose voice it was, and was surprised to learn it had been my own.

Suddenly, Mary Kay changed the subject. "I've been wanting to talk with you about something, Jackie, if you have a little time." I glanced at my watch and told her it was okay. "There's a group of people in California, near San Francisco, that is interested in joining our company. I'd like you to go out and spend a couple of days with them—show them the products and explain the marketing plan."

Surprised, I asked, "Where did they come from? How did they hear about it?"

She chose her words carefully, and I wondered why she would have to for such an innocuous question. "They're people I knew in the past." She failed to make eye contact as she went on to explain that she would pay all my expenses and a little something extra to boot. "Based on what you've just told me," she added, "I think it would be good for you to have a change of scenery, don't you?"

I'd never been on an airplane before, nor had I been to California, so the idea intrigued me, but in all honesty I had to confess that Marjie or Dalene would probably do a better job, since I wasn't in my best form. But she insisted that she wanted me to go. I said I'd have to discuss it with Ned first. "When, exactly, would I make the trip?"

"Probably three or four weeks from now, when all the arrangements are made."

Ned, unfortunately, was like a brick wall. He didn't want me to go because he was concerned that it was such a long trip for me to take alone, especially since I had never flown before. I hugged him to let him know I appreciated his concern, then told him I agreed with Mary Kay—a change of scenery as well as pace would do me good. Although he was still reluctant, he agreed that it was my decision and wouldn't stand in my way.

Before we had a chance to discuss it further, a few days later Ned got a call from his mother. His dad had been having problems with his heart for some time, and suddenly he had died from a heart attack. We usually visited them every summer, but we'd had to miss the last one because we were so busy. We should never put such things off, I thought, regretting the fact that we missed our one last chance to see him. Still, I didn't feel up to the emotional strain of a funeral or the long car trip to Florida. Ned agreed and decided to go alone and to fly. We talked every day by phone while he was gone, and I could tell he loved being with his family, but he hated being there without us.

When we met him at the airport a few days later, he hugged Sharon and me and said it was the last time he was going to be separated from us, at least until after the baby was born. I hated to break the news to him, but Mary Kay had already bought my tickets for the trip to San Francisco. I was to leave the following week. At first he looked as though he was going to object, but then he sighed and said nothing more. I assumed it was because he knew he had already agreed to it.

In spite of the constant nausea, I found myself looking forward to the trip. It didn't seem to matter where I was or what I did, the nausea was ever-present. I simply went on with my life in the best way I could. There were only two things I could not tolerate at all, and even their smell triggered the nausea: coffee and popcorn. Instead of coffee in the morning (which I had always loved), Ned brought me a glass of V-8 juice filled with ice cubes. This was long before automatic icemakers, so the cubes had to be pried from a metal tray in the freezer, which was not an easy task. He never complained and did everything he could to make life more comfortable for me. Avoiding popcorn was much easier; we simply stayed out of movie theaters.

Marjie helped with my trip, too, saying she would drive me to the airport. Since it was my first flight and I had to take additional baggage full of products to show, I accepted gladly. She and Stan flew a lot, and she knew the routine by heart. We drove into the area at Love Field where I was to board my flight, and she pulled over to the curb to unload my luggage. Suddenly the door was jerked open, and looking up I saw Ned and Sharon standing there, grinning like Cheshire cats.

"We're coming with you," he said, as Sharon ran up to me saying, "Are you surprised? We wanted to surprise you."

'Well, you certainly did that!" I turned to Marjie. "You were in on this, weren't you?' Her facial expression told me she was, and I could tell she was pleased with herself that they'd pulled it off without me suspecting a thing. I had one more question, "Does Mary Kay know about this, too?"

"Oh, shoot," Ned said, "we forgot to mention it to her."

The flight was so turbulent that the seat belt sign stayed on constantly and I spent a great part of the trip in the bathroom being sick. Even the Butternut candy bar that I kept in my purse for such emergencies didn't help.

I tried to smile as I spotted Lois in the crowd, holding up a Mary Kay sign. After we introduced ourselves and recovered our bags, Lois suggested, because it was already late afternoon, that we go to dinner at the famous Fisherman's Wharf for seafood before driving out to our motel in the suburbs, where she lived as well. Being from Florida, Ned loved fresh seafood and wanted to go. Fisherman's Wharf was a temptation even to me, even though I knew the nausea would keep me from eating a single thing on the menu.

I could tell Lois had sales experience. She was warm and friendly and easy to talk with. She apologized for not bringing her husband along but said she hadn't realized Ned would be coming. We all laughed at that as I told her the story of how they'd surprised me with their last minute plans. "That's the sweetest thing I've ever heard," she said, looking at Ned in appreciation.

"Well, I hope Mary Kay agrees with you," I said sincerely. I knew that for her, this was supposed to be all business.

Shocked, Lois replied, "You mean she doesn't know?"

"Do you think Mary Kay will mind?" She had known her much longer than I had, and I was interested in her opinion.

In answer, she seemed to deliberately neutralize her voice, "I'm not sure," and quickly changed the subject.

We sat in an open-air section of the restaurant. Everyone else ordered a full seafood meal, whereas I simply asked for a tall glass of iced tea. When Lois shot me a look, I had to explain about my nausea so she wouldn't think we were just weird people from Texas. Lois kept the conversation going and by the time the meal was over we were all comfortable with each other. She gave Ned and Sharon tips on sightseeing to keep them busy while we worked. I kept waiting for an opening in the conversation so I could ask her how she and Mary Kay knew each other, but none came.

I had her stop at a grocery store for V-8 juice before we reached our motel. By the time we registered and unloaded the car, I was so tired I considered flopping into bed with my clothes on. Lois saw it and immediately said she would see me tomorrow.

The next morning at 9:00 a.m., eight women would be showing up for facials. After cleaning my face and falling into bed, my last thought for the evening was, This stress couldn't be good for the baby or me. I must have been crazy to agree to this trip.

The next morning Ned and Sharon left for their day of sightseeing. Lois and her crew were right on time and were anxious to get started. When I began the show, asking each one of them to tell about themselves, including where they worked, as I always did, they seemed strangely evasive. They all said they were in sales, and had been for several years. Then they quickly changed the conversation to the cosmetics, as they picked up and smelled each item, eager to begin the facial. This had never happened before.

They listened politely as I went through the presentation and the hide tanner's story. They didn't have the same transfixed look that people usually had who were hearing it for the first time. I thought immediately: They've heard this story before. Yet I continued as if everything were normal. Afterwards, I would find out just what was going on.

Even though there were eight people having facials, it went smoothly. They liked the skin care, but they loved the glamour

127

products, as if this was the part that was new to them. They spent a lot of time with the mirrors. When I brought out the before-and-after photographs, they smiled slyly at each other, and that did it. They'd obviously seen them before. There was a lot going on here that I didn't understand, but I decided I would before leaving for home.

After the show was finished, they all filled out orders for the products, even though I had explained this was just a mock show, so they could see how it worked. I had stayed seated the whole time (something I did not usually do), but was exhausted anyway. We spent a little time talking about some of the basics, such as booking shows and percentages for hostesses. Because I felt so drained, I didn't think I could talk one more minute, so I asked them if they could come back in the evening to discuss recruiting. Lois looked at me, recognized my problem, and quickly agreed. She walked people to their cars, but then returned. I could tell she didn't want to leave me alone.

After a few minutes, I pulled myself together and decided it was time for some straight talk. "Lois, what's the story? All I know is that you have known Mary Kay in the past. Did you work with her, or what?"

She was silent so long I'd begun to wonder if I had even asked the question. Finally, she answered, "I'm in an awkward situation here, and I know you are, too. Sooner or later you will hear the whole story, but I can't be the one to tell it, at least not right now. I can tell you I have known about Mary Kay for many years, but not on a personal basis. What do you know about her past?"

"Not much, really," I answered. "I know that she's been married twice, and I've heard about her last husband's death in 1963. She has a daughter and two sons, and she worked for World Gift before starting her own company. I keep hearing other rumors, but I don't know what to make of it all."

Next, she asked me if I knew that Mary Kay and Mary Crowley were friends and at one time had also been sisters-in-law. I couldn't quite figure out where she was going with this, so I asked as plainly as I knew how, "Tell me exactly what you mean. Was Mary Crowley married to Mary Kay's brother?"

"No," she answered, "it was the other way around. Mary Kay was married to Mary Crowley's brother."

How could this be? As far as I knew she'd been married only to Rogers, the children's father, and Hollenbeck, who died in '63, and neither was Mary Crowley's brother. Then I remembered the sheet off her notepad with the name Mary Kay Weaver on it.

"What was his name? I asked, knowing what she was going to say.

"Weaver," she answered, "and she married him twice."

"Twice!" Stunned, I couldn't make sense out of it. I wondered why this information would be kept secret, so I just decided to ask. "Why the secrecy? It just causes more talk when it comes out."

She waited a while to answer but then said, "Because there is a whole lot more to the story." This was all she could tell me, and she hinted that it had probably been too much anyway. She said she had been told not to discuss personal information about Mary Kay, but she didn't say by whom. I was frustrated but had to let it go at that.

The other ladies came back in the evening, and I gave them a full training session on recruiting. They seemed to have a hard time accepting how much money could be made. I happened to have the stub off my last director's check with me, showing an amount over $3,000. "For one month?" they asked in unison, and I nodded.

By the time they left, I felt as if I had a new group of friends and after they saw the check stub, I was pretty sure they would sign up with the company. They said they wanted to use the products (which were being mailed to them) before they made a final decision, which I thought a smart move. On a personal note, they asked me to let them know when our baby came. I felt a little guilty that I hadn't explained about the pregnancy problems, but I just couldn't even though they seemed like true friends this quickly.

The next morning Lois was at our motel bright and early to take us to the airport. While Ned was loading the car, she pulled me aside and said, "I don't think it's fair that Mary Kay didn't give you the full story about this trip. If she doesn't tell you when you get home, then I will." I decided not to mention anything about this to Ned. He had enough on his mind.

It had been a great trip, but we were very happy to be home. Sharon couldn't wait to tell her school friends all about seeing the Golden Gate Bridge; the high spot for Ned had been the Fisherman's Wharf. Mary Kay called me early the next morning and related that the reports from Lois about me were glowing, and she was pretty sure they would join the company. She also mentioned, rather unhappily, that she was surprised to hear Ned and Sharon went along; I explained that it was a surprise to me as well. Given her sense of disappointment, I found her to be a lot nicer than I'd expected. As she talked, I kept waiting for an explanation about what company the people were currently with, but it was not mentioned.

A few days later I took Lois up on her promise and asked for the story. All these people were with Home Interiors, Mary Crowley's company. On hearing that, I felt that Mary Kay had sent me out to steal people away from her. I was horrified but knew why Mary Kay hadn't told me. Mary Crowley and I went to church together, and if I had known this in advance, I wouldn't have gotten involved or made the trip.

There were two people who joined the company during this time that made major contributions in an area other than just cosmetic sales. They were former modeling instructors and helped to add a new layer of confidence for our beauty consultants. One was Suzanne Collins and the other Betty Myers, who was my personal recruit.

Looking good ourselves, as well as knowing how to help others do the same, was an important part of our job. Sometimes as a part of our training in a sales meeting, Betty taught our group the proper way to sit, stand (body alignment), walk, enter and exit a car, and much more. For me personally, Betty addressed the importance of balance in our overall appearance. That information led me into a deep study on how to improve the total physical appearance (ultimately studying with experts in Hollywood, New York, and Europe). As a result of that study, I would one day be considered an "image specialist."

Suzanne was a beautiful blonde and a fashion trendsetter. She wore hats to match her outfits and never succumbed to our obsession with wigs. Instead, several of us started showing up at events wearing hats, copying Suzanne and adding even more glamour to our job. Although usually we still wore wigs, they were just too easy. Mary Kay was not one of the people who wore hats; she always stuck to her wigs.

Even though Ned strongly objected, I occasionally continued to hold shows out of town. Ned felt that if I should suddenly need medical attention when I was many miles away, it could be bad for our baby. But I reassured him that I would be extra careful and wouldn't make such trips often. Sharon was in school and I scheduled the shows so I could be home by 4:00 p.m. to make sure she wouldn't be home alone.

One morning I was going to Winnsboro, Texas, about 100 miles from our house. Looking at the array of maternity dresses in my closet, I chose a pink one that flared out in tiny pleat from the bust line, which was concealing and flattering at the same time. As was the fashion of the day, I chose matching pink shoes and bag to complete my outfit. Since the weather was warm, and I wanted to stay as cool as possible, I wore an extra short brunette wig.

The show went smoothly, with everyone purchasing the product. I booked more shows but explained I might have to send someone to hold them. My nausea wasn't any worse than usual, and I felt okay as I headed home. I was running a few minutes behind schedule so I had to drive a little faster than normal in order to be home before Sharon. These are the times this Cadillac comes in handy, I thought, pressing a little harder on the gas pedal. As the car purred along, the sun was warm on my face and I felt a little sleepy. I shook myself and turned up the radio, hoping to clear my head. I was only about three miles from home when I decided to take a short cut through a shady neighborhood with tree-lined streets. Although I had been in the neighborhood before, I had never been on this exact street, and glanced quickly at the houses as I hurried toward home.

The last thing I remember hearing was huge explosion before everything went black. When I regained consciousness, a policeman was standing at my window yelling, "Get out of the car, lady! It's on fire." Confused, I looked around to see what had happened. My wig lay on the floorboard and I wasn't sure where I was or what was going on. People do strange things when they're in shock. My car was about to blow up, but there was no way I was going to get out of it without my wig back on. As I secured the wig into place, I felt blood running down my forehead. Then I saw the smoke billowing out from under the hood of my car, which was smashed against a telephone pole. The pole had broken in two from the impact. As I tried to push the door open, I heard the officer saying to someone, "That big, heavy car probably saved her life."

He wrenched the door open and pulled me out into the yard. As he helped me toward the house, which was in front of the wreck, I looked back and saw my once beautiful Fleetwood Cadillac, which now resembled a crushed tin can.

The woman who lived in the house was standing next to the policeman, crying. "Are you okay?" she asked. I nodded and said as coherently as I could, "But I have to call my daughter."

The officer announced that the ambulance was on the way here. "You'll have to wait to make the call. Right now we need to get away from the car. It's in immediate danger."

"No, I have to call my daughter; she's waiting for me," I yelled. The sympathetic lady took me into her house and dialed the number I gave her. I told Sharon I had been in an accident, and then the lady took the phone and assured her I was okay, but an ambulance would take me to the hospital. Then she added, "Your mom wants you to go next door and stay with the neighbor until your dad gets home."

Before hanging up the phone, the woman gave Sharon the address of her house. Back in the yard, I heard her whisper to the policeman that Sharon was hysterical. I couldn't clear my head enough to think what to do. I felt something on my legs and looked down to see blood streaming down both of them from large gashes in my knees. And my dress was torn almost in two.

The words, "what happened," kept running in circles through my head, but I couldn't find the answer. Then I suddenly realized that another car was involved, but I couldn't see it in the area. In what seemed like just minutes, the ambulance was there, and Sharon and our neighbor were there as well. I was horrified that Sharon would see me like this, but I learned later that she begged the neighbor until she agreed to bring her. She ran to me crying, "Oh, Mommy, please don't die."

Ignoring the blood all over me, I hugged her and said, "Oh honey, I promise I'm okay. It's not as bad as it looks. I just have to go to the hospital to be checked over." As I said the words, I hoped it was the truth. The ambulance driver rushed us to finish the conversation and loaded me into the ambulance. The last thing I saw as the door shut was Sharon's stricken face. "Take care of her, Lord," I prayed, as the ambulance sped away.

The attendants in the ambulance began taking my blood pressure and checking my pulse. I turned my head and saw another lady lying beside me. The other person in the crash, I thought. The attendant saw me looking at her and leaned down and whispered, "She's going to be all right, don't worry."

I heard the scream of sirens all around us, and wondered if they came from the ambulance I was in. The attendant explained that he couldn't give me any pain medication because of the baby. Oh, God, the baby, I thought.

"Where does it hurt?" he continued.

"Nowhere," I answered. Once again, in what seem to be an extremely serious situation, I didn't feel a thing.

The emergency room crew at Baylor Hospital was waiting for us. They took the other lady out first, before I could wish her well, and I hoped I would have a chance to do so later. Then four men laid me on a stretcher and carried me as gently as possible into a private room; I knew the extra care was because of the baby. A doctor and a nurse were instantly beside me and they cut the dress away from my body before starting their work. The nurse began extracting shards of glass from my face (it had collided with the windshield) and gently wiped the blood away so that it could be stitched up later. The doctor said he was going to check my arms and legs to see if anything was broken and when he raised my right arm, he said, "Well, well, what have we here?" I glanced over to see what he was talking about, and saw that someone had tucked my wig under my arm, probably for safekeeping. Apparently it had fallen off again. Everyone in the room laughed, and I wanted to laugh with them, but I was finally feeling the pain and couldn't make the effort.

After the nurse finished cleaning the cuts and they were stitched and bandaged, she told me that they had called Dr. Jordan, who was coming to check the baby's condition. I prayed without ceasing that it wouldn't be in more danger because of the accident, which I'd already decided must have been my fault because I wasn't as alert as usual. I learned later that a tree branch was covering a yield sign, causing me not to see it.

Dr. Jordan, Ned, Sharon, and Richard Rogers all arrived at the same time. They let Sharon come in even though she wasn't twelve yet (the required age for children to visit). In regard for my privacy, Dr. Jordan asked Richard to stay in the waiting room for a few minutes while he checked me over. Ned and Sharon each held one of my hands during the exam. After the doctor finished, he said, "You're very lucky, Jackie. I don't see any evidence that the baby has suffered from this. We'll do further tests, of course, but I think it's okay."

As he finished speaking, the baby kicked hard, for the first time, and everyone could see it through the sheet that covered me. In my heart I knew it was a sign that all was well, for now.

Even though nothing appeared to be seriously wrong, Dr. Jordan decided I should stay in the hospital overnight as a precaution. Richard came back in the room and pulled up a chair beside my bed. He seemed uncomfortable, and I suspected he hadn't had much experience in situations like this. To make it easier, I asked him how he found out I was in the hospital and he relayed the story: When Ned had returned from work and was leaving to come to the hospital, a Mary Kay consultant had called the house. When Ned explained the situation, the consultant passed on the information.

"Mary Kay is right." Richard said, laughing, "If you want to get the word out, just tell a woman; it's all over town by now." As the laughter died, for a few minutes the room was silent. But then Richard blurted out what he came to ask in the first place. "Jackie, do you have any idea when you're going to be able to get back to work?" Ned actually gasped at the insensitivity of the comment, but I shot him a stern look and he kept quiet. Richard still waited for an answer. I looked him straight in the eye and wanted to say, "You are kidding, aren't you Richard," but instead I just shrugged my shoulders and said I didn't know as he left the room.

When we were alone again, still shaking from anger, Ned said, "Do you believe that guy? Does he not realize how that conflicts with their motto, God first, family second?"

And I replied, "Oh, I think they do, and it's why Mary Kay sent Richard to say it instead of her saying it herself."

CHAPTER TEN

Race to the Top

The climate at Mary Kay Cosmetics in the summer of 1965 was much like the weather: bright and sunny one day and threatening the next. This must have been especially true for Mary Kay herself, since so many rumors were flying about our chief. Bits of gossip circulated faster and faster as the company grew by leaps and bounds. Some was about the business, but some concerned her personal life, which I was certain, bothered her even more. She was a very private person.

One of the most intriguing tidbits came from someone who still worked with World Gift; she said that Mary Kay had actually gotten her formulas from them and not from the original hide tanner's family as claimed. World Gift had a cosmetic line very similar to Mary Kay's, which seemed to back up the idea that they had the formula first. Another rumor was that Beauticontrol was still in business, even though Mary Kay said she had bought them out. If these were true, it meant that she had lied (today she would have simply "misspoke"), although none of us could guess why.

When this rumor surfaced, I remembered what Stan had tried to tell us months earlier. I called him and related this story. He then confirmed that what he had heard from a personal friend of Dick Kelly's supported this one. Because the rumors were so strong, I couldn't automatically decide they were untrue. With this much smoke, I knew that somewhere there had to be fire; but still loyal, I jumped to Mary Kay's defense, condemning the gossip as well as the people spreading it. For whatever reason, at this point the rumors did not yet appear to have a negative effect on sales, recruiting, or morale.

My director's check had grown steadily from one to two to three thousand dollars each month. By the next seminar, it could well reach four thousand. I never would have dreamed I would enter that income range, given my background. I was now in a financial category that I thought only bankers and financiers achieved.

My heart wasn't in it as much as it had been before, because of the dark cloud hovering over my own life. On the other hand, I could not afford to have the fairy tale I was living blow up in my face. The money had made our lives so much easier. Not only did we have money for a much better life style than we'd ever had before, we were actually saving money each month.

In addition to all the other perks that money had provided, I also had a whole new wardrobe of elegant maternity clothes, with accessories to match, from Neiman Marcus. So, instead of buckling under the rumors, I went on the offense. I took a page from Mary Kay's own book and at every gathering I lavished her with praise: for rescuing the formulas from obscurity, for giving all of us the opportunity to excel financially, and for making sure we received recognition for a job well done. In conversations with other consultants, I ended with, "And she keeps all of it in proper perspective: "God first, family second, and job third." I was no longer totally convinced that this truly represented the company, but I held onto it anyway.

We were all shocked when Barbara Acker resigned as secretary at the beginning of summer to sell Mary Kay Cosmetics full time. She had been with the company since it opened, but seeing the money we were making in sales, she chose to join us. Anna Arnold, who would become an important player in the story, took her place. Anna was a cute, vivacious redhead with an easygoing personality, and we all liked her. We soon found that she had a hidden talent that was nothing short of remarkable. She was a songwriter. She could turn any song into one about Mary Kay and could write original music and lyrics, as well.

She was given an extra duty—to take care of Mary Kay's miniature black poodle, Monet, which was now in the office every day. Mary Kay had brought him in on occasion; now he was a regular fixture and had to be seen to. It was a huge responsibility. Mary Kay was more attached to this dog than anything in her life—even her children—so the stress on Anna was considerable. God forbid anything should happen to the dog on her watch. (It was many years later, after I was alone, that I really understood how much joy and comfort a little poodle could provide when you are lonely.) We were all surprised, however, that when Mary Kay was going out of town she was letting Anna take Monet home. It indicated that Anna must have an extremely close connection to Mary Kay and was probably privy to the best-kept secrets. Yet letting go of the dog on those occasions also showed us that something had changed for Mary Kay. She seemed to have a whole new lease on life and no longer needed so much comfort from her little poodle.

Marjie had liked Anna right away and introduced her younger brother, Fred, to her soon after she joined the company. After a whirlwind courtship, they were married before summer was over. Nobody was surprised when Anna started selling cosmetics in the evening in addition to her regular job. Marjie, as her sister-in-law, now gained access to a great deal of inside information that she otherwise would never have heard. We found out how Mary Kay and Richard indeed conspired to play certain roles. It hadn't been a great secret before, but now we knew that it was planned and intentional. Mary Kay, from the start, was to be the compassionate, understanding one in the company, and Richard was to be the heartless one. Whenever he heard what he casually referred to as a bleeding heart story, he would say, "Please don't bleed on my carpet." Those of us who knew him came to expect it. Nevertheless, it was still shocking to hear it said out loud.

The rumors may have been a headache for me, yet surprisingly Mary Kay seemed oblivious. To the contrary, she looked prettier and happier than I had ever seen her, and I wondered vaguely if the gossip that she had met a man was true. One Friday morning, when I was walking past her office for my regular training meeting for new consultants, the door was open. She was on the phone, laughing and speaking quietly. The tone was flirtatious as though she were sharing a secret with someone special. For some reason, it stopped me. I hadn't ever heard her talk like that before. I waited out of sight until she finished, then stepped into view. As a lure, I told her she looked great and asked what the occasion was.

"Nothing special," she answered, but the smile belied the answer. "Come on in for a minute." I wasn't lying about how she looked. Her bright blue silk suit was in stark contrast to the usual dark ones, and the effect was stunning. Her eyes were bluer, her skin smoother and, as an overall result, she looked years younger. She seemed, for some reason, to have the confidence to suddenly change her look. "Would you like to have lunch with us today, after your meeting?" she asked

She had never before asked me to join her and Richard. She meant we would eat in the tiny kitchen in the "new" building. Recently Mary Kay had hired a full-time maid, who served lunch to the chosen few. Mary Kay's older son, Ben Rogers, who had just joined the company so he could relieve Richard of the burden of some of his duties, would be there too. The two men didn't look much like brothers. Richard was tall and thin; Ben was shorter and had a stockier build.

The three of them lunched together almost every day, sometimes with invited guests. I had often, through closed doors, heard them laughing and talking among themselves. It always sounded like everyone was having fun, just one happy family eating lunch together. Dalene had been invited a few times, but it was the first time for me. I used to wonder why she and Mary Kay had formed such a tight bond, but it didn't bother me much anymore.

I told Mary Kay I would love to have lunch with her, and for a moment I felt special as I had before. It wasn't the food I was looking forward to, because my stomach wouldn't tolerate a fancy lunch. About the only things I could still keep down were V-8 juice, milk, hot dogs with mustard, and Butternut candy bars, which I kept in the car for emergencies. I took vitamins as my doctor suggested, but they didn't always stay down either. Now what I looked forward to was the camaraderie.

Lunch wasn't particularly eventful, and yet I did find out that I wasn't wrong about the phone call. Mary Kay had met a man. I knew it for sure because Richard and Ben teased their mother about it. She offered no information of her own; she just laughed it off without comment.

It took only a few weeks for the rumor mill to buzz with the truth. Mary Kay brought him to a party thrown by one of my youngest new directors, Peggy Price. I was a little surprised to see Mary Kay at the event although I had noticed Peggy in Mary Kay's office lately and surmised that they had become close. The name of Mary Kay's escort was Mel Ash. Even though Peggy had asked us to dress casually, Mary Kay was decked out in a low-cut blouse that showed off her silky chest, and a bright turquoise skirt that reached almost to her ankles. Never one to forget about accessorizing, she had worn flat shoes of a matching color. Mel's clothes were more in keeping with the occasion.

They danced together on the patio. Mary Kay's skirt swirled softly around as Mel held her in his arms. We had to admit that they did make a great looking couple. At just under six feet, Mel was the perfect height for her. His light olive skin contrasted with her pale complexion and both had snow-white hair (even though hers was a wig). He had a broad chest and shoulders, making him appear strong and virile, qualities that many women find attractive in a man. I asked Peggy where they had met. Although she wasn't sure, she speculated that it was "at a dance class."

"Really?" I answered, surprised that I hadn't heard a word about him. "What does he do?"

"I believe he's in sales of some kind," she answered confidently.

That wasn't a big surprise. Mary Kay was the ultimate salesperson. After that day, we didn't see Mel a lot, yet we knew he was always in the wings. We were happy for Mary Kay because she was happy. We thought he seemed like the kind of man that would never hurt her. We would soon find out how wrong we were about that assumption.

My baby was due soon after Mary Kay's second seminar, which was still several weeks away. While I wasn't able to do what my doctor suggested, pretend I wasn't pregnant, I had developed some sort of protective shield that kept me from dwelling on the horror that could happen. Much of the time I felt only the numbness that had set in the minute I heard the verdict. So, instead of pretending I wasn't pregnant, I held onto each moment, not wanting time to pass, since the pregnancy was probably the only time I would ever have with my baby. But in many ways, life seemed so normal that sometimes I had to remind myself that the doctor had told me the problem wouldn't become evident until near the end of my pregnancy. The baby was active, especially when we sang the Mary Kay songs at meetings. It was almost as if it was keeping time with the music. When I related this to my doctor as evidence that the baby was okay, he listened but answered gently, "Don't get your hopes up, Jackie. As I said before, it would take a miracle for your baby to be all right." I knew that miracles happened, but so far, not for me.

Ned thought I was working too hard and wanted me to slow down. To make a stronger case, he got Dr. Jordan to agree with him. I wasn't really convinced it would make a difference, but I agreed to talk with Mary Kay about it. Every Monday at 10:00 a.m., I held my unit sales meeting, and I was resolved after the next one to talk to Mary Kay. I tapped on her office door, stuck my head in and asked if I could see her for a few minutes. I pulled a chair up slowly to her desk, trying to decide how to begin. She sat behind it and waited. After a few minutes, she raised her eyebrows, as if to say, "Well?" and I had to begin.

"My doctor and Ned both think I should slow down until after the baby is born." I rushed to get the words out. Somehow I knew this wouldn't be well received.

"Oh?" she said, eyebrows raised again.

I hurried on. "I've already told you about the problems we're facing. They really think this is the best thing for me to do." As she held the same expression, I wondered how she did it. She knew I was trapped in a disastrous and tragic pregnancy and so far had missed only a couple of days of work after the auto accident. Yet with this one look she made me feel like the world's worst slacker, trying to get out of doing my job.

"What did the doctor say, exactly?" She asked, and I wondered to myself, is she looking for a loophole? When I didn't answer right away, she continued, "Did he actually tell you that the work would put your baby in more danger?" I realized that he hadn't said that precisely, but I was sure it was what he meant. It was certainly implied. Mary Kay used the fact that I had made an assumption fully to her advantage.

"Why don't you call him back and ask him that question specifically." She straightened some papers on her desk and added, "There's more than one way to look at this. I think that staying busy is the best thing for you. It is certainly best for your salespeople." Then she added her final shot. "If you take a lot of time off, Dalene will gain on you."

I almost laughed in her face. Was this the best she could do, this tired old line? For one thing, she didn't have a leg to stand on. I was so far ahead of Dalene at this point, there was no way she could catch up. Yet, Mary Kay was still trying to engage my competitive spirit. She wanted to keep me working hard, pregnancy or no pregnancy. This technique had become so familiar that I would probably have been disappointed if she hadn't brought it up. However, staying busy didn't seem so far-fetched. The last thing I wanted was time to think about my condition.

Mary Kay took my silence as an opportunity to make a stronger case. "I've already been looking at mink stoles, you know, trying to pick the right one for the 'director of the year'." She was practically gushing, trying to entice me with the top prize. "You said you wanted an autumn haze one, right?" she added, almost as if thinking out loud. Material things had dimmed in importance for me in the last few months; still, I had to admit that a mink stole did hold a certain appeal.

"Okay," I agreed. "I'll call my doctor, just in case I misunderstood."

"Before you go," Mary Kay added quickly, "you should be considering what you need to do, if the baby does live."

"And what's that, Mary Kay?" The comment was inappropriate and premature, to say the least.

"If the baby does live, you will have to hire a full-time nanny. Your sales organization is so large that you need to give it your full-time attention."

Her insensitivity was staggering, but I said nothing. I tried to keep my thoughts as even and business-oriented as I could. "Whatever happened," I muttered to myself, "to the idea that I was an independent business person and could make my own decisions and set my own hours?"

I called Dr. Jordan as soon as I got home. He quizzed me extensively about the type of tasks I would be doing. After listening carefully, he finally replied, "Ned really wants you to slow down, but based on what you've said, I don't think the work itself will harm the baby's chances. If you use common sense and don't lift heavy objects or drive when you're exhausted, then I think you'll be fine."

I prodded him, "You're sure that it won't add more danger for the baby?"

"I don't think so, and it might even help you keep from thinking about it so much."

That's the clue I was waiting for. I decided to give it a try. From somewhere deep within, an idea took root; if I worked long and hard enough, perhaps the familiar black cloud that always seemed to hover just above my head wouldn't swoop down and swallow me whole. It was a desperate grasp for hope in an otherwise hopeless situation.

Ned was not happy with the decision. I hadn't expected him to be, but I realized that he was angry for more reasons than this. He was frustrated by our whole situation and the fact that there was nothing he could do to help. I explained carefully what I wanted to do and assured him I wouldn't take any risks that could harm our baby, so he got on board (again) and he and Sharon helped even more. The woman we'd hired to clean on Saturdays now came on Fridays. That way Sharon could be home for a day during the summer and not have to go to work with me. (She wanted to stay home alone, which we never allowed.)

Ben Rogers helped too. He began delivering my orders to our house. At first, I thought he did that for everyone until I realized that he was trying to make my job easier. I was touched by his thoughtfulness and, from this beginning, he became one of my favorite people. Sometimes he stayed to visit with Ned, talking openly and freely about how he had taken over the mundane jobs in the warehouse so Richard could spend time on more important things. It was never discussed what those "more important things" were.

So instead of slowing down, I actually speeded up for the rest of the summer. In Southern vernacular, "I met myself coming back." I returned to booking three shows a day. But I kept my word, and when it was more than I could handle, I dovetailed them to my people. The worst part of holding the shows was the constant nausea. I made at least two trips to the bathroom at each show because of the smell of coffee from the hostess's brewing pot. It was exhausting as well as a little embarrassing, even though no one seemed to think it objectionable. Everyone knew of the prediction for our baby, but there seemed to be a pact not to mention it.

What actually made the pace possible was the fact that I usually had three new consultants in training attending the shows with me. They met me at my house (even though they lived in areas all around Dallas) and assisted me in every aspect of the show, including loading and unloading the car, filling orders, and helping guests with their make-up. The care and concern shown for me during this difficult time left an imprint on my heart that is still there today.

Sunday was our only day of rest. We had accepted an associate teaching position for the Young Married Department at our church, but Ned did most of the teaching. He was an excellent teacher, and it gave him a break from our stressful routine. This was almost the only time we got to spend with our church family, and their love and support strengthened us.

One would think I'd experience lowered sales while pregnant, but paradoxically, the heightened activity resulted in exploding sales and recruiting. I learned ways to make my time more effective, such as conducting interviews with potential recruits before or after the shows, which saved a lot of time. I had also discovered an effective way to close prospective new recruits. As I listened to myself during a recruiting interview, telling about the wonderful potential of earning money, an idea struck me: If someone promised me all of that, I would want proof. So I started giving copies of the check stubs from my own paychecks to the prospect and her husband. Since they ranged from $400 to almost $4,000, it got the point across: a lot of money could be made in Mary Kay Cosmetics.

It was during this time period that I recruited Kay Dickson. From the moment I met her, I knew she was truly special. Polished, sophisticated, and attractive, she was a single mother with a young teenage daughter. She had just sold her travel agency and was looking for a new career. From the beginning, I knew she would play an important role in my unit. Other than Mary Kay, I had never met anyone who made a better first impression. She, Marjie, and I became a threesome almost immediately.

Like Marjie, Kay hit the ground running. She seemed to master all the basics immediately, and within weeks brought in her first recruit, Helen McVoy, who lived in Highland Park, the same prestigious area where Kay lived. She and Kay looked alike. Actually, almost everyone in Highland Park had that certain look. The joke around town was that when you moved to Highland Park you had to take a class to learn how to look rich and understated at the same time. The rumor was based on envy, of course. Helen was even higher on the social scale than Kay, and she had extraordinary contacts. She was to become one of the wealthiest of all of Mary Kay's National Directors, reportedly earning in excess of a million dollars a year.

But the most important thing I did to keep my unit on top was to remember what Mary Kay had taught me: "Praise them to success." At every meeting, I looked for reasons to praise them: a good show, a new recruit, extra bookings, and anything else I could find. I watched them respond and grow, just as I had, to recognition of any kind. And the interesting thing about this practice was that it helped me as much as the ones I praised. I developed the habit of looking for good in people, which has served me well to this day.

As seminar time neared, I had ten directors working under me who had already qualified, plus other DIQS (Directors In Quali-fication) as well. In addition, some of my directors, including Marjie, already had people in qualification. This meant that I had to hold meetings for my directors (which we called sub-units) plus take care of my regular duties. I was getting close to the "third tier" Richard kept hinting about, and I resolved that once my pregnancy was over I would take steps in that direction.

Because we were growing so fast, we fine-tuned our training program for new recruits. When close personal contact became almost impossible, the training program had to ensure that new consultants got off to a strong start. So we instigated a three-step program. We told them how (training sessions), showed them how (they had to attend three shows before holding one of their own), and then they had to show us they knew how (they had to hold five shows their first week and the recruiter or director attended at least one of them). This training program produced a group of people that was to lay the foundation for the huge empire Mary Kay Cosmetics was to become.

My director's checks continued to grow and by seminar time, I now expected them to surpass the $4,000 mark. When-ever Richard or Mary Kay handed me my monthly check, I could tell by their expressions that they were as surprised as I was by the amount. I remembered that Mary Kay had been mak-ing only $2,000 a month at World Gift, prior to opening her own company. I did actually wonder, at one point, if I was making more money than both of them put together.

I should have been ecstatic, but instead it still seemed unreal, as if it were happening to someone else. But that was far better than dwelling on the horrible possibility of what could happen in the weeks ahead. Sometimes I felt hopeful that it wouldn't be as bad as expected, but then I would hear my doctor's warning in my head "Don't get your hope up. Don't get your hopes up."

Disturbing rumors continued to crop up about Mary Kay that made us wonder if she were hiding a level of deception that was genuinely troublesome. I was still upset that I had unknowingly played a role in "stealing" Mary Crowley's people. When I had finally confronted Mary Kay with this fact, mentioning that Mary Crowley would be furious with me, she replied, "She can't say a word. She's done far worse things than that," leaving me with many more questions than answers.

On another front, my accountant, Bob Hurt, also did work for Mary Kay. He hinted that there had been more men in Mary Kay's past than we could imagine and there had been a huge problem with her former employer, World Gift. Sick of the innuendo I told him that if he had something to say, to say it. I added that I kept hearing rumors but so far nothing concrete. When I came on that strong, he backed off, muttering, "I guess I shouldn't get involved."

Frustrated, I called Stan and reported the conversation. Immediately he said, "It's time to go see Dick Kelly about this. We need to get to the bottom of it all. "

"What for, Stan?" I was nearly shouting. "It seems like I'm already spending half of my time defending her. I think we need to concentrate on work."

"Don't you think we need to know what's going on?" he persisted. Even though he had only hinted at it, I knew Stan was itching for Marjie and me to break with the company and start one of our own. He had his own agenda for checking out the rumors, but at this point it wasn't mine.

"What's going on is too much gossip," I said, closing the discussion. At my next sales meeting I preached a little sermon on the evils of gossip. It didn't stop the gossip, but it helped me feel a little better.

It was ironic that I had become Mary Kay's main defender, given what the future was to hold. I had personally seen her duplicity and had more reasons than anyone to wonder if the rumors were true. I simply couldn't bear the thought that I had idealized her when she didn't deserve it. I'd accepted her as the woman I aspired to become, and I didn't want that image to crumble.

One night, not an atypical evening, I pulled my cream-colored Cadillac DeVille (which had replaced the green one

I'd totaled earlier) into the garage. It was ten o'clock, and I was so tired I could hardly speak. The new recruits with me sensed my condition and quickly left for home. Sharon was waiting up with Ned, even though she should have been in bed. They quickly unloaded the car for me, and as I climbed the few steps to the second level, they followed closely behind. I could feel their love and concern and I tried to perk up to reassure them. A tall glass of cold V-8 juice was waiting for me on the kitchen counter. As I sipped it eagerly, feeling the cold liquid find its way to my stomach, the baby kicked and it made me laugh. "What's so funny?" Ned asked, bewildered by my sudden change in mood.

"Here," I said, reaching for his hand and placing it on my stomach. "Feel this." And sure enough the baby kicked again, even harder.

"Can I feel, too?" Sharon asked excitedly.

"Of course you can, this is our baby, you know." For a few minutes we shared the feeling that all was well.

Soon afterwards we were upstairs, getting ready for bed. The downside to wearing wigs all the time was that my head itched terribly when I took one off. So it had become a regular routine for Ned to massage my head while the three of us sat on our bed, discussing the day. The tension melted away, and for a while we were just an ordinary family sharing stories.

"Does the baby usually kick that hard?" Ned asked suddenly.

"I know what you're thinking Ned; I thought the same thing. I even called Dr. Jordan and told him about it."

"He told you not to get your hopes up, right?" I could tell by the stricken look on Sharon's face that she'd been hoping, too.

I didn't want Sharon to worry anymore, so I said quickly, "It's late, honey, and time for bed. Don't forget to say your prayers." She kissed us both goodnight and whispered in my ear, "I wouldn't let you go for a dollar," the same way she'd been saying, I love you since she was three years old.

As far as I know, Sharon has never missed a night saying her prayers. We had taught her in the beginning to kneel beside the bed, place her hands together, and bow her head before praying.

She always prayed aloud. As I heard her getting into position, I got up quietly, motioning for Ned to follow. I did this often because I loved the unique way she talked with God. We crept into the hallway and stood, unseen, outside her door.

"It's me again, God," she began in way of greeting. Then she thanked him for everything in her life: food, shelter, friends and, of course, her dog Sniffles II. Next, she said, "But thank you most of all for sending your son, Jesus, to save us." This part had been added after she'd made a profession of faith at camp a year ago. She went on to ask God to bless every single person she knew. Then her voice changed and she began to cry softly. Quietly, she added, "And now, God, I have a big problem and you're the only one I know who can help. The doctor says we have to have a miracle for our baby to live. And I know miracles come only from You. I've always wanted a brother or sister more than anything. And God, if you will let me have one, I will help all the time. I can babysit and do a lot more to help around the house." Now the soft cry turned into a sob. "But I'm asking this, God, mostly because my mommy and daddy are so sad all the time. It would make them so happy if just this once, we could have a miracle."

Fighting back the tears, we tiptoed silently back to our bed, neither of us able to say a word. As he always did when I need comforting, Ned took my hand and we lay in the darkness, lost in Sharon's prayer. Finally I whispered, "Surely God must pay close attention to prayers like that, from an innocent child with a pure heart. Don't you think?"

After a while, he croaked, "I'm sure of it."

Two weeks before seminar time I had finally been forced to slow down. In addition to my never-ending nausea, my feet were swelling badly and in the intense heat I had trouble breathing. I hadn't gained weight until I passed the six-month mark, but now I was so big I couldn't see my feet. In spite of my condition, I still held all the meetings, talked on the phone almost constantly, and sometimes even held recruiting interviews with prospective consultants. All of this activity was primarily to keep me from thinking of what lay ahead.

The next Monday, Mary Kay invited me again to have lunch after the meeting. I agreed mostly for the distraction. Afterwards, as I was headed toward my car, Mary Kay stopped me and asked me to come into her office, saying, "I need to talk with you about something." Now what? I wondered as I took my seat in front of her desk. Lately, Mary Kay had appeared to want to be almost chummy, and I had let my guard down. Now it was up again. I didn't like the vibes I was picking up. Her face looked perfect at first glance; then I saw the tension lines around her mouth.

Mary Kay sat there fidgeting, crossing and uncrossing her legs, and pulling at her skirt. It made me nervous and I knew that whatever she had to say, I would rather not hear it. Then she began searching for something on her desk. "Oh, there it is." She laid a pad and pencil in front of her, as if getting ready to take notes. As I moved my chair closer to her desk, the praise began: "You know, Jackie, you have done a truly remarkable job. In just one year you already have all those sub-units under you. I'm not sure I've ever seen anything like it before. And," she added laughing, "as I've told you, you're making more money than I am." I wondered if she resented it and expected me to apologize, but I said nothing and waited for the other shoe to drop.

"You know I've been telling you how close you and Dalene are in the contest for Top Unit." My mouth must have fallen open. We weren't close at all—I was miles ahead. Mary Kay held up her hand and quickly hurried on. "If we don't count your sub-units, then it's very close between just your unit and hers. Actually, we could call it a tie."

What she was trying to do was compare one part of my group to all of Dalene's, which made our sales look about even. It was so outrageous I could hardly believe she was saying it. "Wait a minute, Mary Kay. That kind of comparison has never been mentioned, and that strategy would be penalizing me and my people for working so hard." Suddenly, I saw her in a new light. Not only did she look different, she had become more forceful and willing to do the hard jobs, especially with me.

"Don't get upset," she said, hurriedly holding up her hand again. "I'm not trying to take anything away from you. I'm just trying to come up with a fair solution that would make you both happy."

I wasn't aware that we needed a solution. I had won. That was it as far as I was concerned.

Mary Kay went on. "Actually, Dalene brought this to my attention, and she's quite upset that you're winning and she isn't getting enough recognition."

Suddenly her voice seemed very far away and the room began to spin around me. "Don't faint," she cried, and yelled "Someone bring a glass of water—now!" The maid came running in with it, and after I drank some and patted some on my face, I felt better. But weariness had seeped through my entire body and into my very soul. Physically and spiritually, I was exhausted. I had used up everything in me. I just couldn't fight anymore. As much as it pained me, I surrendered. "Okay, Mary Kay, what is it you want to do?"

"Well, I was thinking that maybe we could call it a tie and give you both mink stoles and lots of recognition."

I didn't have the strength to point out that this had been a competition, and only one person had won it. Now it seemed to no longer matter that much to me, anyway—not the mink stole, not the recognition, and not even the money. But I couldn't let her think I didn't know what was going on, that the contest had been rigged from the beginning. I mustered up all the energy I could and said, "It was all a ploy, wasn't it, Mary Kay? You never intended to let me win, no matter how good my people did or how hard we worked?"

Flustered, she started to deny it, "I wouldn't do that, it's just that . . ."

This time I held up my hand. "Don't waste your breath saying another word. Do what you want; it doesn't matter to me. The only thing that does matter is that my people know the truth: that they are the best of the best and nobody came close to them. And believe me, they will know. Don't forget I have the computer printouts to prove it, as well as Dalene's weekly totals listed in your newsletter." I didn't want her to see how weak I really felt, so I pretended to be looking for my purse, giving me time to ease out of the chair and then out of her office.

I was waiting for Ned when he got home. Sharon was in her room doing homework. I didn't want her to hear the conversation. He took one look at me and asked, "Are you all right?"

"I am, but I'm not sure you will be when I tell you what happened."

He dropped into a chair and demanded, "Tell me." I tried to relate the exact conversation with Mary Kay. When I got to the part where she wanted to pretend that Dalene and I were tied for the top unit, he jumped up and yelled, "Is she crazy? That's dishonest. Why would she want to do that anyway?"

I answered quietly, hoping to defuse his anger. "Because Dalene is really upset that I'm so far ahead. That's why."

He jumped up again and started pacing the floor and yelling. "I don't give a fat rat's butt how upset Dalene is. That's not fair, and we're not going to stand for it." Hearing the shouting, Sharon came running down the stairs.

"Daddy, Daddy, what's wrong?" she cried, almost in tears.

I assured her that everything was okay and she should go back upstairs and I would explain it all later. Then I turned to Ned. "Listen to yourself. Is that any way for a Sunday school teacher to talk? And you're always calling Mary Kay a hypocrite."

But Ned refused to calm down. He demanded that I go back the next morning and tell Mary Kay that we would not go along with her ruse. "Tell her we absolutely forbid it," he yelled.

I waited until he calmed down a little, then replied, "I won't use those words, Ned, because this is her company. If that is what you want to say, you'll have to go tell her yourself." As I suspected, he didn't want to do that.

At 10:00 the next morning I was back in her office. I hadn't slept at all and it didn't look as if she had either. But she was still "prettied up." I knew this meant Mel was entrenched in her life, perhaps even more than before. This time I was prepared for a confrontation. I began simply, "Mary Kay, Ned says that we won't go along with your plan to say that Dalene and I tied for the top unit. He feels it's dishonest and unethical."

She listened, showing no reaction at all to what I'd said. Then she answered in a firm, matter-of-fact tone. "It's too late. I've already told Dalene that's what we're going to do. We're calling it a tie."

I really wasn't surprised. I knew yesterday that she'd made up her mind. But I was surprised at what she said next. "I guess I should go ahead and tell you that we had to do what she wanted, because she was going to quit the company if we didn't."

I thought silently, She doesn't think I will quit if she does this; or, she doesn't care if I do.

"While we're at it," Mary Kay added, a little haughty, "I would like to know why Ned didn't come himself, instead of sending you to take care of this."

I paused for a few seconds, then answered, "I suppose he's like the rest of us, Mary Kay. He wants someone else to do the dirty work."

There was nothing left to say. I picked up my purse and made it to the door before she stopped me and said, "Jackie, he's using you, you know."

As I walked out the front door, I said quietly, "And so are you." When I reached my car, I was surprised to see that the bright sunshine, present when I went into the office had been blotted out by a dark, threatening cloud. There was a major storm brewing, and it was headed our way.

CHAPTER ELEVEN

The Sparks Ignite

The sparks of ambition that began at the first seminar positively ignited the second. Rather than just two directors, there were now dozens (with more in qualification) and hundreds of consultants. There wouldn't be any home-cooked meals at the second, and it wouldn't be held in a decorated warehouse. Instead, it would take place in the posh Adolphus Hotel in downtown Dallas, and the awards banquet would be held in the Grand Ballroom, complete with plush carpeting and sparkling, iridescent chandeliers. There was much speculation about the awards banquet, where the top producers for the year would be honored in a spectacular way. But when asked specific questions, Mary Kay and Richard only smiled and said "You'll see." We were told only it was to be a formal affair, so I had already purchased my maternity evening gown.

As Mary Kay, Dalene, and I planned the program, I couldn't help but get caught up in the excitement. During the last year, Mary Kay Cosmetics had become well known not only in the Dallas-Fort Worth area, but also throughout Texas, and people from other states were coming, too. As a special treat, Mary Kay booked hotel rooms for all the directors so we could settle in for the whole affair. Since the provision didn't include the husbands (which they weren't happy about), we didn't need private rooms. Jan Jack and I decided to share a room and checked in on Thursday evening. The seminar was to begin on Friday morning and end on Saturday night after the awards banquet. It would basically follow the same format as the first one, with speeches and demonstrations on how to sell the products.

I now had twelve wigs of all colors lined up around my bedroom at home. Even though some of us occasionally wore our own hair with a hat, most of the time we still wore wigs. For the two days of seminar, I carefully chose a blonde and a brunette. Jan had also brought two for herself, so we had an array of wigs in our room. Soon after we finished unpacking, other directors from our group began dropping in. The very first one who walked in the door saw the wigs sitting on their Styrofoam heads and said she'd brought a couple herself, and the second arrival said the same, which made us laugh at how predictable we had become. It didn't bother us in the least. We were like an ultra-successful girls' club; the wigs were part of the uniform.

And so it went—almost every new arrival made a similar comment. With each one, it just seemed funnier and funnier and by the time everyone had arrived, we were laughing hysterically. As I looked around the room I thought, This reminds me of a high school slumber party with a group of good friends where everything is funny.

We were, indeed, a close-knit group. We'd been through the fire together during the qualification process. Each director had experienced the stress of meeting quotas, as well as the joy that came with succeeding. However, the thing that kept everyone going was that one of us was always there to help every step of the way. No matter where we were, business or social, we always seemed to seek out the others in our group. I felt a particularly close bond with each one, because we had walked the entire journey together.

I had already told them about Mary Kay's decision to call it a tie for the top unit. While they didn't like it anymore than I did, we all agreed that we knew the truth and that was all that really mattered.

Very much like family, we kept up with what was going in each other's lives. When they asked me if I had any news about the baby, because I wanted to keep the mood light and not share how worried I actually was, I responded simply "So far, so good." Not a lie, but not a subject I could talk about.

Jan left to check on her people, who were coming in from out of town, and gradually the others left as well, except for Marjie. "I'm glad you stayed, Marjie. I want to ask you something if you have an extra minute."

"What's on your mind?" she answered, settling into a chair to show she was in no hurry.

"There's a question that keeps bugging me, and I want to know what you think about it. If either Dalene or I had to be allowed to quit over the top director situation, wouldn't you think it would be Dalene, since my group produces far greater sales than hers does? It's so confusing. Mary Kay always chooses Dalene over me, and I can't for the life of me understand why. I know that the bottom line for her is money, and I'm clearly the cash cow, so what is it?"

Marjie looked at me for a while before answering. Then she said, "You mean other than the fact that you wouldn't let her spike the punch?"

As we both laughed I said, "Yes, other than that."

She thought it through before answering. "Maybe Dalene knows where all the bodies are buried," (figuratively speaking, of course.) Seeing the shocked look on my face, she hurried on. "Well, we've been told she worked with Mary Kay's husband and probably knows a lot more intimate details about her life than we do. We've all heard rumors, and it appears that Mary Kay is keeping a lot of secrets. Doesn't it make sense? That could be the reason she caters to her."

For the first time, it did seem like a possible explanation and I hoped that one day I would know the whole story.

Then she changed the subject. "Now, I want you to tell me the truth about something. How are you coping with your situation?"

It took a while to answer because I didn't know how to put my tumultuous feelings into words. I needed to talk, but so far I hadn't really confided in anyone. Marjie was a trained counselor, so I knew she was great at listening. I decided to level with her. "The truth is that this is a burden I'm not sure I can bear. The closer I get to my due date, the harder I have to fight to keep from panicking. So much can go wrong." Then I explained the series of events that would begin the next week: "Every five days I'll have my blood checked for antibodies. If the count accelerates, I have to go into the hospital immediately, because it could mean the baby's blood would need to be changed as soon as possible. Dr. Jordan will then induce labor, and a team of doctors will be standing by to change the baby's blood if necessary—Dr. Jordan expects it will be."

Marjie listened with deep concern. "Because I've already lost one baby due to this same problem, I'm having difficulty imagining a healthy child, which I so desperately want." I waited for a comment, but she remained silent and I added: "This might be the only time I will have with the baby. So I've developed a super strong attachment with it. I know this sounds strange, but the way I see it is that I'm a mother right now, and no matter the outcome, I wouldn't have missed this experience for anything."

When she still didn't answer, I looked up and saw her eyes were filled with tears. She was sharing my burden, not as a counselor, but as my best friend, and my burden was lighter because of it. Everyone thinks you need advice at times like this. They don't understand how powerful it is to just have someone listen with an open heart.

Jan and I were up early the next morning. I had my usual glass of V-8 juice, and Jan had a cup of hot tea. No appetite for either of us. Although I was still nauseated, it wasn't nearly as severe as usual, and I prayed my reprieve would last for the next two days of the seminar so it wouldn't drain me of all my energy.

Jan chose to wear a simple red suit that was sophisticated, yet businesslike, and looked great because it was an excellent contrast with her dark wig. My choice was a far greater challenge because of my advanced pregnancy. I knew light colors drew attention to a particular area and dark colors were supposed to not draw attention. So I chose a lightweight, deep teal suit with a long jacket and accented it with a layered gold necklace and earrings, hoping it would draw attention away from my bulging body.

As the elevator doors opened on the ground floor and Jan and I stepped out, we could hear the "Mary Kay Enthusiasm Song" vibrating throughout the lobby. Mary Kay had hired an organist for the seminar and he was already on the job in the meeting room. The song, appropriately, was to be the call to arms throughout event, and when we heard it we knew it was time to gather for the meeting. Jan and I looked at each other, and it was as if two people running on low batteries had suddenly been plugged into an electrical circuit. Our smiles were brighter and our steps energized as we hurried toward the music. Other songs would also be sung this year, many of which were written by Anna Kendall. But the Mary Kay theme song was the one that set the pace and sparked the excitement.

Consultants, like bears after salmon, gravitated hungrily into the huge meeting room, clapping, singing, and marching more enthusiastically than ever before. As the organist increased the tempo, the excitement picked up momentum. The magic was back, and there was no doubt that it was going to be an enchanting two days.

I had spotted Mary Kay outside the meeting room and saw that she was wearing a smart rose-colored suit, not the color of more subdued pink associated with her products. This was definitely an "after Mel" (more daring) choice of colors, and it made her look even more glamorous than ever. Although I didn't see him anywhere, I figured he was around and would show up—at least for the banquet.

Mary Kay took the podium and the seminar began. The crowd went wild—she was so glamorous, almost like royalty. People were clapping and cheering, keeping time with the theme song playing in the background. After she finally quieted them down, her magical touch kicked in. She began with an effusive welcome. First, she had everyone from the Dallas-Fort Worth area stand, which was the majority of the crowd. Next she asked the rest of the group to stand. They were mostly new people attending a large function for the first time. As they rose, they seemed a little nervous and unsure about how to act.

Mary Kay saw this and immediately took steps to put them at ease. One by one she had them introduce themselves and say where they were from. Of course, there was rousing applause after each introduction and by the time they were finished, Mary Kay had begun forming a bond with each one just by giving them a little special recognition. It might have been a big group, but she deemed them worthy of individual attention. As I watched her "working her magic," I was impressed all over again.

Out of consideration for my condition, Mary Kay had scheduled me as the first speaker of the morning; I suspected it was because she knew I tired easily as the day went on. (In later years, she always put top-notch motivational speakers, like Zig Ziglar, in this spot.) For the introduction, she quickly reviewed the story of how I joined the company and then moved into how I hadn't allowed a difficult pregnancy to slow me down. Instead, I had actually worked even harder. I appreciated the fact that she was recognizing my efforts, in a way, yet I realized for the first time what she was really doing. There wasn't a woman there who might not decide to have a baby, and Mary Kay didn't want that to continually gum up the works. She was using me to show that there was no need for anyone to cut back on work because of a pregnancy. She doesn't miss a trick, I thought. She used my condition to promote her own business.

As I approached the podium, my people, who filled the entire right side of the room and even spilled over into the other side, rose and gave me a welcome of the same magnitude as Mary Kay's. Genuine emotion has always overwhelmed me, and I was truly moved. I looked around the room, trying to get control of myself and my glance fell on Mary Kay. The look on her face was not sympathetic, but I couldn't determine just what it was.

I, of course, said nothing about the fact that Mary Kay's remarks flew in the face of the company motto about family before work. Instead, I promised the audience that I would keep my talk short and sweet; I wanted to make only one major point about what this seminar could mean to them. Then I shared the lesson of how it always begins. We have to struggle to find our own way, and it's mostly through trial and error. When we are alone in this endeavor, the only thing we can do is to learn from our mistakes and keep moving forward. As I spoke, my people were going down the aisles, handing out small candles and matches. The people on the ends of each row quickly lit their candles. Within seconds, I motioned to the person at the wall switch to turn off the overhead lights. Then the only lights visible were the candles on the ends of the rows, in preparation for what would happen next.

The darkness lent my voice a slightly dramatic tone and I continued, "You have a candle and a book of matches in your hand. Now, you can choose. You may light your own candle, or you can take a light from the ones already lit." The women made their choices and suddenly the room was filled with light. "How many of you took a light from someone else?" I asked. The vast majority held their candles high by way of answering yes. "You chose that because it was easier and faster, right?"

"Right," they yelled, almost raising the roof with their voices.

"That's what this seminar can do for you. The speakers you will hear during the next two days have had to find their own way to get where they are today. They are here to 'share the light' with you, to light your candle, so your pathway to success will be much smoother than the one they traveled. Accept the help so you don't have to reinvent the wheel, or make the same mistakes.

"My final word of advice is this: Absorb everything you can at this seminar. Seek out the top producers at every opportunity. Don't be afraid to share your goals with them and ask their advice for achieving them. Then, even if you are brand new with the company today, next year you may be sharing your success story with others."

As I returned to my seat amid even stronger applause, I thought, This has got to be the best job in the entire world.

Not surprising, Dalene was the next speaker on the program. As she walked toward the podium I noticed that she looked especially sharp. She was wearing a gray silk suit, accented with a bright red necklace and matching earrings. I had seen her talking with Suzanne Collins at the office lately, who was an expert in fashion and I wondered if Suzanne had helped her with the look.

I couldn't wait to hear Mary Kay's introduction. Since she had bestowed so much preferential treatment already on her in spite of the fact that she was far behind me in sales, I wondered if this introduction would leave mine in the shadows too. I wasn't wrong. She raved and raved as if Dalene was about to put the company on the stock exchange. She reiterated that Dalene had been the very first consultant and had benefited the company tremendously because of her vast experience in sales. Mary Kay stretched Dalene's accomplishments so far that I looked around to see if anyone else noticed the stretch marks. But the exaggeration was apparently lost on them; in fact, they were eating it up. Mary Kay's performance left me stunned. To me, Mary Kay already had Hollywood glamour. Since she's this good at acting, I thought, she should head straight for Movieland.

Apparently because she was such a veteran sales person, Dalene talked about the power of perseverance, stressing the importance of not saying if I reach my goal, but instead to say when I reach my goal. She went on to explain the IF is just a crutch and almost a sure road to failure, whereas WHEN is a powerful positive word and will help to ensure reaching a goal. She added that once a goal was set, it could only be accomplished by persevering every day, not just making an effort spasmodically when you happened to be in the mood. She closed with the punch line: "Winners never quit and quitters never win." Even though the statement wasn't original, it was definitely true. Actually, her speech was good, and I joined the group in applauding enthusiastically. Suddenly, I wondered whether we might have been friends if Mary Kay had not constantly pitted us against each other. As she left the podium, I noticed she was smiling broadly.

Since one of the most beneficial parts of training was "showing them how," it was important that all those in attendance got to see an example of what a top-notch show should be like. Because the majority of my directors were among the most successful, on Saturday they would hold "mock shows" for the consultants to observe; it would take almost half of the day. During that time, there would be a separate meeting for the husbands—a much larger group than had attended last year. The husbands had become strong supporters of their wives' businesses, and the word had gotten around how beneficial last year's meeting was for those who attended.

Ned and Stan would play a key role in the meeting, leading discussions and answering questions about how they could contribute to their wives' success.

As always, there were talks on all the basics of the business. The main addition since last year was a talk by Elwood Goodier, the chemist who manufactured Mary Kay's cosmetic line. By supplying information about how the products were actually created, he provided a here-to-fore missing link in the total process of the cosmetic business. Mr. Goodier also manufactured what appeared to be the same line for World Gift (which he didn't mention, but Dick Kelly, the president of the company, later confirmed). Although the talk may have been a little technical for women, the men in the audience loved it.

During both days, there were short breaks in the morning and afternoon, as well as an hour for lunch. But by late Friday afternoon everyone was tired, mostly from the intensity of the whole affair. Richard was to give the last talk of the day and for weeks he'd been hinting it would be "new and exciting information."

As Mary Kay returned to the podium to introduce him, I wondered how she could top last year's introduction. But she did. Not only did she restate his talents as a "computer genius," and the endless hours of hard work he put in taking care of details, but she also gave him credit for the astonishing growth of the company in the last year. Ben had not been mentioned at all; I looked around to see if he was present. He wasn't, and I realized that he was probably at the office, taking care of "less important" matters, the kind that helped to make the company grow.

As her introduction ended and the organist again burst into the Mary Kay Enthusiasm Song, Richard ran from the back of the room and jumped up onto the stage, rather than walking up the three steps provided. As intended, it got everyone's complete attention. He was wearing a navy blue suit, a starched white shirt and a red, white, and blue tie. He was the spitting image of what a successful young executive should look like. "Welcome to our second annual seminar," he said, almost shouting, his voice full of energy and excitement. In response, we rose to our feet, then clapped and cheered, forgetting all about being tired.

"Okay," he continued, "today we're going to talk about how to make the BIG, BIG money." That made the crowd straighten up in their seats even more, as they strained to hear his every word. "First, I would like those who were directors last year to stand up." Of course, Dalene and I were the only ones to stand. "And now," he continued with his voice rising to a higher pitch, "would everyone who is a director today, as well as those in qualification, join them?" The sound of chairs being pushed back filled the room as people all over stood up. "Finally, every-one that would like to join this group, stand as well." From where I stood, I couldn't see a single person still seated. Again the organist started playing, and all of us began to sing the song at the top of our lungs. And Richard hadn't even gotten to the "new and exciting" part yet. I had to give the man credit. He knew how to work a crowd.

First, he pointed out that everyone was probably aware of the benefits of recruiting and becoming a director (from seeing it happen). Then he added that there was good money to be made on that level. "But that's only the first tier." It was a tantalizing opener. I could hear paper rustling all over the room as everyone prepared to take notes on what he was about to say next.

On the blackboard beside him, he drew the circles to rep-resent the first tier. Last year he had used Dalene and me as examples because we were still on the first tier. Since I was now so far ahead and strongly into the second tier, I held my breath waiting to see how he would handle it now. Without mentioning examples at all, he then drew fourteen circles extending from circles on the first tier. "This is the second tier, and the circles are directors. When a director has consultants who become directors, they are called sub-units." At this point a man in the audience stood up to ask a question. "Has anyone reached the second tier yet?"

I watched closely as Richard hesitated, but then he replied, "Yes, Jackie has." I avoided Dalene's eyes by staring directly at Richard. Not wanting to dwell on the point, he hurried on to draw from three to ten circles under each of the fourteen on the second tier. There were so many circles they almost filled up the entire blackboard. "These groups are called sub-sub units, and this is the third tier." I almost gasped out loud. From what he'd just shown, it appeared I was already there.

Silence filled the room as everyone waited to hear what kind of money that level would bring. I had drawn every circle that Richard had shown, complete with notations. I already knew the percentages up to this point, and I was ready for the total picture.

"A director makes commissions on her unit and sub-units. But as you can see, the third level can consist of more than a hundred new units." And I would make a percentage on every salesperson in them, I suddenly realized, stunned at the thought. Then Richard continued, "This is the pot of gold in our marketing plan. In order to make money on the third tier, a director will give up her personal unit and move into a management position, which will probably be called National Director. While she makes an additional 2 percent, she still makes 4 percent on her sub-units, which sounds like less. However, the volume at this point is so huge that it will at least double her prior earnings. Ladies, the potential is unlimited."

The same man stood up again and asked as he had before, if anyone had reached that level. Richard hesitated but finally said, "Jackie is very close."

As they talked, I had been figuring in my head what this would mean to my monthly paycheck. I quickly concluded that it would almost double my earnings, putting me close to $10,000 a month. (In 1965, that was about as good as it could get. Today, the equivalent would be more than $50,000.) I had thought I had already reached the top of the mountain, but now

I could see and feel that there was a pot of gold waiting for me on another peak.

I looked down at my sheet of circles and notations. I had already experienced the power of this marketing plan, and I had no problem believing I could capture the top level. I looked around, hoping to see how Marjie was taking this, and saw Kay Dickson looking at me. She held up her note pad with circles resembling mine, and with her thumb and pointer finger made circle. I got the message; it was "Let's do it."

It is a shame that human beings cannot see the future. If I could have, I would have had Richard sign and date the diagram I had in front of me. It would have saved me years of trouble. But I was still trusting and thought your word was your bond. I paid a high price to learn that wasn't always the case.

When the day ended, I hurried to my room as quickly as possible. Not only was I tired, but also my back was hurting from sitting so long. I crawled into bed, lay back on the pillow, and almost immediately dozed off. My baby had been kicking steadily all day while the music was playing, and now it began again. For a while I just lay there, sharing the moment with this little person I would, I hoped, soon see face to face. And I prayed Dr. Jordan was wrong in his prediction.

The ringing of the phone brought me fully awake. It was Ned, already home from work, checking up on me and asking about the day. I told him about the exciting news concerning the third tier, but his only comment was, "We'll see how it plays out." Because of the way I'd been treated (especially the latest of counting Dalene and me as tied for top unit), Ned didn't trust what Richard said at all, and I was not surprised at his skepticism. Then he reminded me he was taking Sharon to stay with my sister, so he could be at the seminar early the next morning. He added, "Did the baby handle all the activity okay today?"

"More than okay. We were just enjoying a little fellowship time when you called, so promise you won't worry."

"I'll try," he said as he hung up.

Jan and I had planned to spend Friday evening with just the people in our personal units. We met downstairs at the coffee shop where we divided into our separate units for dinner. As my unit ate their meal (I'd had a Butternut candy bar before joining them), we discussed what to do for the rest of the evening. They knew I was limited in my activities, and someone suggested that since Neiman Marcus was only about a half a block away, we ought to walk over there.

Several in the group were from out of town and had only read about the famous store, so they were eager to go. Downtown Dallas in September is usually still hot, but tonight the evening was pleasant, with a soft breeze blowing. Music was drifting from small restaurants up and down the street; the mood was light and we were happy to be together.

A woman's first trip to Neiman Marcus is equivalent to a child's first trip to Disneyland. I watched their dazed expressions as they gazed at the hundreds of butterflies that had been hung with invisible strings over the entire cosmetic department. Then they combed through various other departments, buying souvenirs with the famous name of the store prominently displayed.

It was a little before 9:00 p.m. when we got back to my room, so we kicked off our shoes and settled in. Jan and her crew hadn't come in yet, so it was just my immediate unit. Since this was the first seminar for most of them, we had a lot to discuss—not only the seminar itself, but also the beautiful hotel and what everyone was wearing (which women always do). But the most exciting topic was the awards banquet to be held the next night. Since everyone there knew they were among the top producers in the company, there was great speculation as to who would make the Top Ten consultants' list. I was like a proud parent to all my children; I wanted them all to win.

Suddenly there was silence in the room. Then one of my newer consultants, Meryl, spoke up. "Tell us what you need for your baby. We've been talking about it and realized that you haven't said much about it. What have you already bought for the nursery?"

I knew I couldn't sidestep the issue any longer. I had to let them in on the possible crisis. So I took a deep breath and told them we'd bought nothing for the baby, because that's what my doctor had advised us to do. In response, Meryl said she'd heard earlier there might be a problem, but since my due date was soon and I seemed calm, they assumed everything was okay. I apologized for not confiding in them sooner and explained that I hadn't wanted to spoil the excitement. As I talked I could feel the mood changing from happy to sad, and I regretted putting a damper on their high spirits. But my baby might not live, and I couldn't think of a positive way to impart that information.

Meryl finally asked, "What did the doctor say you could do?"

And I answered honestly, "He said to pray for a miracle."

Soon after this conversation, someone suggested that we should call it a night and everyone rose to leave. Each one hugged me silently as she left the room. Filled with emotion, none of us could speak a single word.

As I undressed and crawled into bed I was glad Jan was still out. The talk about the baby had jarred me back into reality. Within just a few days, I was going to have to face the cold, hard truth, whether it would be life or death. The protective wall I'd built around me came tumbling down, and I let the tears that I'd held back for months flow. Totally exhausted, I finally fell asleep.

The next morning I felt a little better, although I still felt sluggish. As we began our routine, I noticed a large pile of bits of paper just inside our door. When I called Jan's attention to it, she said they hadn't been there when she came in last night. So, with curiosity, I picked one up and read it. Someone had written "I'm praying for a miracle." There were far more pieces of paper than there were people in my group. The same sentence had been written on them all so I knew the news had traveled throughout the whole company. Not wanting to upset Jan, I quickly went into the bathroom and cried once again.

As we walked through the lobby on our way to the meeting room, we passed Richard, who was talking to a group of consultants. We heard him say, "Jackie makes one hundred dollars before she even gets out of bed in the morning." Jan and I laughed with them, but I thought, That's probably true. I looked around to see if Ned was here yet, but didn't see him. I decided to let him take care of himself, and I would do the same. Stan was already there and I knew they'd find each other.

Excitement continued to mount as the day wore on. At the noon break, people in small groups were speculating about who the winners would be that evening. And the men were discussing the money that Richard had promised could be made in the third tier. Women had never before had the opportunity to earn that kind of money, nor had they ever had the recognition or the lavish prizes for a job well done. I must say that as grand as this affair was, it was nothing compared the ones to be held in the future, where the queen of sales was carried in like royalty and crowned with a rhinestone crown. Nevertheless, I seriously doubt that they were more exciting than this one or even the first one the year before.

For the banquet, Jan chose a simple black, beaded evening gown. Her make-up was perfect and the finished look was elegant and expensive. My look was far less remarkable. Choices in maternity evening gowns back then were in short supply, and I had to take what I could get. Of course I looked for a dark color but the only one I could find that fit was made of shiny taffeta the color of champagne. There was no way I could conceal my condition so I decided not to worry about it. I wore my platinum wig, in a small attempt to draw attention to my face and away from my body. (In the mid 1990s when I looked at pictures in Mary Kay's Hall of Fame, I was horrified at the picture of me at this very event. If I had realized I was really that large, I would probably have stayed home.)

Ned, in his black tuxedo, was waiting for me outside the ballroom door. The organist was already there, playing soft dinner music, which was a nice contrast to the Mary Kay music we'd heard all day. The round tables were covered with fine linen cloths and were set with china plates and lead crystal glassware. An arrangement of fresh flowers, in various shades of pink, graced the center of each table. It was the perfect setting for honoring royalty. Ned whispered to me, "I'll bet this affair set them back some." While there was a nominal fee for attending the seminar, there was no way it could have covered such a lavish evening. Even the waiters, in their splendid white dinner jackets added to the décor. Any critic would have given the entire event four stars.

While Mary Kay always looked like the star of the show, to use a colloquial expression, "she'd put the big pot in the little one" for this one. She wore a soft blue evening gown that appeared to be covered with the same color of iridescent stones. She literally glittered and sparkled. I tapped Ned on the hand and whispered, "If she had a wand and a tiara I would think she was the proverbial fairy godmother." He simply nodded in agreement. I couldn't help thinking there was truth in her "costume"—she was to play the role of fairy godmother for millions of women worldwide for years to come.

Mel and Richard, both wearing black tuxedoes, were seated with Mary Kay at the front of the ballroom near the podium. They seemed relaxed, laughing and talking with everyone at the table, as if this were just an ordinary night out.

As Mary Kay and Richard began the awards ceremony, the feeling that I was watching it all happen to someone else returned and left me in a dazed state for the rest of the evening. As always, Mary Kay lavished praise on each one of the Top Ten in sales as she presented each of them with their prize: a genuine alligator handbag, which would be worth a small fortune today. While they all received a bag, each one appeared to have been chosen with the winner in mind, which was evidence that Mary Kay had added her "special touch" by making the purchases herself. But as expensive and elegant as the prizes were, it was still the praise that was the real reward for their accomplishment.

Although I could see and hear it happening, because of my dazed state, it all seemed to come from far away. Ned leaned over and asked if I was all right and I nodded to show I was. The majority of the winners were once again from my group, and I felt a great surge of pride.

When it came time to announce the top unit, Ned again looked at me to see how I was going to react. "I'm fine," I whispered as Mary Kay began her meticulous account of the dilemma they'd had in determining the top director for the year. She went through the song and dance she'd given me, that when they added it one way, it was a tie between two people, instead of a clear-cut winner. Then she added: "So that's what we decided to do—call it a tie." Ned immediately grew tense at the injustice. This was just wrong, and he knew it. I reached out, took his hand, and held on tightly. Suddenly Dalene and her husband were at the front, standing beside Mary Kay as Dalene's group cheered loudly. Then I felt Ned pulling on my hand, and all of us stood and joined in the applause as Mary Kay placed a ranch mink stole around Dalene's shoulders.

Mary Kay began talking again but I couldn't quite comprehend what she was saying until she called my name and Ned was guiding me toward the front of the room. Everyone was standing and giving thunderous applause as we reached Mary Kay's side. Then, the look I'd seen earlier was back on her face and I suddenly realized what it was—irritation. But it was so fleeting, I thought I must surely have imagined it. The noise had brought me out of my stupor, and I was more alert as Mary Kay began her presentation.

She was just as illustrious with her praise for me as she'd been with Dalene. When she finished, she handed me a bouquet of red roses and a silver wine cooler, engraved with the words "Brown Unit, Top Unit, 1965. (I later wondered if the wine cooler was supposed to have a hidden message and to this day I don't remember if Dalene received the flowers and wine cooler, too.) Next came then the moment I would never forget: Mary Kay placed an autumn haze mink stole around my shoulders. Again, the crowd rose, cheered, and clapped until Mary Kay asked for their attention.

She asked me if I had anything I wanted to say, and handed me the microphone. Ned squeezed my hand for encouragement and I quickly pulled myself together. I held the wine cooler up as high as I could and said, "I want to say to my entire sales organization that this is your award, not mine. It is in recognition for your outstanding efforts and accomplishments, and I will always be grateful for being a part of your success. You are truly the best of the best."

In conclusion, I added, "And now, I want to thank all of you for your concern and your prayers for my family and me. It has touched us deeply, and we will never forget your thoughtfulness. And as we go our separate ways, my prayer for each of you is that God will richly bless you for your sweet, caring spirit, and until we meet again, hold you in the palm of His hand." As I said these words, I had no idea how soon this warm wonderful feeling would turn into one of intense hurt and brutal betrayal.

Jan went home directly after the banquet, but Ned and I decided to spend the night at the Adolphus. Sharon was at my sister's, and a night of total relaxation sounded good to both of us. I hung my mink stole in the closet and left the door open, so that I could see it if I awoke during the night. As Ned watched me do this he said, "Remind me to tell you what Gene Brewer said during the break."

Intrigued I asked, "What was it? You know I can't stand that kind of suspense."

He laughed and replied, "In essence, he said Mary Kay was trying to drive a wedge between his and Dalene's marriage. But come on to bed. We'll talk more about it later." I knew that must mean it would be a long story.

The following Monday, The Dallas Morning News printed a large article about Mary Kay's phenomenal success. Rosalie McGinnis wrote the story and quoted Mary Kay as saying that she was the actual daughter of the hide tanner and heir to the magical formulas. Reaction to the article produced a bedlam of activity, both good and bad. At first the controversy over the article appeared to be just a minor nuisance. However, in the future, it would turn out to have far more serious repercussions.

On the bad side, people who knew the real daughter of the hide tanner, Ova Spoonemore, cried "foul" and demanded a public retraction. Mary Kay vowed that it was Rosalie McGinnis's error, that she had misquoted her, and that she had never made such a statement. (Rosalie McGinnis later told me personally that she had quoted exactly what Mary Kay had said.) A retraction was never made and until much later many people continued believing that Mary Kay was an actual member of the hide tanner's family. Stan jumped all over this fiasco and wanted to dig deeper into all the other rumors, but Marjie and I were flying high from the seminar and didn't want our balloon deflated. We told him to cool it, which he did for a time.

The good side from the publicity was that the telephone rang off the wall with people wanting to try the products, and many were interested in selling them as well. Even though I was expecting to give birth in just days, I didn't pass up the opportunity to recruit Martha Weddle, who was to become a major player in the rest of this story. She called right after she had read the article. The first time I saw Martha, I was struck by her resemblance to Mary Kay. She was a real platinum blonde with a flawless complexion and bright blue eyes. On top of that, she was highly ambitious. After she tried the products and decided to sign up, I had to add a whole new category for the size of cups in my unit: Martha was a giant mug.

CHAPTER TWELVE

The Miracle

It was time to face what could be the biggest crisis of my life. For nine months I had hidden behind a protective wall I'd built around myself so that I wouldn't have to think about the possibility (which the doctor called the probability) that my baby would not live, as well as the fact that I might not live myself.

A few days before the end of September, I went for my doctor's appointment to check my antibody count. I was concerned because my baby hadn't been as active lately. I hadn't mentioned it to anyone, even Ned, because I knew he was just as frightened as I was, and more stress wouldn't help the situation. After the technician took my blood, I had to wait for the results and as I waited, I reviewed in my mind what I'd learned about my problem.

While the information about the danger of my antibody count rising was in highly technical terms, I had already broken it down into cold, hard facts. If by some miracle the baby had the same Rh-negative factor I had, then it would have a good chance of being okay. On the other hand, if the Rh was positive, as our first baby's had been, then my body would consider it to be a potential deadly infection, and use its strongest power—antibodies—to kill off the threatening invader. That's why my antibody count had been watched so closely. The minute it escalated, it was a sign that the fight to kill off the invader had probably begun, and as soon as this happened the doctor would need to induce labor.

Instead of the technician coming to tell me about the results of the test, Dr. Jordan came himself, and I froze. This couldn't be good.

"What's wrong?" I asked as soon as we were in his office.

"Don't panic," he cautioned "your antibody count has risen slightly, but not to an extreme. I want you to come back in three days for another test, and this time bring your bag for the hospital, just in case the count has jumped again."

On the way home I could hear my heart beating in my chest, and I knew it was because of the stress from the dreaded news. Yet, I decided not to alarm Sharon and Ned. Instead, I would prepare myself for accepting the unacceptable. While I knew my family would do anything they could to help me, I also knew that fundamentally, I would have to walk this valley alone.

On September 29, 1965, at 10:00 a.m. I was back in Dr. Jordan's office for another test. I'd stuck to my decision and hadn't told anyone the count had elevated on the last visit, hoping it wouldn't be important. But as I sat waiting for Dr. Jordan to give me the results, I wished desperately that I'd asked Ned to come with me. And when Dr. Jordan came through the door with a somber look on his face, I braced myself for the verdict.

"Did you bring your bag with you?" he asked. I nodded and he continued, "We need to go straight to the hospital so I can induce your labor. But you should call your husband first and have him meet us there as soon as possible."

I finally found my voice and asked, "How high is the count?"

He hesitated as if deciding whether or not to tell me the truth. Then he said, "It's way too high. But remember, we're prepared for this, and I've already called the team that is going to stand by to change the baby's blood." This would replace the blood that contained antibodies with clean, untainted blood. It was a risky procedure but was the only way at the time to save a baby with this problem. "So we're not giving up here. Okay?" I tried to smile as I nodded.

Baylor Hospital was just across the street from his office, so I was quickly settled into a room. After he did an examination of the baby and me, he pulled up a chair beside the bed and said, "We have to talk about your labor, Jackie. I haven't said anything about this because I didn't want you to worry, in the hope we wouldn't have to do it this way. But now you have to know the details. Because we need to give the baby every possible chance, I won't be able to give you any pain medication." The baby would also receive anything given me, and pain medication would be far too strong and weaken the baby even further. "Do you think you can handle that—giving birth without any medicine for pain?"

Without hesitation I replied, "My mother had ten without medication. Surely I can manage one."

He smiled and squeezed my hand. By noon an intravenous drip was in my arm and he explained that labor pains would begin soon. Then he smiled and said, "Just relax and everything will be fine." I looked at him and thought that was a typical comment from a man who doesn't have a clue what this is really like.

By 2:00 p.m. Ned had arrived and the pains had begun, but they were still mild. He was as pale as a ghost, and I knew intuitively that he was reliving our last experience. "Don't worry, Ned," I said, "just pray. That's what I'm trying to do. Is Sharon okay?" Sharon knew only that this baby could possibly have the same problem as the other one, and she still had vivid memories of that experience.

After he assured me she was fine and settled in with my sister, he told me he had called our families and they were praying the baby would be okay. He had also called Marjie and she was calling my directors and others, including Mary Kay. In knowing we were covered with prayer, a sense of calm washed over me and I did relax, at least a little.

By six, the pains had begun in earnest. Dr. Jordan took my pulse and listened to the baby's heartbeat every thirty minutes, and each time I tried to read the expression on his face. It was always passive. Like a child anxious to arrive at a destination, I wanted to say every time "Are we almost there yet?" But I managed to keep silent and just watch the clock on the wall over the foot of my bed; its hands seemed to barely move. Ned, on the other hand, did nothing but move. He paced the floor in the little room and made constant trips outside for coffee. I fought the feelings of despair that kept trying to engulf me, and thought, It's going to be a long night.

By ten, the pain was almost overwhelming, and I asked Dr. Jordan if it would get much worse. He replied softly, "I'm afraid so." Then he brought in a woman. She was very large and low-ered herself into a chair on the left side of my bed. He explained that she was there to do whatever I wanted her to do, such as getting a cool cloth for my head or a drink of water. Ned was seated on the right side for the same purpose. When Dr. Jordan turned out the lights, both Ned and the woman dozed off almost immediately.

By midnight the pains were so strong I could hardly breathe, and to make it worse Ned and the woman were snoring so loudly I was sure they could be heard in Siberia. And they weren't even in unison; when one finished the other began. Finally I pushed the buzzer and Dr. Jordan came into the room. I looked at him sternly. "I'm trying my best to handle the pain, but I cannot stand listening to these two snore any longer."

He dismissed the woman for the rest of the night and took Ned to the waiting room so he could sleep on a couch. Then he came back and sat with me. There was no way I was going to fall asleep, so he talked to me constantly, trying to distract me as the pains grew worse. And when they became so severe that sweat drenched my face, he had a cold cloth ready for me to wipe it away. After one such pain, I gasped, "Why is it taking so long?"

"The baby isn't in the right position yet; are you still okay?" I nodded but I was no longer sure I could hold on, and I won-dered what had happened to the protective wall that had shielded me early in my pregnancy.

By 5:00 a.m., I was gasping for breath and I could feel my life slipping slowly away. Drawing on my last ounce of strength I whispered, "Dr. Jordan, I just can't hold on any longer, but it's okay. Tell Ned . . ." He sprang from his chair. In moments the room was full of nurses, and they were pushing my bed as fast as it would go toward the delivery room.

"Hold on," Dr. Jordan commanded, "we're not giving up. You've got to stay conscious so you can help. Will you do that?" As he talked he was gently slapping each side of my face, pre-venting me from slipping into unconsciousness. I remember wishing Ned was with me, but this was long before anyone other than medical staff was allowed in the delivery room.

I could hear the team of doctors talking quietly as Dr. Jordan worked to reposition the baby. And finally, the detached feeling I'd had much earlier in my pregnancy returned, and I felt no fear as I struggled to follow Dr. Jordan's instruction. Even the pain lessened. Then suddenly I heard a baby crying and tried to raise my head, but Dr. Jordan was already at my side holding my tiny baby girl, with wet, black, curly hair.

"Is she okay?" I croaked. "Is she okay?"

"We'll have to run tests, of course, but I actually think she is," he said as the other doctors in the room clapped and cheered.

Dr. Jordan leaned closer to me and said, "We're going to let you sleep now."

Thank you Lord, I prayed as I felt myself drifting away. Suddenly the room was filled with the most beautiful music I'd ever heard, and my final thought was that it must be angels singing.

It was past noon when I awoke in my hospital room. I was greeted with the sight of the flower arrangements, from a single rose to lavish bouquets, that filled my room. As I was still trying to get my bearings, a nurse walked in and said cheerfully, "Hi there, I see you're finally awake and I'll bet you're starving. Just tell me what you want and we'll take care of it."

Straining to focus, I said, "First, I need to see my baby; can you bring her in now?" She explained that the doctor was still doing tests, but promised that she would bring me my baby as soon as possible. Then she asked again if I was hungry.

Suddenly I had a tremendous craving for something I hadn't had for nine months and asked, "Could I have coffee, and not just one cup?" She was back in minutes with a full pot and said that coffee was always available in the nurses' lounge. Then she asked if there was anything else I'd like. After thinking for a moment and feeling a little foolish I added, "Is there any place I could get some popcorn?"

"That's a new one," she said, laughing and added, "coffee and popcorn" She thought about it or a minute and said, "I think there is popcorn on the children's floor."

When she returned with it, I asked her if she'd seen my husband. She smiled and replied, "That must be the man with his nose against the nursery window until they took your baby for more tests. When he shows up again, I'll tell him you're awake."

A little later Ned opened the door to the room, and when I saw the expression of joy on his face I burst into tears. Without a word, he climbed into the hospital bed with me and held me close as we cried together with thankfulness and relief.

Keeping her word, the nurse brought our baby in a little later and put her first in Ned's arms. Although the look on his face is permanently imbedded in my mind, I wish I'd had a camera. The look said "I'll never let you go," and I knew he never would. When he finally put her in my arms, and I gazed down at her face the same protective feeling I'd had when I first looked at Sharon consumed me. It was as if I was suddenly filled with super-human strength to care for them and keep them safe; I thought, Heaven help anyone who ever tries to hurt my children.

Then the baby opened her eyes as if she wanted to see me as much I had wanted to see her. As I held her close to me, I vowed silently, "I will never again put anything ahead of my children."

I couldn't believe how tiny she was, just six pounds and, even though she looked a little like she'd been in a welterweight fight, she was beautiful. She had gashes on her nose and temple from the instruments, and we later learned her nose had actually been broken. I removed the pink blanket and checked her fingers and toes and found that because she was a few weeks early, her fingernails and toenails were not yet developed. Other than those minor things, she was perfect.

"Has the doctor explained to you yet how she happened to be okay?" I asked, and Ned shook his head. I looked at him and knew we were thinking the same thing: It was a miracle.

We decided to give her the name we'd chosen for our first baby—Shannon, with no middle name. We also decided that Ned would buy a baby bed and a few tiny clothes as well as sign up for a diaper service. Marjie had already called to say they were giving me a huge shower as soon as I was able to attend, and for me not to buy anything else until after that.

Ned had talked to Sharon and our families, and everyone was just as excited as we were. He'd also made special arrangements so Sharon could visit us that evening. After he left, the nurse kept bringing in bouquets of flowers, and finally even extra tables to put them on. She said the telephone was ringing off the wall with people checking on us and finally she asked, "The nurses want to know what this is all about? Are you someone extra special?"

The tears started all over again, but I finally answered, "Yes, I'm very special. I've just been given a miracle."

Marjie, Kay Dickson, and Suzanne Collins came that afternoon. Suzanne brought Shannon a very small pillow with a pink pillowcase that had been hand embroidered with tiny flowers. It was exquisite (and Shannon still has it today). After Suzanne left, Marjie, Kay, and I settled in for a heart-to-heart conversation. We'd become close friends, and we speculated about the wonderful future that lay ahead for all of us, now that I'd had my miracle.

I don't remember ever being as exhilarated as I was that day. During a lull in the afternoon when no one was visiting, I was listening to the music piped into the room. Doris Day was singing, "I'm sitting on top of the world, just singing a song," and I thought, she's singing about me.

That evening, Sharon came in carrying the large silver wine cooler, and it was filled to the brim with red roses. And of course, the three of us shed more tears of joy. As I hugged her tight, I whispered in her ear, "God was listening to all those prayers." And she nodded as she cried. She had already been to the window to see the baby, and she was anxious to hold her. As we discussed when that might be, Dr. Jordan came into the room. Smiling from ear to ear, he said, "I see you're celebrating, and I'm celebrating with you. Things couldn't have turned out better." We knew he was referring to the fact that the tests had all been good. They revealed that Shannon had the same Rh factor as me, which was the reason she had survived without the blood exchange.

I interrupted the conversation because I'd been waiting all day to ask the question, "What caused my antibody count to jump like it did? It should have meant her Rh factor was positive or there was a major infection in my body, yet she turned out to be just fine?" He was silent for several minutes, as we all waited breathlessly for the answer.

Finally, he said, "I've been going over that in my mind all day. We double-checked each count we took, and I know that for certain it did jump drastically. As a doctor I'm supposed to come up with a scientific explanation. I guess it's possible that you could have had an infection somewhere that we didn't discover. It had to be that or . . ."

I finished the sentence for him, "Or it really was a miracle."

As he was leaving, he stopped at the door, turned, smiled, and said, "Even though doctors won't usually admit it, I do believe in those, too."

Bending the hospital rules, the nurse brought Shannon in while Sharon was in the room with us. I wrapped the blanket snugly around her and put her in Sharon's arms. The look on her face as she gazed down at her baby sister melted my heart. She looked up at Ned and me and said "I'll babysit all the time if you want me to." Ned and I laughed, suspecting that attitude wouldn't last long, but for the moment we were probably the happiest family in the whole world.

There was a constant stream of visitors at the hospital, yet two people were conspicuously absent. Mary Kay and Richard never showed up at all. I felt a little sad that Mary Kay hadn't even called, but I was so full of joy there wasn't much room for anything else.

Almost the minute we got home from the hospital, I started combing through the want ads, looking for a nanny. On the second day, I found an ad that looked interesting. It read: "Responsible middle-aged woman needs full-time work, caring for children and house." It caught my eye because I wanted someone who would do both, and this was the only one that indicated she would.

As soon as I read it, something clicked in my head and I called the number listed. She said immediately, "I'm colored," and then asked if that mattered. "Of course not," I replied, and we made an appointment to meet the next day. It was a one and one-half hour bus ride from her house to ours, but she was right on time. Just from her appearance, I almost hired her before she ever said a word. Her hair was perfectly groomed, and she wore a spotlessly clean pink uniform. She had a soft voice and spoke only in answer to questions. When she saw Shannon lying on her stomach asleep in the baby bed, her face softened and she reached over and patted her gently. "When can you start?" I asked.

She came to work the very next day and stayed with us for twenty years. When my friends commented on how lucky we were to find such good hired help, I only smiled, but I thought, It didn't have anything to do with luck, and she wasn't just hired help. God sent us an angel to help care for our little miracle and the rest of us as well. Her name was Marie Johnson, but when Shannon began to talk, she renamed her Re Re, and that's who she was to us for the rest of her life.

My shower on Sunday afternoon was held in the meeting rooms at Mary Kay Cosmetics. I'd gained very little weight during my pregnancy and was pleasantly surprised that I could still fit into a light olive green crepe dress that I had bought earlier. I was happy and carefree as I arrived for the shower. All the demarcation lines came down and everyone showed up, including Dalene and many of her people. We literally got everything we needed for Shannon, and a lot we didn't really need at all. Bath-a-nets (designed for bathing a baby) were the new rage for babies that year, and the one given to Shannon was grand. Mary Kay did come to the shower. She brought Shannon a sterling silver cup and spoon to match. Even though she stayed only a little while, she seemed genuinely thrilled that Shannon was healthy, and I thought again what a special person she was. I knew that Ned wouldn't think her just showing up for a few minutes was special, but I wasn't ready to give up the picture I'd kept of her in my mind: a role model that was special in every way. The shower is still fresh in my mind. There was not a hint of ill will of any kind, and instead the time was filled with thankfulness and good wishes for my family and me.

When Shannon was three weeks old, we took her to church. There was a special nursery just for newborn babies that had a large picture window in front. Because it was the very first time in church for her, Shannon, in a bassinet, was placed in the window for everyone to see. All of our friends, who had prayed so faithfully with us for a miracle, joined us as we admired Shannon through the window and thanked God for answering our prayers.

I returned to my Mary Kay duties almost immediately, even though this was the era when we weren't allowed to drive until six weeks after giving birth. For a period, I had to have someone drive me everywhere, but because many consultants now lived in my area, it wasn't much of a problem. Ned and I had long talks about my work schedule. Even though we had full-time help, I was no longer going to schedule three shows a day, and I was going to reserve at least two full days a week for my family.

But I still met myself coming back, because I had not only so many people in my unit, but also new directors qualifying every month. More people simply meant it would take more of my time. Even when I was home, the telephone rang constantly, and people were always showing up at my door. I began to think seriously about moving up to the third tier. If I gave up my personal unit, it appeared that I wouldn't be spread so thin. Truthfully, what I really wanted was to be at home a lot more with my children, and the idea of a simple eight-hour-a-day job sounded better all the time. The gold had lost a great deal of its glitter, and I was no longer willing to give my whole life to Mary Kay Cosmetics.

After discussing the problem for hours, we had to admit there was no easy solution. My checks had grown even larger and Ned cautioned me not to make any hasty decisions. I was amazed at how he'd done a complete about-face. He now believed my job, or something like it, was our chance of a lifetime.

After her training, Martha Weddle had gone to Miami and held shows for her friends there. Her sales had exceeded $1,000 for the week, plus she got a new recruit. She had prospective recruits in Fort Worth as well. I was presently making 16 percent on her sales because she was my personal recruit, and Ned pointed out this was only the beginning of what could happen from this new "giant mug."

In addition, Kay Dickson and Helen McVoy had taken Highland Park by storm. Kay was just finishing qualification for director, and with her entourage of outstanding recruits, Helen was getting close to beginning qualification as well. The company was growing so fast, thanks primarily to my group, that the meeting rooms at Mary Kay were filled almost every day with unit sales meetings. When I really thought about how the company, as well as my paycheck, had grown in just one year, I was overwhelmed.

By the end of each day, I was desperate to get home to my children, but I wasn't the only one. Ned would walk in the door each evening and head straight for Shannon's crib. He'd pick her up, take her to the recliner, and rock her for hours.

Once the late news came on, I had to insist that he put her to bed. It was like a contest to spend time with her. When I did get to rock her, I sang the Mary Kay songs to her, rather than lullabies, because she had always seemed to respond to them at meetings even before she was born. And now, if she was crying as I began singing, she would stop immediately, kick her feet, and after a little while she'd fall asleep.

Soon after we had brought Shannon home from the hospital, I saw Sharon watching as Ned rocked her, looking at her adoringly. My heart ached for her, because I could guess what she was feeling. That night when I went in to hear her prayers and kiss her goodnight, I sat down on her bed and said, "I don't think I've ever told you about the night you were born, have I?"

She shook her head no and said, "Can you tell me now?"

As she lay in bed, propped up on one elbow, I told her the story. "You were born in the small hospital in the town where your grandparents still live. During the afternoon we had a constant stream of visitors who couldn't wait to see you. Even on your very first day of life, you sucked your thumb and looked at everyone with your big round eyes wide open. As they gazed at you through the window of the nursery, they all said you were the most beautiful newborn they had ever seen."

"What happened next?" she asked, smiling happily, completely into the story.

"Well, when everyone left, your dad refused to go home and said he was staying the night. Since the hospital bed was narrow, I knew we wouldn't sleep too well, but we were so excited about you, we didn't care. During the night a terrible thunderstorm came up, and your dad rushed to the nursery and brought you back to be with us. He couldn't stand the thought of you being alone in the storm. The three of us slept in that narrow bed the rest of the night."

"Is that really true?" she asked, laughing out loud.

"Every word," I said. "I'm telling you this because I want you to know that your dad thought you were the most precious gift anyone ever received."

She looked up at me with tears shimmering in her eyes, and said, "I wish I could remember that."

And because I, too, had no memory of being adored by my father, I knew she was feeling she'd missed out on something wonderful. But all I said to her was "I wish you could, too, sweetheart." Then I added as I touched the place over her heart with my finger, "But that love is still right here with you, because a love like that never dies. But it's time to go to sleep now; tomorrow will be a busy day." I tucked the covers around her and added, "Sweet dreams and sleep tight."

"And don't let the bed bugs bite," she said, laughing merrily, returning to a habit of earlier days.

As my business continued to spiral upward, my family realized how fortunate we were. Marie was exactly what we needed. She'd told me that she cooked only "plain food," but when walking in after a hard day to a prepared meal, it tasted wonderful to us. One of her specialties was ground beef with pinto beans, all of which she cooked and seasoned from scratch. When that was served over rice with fresh sliced tomatoes and corn bread, as far as we were concerned it was food fit for royalty. Sharon and

I still talk about how wonderful it would be to have that exact meal one more time.

Rumors were flying that Mary Kay and Mel were very serious and there might be a wedding soon. Marjie and I pumped Anna for information, but she would only smile and say "Could be." But there were signs—Mary Kay was especially cheerful in the office—so we suspected the rumors were true.

When Shannon was about six weeks old, I was at the office one day picking up merchandise. As I walked past Mary Kay's office she called out, "Jackie, come in for a minute." I pulled my chair up close to her desk and waited. Smiling broadly, she continued, "I guess you've heard the rumors?"

"Are they true?" I asked, smiling back at her. In answer she held up her left hand and the diamond on her ring finger was the largest I'd ever seen. I wanted to say "Congratulations!" but I knew that was supposed to be for the groom, so I said, "I take it that means 'Yes.'"

As she continued to smile from ear to ear she replied, "Absolutely," and then shocked me with her next statement. "I want you, Marjie, and Dalene to be in my wedding. What do you think?"

The warm feelings I'd had for her in the beginning returned, and I answered, "I'd love to, and I'm certain they would as well. When is it going to be?"

"Soon, very soon; but we haven't set the exact date yet." She then explained that she'd talked with Dalene but hadn't yet spoken to Marjie. She looked happier than I'd ever seen her, and because of that, I was happy, too. We continued to talk and giggle like two schoolgirls as she discussed her plans, and I wished our visit could go on and on.

As soon as I got home, I called Marjie. She was just as excited, and we discussed what we would wear. I hadn't bought anything other than maternity clothes in a long time and I couldn't wait to go shopping. While we were on the phone, we decided to get together with Dalene as soon as possible and decide on a wedding gift for the two not-so-young lovebirds. Those ideas led to getting all the directors together and having a dinner for Mary Kay and Mel—and presenting the gift at that time.

When I told Ned the news that evening he looked at me as if I had totally lost my mind. "What?" I demanded.

"Don't you think it's a little nervy, that she didn't even come to the hospital to see you, but now she wants you in her wedding?"

"Ned," I answered, "don't you see? That's why she didn't come. She's in love, and that's all that's on her mind. And I think you're a little paranoid."

He just rolled his eyes, as if I was a hopeless case, but the look on his face said, "We'll see."

The entire company was abuzz about the wedding, and after talking with Dalene, we put our plan for the party into effect. First we notified all the directors, pooled our money, and bought a luxurious set of luggage. It was elegant and would be appropriate for anywhere they would go (the honeymoon destination was kept secret).

Mary Kay gave us free rein on what we would wear for the wedding, explaining she had no special color scheme. Marjie and I went shopping together and I bought a turquoise "after-five" dress with matching shoes. It was sleeveless and if it were cool enough, my mink stole would be the perfect evening wrap. Marjie, as usual, chose all pink, but her dress had a matching coat, and the pink and turquoise looked great together. We asked Mary Kay several times what she was wearing, but she wouldn't even give us a hint; she just said, "It's a surprise." We'd also asked Dalene what she was wearing but she said she hadn't made a decision. I didn't know if that was the case or if, like Mary Kay, it was going to be "a surprise."

The dinner took place just two days before the wedding. It was a true gala event. Spirits were high and laughter rang throughout the room all evening. No one paid much attention to the food. Mel, however, was the one person who seemed a little quiet. He did make one memorable comment—that he would probably end up being known as Mr. Mary Kay. We all laughed, including Mary Kay, and she picked up the conversation and entertained us with funny stories about how they'd met and how they'd come to the decision to spend their lives together.

At the close of the evening, Dalene presented the luggage to them, with our love and best wishes for a long and happy life together. Accepting the gift, they said the luggage was the perfect choice and just what they needed. As we prepared to leave, someone called out, "The next time we're together, it will be to watch you become Mr. and Mrs. Mel Ash," and we all cheered as they closed their car door and waved good-bye.

The next afternoon, everyone who had been present at the dinner, got an alarming phone call from Anna Kendall. The wedding was off. The groom had gone missing and there was no further explanation, leaving us all with the obvious question: "Why?"

CHAPTER THIRTEEN

She Always Gets Her Man

We waited anxiously for news about the mysterious disappearance of Mel, but none came. To make it worse, Mary Kay was rarely seen herself, contributing to the notion that the situation was dire. Her absence meant she was too mortified to talk about the incident with anyone. Our telephone lines were busy, with all of us discussing how to make things easier for her. In the end, we settled for "the less we said the better." No one really knew anything for sure, and the last thing Mary Kay needed was more wild stories to deal with. But as with any mystery, at times we couldn't help speculating amongst ourselves about why he left and where on earth had he gone.

I wasn't sure how much the public was aware of what was going on, but business continued as usual. Whenever someone asked directly about Mary Kay's whereabouts, we answered vaguely that she was "taking care of personal business." Shows were still held, products were sold, new people were recruited, and of course my commission checks grew even larger. Momentum from the last two years of hard work had kicked in and it was like a huge ball rolling down hill so fast that nothing could stop it.

While Mel's disappearance was by far the biggest concern for the company during the final months of 1965, mine was the hectic pace I kept. As had been said many times, "Everything has a price," and there was a huge one for me as my sales organization continued to mushroom. I was a new mother, yet I was spending even more time at my job. I had begun to resent the fact that the only time I got to see Shannon was when she was sleeping. She was well cared for, but I wasn't the one who got to do it.

At one point I mentioned to Ned that if I had to, I could give up the cosmetic business and go back to college. When we first met I was taking courses at night toward a degree in English, so that I could one day become a writer. And he knew I still wanted to pursue that goal. He was doing great in his job, actually earning far more than he ever had before. To say that our bank savings were healthy was an understatement, so I could afford not to work for a few years. However, Ned had grown used to the high-octane income and didn't want to go backwards. When I mentioned my plan to him, he looked as if I'd completely lost my mind and said, "You're being absurd."

"And how is that, Ned?" I asked. In two years, he'd gone from thinking I was crazy to get into the business to thinking I would be crazy to get out. There was no return comment for several minutes.

Finally, he spoke. "Just go out and tell Richard Rogers you're going to step up to the third tier, and that you're giving up some of the long hours you're putting in." I was shocked at the forcefulness of his reaction, but I decided to at least give it some thought.

The next time I was in the office, I caught Richard alone and tapped on his door. "What's going on?" he asked in his usual energetic voice when I came in. I looked at him in amazement. He was so calm and collected: business as usual. No one would ever suspect that his newest potential stepfather was AWOL after a wedding had already been planned. Nothing seemed to be amiss in his perfect world. I gathered my thoughts and tried to get him to understand how unbearable my situation was. Suddenly, his mood changed. The normally enthusiastic persona was replaced with one that appeared to be boredom. This was intensely personal to me, and he seemed to be thinking, Don't bleed on my carpet.

I persevered anyway and told him I was thinking seriously of moving up to the third tier. I expected encouraging words like "go for the gold," which was his usual approach, but he just let me talk. As I started to give him more details, his phone rang, and he motioned that he had to take the call. I got up and quietly left his office. Mission not accomplished.

On my way home, it struck me that Richard hadn't said much at all. And he wasn't like the Richard I knew. I wondered if it had anything to do with Mary Kay's problem with Mel or was it a problem with me? Or was he just a young man who couldn't understand how a mother felt?

The days went on. It seemed as if Mel had vanished into thin air. I had never seen anything like it. Then one night on the 10:00 p.m. newscast, a reporter came on the air with "breaking news." He said, "Local cosmetic mogul Mary Kay Hollenbeck's home was burglarized this evening. She was bound and gagged for hours while two men ransacked the house." He went on to say that very little was taken, and Mary Kay was unharmed. Then he suggested that the men had been looking for something, which they apparently didn't find.

In spite of the late hour, telephones began ringing off the hook all over town. The word was out that what the two men were looking for was the gigantic diamond engagement ring. Fortunately, at the moment it happened to be at the jewelers being sized. Even more interesting, it was the consensus of almost everyone that Mel had sent the thieves to get it. No other explanation accounted for such a strange break-in. The next round of information that passed among us was that Mary Kay had hired Gene Brewer to find Mel and bring him back. We held our breath waiting for the outcome of this caper. It was all beginning to seem like a movie script. After all, we were just normal people. The oddest thing that ever seemed to happen to us was if the newspaper boy threw the paper on the wrong lawn in the morning.

A few weeks later, Mel magically reappeared. He acted as if there was nothing unusual about the whole affair. The next thing we knew he and Mary Kay had quietly gone away and gotten married. As far as I know, no one ever gave away the mystery. What I found odd was that Mary Kay went ahead and married a man who might have had her held at gunpoint as her house was ransacked.

In spite of all the drama, they acted as though nothing unusual had happened and appeared to be the normal "happy couple." Soon after they settled into married life, my sales organization scheduled a joint meeting. Since we'd heard a lot about how successful Mel was as a salesman, we asked him to be our guest speaker. Curiosity was still high about this new man in our chief's life and because of that, every single person in our organization showed up. Who wanted to miss an event like this? Although the room was packed, there was none of the talking and laughing that usually went on. Instead, it was as silent as a wake.

Mel still wasn't letting on that anything had gone amiss in the past month. He appeared totally relaxed, sharing his experiences in sales and relating funny stories about things that happened along the way. I finally realized that he knew he was talking to the top sales people in the company, and he was steering clear of telling us how to do our job. Instead, he was just entertaining us.

Then he suddenly switched gears and said seriously: "If I had to pick one quality that is the key to getting you what you want out of life, I would have to say it's determination. And you have the perfect example of someone with that quality right here in the company. You may have already guessed that I'm talking about Mary Kay." I listened intently as he spoke, thinking how sweet it was for him to praise his new wife. Then he finished with an unforgettable statement. "Not only does she have determination in business. From my own experience I can testify that she has even more in her personal life. Actually, she's just like the Mounties, she always gets her man."

We were so stunned we didn't know how to react. So we lapsed into silence for a few seconds. It was such a highly personal and revealing statement, almost as if he wanted us to know he'd been trapped. Finally, we rose to our feet, clapping, cheering, and laughing. Mel had just been royally accepted into our group, and from the smile on his face, he was pleased. In spite of the scandalous episode of his skipping town before the wedding, Mel and Mary Kay had a grand finish. They stayed married for the rest of their lives.

I began talking with my directors about the possibility of moving up to the third tier. We discussed what would happen when I did. The people in my personal unit would be given a chance to choose which sub-unit they would go into, and I promised to keep distribution as even as possible. So they could get more familiar with each other, some of my directors would attend all of my meetings, both sales and training. They seemed excited about the possibility of getting new people in this manner, and I remembered how happy I had been when Mary Kay had done the same thing with Dalene and me. Since there were far more people to divide up than Mary Kay had at that time, my sub-unit directors would receive a healthy boost in income.

Because no one else was even close to being qualified for this top position, once again I had to figure it out for myself. My main responsibility in this new position would apparently be to work with my directors and their directors. Most of my efforts would be toward adding even more new directors with new units under them.

I had a long talk with Marjie and Kay, since they would most likely be next in line for advancement. Marjie's interest in it still seemed to come from Stan's eagerness for her to advance, rather than her own sense of competition.

Kay, on the other hand, was in hot pursuit of the position because she understood the advantage of being among the first to achieve the level. The first ones to reach the level would become the foundation for all the growth that would come in the future. Not only would it add income, but also prestige. And since she had the rich folks in Highland Park behind her, it was within her reach. In a nutshell, we could see that all of us that reached this position first could receive 2 percent on millions of dollars, which was by no means pocket change.

Another Christmas was fast approaching, and I rushed from one thing to the next, with little time to enjoy my baby's first Christmas. I promised myself that I would get everything settled about moving up to the third tier before the end of the year, so I could begin the new year and the new job under less pressure.

As we had the year before, my group planned to hold another elegant party at the country club. Many new people had joined us since then, and they were eagerly anticipating the event. While I tried desperately to put on a good front, I was always in a state of exhaustion, and this year I would have preferred a quiet evening at home instead. But in the end, it was worth it. Everyone had a great time and talked about it for weeks afterwards.

Shannon was almost three months old. I loved the way she stared at the lights on the Christmas tree as though she understood what it was all about, but she still preferred I sing Mary Kay songs instead of traditional tunes when I did get to rock her. As usual, she started kicking when I sang. Since we had been so blessed, we decided to focus on giving to others this year. A healthy baby was the best gift anyone could have and we couldn't think of anything else materially that we really wanted. So we concentrated on our parents and the children in the family. We did buy Shannon and Sharon Christmas dresses. Both were red, but Sharon was almost twelve and her dress had to look like the ones her friends wore or apparently she would be a pariah. It was simple with a bolero jacket. Shannon's was her first "little girl dress" and was frilly with a petticoat underneath.

Sharon's grandparents, the C. D. Franks, always visited us at Christmas. This year we took them shopping at Neiman Marcus for complete new outfits, and we sent Ned's mother one as well. I bought my mother a long cashmere coat, with a fur collar; it was the only full-length coat she ever owned. And, for Marie, who was now almost like one of our family, we started a tradition of giving her a cash bonus every year. We agreed the looks on all of their faces upon receiving the gifts was by far the best Christmas present we could have received, and even Ned had to admit that Mary Kay had made it all possible.

On Christmas Eve, again we concentrated on family. We had my sister, Geneva, and my brother Gene, along with their families over for dinner. While there were gifts for the children, the evening was basically reminiscent of the ones we'd had as children: good home-cooked food, old-fashioned Christmas carols, and stories from our childhood about growing up on the farm. Because everyone in the family used Mary Kay cosmetics, the subject did come up, but only briefly. For once it was just a simple, cozy family gathering on Christmas Eve, filled with love and good will for each other—the kind of Christmas that lives forever in our memories.

I set up an appointment with Richard for the Monday following the holiday to continue the discussion that we'd started earlier. Mary Kay was having a workshop (again in the Adolphus) the first week in January, and I wanted to have the fact that I was moving up to the next level of management finalized by that time. I took along my yellow pad with the diagram that Richard had drawn at the seminar so I could show him I understood the requirements that had to be met.

As soon as I sat down in my usual chair in Richard's office, I could feel the tension in the room. His mouth was set in a firm line like the edge of a sword, as if he were preparing for a confrontation. I tried to shake the ominous feeling and began. "Your speech at seminar sold me on the idea of moving up to the third tier, and I have all my notes. I've met all the qualifications and I'm ready. I've already discussed it with the directors of my sub-units and I want to get it finalized as soon as possible."

He gazed at me as if he had no idea what I was talking about. What is going on? I wondered. He looks as if I'm speaking Greek and he doesn't understand a word I'm saying. Nevertheless, I steadily returned his gaze.

Finally he spoke, "What did you think you would get in that position?"

I paused. "Just what you said I would, of course: 2 percent of the third tier. I understand that I will have to give up my own unit, and I've already informed my directors." I went on to explain the details about how I was going to handle dividing up my people. He let me rattle on until I had to pause for breath.

Then he said, "Stop right there, Jackie. I'm afraid you've misunderstood the whole thing."

I actually shook my head, thinking I hadn't heard him correctly. So I asked, "What did you just say?"

He leaned forward in his chair and said loudly, "I'm afraid you heard me wrong, there is NO 2 percent on the third tier."

He can't really be saying this. So many people were there. But the look on his face told me had had no intention of delivering on his promise. This must be a nightmare, I thought, and I'll wake up soon. When I realized it was real I said it, "You're joking, right, Richard?"

"No joke, you misunderstood."

He wasn't fooling anyone and certainly not me. I knew he didn't even believe his own words. He absolutely did not think I misunderstood anything. Something else was going on. It finally sunk in. Pieces of the puzzle began to snap together in my mind. "All right then," I said in a steely voice, "let me see if I now understand what you're saying."

Then I held up my yellow pad with the same diagram that he had drawn at the seminar and said as loudly as he had, "You're saying that I and all the other people in the room that drew this same diagram misunderstood the advantages of the third tier?"

He mumbled something about how he didn't know about the others, but I had misinterpreted the whole thing. As I continued to stare at him in disbelief, he added, "Besides, nothing has ever been put in writing about that level."

"I suppose Dalene knows all about this, and it's okay with her?" I asked, sarcastically, already knowing the answer. With a smirk on his face, Richard nodded yes. Even though Dalene wasn't anywhere near reaching this level at this point, in the future it would also affect her. Suddenly another thought hit me, Maybe they just wanted to get rid of me. If that was the reason behind this, they could always restore the 2 percent later. "And Mary Kay, she thinks the entire organization misinterpreted it also?" I asked, unable to keep the anger and sarcasm out of my voice.

"Of course," he replied.

I was being conned and I knew it. I just didn't know what I could do about it.

"Then go get her and bring her in here. It's time we had a heart-to-heart talk," I said, slamming my yellow pad down on his desk. He hesitated, and I added, "I'm not leaving until you do."

While he was getting her, I tried to control the shaking anger boiling inside me. Within minutes, the three of us sat staring at each other. I couldn't remember the last time I had been so enraged. These were people I trusted, people who preached the same values I believed in. And yet here they were betraying me, betraying all of us. Without letting them say a word, I began. "Mary Kay, Richard says you also believe that I misunderstood about the 2 percent and the third tier. Is that correct?"

My bluntness seemed to throw her off guard so she simply nodded yes. Then, as if she felt she had to back up Richard in a stronger way, she added, "Do you REALIZE that 2 percent of that kind of volume could ultimately mean millions of dollars? We couldn't do that!" The way she spit the words out suggested that I was even dumber than she'd thought. All at once I had a realization: "What it could ultimately mean" was precisely what they hadn't thought out when they hatched the plan. Or perhaps they never figured anyone would actually reach that level so it was a problem they'd never have to deal with. In any case, once I posed my plan to Richard, and he shared it with his mother, the implication of how much money they'd have to shell out suddenly dawned on them. And they decided to wriggle out of it. Hence, the "You misunderstood" approach. I was fighting mad, so I let them have it with both barrels.

"I guess you two think because I went along with your charade that Dalene and I tied as top director, I was stupid enough to go along with anything. If that's what you think, you're about to find out that you've made the biggest mistake of your life. I've already told my directors that I am dividing up my unit among them, and I don't go back on my word. So what you're saying is, when I do this, then my income will drop to 20 percent of what it is now. Is that right?"

They both nodded a little sheepishly, and I added, almost yelling, "What do you expect me to do?"

Mary Kay replied, in a weaker voice than before, "Well, you could start over and rebuild a unit."

That was so ridiculous that I pretended I hadn't heard what she said, and I continued. "Or, I'm thinking this whole thing is a ruse. That you're hoping I will just quit, which I've thought you wanted for some time. If that's the case, you could have just told me. But on second thought, Mary Kay, you could be right; maybe I should start over. But remember, I'm an independent contractor and when, where, and if I do, it will be on my own terms."

I rose from my chair, walked straight to the door and looked back at them. "And I'm afraid those terms might not suit you." The transfixed look on their faces was shock. I had always been such a polite Southern girl. They had just met the new Jackie. As reinforcement for what I'd said, I slammed the door behind me as I left.

I stopped at the nearest coffee shop and called Marjie and Kay. I explained briefly what had happened and asked them to meet me as soon as possible. Within thirty minutes the three of us were seated in a booth in the back of the coffee shop. Now I related the details of the whole encounter, and when I was finished, Kay said, "Well, that's it, then. There's no future there for me."

Marjie and I agreed that was true for all of us. Then Kay said, "You know, the three of us could start our own company. We're the ones who brought in all the good sales people anyway."

We looked at each other and time seemed to stand still. A new company. I hadn't seriously considered it before, but now that she brought it up, I knew it was a definite possibility. But it was just an idea and there was no point even discussing it any further right now.

Kay left first, and Marjie and I sat drinking coffee for a while longer. I told her that whatever we decided, I wanted to proceed slowly and not do anything until I was sure what direction to take. Marjie agreed and said she wanted to say something to me, but didn't know how to put it.

"Just say it, Marjie, no matter what it is."

She was afraid that if three women were in business together on equal terms, it could be almost impossible to make timely decisions—you could always end up at a stalemate. As usual, she had a very good point and it was something to carefully consider.

And then she added, "Kay is strong willed, and I think she is used to being in total control." I could see where she was heading, and it was going to entail another long and serious discussion. Suddenly it was all too much, I was so tired I couldn't think straight. There had already been far too much strong emotion for one day.

"Thank heavens we don't have to decide anything right now," I said. "We have a lot to tell Ned and Stan, so let's start there."

Three days later, I got a call from Stan. He'd already heard from one of his "sources," that Richard was looking for a legal way to get me out of the company. Because I was an independent contractor, that could be a lot easier said than done.

Ned was furious over the act that Richard and Mary Kay put on about me misunderstanding the marketing plan, and nothing I could say calmed him down. But when I added we needed our income to remain as it was until we decided what we would do, he finally nodded in agreement.

Incredibly, we all went on as if nothing had ever happened. I knew Mary Kay and Richard played along because they had the most to lose from a major public confrontation. The whole thing could blow up in their faces if they weren't careful, and they knew it. For the first time, Mary Kay planned the workshop program herself. I wasn't surprised when I was given a token part, introducing the speakers that were part of my sales organization. Dalene would do the same for hers, so it would simply appear that it was time to put the spotlight on others. No one seemed to think there was anything unusual about the change in format.

However, Kay Dickson was assigned a major speech on recruiting. Because she was the new star in this area, everyone was interested in what she would say. I also thought Mary Kay was gently moving her up to possibly take my place in the ranks.

The crowd for the workshop was expected to be almost as large as the one at seminar, and I had mixed emotions. I was pretty sure it would be my last event, and I planned what I would wear carefully because I needed to camouflage the fact that I was a nervous wreck over the whole affair. I chose a red, wool knit suit with large gold buttons and gold earrings as an accessory. My shoes and handbag were black genuine alligator and altogether the look was bold and suggested confidence.

The "Mary Kay Enthusiasm Song" was playing loudly and the crowd was singing, clapping, and marching as I walked into the meeting room. It certainly didn't entice me the way it always had before. I found a seat close to the front. Mary Kay was standing at the podium and looked as glamorous as ever in a winter white wool suit with long sleeves and leopard skin cuffs. I looked at her face closely and saw tension lines around her mouth. Apparently, I wasn't the only one who wasn't gung-ho for this event.

The format for the day was similar to all the others. Mary Kay gave lavish praise to each speaker, and the crowd responded as usual, wildly clapping and cheering for each one. The cheering was magnified for Mary Kay herself each time she returned to the podium. There was no doubt the magic was still there for them, but it was quickly slipping away for me.

Kay's talk was the highlight of the day. She based her entire speech on six words, "Can you use some extra money?" In spite of the fact she was recruiting people primarily from Highland Park, which was the richest area in town, she asked all of her prospects this question. And many of them answered yes. Instead of being intimated by this elite group, Kay simply assumed everyone could use some extra money. Of course she also made sure they liked the products and appreciated the recognition they would receive from succeeding, but she credited this one sentence with her outstanding success in recruiting. When her talk was finished, the crowd gave her a standing ovation, and I was very proud.

The most conspicuous thing missing from the day was that Richard didn't give a talk at all. Since he'd always talked about the marketing plan and the money that could be made with it, I suspected he didn't have the guts to do it with me looking him right in the eye. He was downright afraid of what I might do.

When the day was over and I said good-bye to my people, I could hardly hold back the tears. Something very important in my life was ending, and I knew it. Light flakes of snow had begun to fall, and as I walked to my car I saw Mary Kay walking to hers. She was wearing a leopard coat (that matched the cuffs on her suit sleeves) and she whirled around to open the door. With snowflakes falling on her face, she looked again like the star she'd always been to me. But this was a star I had to walk away from. Mel was right. Mary Kay really did have determination. But in my book, if you didn't have integrity as well, so what? A feeling of intense sorrow consumed me. I was coming to the end of a glorious ride as well as an intimate relationship with a remarkable woman.

Snowflakes covered my windshield as my car purred into action, and I thought of my family waiting for me in front of a fire. Suddenly I couldn't wait to get home.

CHAPTER FOURTEEN

The Visit

It was definitely time for Mary Kay and me to go our separate ways. The final straw was when she and Richard had decided to renege on our deal when they figured out just how much money I would make under the marketing plan. The minute they told me I had "misunderstood" company policy and there was no third tier, or 2 percent, after I had qualified for the position, there was only one direction to go: out the door.

Once I accepted that I had to leave, it took a gigantic burden off my shoulders. However, I couldn't afford to make a move yet. I still needed the money and, until I was ready, my plans had to be kept secret. But I was aware that when and how I left might not be up to me. Richard was trying to find a legal reason to terminate me, something Stan had already told me he'd heard from his business contacts. This was no doubt brought on by the colossal fit I threw over the deception; Richard knew there would be a ripple effect throughout the entire company and others would begin complaining. A few competitive companies that had also heard about Richard's plan had contacted me to come in for interviews. This was the clincher—it meant the rumors Stan heard were correct.

Several things had to be done before decisions could be made about my future, and they had to be done in the proper order. First, I had to confront the legal issue of whether Richard actually could terminate me; I absolutely did not want to leave the company before I was ready. I called Henry Baer, the attorney I had worked for before joining Mary Kay. When I told him it was kind of urgent, he worked me into his schedule the next day.

It was close to lunchtime when I arrived, and he was alone. I hadn't seen him in almost two years and was surprised that he looked the same as he had back then. He was still unpolished, which made him different than most lawyers. During my tenure with him, I had tried to freshen up his look by keeping clean shirts and ties at the office for a quick change when necessary, but apparently the idea hadn't stuck. What he had, however, was even better than "a look." He had a friendly smile and kind, brown eyes.

"Tell me what's going on," he said. "All I've heard is how rich you've gotten."

"I've made more than I did as a legal secretary for sure," I said, laughing. Then my voice grew serious, "But it came at a high price." I made eye contact with him over the pile of papers on his desk, and the words came tumbling out easily because I trusted this man. First I told him about Richard wanting to find a legal way to terminate me. He stopped me there and said, "Let's talk about that first. You're an independent contractor, aren't you? They can't 'fire' you unless you've done something drastically wrong."

"In theory, I'm an independent contractor," I answered, "but their rules are so hard and fast, you would think we were employees."

"Do you have any sort of contract that enforces those rules?"

"No contract at all."

"Okay, so officially, they just have requirements, not rules. And you haven't violated any requirement that they have in writing. You haven't neglected your responsibilities?" he persisted.

"Absolutely not," I answered, thinking of how utterly responsible I had been when I'd returned to my duties less than a week after Shannon was born.

"Well, then, I doubt that they can legally terminate you. Remember, Jackie, you're in the driver's seat. Take your time and don't let anyone push you into a hasty decision about leaving. They can't make you go."

That was a relief, but there was still the controversy over the 2 percent category. I explained carefully why I knew it to be true. Richard had drawn the diagram on the blackboard several times, always in front of the whole group. He clearly showed how the position could be attained. "Yet, now they're blatantly lying about it. Kay Dickson has already left the company because of this. It's outrageous."

"But it was not in writing?" he queried again.

"No, not in 'their' writing, but all of us have it in our notes. What would they claim—that it's a conspiracy?"

He was silent as he gave this some serious thought. Henry had a brilliant mind, and I was confident that he would know what to do.

Finally he said, "If it should go to court, you may have a case that you had a verbal contract. But that's risky, and depends on the judge's evaluation. The best thing for you to do is to go talk with Mary Kay. Surely, you can work this out. As you well know, court is the last place you want to go to settle anything. I can't believe she wants you to leave when you've been so instrumental to her success."

"She does." I said, looking him directly in the eye. "I committed the unpardonable sin."

He leaned forward in his chair. "What did you do?"

"I stood up to her." I didn't go into details, but between forcing her not to spike the punch and insisting that they honor the 2 percent deal, I had become more than a thorn in their side; I was a four-inch nail.

Now I know that, a few years later, they were forced by the directors to restore the 2 percent rule, as well as to add many other incentives to attract good people. They came up with the pink Cadillac program, a retirement plan that enabled the national directors to retire wealthy, and glamorous trips to exotic destinations, to name a few. All of this supported my belief that the determining factor that caused me to fall from grace with Mary Kay was the strong stand I took when I disagreed with her tactics.

Henry refused payment for the session and I thought, not for the first time, what a nice man he was for a lawyer. Since he wasn't a courtroom attorney, we both knew he couldn't help me further, regardless of the course of action I would take. I knew this was probably the only time I would contact him, and I knew Henry also had been thinking it was sad that it had come to this.

But Henry was wrong about one thing: I could not go to Mary Kay and talk this out. I had, in the course of my dealings with her, learned an important lesson about relationships. When a conflict centers on a lack of trust and respect, it probably cannot be resolved. You can never arrive at an agreement that's fair for both sides when one side doesn't believe in fairness. It would take a miracle to settle this amicably. I'd already been given one of those when my baby arrived healthy, and I didn't dare ask for another.

Kay Dickson's decision to leave the company had occurred as soon as she heard about Mary Kay's refusal to make good the promise of the third tier. She, Marjie, and I had discussed starting a company of our own, but before we had a chance to explore the idea, Kay was offered a top position with a prominent cleaning supply company. She was to head up a new division, which would use direct sales to market products for the home and yard.

She invited us all over to hear about it, of course, but something was missing. I realized what it was immediately—magic. The magic of Mary Kay was like a spark that had permeated every area of my life—physically, mentally, and spiritually. It was the key ingredient that provided the staying power to keep me loyal to her through all our ups and downs. And that spark didn't affect just me; it passed from person to person. The more people there were in a room with it, the larger the flame. That's why there was such a magnetic frenzy that kept the company going.

Kay's overall plan might have been good, but I knew it wasn't right for me. However, I understood why Kay had accepted the position. She knew what it took to build a company from zero to where Mary Kay was presently; it required a superhuman effort and total commitment.

Kay's leaving left one little problem to be solved: the distribution of her salespeople who were still left at Mary Kay.

The policy had been that the people would return to the parent unit, which was mine. But Mary Kay decided that she wouldn't allow that and would put them all into an office unit, which would effectively make the unit the company's. (And Mary Kay wouldn't have to pay out commissions.) My directors stood up to her and demanded that they be returned to me, and they were. Since this group included Helen McVoy, who was already in qualification for directorship, this was a major concession on Mary Kay's part.

Next on my "to do" list before I left the company, was to get to the bottom of the relentless rumors about Mary Kay. I knew I could find out more while I was still working there, so I decided to get busy. I telephoned Dick Kelly, and he confirmed that Mary Kay had taken the cosmetic formulas from his files, the ones he had bought years earlier from Ova Spoonemore herself. He also confirmed that Beauticontrol products were still on the market and had always been, although in a very limited manner. With that settled, I asked him if Mary Kay had "stolen" any of his people. He said, "Not really. A few of mine went with her, but as far as I know, they contacted her." I was about to hang up the phone when he added, "But Mary Crowley is another story."

"What do you mean?" I asked, more than a little intrigued.

"It's a long tale. Let's get together sometime and I'll tell you." I made a mental note to check into this later.

Marjie and I, at the urging of Stan and Ned, were seriously beginning to consider checking into Beauticontrol as a possible way of going head-to-head in competition with Mary Kay, using all the skills and the networks we had developed at Mary Kay Cosmetics. Right now though, to put it in the most generous terms, Beauticontrol was a stalled company. I still had reservations because I knew the pros and cons about building a company from the ground up, and mostly it was cons. Marjie urged me to at least try the products, if Stan could get samples.

I agreed, seeing no harm in going that far, but it would take a lot to convince me to go ahead with this project. If I could follow my heart, I would stay home with Shannon, who was just five months old and was our little miracle. In spite of all the dire predictions, she was perfect and beautiful. Since Ned had made it clear he would not agree for me to go back to school, I wanted to simply be a homemaker, at least until Shannon started school. Ned's job was sound, and while we wouldn't be able to maintain our current financial position, we could certainly manage. But I was stuck with the same old problem. Ned again made it clear that it was my responsibility to support Sharon, not his. Sharon would be in college in a few years, and I had to plan for that. So I was back to square one. Where would I go and what would I do? The answer would come far sooner than I could ever have imagined.

Early the next day I got an urgent call from Marjie. "Can you meet me right away?" she asked, sounding more excited than I had ever heard her.

"What's going on? You don't sound like yourself."

"I can't tell you on the phone; I'm not at home. Meet me halfway in forty-five minutes," she said and hastily gave me the name of a coffee shop.

"Wait a minute, Marjie," I cried, but it was too late. She'd hung up.

I was so grateful for Marie. Because of her, I could go out like this on a moment's notice. I still felt this perfect nanny was an angel, sent to help take care of our precious baby girl.

I threw my clothes on and hurried to meet Marjie, who was already there when I arrived. She motioned to me to hurry, and as soon as I sat across from her in the booth, I said, "What on earth is it? You sounded so urgent that I only got half dressed."

"Sh-h-h," she whispered, "you never know who's listening."

I suddenly grew very concerned and asked if we should go sit in the car.

"I think it will be okay in here, we just need to be careful."

"About what?" I persisted.

"About these," she answered, opening up a paper bag and taking out a group of jars and bottles.

"Is that . . ." I began, but she put her fingers to her lips to stop me. But I wondered if these were the original Beauticontrol products, the ones Ova Spoonemore had kept in the family.

"Yes, it is." And just wait 'til you try it. You think what we've been using is good, but you won't believe how much better this is." An old, once familiar, tingle of excitement ran through me, and a tiny ray of hope returned.

"Really? It's actually so much better that you can tell the difference?"

"Really," she said quietly, smiling from ear to ear.

She began to show me the products, one at a time, pointing out the differences between them and Mary Kay's. They smelled of lavender, like fresh flowers after a spring rain. As I sniffed them, the words clean and pure came into my mind, and I could visualize the words on a product brochure.

"Is this set for me?" I asked, suddenly eager to get home and try it.

"Yes." she said laughing. "I almost called you last night. I tried them after Stan got home, and I can't wait to hear what you think." She quickly put the jars back into the bag, handed it to me, and we paid the check and headed for the door.

The waitress called after us, "Was there something wrong with the coffee? You didn't even touch it." We just smiled and waved to her as the door closed behind us.

Marjie was right. Even though the products were similar in some ways (both cleansing creams liquefied when applied to the face), they were incredibly different in other ways. Because ingredient labeling had not yet become a legal requirement, we couldn't tell the exact difference until we had them analyzed. One obvious and significant difference was that Beauticontrol had a separate masque for skin problems like acne. Mary Kay only had "one size fits all."

Beauticontrol's masque was the one used by the people in the before-and-after pictures that had now become famous. A new thought struck me: when I had first asked Mary Kay about the before-and-after pictures, she said that Ova Spoonemore had made them. Yet Mary Kay didn't even have the product used by the people in the pictures. Suddenly a cold chill engulfed me, as I realized Mary Kay's deception was even deeper than I had thought.

The proof that these were products worth building a company on came in less than a week. My skin was smoother, softer, and more glowing than it had been after years of faithfully using Mary Kay's products. If Marjie and I were that impressed, surely our customers would be too. The only way that Mary Kay products appeared to be superior was the packaging. The jars that Marjie handed me were plain white, without labels. This was minor, however, and easily corrected.

"Let's go meet Dathene," I said to Marjie on the phone. "We can sell this product. But first we need to get the rest of the story."

Stan had already hunted down Dathene Dark while on a business trip to Tyler, Texas, about 100 miles from Dallas. Dathene was Ova Spoonemore's daughter and the hide tanner's granddaughter. When Stan told her we were interested in entering a joint venture with her and selling Beauticontrol on a much larger scale, she was ecstatic over the idea. Stan explained that this was just a possibility and not to expect anything at this point. He added that was why he wanted the products so we could compare them with Mary Kay's.

When we decided to pay her a visit, we knew where Dathene lived, but not much more about her. In mid-March of 1966, in late afternoon, Marjie and I drove to Tyler to check out what was going on with Beauticontrol Cosmetics. The wind howled ominously and sleet pelted the windshield. It was hard to believe that spring was only one week away. Marjie always insisted on driving (I suspected she was afraid of mine). In weather like this, she was welcome to the job. We both wore jeans and sweaters with trench coats to ward off the chill and I pulled mine more tightly around me.

From the beginning, Marjie and I had been good friends as well as business associates. We agreed on almost every important subject like family values, Christian principles, and even politics. But when it came to mundane matters, such as which direction to take to a certain area or where to go for lunch, we could almost come to blows if we weren't careful. Our relationship remained this way for more than forty years. I tried to stay away from idle chitchat especially tonight. But after several minutes of silence, Marjie said, "Penny for your thoughts."

"I was just thinking that we need to discuss what we want to ask Dathene when we get there." I had brought a notebook and pen because Mary Kay had pounded into us the concept that "the faintest ink is better than the most retentive memory." We quickly made a list of things we wanted to ask. Stan had tried to warn us about what we were in for with this character. All he said was, "She marches to a different drummer." That didn't quite prepare us for what we actually found.

We finally located Dathene's small house in the freezing rain. The carport was bulging with "stuff." It was literally spilling out of the small building, leaving no room for her car, which was on the street. The car appeared to be full of junk as well. We knocked on the front door, and although we could hear her inside, it took awhile for her to open it. She was a little taller than I, but shorter than Marjie, and she was wearing a work uniform I'm sure was white at one time. Now it was sprinkled with bits of various colors. Her dark hair was mixed with gray and drawn into a bun on the back of her head. She looked tired and weary from a long day's work, which accented her wrinkles. She wore no make-up and looked much older than Mary Kay, although I knew she was quite a bit younger.

"Come in," she said, laughing nervously. "I was getting worried about you being out in this weather." She led us through the maze of boxes filling the living room. I didn't dare look at Marjie, for fear we would start laughing. The place looked like a tiny warehouse more than it did a home. We made it to the kitchen and Dathene motioned to us to sit around the table. Actually it was the only place we could sit; every other spot was filled with boxes. "I'm going to have to move, and I'm trying to get things ready," she said by way of explanation. But moving did not explain the extent of the chaos we saw.

Dathene made coffee. Quietly sipping it helped reduce the awkwardness. Soon, Dathene was smiling and telling us about her five children. The two older ones, a boy and a girl, were almost out of school and would soon leave home. Apparently those two had the same father; it was less clear who had fathered the youngest three. We only knew that at this point in her life, she was a struggling single mother. Looking around the small house, I wondered where the children were and how she could fit them all into this place. As if reading my mind she said, "I farmed them out with friends, so we could talk."

We broke the ice by telling her we loved her products. She was totally at ease with that subject and jumped in. "My mother insisted that we follow a strict manufacturing procedure. They are made from U.S. pure ingredients, which means the finest available, and there is a secret ingredient that makes them unique from all the rest." This was something Marjie and I had never heard before. I made a quick note to ask more about this later. First I wanted to ask the all-important question of how Mary Kay had ended up with the family formulas. Before I could get the words out, Marjie asked where the products were actually made. Dathene looked at her as though it were a ridiculous question and replied, "Right here, of course," waving her hand around the kitchen. Aghast, Marjie and I just looked at each other.

I interrupted, because I didn't want the conversation to head off in another direction before we got what we came for. "How did Mary Kay end up with your formulas, your company, and even your family story about the hide tanner?"

"I've known Mary Kay for a long time," she said, then giggled and added that they had a lot in common. "We've both had a lot of husbands." Her mother had trusted Mary Kay and asked her to be a spokesperson on a television show for them, promoting Beauticontrol. "We sold so much we couldn't make it fast enough, so we had to stop the TV program." That was my first clue about her ways of thinking. Why didn't she just find a way to produce the product faster?

Mary Kay had sold Beauticontrol along with other products she was pushing at the time, such as Stanley home products and World Gift items. She soon liked the products so much that she talked Dick Kelly into adding a cosmetic line to his company. That was when Ova had sold him the formulas for a few items.

They apparently weren't, however, "the gold standard," the ones made from the original hide tanner's formulas. Ova was a cosmetician and had apparently made up a few variations of the products. She didn't mind letting those out of the family. I asked if she had anything in writing about the transaction with World Gift.

"Sure, I've got it right here," she said, opening a folder in front of us. We already knew two important things about Dathene. The worst thing about her was that she never threw anything away. And the best thing was that she never threw anything away. Marjie moved her chair closer to mine, and we perused the simple document. All it really did was list the products that she provided formulas for. There was no mention of them being the hide tanner's formulas, nothing that would indicate they were buying exclusive rights to anything. Dathene could have sold those formulas to a hundred people, given the wording of that contract. Marjie and I just looked at each other in disbelief.

"Do you have a copy of the contract with Mary Kay?" Marjie and I asked at the same time.

"I do," Dathene answered, "but it's the same as that one. She just changed the names when she copied it. I didn't give her any formulas, though, because she said she had already gotten them from World Gift. She just wanted this piece of paper. I wasn't sure what was going on, but she said it was just in case Dick Kelly sued her. If he did, I was to say that she'd bought the formulas from me." She handed the contract to us and sure enough, it was the same, except the names had been changed. It was becoming clear to me that the only thing Mary Kay ever had access to were the second-rate formulas that Ova had come up with, not the original ones from the hide tanner. Those, as far as I was concerned, were the treasure. But I had to be sure about this, so I asked more directly:

"Did you ever sell her Beauticontrol formulas specifically? Or the company itself, or your family history? Or your grandfather's story of how he came up with the idea in the first place?"

Dathene took the sheet of paper and shook it at us as if we couldn't understand anything and said, "This is the only thing there is. She gave me $500 and I didn't give her anything in return except for a piece of paper. No formulas, nothing. I thought it was the easiest five hundred I ever got, and I thought it had to be a gift from God."

"What about the before-and-after pictures taken by your mother using Beauticontrol products? What is Mary Kay doing with those?" I demanded.

"I loaned them to her, but she never gave them back. She was supposed to get her own before-and-after pictures." Suddenly, a strange look came over Dathene's face. It seemed to be sinking in that not only had Mary Kay taken the family pictures, she had also taken the family history. "Is Mary Kay saying I sold her everything? The Beauticontrol formulas, the company, and my family's history?"

"That's exactly what she's saying," Marjie said emphatically.

"I would never do that!" Dathene cried. "My mother made me promise two things: that I would always bless every jar of cream that came from Beauticontrol—that was the secret ingredient—and that I would keep the formulas in our family."

I'd thought the secret ingredient would be something more scientific and marketable. Years later, after we began producing the products in huge stainless steel vats, I had to convince Dathene that blessing the entire batch was just as good as blessing one jar at a time. It was not an easy job; I knew beyond a doubt that she would never have gone back on her promise to her mother.

"So," Marjie said skeptically, "you really thought you were getting all that money for nothing?" Nobody ever accused Marjie of being subtle.

Flustered, Dathene lamented, "We're Christian Scientists and we believe that God always provides. And I thought that was what He was doing."

I'd been listening to the exchange with a feeling that I'd heard this story before. It was the one about Jacob and Esau where Esau sold his birthright to Jacob for a bowl of porridge, not really believing it would ever come back to haunt him, which, of course, it did.

And then another important question popped into my head. "Dathene, was your company called Beauticontrol, Incorporated?"

"Of course," she answered, puzzled.

"Is the corporation still in good standing?" I asked, afraid to hear the answer.

"Well, no," Dathene admitted. "I couldn't pay the fees to keep it active."

"Could Mary Kay have possibly reserved the name in the state of Texas?" I asked.

She hung her head and answered softly, "I don't know."

Marjie and I exchanged glances again, and I made another note on my pad. "Check the status of the corporation." This was serious. If it turned out that Mary Kay did own that name, then it was the end of our plans to resurrect this company.

Dathene was burdened by the conversation. She could not escape the fact that she had been taken for a ride. Anxious to change the subject and lighten things up, she asked us if we knew about all of Mary Kay's husbands. We shook our heads.

"Do you?" Marjie asked her point-blank.

"I've got letters and contracts right here with most of them," Dathene said proudly. Marjie and I moved in closer to her. Mary Kay was a die-hard Baptist and vehemently proclaimed to put God first. Because of this, we never really believed the rumors that she had been married many times. Again, Dathene pulled out papers for us to see. One was signed with the last name of Eckman, another was Miller, and still another one was Louis. Speechless, Marjie and I just looked at each other. "And," Dathene added, now excited, "she married Mary Crowley's brother, whose name was Weaver, twice." And I suddenly remembered that was exactly what Lois (from San Francisco) had told me.

"How many times does that make?" Marjie asked, excited.

"She's been married nine times, I think," Dathene answered, "and I know for sure eight."

So we started counting: Rogers (the children's father), Louis, Miller, Eckman, Weaver, Weaver, Hollenbeck, and Ash. Marjie and I burst out laughing. "What's so funny?" Dathene asked, probably thinking we were laughing at her, too, since she'd admitted to numerous marriages as well.

I said, "I couldn't find that many husbands no matter how hard I tried."

"Does this make her tied with Elizabeth Taylor?" Marjie added.

"I guess it does. What I don't get is how she can remember the right name of her present husband. I can't even keep my two children's names straight," I said, still laughing.

"She could call up Liz and see what she does," Marjie suggested merrily.

Finally Dathene joined in and said: "Or, she could do what I do." Marjie and I looked at her expectantly. "Whenever I can't remember my current husband's name, I just say 'Hey, you,' and it works just fine."

And then the three of us had one great laugh together. After that, the conversation turned serious again. Dathene broke down and told us how desperate she was in trying to provide for her children. She worked as a cosmetologist all day and made and sold Beauticontrol at night to make ends meet. She couldn't afford to buy new jars, so the customers sent back their old ones. She had to sterilize them, refill them, and send them back to the customer. And, even with both jobs, she still couldn't make enough to pay her bills. She explained that was why she was being forced to move. Her mother had a little house in Oak Cliff in Dallas, and she was going to move back there to save rent.

Marjie and I were both thinking of the lavish lifestyles we all lived in comparison with hers. Especially Mary Kay, with her Cadillacs, fur coats, and diamond rings. "It's not fair" seemed to vibrate through the room, although not a word was spoken out loud. I knew I wanted to get involved, to help right this wrong.

Dathene refilled our cups from a second pot of coffee. I looked at my watch and knew we had to head home soon. "Dathene, there is a question I have to ask you, and I have to have an absolutely truthful answer."

"What is it?" she asked with a puzzled look on her face.

"Is the story true about your grandfather, the hide tanner, and how he came up with the formulas?"

She didn't hesitate. "Absolutely, and I can prove it." We waited as she again withdrew papers from a folder. She held up a picture of her grandfather, with his wife and several children. "Look at his face," she said, "then look at his wife. He used the product on his own face, experimenting, and she did not. She looks like his mother." Marjie and I both peered carefully at the picture. She was right; he looked many years younger.

Then Marjie, looking at the picture with her keen eyes, said excitedly, "And look at his hands; they look even younger."

"That's right," Dathene agreed. "That's how he got the idea in the first place. He noticed that his hands were looking younger from using the tanning process, and eventually that led him to try it on his face."

Marjie and I both knew that this would make powerful marketing information, and I asked, "Why haven't you ever used this in your literature?"

"I guess we just didn't think of it," she answered. Marjie and I certainly wouldn't be putting her in charge of the marketing department.

"While we are on the subject of using the product, why don't you use it yourself, Dathene?" I asked point-blank.

"How do you know I don't?" she asked testily.

"Are you kidding? Anyone who knows how good your products are can tell by looking at your skin that you aren't using them." (I can be a little blunt myself).

Embarrassed, she mumbled, "All these kids . . ." her voice trailing off.

"I want to be up front with you, Dathene, IF . . . and that is a big IF right now, we join you in this business, you will have to use the products faithfully. Understood?"

"I'll do whatever you say, if you will only help build this business," she said with fear in her voice and hope in her eyes.

"I'll bet you were a real beauty when you were in your teens, weren't you?" Although I said this partially to soften the criticism, I also meant it. She had good bone structure and good features. With a little work she could restore a much younger look.

"Here's a picture when I was about twenty," she said, proffering it. "I actually won a beauty contest in Mena, Arkansas, that year," she said shyly. Marjie and I looked at it a long time. She had been a real beauty. Strange that she had access to the fountain of youth and had ignored it as if her looks didn't concern her. Yet she was pleased at our response. It made me sad. Somehow I knew she hadn't had a lot of "warm and fuzzy" moments in her life.

Marjie and I began gathering up our things. The sleet had let up temporarily and we wanted to use the opportunity to head for home. Before we left, Dathene gave us the names of a couple of people who still sold Beauticontrol, just in case we needed further proof of its benefits. One of the names was Pauline Hill, who turned out to live in my area. Her son was actually in a class with Sharon. The other was Nell Davis, who had been a close friend of Ova Spoonemore and would ultimately become one to me.

"How soon do you think you'll know what you're going to do?" Dathene asked, anxiously, as we stood at the door, buttoning our coats. The emotion in her voice was unmistakable, and Marjie and I had to struggle with our own. It was hard to see this good, honest woman struggling, knowing how much she had been taken advantage of, knowing how much money others had made off her heritage.

"As soon as we can," I assured her. We hurried to the car, anxious to get out of the bitter cold. As we backed out of the drive, Marjie noticed that Dathene was still in the doorway. "You can tell she doesn't want us to leave." She generally considered herself to be the hard-nosed one and me to be the emotional one, yet at this moment in the dark car we were both touched more deeply than either of us would admit.

"What do you think?" she asked, the minute we were on the road.

"We have a lot to think about, that's for sure," I answered. "Do you remember the truck stop we passed about halfway here? It stays open all night, I hear, and they are known for their homemade pies. I've had all the coffee I can take, but I'm starving. I thought maybe we could stop there. I didn't eat anything before we left."

"Neither did I."

About an hour later we pulled into the truck stop. These were the days before women always chose a salad, no matter how hungry they were. After everything we had heard that evening, a little bit of sweetness was in high order. The pies looked mouth-watering in their display case just inside the door and we took our time deciding which one we'd try. Marjie took the chocolate and I picked the fresh coconut cream, hoping that we'd exchange bites.

We ate first, barely saying a word. Finally Marjie began, with an odd comment. "Do you really think that blessing each jar of creme helps?" She had something of a smirk on her face, and I knew I didn't want to go there; so I was silent for a few minutes. This was one of those subjects I had to answer carefully. I took anything religious far more seriously than she did, and I didn't want to have to defend it. The truth is, I didn't know if blessing something helped it or not, but my deep beliefs told me there was something to it. I gave the most noncombatant answer I could think of. "Well, it certainly can't hurt, can it?" She hesitated, as though she wanted to say more, but finally mumbled, "Guess not." Fight averted.

She took another bite. "My head is spinning. We have so much to sort out. Do you think Dathene is telling the whole truth?"

I hesitated for a long time because it was a hard question. The sticking point was the $500. Was she really naïve enough to think someone would give her that much money for virtually nothing? Did she mean it when she said she thought of it as a gift from God? I realized that I simply believed her. She wasn't disingenuous enough to lie. But as I pondered it further a new revelation came to me, and a missing piece of the puzzle finally clicked into place.

I said, "You know, Marjie, we keep wondering if Dathene actually believed she was given $500 for nothing. Let's look at it another way. You and I both know that Mary Kay spends more than $500 a year on her little poodle. She considered giving Dathene $500 nothing, as well. So I think it went both ways; they both thought they were getting something for nothing."

Marjie sat silently, thinking about what I'd said. Then she answered simply, "Maybe so."

I picked at the last bits of coconut with my fork and debated ordering another piece. "I'll tell you the thing that bothers me the most. Mary Kay built her entire empire on the hide tanner's story being her story. She told the reporter that she was the granddaughter and this was her family." When challenged, Mary Kay explained this by saying the reporter was the one who had written it incorrectly. That, in itself, seemed troubling enough. But I knew there was even more. "She also told all of us that she bought everything, the company, all formulas, and the family history. And yet she has to know there is a contract—something in writing—that says otherwise."

"Exactly," Marjie agreed. "For all of this to not be true is shattering to people who are loyal to her and look up to her. I don't understand how an intelligent woman would think that she could keep all this shocking information from coming out. Ever. She'd have to be stupid, and one thing we do know is that she and Richard are not stupid."

"And then there's all those marriages," I pointed out. "It just doesn't look good for her to have gone from man to man to man, even if she did have the respectability of a marriage license."

We sat without speaking for several minutes as we stared out the window into the black, cold night.

"Maybe she just thought Dathene would stay in her little corner of the world and the truth would never be told," Marjie speculated.

"Well, that was a mistake, if it's what she thought. If no one else tells it, I'll tell it myself."

"It's so directly opposite from everything she says she believes in, about God and family. How do you explain the chasm?" Marjie continued.

"Maybe in her heart of hearts, that is the way she wishes her life was," I answered softly.

Marjie just rolled her eyes, as if to say, "Give it up."

We talked very little the rest of the way home. I reviewed in my head the situation with Dathene and the desperate place she was in with her children. As the thoughts turned, I listened to the noise the tires made on the wet road: bumpty-bump, bumpty-bump. And then the noise seemed to turn into words, "Make it right, make it right." And I knew that was what we had to do.

CHAPTER FIFTEEN

The Cat Is Out of the Bag

The stunning information we'd gotten from Dathene on our visit to Tyler required a mountainous decision that would change our lives. Before deciding whether or not to take over Beauticontrol, we had to thoroughly understand what we would be getting into. So, Marjie, Stan, Ned, and I hashed and rehashed the situation for hours on end. Marjie and I were totally sold on the products and felt they were far superior to Mary Kay's. That fact, along with possession of the real history behind the products and a few stainless steel mixing vats, would be the extent of the assets we would own to begin with.

The long-time customers that Dathene still had were true believers in the product, but their purchases would produce very little income. Dathene hadn't made any effort in years to add new customers, so it was nothing short of miraculous that she had any left at all. As I digested all of this information, the burden grew heavier when I fully realized that we would be starting from scratch.

Remembering how it was when I first began with Mary Kay, I shuddered at the thought. The long hours and the constant pressure to work and never to take a break were still fresh in my mind. And it would probably be even worse, because I now had two children who needed my attention.

Even as I had the thought, an idea popped into my head. When Kay Dickson left the company and Mary Kay had tried to prevent her people from returning to my group, as was the custom, my directors had intervened. As a group, they went to Mary Kay and demanded that she return the people to me, and she did. Now I realized that if I asked them they would probably go in and demand that the 2 percent be reinstated or else we would all leave. But even as I considered it, I knew it would not be the same.

My directors had made the first demand on their own, and I was not willing to ask them to put themselves on the line this way for me. And even if they did and Mary Kay complied, what kind of future could we have? If she would renege on this deal, she would probably do the same on others. So I scratched the idea and never told Ned that I'd even had the thought.

Our first priority was to find out if the name Beauticontrol, Inc. was available for us to use for our corporation. If Mary Kay had somehow made that impossible by reserving it for herself then it would cancel the entire idea because our whole premise was that the name of our company needed to be the same name used by Dathene's family since 1933. So Stan called the Texas State Comptroller's Office and tracked down the information we needed. The name was available, and Stan got the paperwork necessary to complete the transaction of reincorporating the company.

Because we wanted to keep our plans that we were probably going to join Dathene in Beauticontrol secret until we were ready to make our move, we decided to visit my brother, J. C., in Arkansas over a weekend. By doing so we could have complete privacy for our discussions. I looked up to J. C. He was the closest thing I had to a father figure, although he was just twelve years older than I was. He was business-minded, and I knew he would understand, as other family members might not, that we were there on business purposes and not on a social visit.

When I was a sophomore in high school, he built a large restaurant in the small Arkansas town where he lived. And he asked me to come live with his family for the rest of my high school years and help out in the restaurant. For the first time in my life, I would get to be a part of a family atmosphere and have the support it would offer. Since it wasn't especially far from where my mom lived and I could still see her often, I decided to go.

It turned out to be the best of my teen-age years. Although it was hard work, I loved being a waitress in the restaurant. I met all kinds of people, good tempered and bad, and I had to learn to deal with them accordingly. Our cooks prepared wonderful food and complete lunches were a whopping sixty-five cents. Of course, I always looked forward to discovering what kind of tip I would get. Usually, it was just ten cents, but sometimes it would be a quarter, and that was really exciting.

But the most wonderful thing of all about living there was that my sister-in-law, Juanita, was a fantastic seamstress. Thanks to her I was among the best-dressed kids in school. For my junior banquet, which was a formal affair, she made my gown out of a shiny-white shadow print organdy fabric with a scooped neckline and tiny puffed sleeves. It fit tight at the waist and the long skirt was a complete circle and swished when I walked, making me feel even more special.

My date, "Red" Franks, (who would one day become my husband) sent me the largest purple orchid corsage I'd ever seen. When I pinned it on my shoulder and whirled around in front of a full mirror, for the first time in my life I felt beautiful. Having clothes that made me feel better about the way I looked helped me to build self-esteem as well as self-confidence, and that would impact the rest of my life. It helped to give me the courage I needed (such as having the nerve to head up a cosmetic company).

J. C. still owned a motel, so we could stay in the cabins (Ned and I in one and Stan and Marjie in another) and have the seclusion we needed. Also, there would be plenty of family to take care of Shannon and Sharon while we worked. Sheryl would stay home with Stan's mother.

On Friday afternoon all of us piled into my Cadillac for the trip. It was early spring and the day was warm and our spirits were high. The kids slept most of the way while the four of us fantasized about where our new adventure would take us, and where we might be in five years. If we could have had a hint of what lay ahead, I have often thought we would probably have turned the car around and ditched the whole idea.

After dropping the kids off at the Franks' house on Saturday morning, we returned to the motel, made a fresh pot of coffee, and settled down to business. The first decision the four of us had to make was the way the stock in the corporation would be split. Ned and I had already spent hours discussing the matter. He felt we should have controlling interest in the company, meaning more than 50 percent of the stock, primarily because he thought we deserved it since the venture would basically depend on my accomplishments. The rest of the stock would go to Marjie and Stan, except that Dathene would be given a minor part, even though we would be contributing all the money and almost everything else for operating expenses. We had already agreed to pay her a monthly salary that was far greater than anything she'd ever had so that she could finally take proper care of her children. But we knew that the four of us could not take anything out of the company until it showed a profit, and we had no idea how long that would be.

Intuitively, I realized that Stan and Marjie wouldn't go along with the split that Ned was suggesting. And in truth, I didn't feel right about it either because the whole idea had been Stan's. How could we give him less? Also, as Christians, for us to demand such a split would be greedy and self-absorbed.

Ned backed up his argument with the fact that someone had to be able to make a decision. In the event of a disagreement, we could bicker endlessly because no one had any real power. He also pointed out that someone not having controlling interest was the number one reason for a corporation's ultimate failure.

I was right. Stan would not agree to our having controlling interest. However, he did say that he thought I should be named president of the company, with all the privileges that came with being the CEO. This would mean that in the case of disagreement, my decision would be final. At this point we decided to take a break, and Ned and I went outside for a walk, so we could talk in private.

"I guess you're pretty excited over the possibility of being president of a company, especially since you're just thirty-two years old," Ned said as soon as we were out of earshot. I couldn't tell from the tone of his voice whether he was sincere or resentful.

"Big deal," I answered, "there's nothing to preside over, and there never will be unless I work my head off like I did at Mary Kay's. But it's pretty exciting all right—no income, no free time, nobody to tell me how great I'm doing. But there is a title." Ned laughed as if he thought I was joking, but I was going for sarcastic, not funny.

Ultimately I was named president, Marjie, vice president, Stan, secretary, and Ned, treasurer. And the stock was split 50/50, after providing something for Dathene, without voting rights. Ned maintained to the bitter end that it was a mistake. A few years later I had to admit he'd been right, after the company had grown to the point that every decision seemed to include a fight.

We did decide that we also needed a Buy or Sell Agreement, so if either couple decided we didn't want to work together anymore, we could present the option to the other couple. The one receiving the option would have to agree to buy or sell, and at what price. It was simply a way to dissolve the partnership if it was no longer working.

In a few days the new incorporation of the company was final, and we were the proud owners of the name Beauticontrol, Inc. Ned and I pledged $10,000 toward operating capital, and Marjie and Stan did the same. We figured that would be enough since Mary Kay had said she started her company with only $5,000. Plus, we would be doing our own manufacturing, which should save on expenses. But there was much more to do. We had to find space for offices and manufacturing, suppliers for containers, labels, and ingredients for the products. There were multitudes of other tasks as well.

Dathene had already moved to Dallas as she'd planned, and she was anxious to get the whole thing going. But we were not ready to resign from Mary Kay, because we had to first be certain everything was ready for us to go directly into business.

Then something happened that forced our hand. Because Stan sold insurance, he was out and about during the day and had the opportunity to call on some of the suppliers we might use. (We would soon learn that there are no secrets in the cosmetic world.) One of the suppliers called Richard and tipped him off about Stan's visit.

It was late afternoon near the end of March when I got a frantic telephone call from Richard. He said that he and Mary Kay had to see me immediately, and they wanted to come over to my house. "Right now?" I asked, shocked. "It's not a good time, Richard. I am here alone with Shannon. How about tomorrow?" Because Marie stayed late so much, whenever I was home for the afternoon, as I was today, I let her leave a little early.

He absolutely refused to take no for an answer, and within thirty minutes they were ringing my doorbell. I knew Ned wouldn't be home for another hour, at least, and even though I was apprehensive about talking to them alone, I braced myself and answered the door.

As they entered and we went into the living room, Richard rattled on about how much he like the house, as if this was just a social call. Shannon was six months old and highly alert for her age. As I held her in my arms, I kept my voice normal and calm, hoping that they would get the hint that I did not want to upset her. "What is it, Richard, that couldn't wait until tomorrow?" I asked with an edge in my voice. As I looked at them closely I saw something in their faces I had never seen before in either of them—fear.

"Well," he began, "this is probably all just a big misunderstanding, but you know how gossip gets around in the cosmetic business, so we decided to come straight to you with what we heard."

"And that is?" I asked, as I looked him calmly in the eye. Still nervous, he related the whole conversation with the supplier. Apparently, Stan had given him the complete rundown about our plans. And I thought, So much for keeping it secret. Why couldn't Stan just have stuck to the necessities?

"So, is it true?" he asked. "Are you going to take over Beauticontrol and compete directly with us?"

I didn't answer immediately because I was watching Mary Kay closely; she hadn't taken a breath for so long I was afraid she was going to start turning blue. Finally, she breathed and spoke.

"It's just gossip, isn't it?" she said before I answered Richard's question. "I know you're unhappy about some things but you wouldn't do that, would you?" She laughed nervously.

"And, if I did, what would be wrong with that? That's exactly what you did, wasn't it? Dick Kelly had a cosmetic line, and you went into direct competition with him."

"But that was different," she said, with a touch of anger in her voice.

"It always is, Mary Kay, when it is you that's been treated unfairly. But I will tell you that nothing is definite yet, it's just one of the things I am considering."

All at once Richard rose from the couch and asked, "Would you mind if I look through your house? I've never seen one I like as much as this one, and I'm thinking of buying one myself." His question took me completely by surprise, and I couldn't think of a way to refuse, so I replied, "Go ahead. The top level is the bedrooms and the bottom one the garage." Even as I heard his footsteps going up the stairs I thought, This is strange, I know women love to look at houses, but not men. Perhaps he just wanted to use the bathroom.

While he was gone, Mary Kay, Shannon, and I continued to sit in the living room. Shannon had been perfect so far, sitting in my lap, but I could tell she was getting restless. "It's getting close to her feeding time, Mary Kay, so tell me what else you want to know."

She hesitated but then said, "If you do leave, Jackie, how would you go about it?"

"If you're asking if I'm going to try to take all your people, then I can assure you I will not do anything underhanded. I've talked with Dick Kelly, and I know what's gone on over there. I got all those people for you, Mary Kay, and if I have to, I can get more for myself. If I do this, I will tell my people what I'm doing and what my company will offer. Then I will suggest they contact me if they are interested."

I glanced at my watch and saw that twenty minutes had passed. Richard was still gone, and I was getting nervous. What in the world was he doing? "Where do you think Richard is?" I asked in what I hoped was a joking tone.

"Here I am," he answered coming down the stairs. "I am so impressed with this place I had to look at every nook and cranny." I looked at him closely; he seemed totally sincere.

Shannon started to cry and as I got up from my chair said, "I have to feed her now. If you have any more questions you can ask them later. Why don't we both agree that as Christians, whatever we do, we will be strictly ethical, and let the best man win." But neither one of them said a word in reply.

As I held the front door open for them to leave, I noticed that the look of fear that had been on their faces when they came in was gone. It had been replaced with one of stark terror.

I quickly fed Shannon and turned her over to Sharon, who had just gotten home. Next I called Stan and Marjie and quickly asked them to come on over so I could tell them what had happened. I said we'd pick up hamburgers from Goff's for dinner.

Just then, Ned walked in the door. "What's going on?" he asked. I told him that Richard and Mary Kay had just left, and I would explain it all as soon as Marjie and Stan arrived. He bounded up the stairs to see Shannon instead of pursuing the matter further, and I knew that left me to go for hamburgers.

As the five of us sat around the table eating our hamburgers, I related every detail about the visit, including Richard's interest in the house. Stan spoke first, "I'm glad it's out in the open, and we don't have to keep quiet anymore about our plans." Thanks to you, I thought.

"There's one thing we have to still keep quiet about until we've actually resigned from Mary Kay," I replied. "I don't want my sales people to know until its official." Ned and Stan both looked horrified at the thought, but Stan put it into words, "But Mary Kay will tell them first, and we won't have a chance at getting them to come with us."

"If you could have seen the looks on their faces, I don't think you would be worried about them breaking the news to anyone. They are terrified."

"Really?" the three of them asked in unison.

I had to laugh at the surprised look on their faces. It was hard for any of us to believe that they were scared of us. As I told them that I had promised Mary Kay we wouldn't pull any dirty tricks and try to steal her people; all three of them frowned. "What's wrong?" I asked, "Surely you weren't thinking of doing that."

"Of course not," Stan answered, "but I did think we might offer some of the directors some stock in the company if they brought their people with them."

Horrified, I gasped, "But Stan, that is stealing people. Please tell me you aren't serious. After the way we disapproved of others doing that to Dick Kelly, I can't believe you'd even think such a thing."

At this point, Marjie joined in. "At least you have to tell your directors we want them to join us. Otherwise they'll feel hurt and left out. If you tell them, they can then decide whether or not to ask their people to come along."

Instead of answering her directly, I explained the rest of the conversation with Mary Kay, that I would tell the local directors personally and write a letter to the out-of-towners containing what we would have to offer them, and then leave it up to them to contact us. One bit of enticing information to be included, which I hadn't mentioned to Mary Kay, would be that our marketing plan would include the third tier and the 2 percent, in writing, as we began so there would be no chance of reneging later on. I added that by revealing what we were doing in this way, there would be no sneaking around or underhanded attempts to take Mary Kay's people. Everything would be aboveboard. They were silent for what seemed like eternity, then Stan said, "I guess that will have to do."

'If you want me involved, Stan, this is how it will have to be. I know you don't agree, but I feel it would be totally dishonest and hypocritical to do the same things we've criticized others for doing. And, I don't think it would build the solid foundation we want for our company to start out unethically. I want you all to think seriously about this and not agree too quickly. I know it would be easier your way, and if you want to proceed on your own, that's perfectly fine with me. These are the kinds of things that must be clear among us in the beginning. You and Marjie talk it over and let us know as soon as possible, maybe tomorrow. If we go ahead, we have to move quickly."

After they had gone, Ned remained silent for a very long time. Finally, I said, "You agree with them, don't you?"

"In a way, I guess I do," he answered. "It would be so much easier to start with a good group of people who were already producing sales."

"Nobody knows that better than I do, Ned, and even though I'm insisting on being up-front, of course I am hoping some of them will come with us. If they don't, it may take us longer to build momentum my way, but I still prefer it. This is where our faith has to come in. If we are in the right here, God will help us make it happen. We don't have to figure it all out on our own."

Ned didn't say anything more about it, but I could tell he still wasn't convinced.

The next day Stan called and said they would try it my way, so we wasted no time. We made a list of things that had to be done immediately. First, we needed a location. A college friend of Stan's, Clint Howard, owned a laboratory on Stemmons Freeway. Since we were going to do the manufacturing, space in that building could be especially beneficial for us.

The four of us went to look at it, and the top floor appeared to be just what we needed. We asked them to hold it (except for one office that we didn't need) until we had officially resigned from Mary Kay. By being in the building, we would have access to a full-time chemist who could help with any manufacturing problems if needed. We considered this a major attraction even though Stan insisted that mixing cosmetics couldn't be much different than cooking.

Producing the products was to be primarily Ned's responsibility, with Dathene's help, since this had been his major in college. Working at night, he would set up the process on a small scale at the beginning but he was already dreaming about how to enlarge it later on.

We continued our business with Mary Kay as usual, until we felt we had all of our ducks in a row. Stan found sources for what we would need for manufacturing, and between us we came up with the furniture from our own houses for the offices. But we didn't actually purchase or contract for anything until after we resigned from Mary Kay because we didn't want to do anything that could be interpreted as trying to harm her company. This turned out to be a very smart move in light of the things to come.

While all of this was done silently, and we continued our business with Mary Kay as normally as possible, I could tell by the way she and Richard avoided looking me in the eye that they were still extremely apprehensive about what we would do. The interesting thing was that the sales people didn't seem to notice anything unusual, which was amazing to me, because I could feel constant tension in the air.

After the last sales meeting I would ever hold at Mary Kay's, some of my directors who now held their sales meetings at the same time decided to have lunch at Howard Johnson's, and they asked me to join them. The group included Jan Jack, Idell Moffitt, and Martha Weddle, who had just finished qualification. I tried to act normal, but I was having intense "separation anxiety," because of the possibility I might not see this group again. While I was secretly counting on Jan, Idell, and Martha joining us, I didn't have a clue as to whether or not they would actually do so. But on this day we laughed and talked as usual until Martha said, "Jackie, is something wrong? You seem a little preoccupied."

There was total silence as they waited for an answer, and I knew they had noticed more than I had thought. "No, everything is fine, I just have a lot on my mind." Even as I said it, I hated the deception, but they would know the whole story soon enough. At the moment, they seemed to accept my explanation.

Ned and Stan would keep their jobs, but they would help out at night when necessary. Marjie would handle the office details and purchasing, and I would be responsible for sales as well as writing all the literature, such as our manual. Dathene would be in charge of actual product production, but we would all help out when needed. The only other person to be hired was a secretary-receptionist.

It was exciting and scary at the same time because it required a major layout of actual cash, and I wouldn't be getting any more huge commission checks at the end of the month. But even worse, I couldn't stand the thought of the possibility that I would no longer have the people I cared so much about around me.

On the rare occasions I got to rock Shannon in the evening, I no longer had the heart to sing Mary Kay songs to her. After a few minutes of silence, she would reach her little hand up to my mouth and try to move it, a signal for me to start singing. I tried to substitute "You Are My Sunshine," but she never kicked when I sang that, as she had always done with Mary Kay songs. Even my baby was losing something that had been special to her.

Marjie and I set up an appointment with Mary Kay and Richard for Friday, April 13, 1966, at 10:00 a.m., at which time we would formally resign from the company. And we both set up meetings separately with our own people for later on the same evening. We would reveal all the information we'd discussed about our leaving Mary Kay at that time.

Marjie's group included the people in her unit as well as some directors in qualification. In addition to expecting several from her group to join us, Marjie also believed her sister-in-law, Anna Kendall, would do so as well, after she heard all the particulars. Anna and Fred now lived in Houston, where she had a thriving unit established with Mary Kay. As Mary Kay's former secretary, she was considered an offspring of the office unit. This meant she was the only person not directly connected to Marjie or me that we would be contacting.

My meeting was to be for the people in my unit as well as all the directors of my sub-units. Even as we made plans for these final events, I was glad one minute and sad the next. My life was going to change radically. My little group would set out on a new path, one we had never before traveled. And we knew there would be unexpected twists and turns along the way. So in preparation for the journey, we armed ourselves with high hopes, strong faith and fervent prayers as we stepped into the unknown.

CHAPTER SIXTEEN

The Resignation

I have never been superstitious, but as Marjie and I prepared for our meeting with Mary Kay and Richard, I began to wonder why we set the appointment to resign for Friday, April 13th. I knew my faith should be stronger than to even think of things from ancient and primitive religions, but we could have just as easily made it a day earlier. However, it was too late now. The day before the meeting, Marjie and I met for coffee to finalize what we wanted to say to the two people that we'd come to know so well. Marjie was as cool as iced watermelon, while I was as nervous as a cat walking on a telephone wire. The only explanation I could offer for this difference was that I was more emotionally attached to these people than she was. But at least one of us is cool and collected, I thought, grateful that she would be with me.

We had already decided to dress to the nines for our meeting, and now we were getting specific. I knew that men never called each other ahead of an event or a meeting to discuss wardrobe, but the women I knew did it all the time. Marjie said she was wearing a new pink silk suit and a hat to match. We were not wearing wigs, as a little reminder that we were no longer following right behind Mary Kay. I was going to wear a new silk yellow sheath dress, and my hat was covered with matching silk flowers. What we were doing, of course, was putting on our armor for the battle we knew was about to begin. We agreed that no matter how hard they tried to provoke us, we would remain calm during the meeting, and keep it professional; and it helped, somehow, that we looked our best. We couldn't control what they did, but we could control ourselves.

As we paid for our coffee and started to leave the shop, we decided, for extra support, to meet there the next morning at 9:30 a.m. and ride to Mary Kay's office together. "And Marjie," I called as she opened her car door, "don't forget to pray about this. We need all the help we can get."

She laughed and called back, "I was waiting for you to say that."

That night, Ned and I talked about the meeting the next day and about how drastically different our lives would become when we weren't with Mary Kay. Change of any kind was never easy, but walking out of the light of the known into the darkness of the unknown was downright scary.

"Do you think Stan and Marjie are as nervous about this as we are?" Ned asked.

"I don't know how Stan feels, but I think Marjie is actually looking forward to the meeting tomorrow. And for that matter, the whole new adventure."

We sat in silence for a while, then Ned said, "Maybe it's because they don't have as much at stake as we do. We're giving up an income ten times more than we ever thought we'd have." I knew he had probably hit the nail on the head. Although we kept our normal routine, spending time with the kids and putting them to bed, we couldn't relax. I hadn't been able to eat dinner and I knew I couldn't sleep; Ned wasn't in much better shape. So we sat in bed in the darkness and relived the last two and one-half years with Mary Kay. In a strange way, it reminded me of a gathering after a loved one dies. Almost all we could remember were the good times.

The next morning my nerves were still shot, so it took me much longer than usual to get dressed. Since I was wearing a hat instead of a wig, styling my hair took extra time. But I was finally ready by 9:00 a.m. and headed out the door to meet Marjie. She looked great in her all-pink outfit, partly due to the fact she also looked rested. She had slept well. "How long do you think we'll be there?" I asked, making conversation to cover my jitters.

"Well, it depends," she answered cheerfully. "If it all goes smoothly, it shouldn't take very long, but if a fight breaks out it could take a good while longer." We laughed at the mental picture her comment produced, making the tension subside as we climbed into my car for our final trip to Mary Kay's.

As we entered the building, the new receptionist (Anna and Fred had moved to Houston months earlier) motioned for us to sit down, barely glancing at us. I wondered what she'd been told. Even though it was a beautiful spring day, the chill in the air made the office feel much more like the dead of winter. Apparently the receptionist had buzzed Richard on the intercom the minute she saw us, because almost instantly he was standing in front of us. "Come on in," he said brusquely, "and we'll get started."

Marjie smiled at him as she stood up. You'd think we were there to discuss the company picnic. But my legs felt like rubber and it took me a few seconds to follow. Finally, we were seated in Mary Kay's office. When the overwhelming feeling that I was going to cry possessed me, I forced myself to focus on details to move all my energy to my head instead of my heart. For the first time, Marjie and I looked better than Mary Kay did. She appeared tired and tense, and even her wig was askew. Somehow the imperfection of it gave her less power. She stared at us, in all of our finery, then launched her opening remark: "Don't you think the hats are a bit much?" It was harsh and left us a little stunned because Mary Kay had never played the heavy; that had been Richard's job. We just looked at her, but I thought, If you'll take off your wig, then we'll take off our hats.

Still in charge of the situation, Mary Kay continued, "What do you two have to say for yourselves?" Her tone sounded as though she had caught two naughty children with our hands in the cookie jar and was chastising us for it.

I felt my spine stiffening and my temper rising as I replied, "We're here to officially turn in our resignations in a professional manner. As far as we're concerned that should be a simple transaction unless, of course, you choose to make it otherwise."

The minute she heard the sternness in my voice, she changed her tactic. "Certainly," she said in a sugar sweet tone. "We're adults here, and we can act like it. Just fill us in on the details." I reiterated what I had told her and Richard earlier, when they had charged into my house after they had heard the rumor I might be leaving, about how I would handle the situation.

And now I explained the actual process. I was having a meeting at my house that night, and Marjie was having one for her people at hers. We would explain that we were leaving the company and why we were leaving as well. Then we would reveal our marketing plan to them so they could compare the two. Immediately, the looks on both Richard and Mary Kay's faces changed to the one they'd had at my house: cold, hard fear. They knew we were referring to the 2-percent level in the marketing plan, and they probably suspected we were going to include it in our plan from the beginning.

At this point Mary Kay spoke again, "We have some concerns about what you're going to do and say as a new business. If it weren't Beauticontrol and wasn't so much like my own products, it wouldn't be a problem. But if you use the name Beauticontrol and the hide tanner's story, and have similar products, then we don't think either company will survive."

Marjie gasped and said, "Are you suggesting that we not use those things? Because our attorney says without question, they all belong to us, so if you feel we can't both use them, then maybe you should do the changing."

That seemed to put Richard and Mary Kay at a temporary loss for words, so I added, as casually as I could. "Apparently, Mary Kay, that $500 you paid Dathene was just for some formulas, and didn't include her family history or Beauticontrol itself, whose products have been continuously on the market since 1933."

Richard and Mary Kay again exchanged looks, and I later concluded that was the moment they decided to try and destroy us at all costs. However, she kept it hidden. She reversed her strategy by smiling sweetly and asking, "Since you say everything is going to be aboveboard, I assume it would be okay for me to attend your meeting tonight?" I knew she was letting me know she didn't trust me to handle it the way I'd said I would. I looked at Marjie, and she frowned and shook her head. But I thought, Maybe if she sees I am going to do exactly as I said, she will let this go, and we can go peacefully about our business.

So after a long silence, I answered, "Okay, Mary Kay, but only on one condition: you cannot say one word, or cause any distraction at all. If you do, I will ask you to leave. Can you agree to that?" Marjie looked as though she might choke over the arrangement. I would later consider it as probably one of the biggest mistakes I ever made.

But now Mary Kay replied, "Of course, I'll be as quiet as a mouse."

Marjie nudged me, without even bothering to be inconspicuous, letting me know it was time to go. We rose and made it to the door before Mary Kay cast her final volley, "Jackie, even with Jesus, there was Judas." The shocked look on Marjie's face from the comment was every bit as great as the one on mine.

That remark did it, and Marjie lost her cool. The minute we walked out the front door of the building, she said with an anger I'd never seen in her before, "What does that remark say to you, Jackie?"

"Volumes, Marjie—absolute volumes. But look," I added, pointing up to the street sign just outside the building, which read, Majesty Drive. "It looks like the Queen chose the right address."

By the time we were back in the car, I could no longer control the emotion that was overwhelming me. It wasn't just the meanness in Mary Kay's remark that my betrayal was equal to that of Judas, but also knowing I'd left her office for the last time. And even worse, I knew that in spite of everything, I would miss Mary Kay herself for years to come, because she had filled a void in me I hadn't even known I'd had: praise and recognition for a job well done. Even though I tried with all my might to prevent it, I couldn't stop the sobs that racked my body.

"You're crying, after the way that woman just treated you, not to mention all the money she beat you out of?" Marjie asked in total disbelief.

After I finally regained control, I turned to Marjie and said, "I got something far more valuable than money from Mary Kay."

"And, pray tell," she said with her eyes open wide, "what would that be?"

After a long pause, I said, "The confidence to do what you and I are about to undertake. If my experience with Mary Kay had never happened, I would probably have stayed an underpaid secretary for the rest of my life. No matter what happens now, I will always have to give her credit for getting me to see I could do anything I make up my mind to do."

As Marjie listened to what I said, her face softened and she nodded to indicate she understood my feelings. By this time we were back at the coffee shop, where Marjie had left her car. A thought suddenly hit me that was so funny I started laughing hysterically.

Again Marjie looked at me in shock and said, "First you cried hysterically and now you're laughing the same way. What on earth is it now?"

I caught my breath and answered, "I'll bet Mary Kay is kicking herself right now for overdoing her praise of me. With all that praise, she got me to stop thinking like a lowly secretary, and instead, now thinking I can do her job."

Marjie joined me in the laughter, and we began to relax. As she prepared to leave my car for hers, she made a final comment. "Did you notice that Richard didn't say a single word?"

"I noticed, all right, and that tells us for certain the good cop, bad cop routine was just an act. Mary Kay has always been the real heavy."

After she was in her own car and ready to leave, I yelled, "Call me after your meeting," but she was already on the move and just smiled and waved, indicating agreement.

As I prepared for the meeting at my house, I wondered why I scheduled both meetings on the same day. Two such events packed with emotion and held back to back, were enough to penetrate the toughest heart. What would it do to a crybaby like me? I learned from this experience that from this point on I would have to think things through more carefully. With that thought came another; I was entering into an even greater unknown than the one I'd had in the beginning with Mary Kay. I had now pledged to build an entire company. The on-the-job training would have to start all over. Because it would involve so many people taking the risk that I would lead them to success, this time the responsibility would weigh much heavier on my shoulders.

It was almost 6:00 p.m. when Ned got home, and everyone else was due at 7:00. I hated to tell him that Mary Kay would be there as well, but didn't dare risk him causing a scene if her appearance caught him by surprise. I tried to explain that I thought it might help the situation if she could see I was telling the truth about not doing anything underhanded. And I added that she'd promised to not say a word. For a moment, he seemed speechless, but then said, "You're the biggest example of a Pollyanna I've ever met; do you honestly think she will keep that promise?"

I didn't respond but I was suddenly afraid that he was right. While I filled him in briefly on our earlier meeting with her and Richard, I left out the part about Judas. I'd have to find a way to bring that up at a less volatile time.

After a quick dinner, we settled the kids in upstairs. We made the coffee and tea we'd decided to serve and brought all the extra chairs we had into the living room. As we worked, Ned said, "Do you think we should have a prayer before anyone gets here? This meeting is going to be filled with too much tension for us to handle alone." I agreed and just as we knelt by the couch, the doorbell rang.

I looked at my watch and it was twenty-two minutes before 7:00 p.m. Ned and I looked at each other in surprise. We certainly weren't expecting anyone to be early. As Ned reached the door and saw who it was, he turned, looked at me, and threw up his hands as if saying, "I give up" before opening it.

"I hope I'm not too early," Mary Kay gushed innocently. "I thought it would take me longer to get here." Ned didn't comment but sent me a look that said she must think we're stupid. I got his message; she didn't want us to have a minute alone with anyone.

As each person arrived and saw Mary Kay sitting there, they looked as if someone had thrown cold water in their faces. All they knew about the meeting thus far was that I was leaving Mary Kay and I would explain why at this time. They had no idea that Mary Kay would be present. Not knowing how to act under such awkward circumstances, they took a seat and said very little. I decided from the look on Mary Kay's face that this was exactly what she was hoping for. They were intimidated and she did not want there to be a friendly, relaxed atmosphere.

As we'd expected, the room was soon packed. All of my directors were present, except Marjie, as well as many members of my unit. It was by far the greatest number of people ever seated in our living room; some people even had to stand, it was so crowded.

I had done a lot of thinking about how to begin, but now nothing seemed right. Mary Kay's early appearance had thrown me completely off guard. Tactically, I have to admit that she was impeccable.

Instinctively, I said to the group, "Would you like to see the baby before we get started? Many of you haven't seen her in months, and she's grown so much." They all seemed to answer at once, saying they would love to see her. Nothing sweetens up a room more than an innocent, beautiful baby. As Ned brought in Sharon, who was holding Shannon, the mood did instantly brighten and I breathed a grateful sigh of relief. Mary Kay was the only one who didn't talk to Shannon or try to get her to smile.

I had copies of the letter that I was mailing to out-of-town members of my unit for the group. It explained when and why I was leaving the company, as well as information about contacting me if they wanted further information. As the letters were passed around the room, I noticed that Mary Kay quickly took a copy for herself.

I began, "There are only a couple of things I want to add to the letter. One is that we will be taking a different approach in our sales presentations. We are calling them clinics, rather than shows. This is to suggest an educational approach, instead of the 'party plan' atmosphere that most direct sales companies have been using." I could tell by the looks on their faces (other than

Mary Kay's) that they liked the idea. Just changing the name would help them be taken more seriously.

But the major positive response from the group came when I told them that the third tier and the 2 percent would be included in writing in our marketing plan from the very beginning. Suddenly they all seemed to forget about Mary's Kay's presence, and excited chatter filled the room. Even with limited information they were now really interested, and my heart skipped a beat at seeing it. I remembered what Mary Kay had taught me in the beginning: "Once the sale is made, stop talking, or you may end up buying it back." I looked at Ned and saw he was smiling. I motioned to him that it was time to bring in the coffee and tea for a more amiable, social time before they left.

I went into the kitchen to help Ned with the drinks and when I returned with a glass of iced tea in each hand, Mary Kay was flitting from director to director. She was whispering to each one "Don't forget, after she's gone you're going to get a share of all that money she's been making each month." When she saw the receptive look on the face of the director she was speaking with change into one of horror, Mary Kay turned and saw me standing behind her. I quickly stepped back, because from the look on her face, I was certain she was going to faint (she obviously thought she could do this in secret).

Although she was undeniably shaken to the core, she did manage to keep standing. As I stood staring at her, astonished that I had actually caught her violating her promise to say nothing, I knew I was too late. Although I'd felt the game was going my way after the news about the 2 percent, it had changed in an instant. Mary Kay had just trumped my high card while I was out of the room.

Using more self control than I ever had in my life, I handed the tea to the directors and said quietly, "Mary Kay, please come into the kitchen with me for a minute—and bring your purse."

In the kitchen, she started to speak but I held up my hand as a signal to stop talking and said, "Anything you say would only make it worse." Then I added, "Ned will walk you to your car."

As I watched them head out the front door, for the first time since I'd met her, I didn't feel a pang of regret when we parted company. Instead, I hoped it would be the last time we'd meet. I had finally seen her duplicity up close and personal, and it wasn't a pretty sight.

Returning to the group, I explained Mary Kay's absence. She suddenly realized she had to get home; this was true, but I simply left out that I helped her with the decision. At first they seemed surprised, but soon the atmosphere in the room became more relaxed and friendly and stayed that way for the rest of the evening. I kept my promise and didn't try to influence them in any way to leave Mary Kay and come with us. Instead, we talked about all the great times we'd had together, as I fought constantly to keep emotion from overwhelming me.

As soon as one decided to leave, it seemed they all had to go as well. Ned had already gone upstairs to be with the kids. I stood at the front door and hugged each person as she left. I knew I would probably not see many of them ever again, but summoning strength I didn't even know I had, I kept my emotions at bay. A few of them, including Jan Jack and Martha Weddle, whispered to me they would be calling for more information.

After I straightened the living room and began to fill the dishwasher, I thought about the damage Mary Kay had done. As soon as I had left the room, she'd dangled the easy money they would get in front of them. And all they had to do for it was stay with her. Since money was one of the main reasons all of us had joined Mary Kay in the first place, it was bound to be an effective bribe. Besides, I thought, leaving the known for the unknown is one of the hardest things in the world to do. As I stood in the kitchen thinking and preparing myself for the possibility that not one single person would actually come with us, the telephone rang.

It was Marjie. "I wish you could have been here," she said, so excited she could barely talk.

"I take it everything went well," I answered in a lifeless voice, already dreading telling her about Mary Kay's performance.

"It was great. I think we'll get quite a few from my unit. How about yours?"

"It certainly wasn't dull," I replied, which was all I could bring myself to tell her at that moment. Then I asked if we could discuss it in the morning, since we were moving furniture into our new offices and would have more time to talk then. Even though it was Saturday, Marie was coming in to be with Sharon and Shannon.

"That bad, huh?" Marjie asked, hearing the exhaustion in my voice. She continued, "What did May Kay do anyway?"

"I'll fill you in tomorrow. See you at 9:00 a.m. And it's not that bad. Not yet, anyway." And even though I could tell she definitely wanted to hear about it tonight, using the last ounce of strength I could muster, I hung up the phone.

Upstairs, everyone was already asleep and for one of the very few times in my life, I went to bed with my makeup on, too exhausted to bother. My final prayer was quick and simple, "Watch over us through the night, Lord, and please let tomorrow be a better day."

CHAPTER SEVENTEEN

Beginning Again

On Saturday morning at 9:00 a.m. the four of us met at our new offices. Even though the night before had been demoralizing, on this day the sun was shining and our moods lightened. Marjie and Stan didn't ask the details about our meeting with my sales people and Mary Kay right away, but I knew it would come up soon enough. We had borrowed trucks and hauled furniture from our houses to furnish Marjie's office and mine. We'd purchased only the basics for the reception area. There were windows behind the desk, which meant there was not a lot of wall space that needed decoration. We were keeping our expenses low and spending money only when absolutely necessary. In comparison to the perfect "Baskin Robbins 31 flavors" décor at Mary Kay's, ours was plain vanilla. But it was ours, and for now it was fine.

We planned to use the lab equipment that Dathene already had for the time being. After helping with the offices, Ned and Stan were going to Dathene's house to pick it up, so production could begin early Monday morning. We'd promised samples of our products to those who called and we had to be ready to keep that promise. All we would have to start with was our reputation. Stan had ordered ingredients to make the products and they would also be delivered Monday morning. So, in Stan's words, "We're all set to tango."

As we stood in our new, rather sparse, reception area, Marjie announced, "I brought the most important thing we need to help us get started," as she began digging through a box and pulled out a coffee maker and four large mugs.

"Oh, good," Ned said, "let's make a pot right now. I'm still half asleep and it's going to be a long day." While the coffee was brewing, Ned and Stan talked a couple of the guys from downstairs to help, and they got all the furniture into the rooms where it belonged. Marjie's office included a closet, which we quickly converted into a coffee bar, using a small table that she had brought with her.

As soon as the coffee was ready, we took it to the reception area and sat on the floor with our steaming cups. "I'd like to propose a toast," Stan said, raising his cup high into the air. After we did likewise, he continued, "To new beginnings, and may they be more successful than we ever dreamed."

"Hear, hear," we echoed as we clinked our cups together. Ned and I exchanged smiles; for non-drinkers like us, this was a new and fun experience.

After relishing the moment for a few seconds, Marjie said, "Okay, Jackie, it's time to 'spill the beans.' I want to hear exactly what happened last night."

"And, don't leave anything out" Stan added. "We need to keep up with everything that happens, no matter how small it might seem to be. If Mary Kay and Richard are as frightened as you think they are, we have to keep our eyes and ears wide open. That kind of fear causes people to do irrational things."

Between the two of us, Ned and I quickly related the events of the meeting, including catching Mary Kay red-handed trying to sabotage all interest in our venture. Marjie looked as if she was going to pop if she didn't get to say something, so I beat her to it. "Go ahead Marjie, say I told you so. I deserve it."

"Okay, I will," she said, and then all three of them shouted, "I told you so." Of course it was all in fun, but I did learn a valuable lesson from it. No matter how badly we want people to act in an honest and fair manner, it is only smart to consider that they could do just the opposite. That way, we wouldn't be blindsided again.

And then we really did get down to business. I passed out legal-size yellow pads and asked everyone to write their names at the top of the page. They looked at me as if I thought they were all back in first grade and I was going to teach them the alphabet.

Laughing, I said, "I know this may be elementary, but if it was good enough for the president of Bethlehem Steel, then it should be good enough for us." Then I asked that each one write down the "six most important things they had to do tomorrow," and to do it each day thereafter. Since we all had specific duties, we could look at the other pads to see where we were in our over-all list of things that had to be done. I realized they knew this, but as a reminder I added that as each task was accomplished, it should be checked off; if something did not get done, then it would be transferred to the next day's list. I then admitted that this information was primarily for me. Since this was my first job as a CEO, using this system I could keep up with what was getting done on a day-to-day basis without constantly having to check with them on each detail. All I had to do was consult the list. Since Ned and Stan were working at other jobs during the day, they had to accomplish their tasks either by phone or do things in the evening. And, in a pinch, Marjie and I would have to pick up the slack.

While the men placed the furniture where we directed in our offices, Marjie and I set up the reception area. I had brought my manual typewriter, along with paper and other supplies and placed them in the desk. Nina Harris, Marjie's friend, had agreed to work with us temporarily as a receptionist-secretary, and she would also be starting Monday morning, so everything had to be in order by then. Our next chore today would be putting the finishing touches on our individual offices.

Marjie used some of her Mexican art objects from their travels there to decorate her office. This was a highly popular trend at the time. Using hot pink and green as her primary colors, her office was trendy, yet smart and professional. For my office, I brought my Thomasville desk with black leather inset on the top and a high-backed matching chair. On the wall behind my desk I hung one of Ned's oil paintings of a sailboat scene, incorporating all the colors in the room. Two chairs, upholstered in bright turquoise fabric, sat on each side of a small octagon Thomasville table. Looking at it from the doorway, I was pleased at the effect. The ambiance seemed to say, "Come on in and visit for a while." And it didn't cost a cent, I thought. Just as we finished with our offices, Stan yelled, "Let's go! It's time to eat."

After lunch, Ned and Stan left to pick up the lab fixtures from Dathene's house while Marjie and I cleaned the lab thoroughly. I soon found that cleaning everything was to be a regular duty for the president and vice president of the company. I wondered if the head of Bethlehem Steel had done that. Unfortunately, without phones, which would be connected on Monday, there was no way to let Dathene know they were on their way. However, since she had promised she would be home all day, we didn't think a call was really necessary.

After cleaning, Marjie and I sat in our respective offices and worked on our lists. We'd already discussed at length what had to be done immediately, so at this point the list wasn't critical, but it would keep anything from falling through the cracks.

The jars for our products were to be delivered Monday. They were stark white with a subtle shine and the labels were made of shiny gold foil. Instead of printing the product information on the labels, it would be embossed, which would give it a much classier look. Marjie and I had done extensive research on packaging and had decided to use a label similar in shape to the Hallmark "crown." We didn't copy it exactly, but it was close enough to look elegant and expensive. When using the product name, BeautiControl would be hyphenated and on two separate lines on the labels. When used as the corporation, it would be simply Beauticontrol, Inc. The only color that was incorporated into our package design was in the skin freshener. Since the beginning of Beauticontrol in 1933, the freshener had always been a medium shade of blue, and it would remain the same; but to give it an updated look, we chose a gold cap shaped like a crown for the bottle. We made every effort to not have any product that looked like Mary Kay's. Actually, our entire approach was that we were better. We knew it wasn't going to be easy to explain the difference between the two, so looking different was important.

When Marjie had mentioned that pink was her favorite color, hinting she would like to incorporate it in some way, we quickly nixed the idea. I looked at Marjie and asked, "What are you trying to do, get us sued?" She laughed at such a preposterous suggestion and let the matter drop.

At 3:00 p.m. the men still weren't back from Dathene's, and Marjie and I started to worry. Since it was a short easy trip, they should have returned by 2:00. I'd told Marie we would probably be home by 4:00, and now that wasn't going to happen.

As a distraction while we waited, we discussed what was first on our "to do" list. Mine was to finish writing the new manual for our consultants, and Marjie's was to order glamour products from Kolmar, a major private label company. Kolmar had already promised that samples of the products we were interested in would be in our office on Monday morning so we could place our order the same day. Because Mary Kay used this same private label company, we were already familiar with their work.

One major difference between our products and Mary Kay's would be that we were going to have separate compacts for the lip colors and the eye shadows. The all-in-one compact of Mary Kay's still did not close properly, even though it had been redesigned several times.

We'd already determined we had to be up and running by June 1. Any delay would give Mary Kay more time to convince my people we weren't capable of following through with our promises so they wouldn't decide to come with us. This meant everything had to be done on schedule, which was another reason the lists were so critical. In thinking all of this through, we'd also discussed Murphy's Law: "Anything that can go wrong, will go wrong," so we knew we always had to have a Plan B ready to go.

Finally, Stan and Ned drove up at 4:30. Marjie and I ran down the stairs and asked as they got out of the trucks, "Where have you been?"

"Three guesses and the first two don't count," Stan said, looking more irritated than I'd ever seen him.

"It's something to do with Dathene, isn't it?" Marjie said in a matter-of-fact tone.

"You could say that," Stan answered, "she forgot we were coming and wasn't at home until about thirty minutes ago." Then Ned explained that she'd decided early in the morning to go "junk shopping," and got so engrossed that she'd completely forgotten they were coming to pick up the equipment.

"But the scariest part of all was that she didn't seem to understand why we were upset," Ned said, shaking his head.

"But I made it perfectly clear to her that she'd better be in the lab ready to work at 9:00 a.m. Monday morning, and I think she got the message," Stan said, in a tone that implied that it wouldn't ever happen again.

By the time the equipment was unloaded, it was after 5:00. We decided to meet again the next day, which was Sunday, to finish up. We'd have to bring our girls, because we would come straight from church. As we gathered up our things to leave the building, I noticed that Ned and Stan had laid their yellow pads on the front desk, with their lists completed. First on both lists, was "Learn to manufacture the products myself." From their experience with Dathene, they had already figured out that they needed a safety net.

The next afternoon, things went more smoothly. As soon as we got to the office, Sharon took Shannon into my office and entertained her with the toys she'd brought along. We quickly changed into "work" clothes before going to the manufacturing-shipping area. The vats and other mixing equipment were set up in a far corner of the large room. Also included was a double stainless steel sink, along with a small stove and refrigerator. Cabinets, where ingredients would be stored, separated manufacturing from shipping.

As an afterthought, a small round table was placed near the stove and refrigerator to be used for a quick lunch when necessary, which turned out to a great deal of the time. While it all needed to be kept super clean, cleanliness in the manufacturing area was the most important. The FDA was known to make periodic checks and that area had to be sterile, similar to hospital requirements.

The last chore of the day was to place the long tables, which would be used for assembling products as well as for shipping, in the center of the room. Open cabinets were lined up along the walls to hold finished product. As we stood admiring our handiwork, Stan said, "Hopefully the worst part is now behind and things will be easier from now on."

But we would soon find out that was not to be the case.

Marjie, Nina, and I arrived at the office on schedule Monday morning. I had a rough draft of the manual ready for Nina and laid it on her desk. She glanced at it briefly, and said, "I'll get right on it, but first things first." Then she went directly to the coffee bar and started it brewing. "Now, we can get started," she said dusting her hands together. Marjie and I laughed, happy to have Nina with us. This was going to be fun.

At 9:30, there was still no sign of Dathene. I looked at Marjie and suspected we were wondering the same thing: Would she show up at all? Suddenly I knew this was not going to work. If we allowed this kind of behavior in the beginning then it would surely get worse with time. So I decided to stop it right here. I walked down the stairs to the office of Arvin Jones, the chemist who worked in the laboratory below us, and explained our situation. He agreed to help in any way he could and told me to call on him any time we needed him to assist us or to actually manufacture the products himself. When I returned upstairs, Marjie was on the phone saying, "That's the most unprofessional thing I've ever heard of," and abruptly hung up.

"Now what?" I asked, afraid to hear the answer.

"That was the salesman from the company that was supposed to deliver our jars this morning. It seems that they also sell products to Mary Kay, and Richard told them if they sold anything to us, he would cancel all his business with them, so he was canceling with us." As Marjie spoke, a slight chill ran through me and I shivered. As kids, when that happened we said, "A rabbit ran across my grave," which was a way of saying it was a premonition of bad things to come.

Shaking off the absurd reaction, I thought, good grief, and wondered if it was too late to refuse the honor of being president of the company.

Then I suddenly remembered that Ned had a Thomas Index, a book that listed all the suppliers of containers, at his office. I'd promised I would call him at his work only when absolutely necessary, and this definitely fit the bill. I asked him to look up another supplier for our white jar and call me right back. In thirty minutes, he called with the information. There was another supplier in Dallas with the same jar. It turned out to be a stock item that they had available at all times.

Marjie quickly took the information and called the order in to them, and they agreed we'd have it that same day. The whole scenario reminded me of a basketball game. We'd passed the ball from one to the other until we reached the goal. That's why it's called teamwork, I thought as a light flashed in my head. And this manner of operating became our "game plan" for the rest of the years we were together.

The jars arrived as promised, and as the deliveryman carried them into the lab, on impulse I asked him if the company had any very small containers that could be used for samples. He scratched his head for a second and then said, "You know we just got a new kind of very small containers that snap together. I guess that's probably what they are for—samples. Would you like me to get you one to see?" I asked him to make it several samples, as soon as possible. They turned out to be the perfect containers for the samples, and we used them for "travel kits" as well.

Just before noon, Dathene showed up. Seeming completely oblivious to the fact she was supposed to be there at 9:00, she was all smiles and compliments about what we'd done with the offices and the lab. She walked into Marjie's office, and seeing the frown of disapproval on Marjie's face, she quickly drew on her best talent to change it. "Marjie," she said, "I see the dark roots in your hair could use a little touch up. Would you like me to do it for you?" The expression on Marjie's face instantly changed from irritation to delight. The transformation was so fast that I had to smile. Coloring her dark roots was one of the chores Marjie hated most, and Dathene had apparently picked up on that fact. She might be different, but Dathene was no dummy. She continued to help Marjie color her hair from that point on, and in turn Marjie was more patient with her unorthodox work habits.

Then Dathene announced that she was going to the lab and would probably work late into the night producing products. Sighing, I asked her to come into my office before she did anything else. She took a chair by the table and asked in a shaky voice, "Have I done something wrong already?"

There was something so touching about her, there was no way I could be harsh, but I was firm. I reminded her about our visit to Tyler and telling her she would have to keep regular business hours, from nine to five. The only time she could work at night was when we were there, for safety purposes. Her face fell and she murmured, "But I always work at night."

We were going nowhere fast, so I said "Dathene, here's the deal. You come in on schedule or we will have the chemist downstairs produce the products. Of course, we can't afford to pay you for not working, so you are going to have to decide if you want to do this or not.

She blinked as if she were trying to wake up from a bad dream and finally said, "I guess it's that way or no way, right?"

"That's right Dathene. It's the way it has to be. The chemist is going to watch you produce all the products, until he learns the process so he can take over, just in case you decide to backslide. Ned and Stan will learn as well, as double insurance the products will be ready on schedule. We must have products available for people to try within a few days. Can I count on you or not?"

"Okay," she mumbled.

"What did you say?" I asked again.

"Okay," she said, practically yelling, and I suspected everyone in the building had heard it because I could hear Marjie laughing in the other room. But the problem was solved, at least temporarily.

I knew the mail had arrived and I went in to check with Marjie on the product samples from Kolmar. She was in the process of looking over them and we spent an hour testing them on the back of our hands and making final decisions on which ones to order. We had already pretty well decided because, except for packaging, they were so much like Mary Kay's. While I sat in her office listening, Marjie placed the order with Kolmar, and they promised her we would have our order in house by the middle of May.

The next thing I had listed to do that day was to gain access to the Apparel Mart and the Trade Center, large wholesalers who were on Stemmons Freeway. We had gone there with Mary Kay a few times to buy sales prizes for people in our units. Now we had to be ready to begin regular monthly contests for our own consultants, which we hoped to have very soon. Marjie and I couldn't wait to go there and spend at least half a day browsing through the showrooms. The craze for wigs had begun to fade, but hairpieces had taken their place, and we were going to offer them as prizes for the first few months. I called both establishments with all the necessary information required for access cards, and they promised we'd have them in a few days. Another fun part of this business, I thought, as I enthusiastically checked it off my list.

The four of us had agreed to touch base several times during the day. When Stan called, Marjie filled him in on Dathene's late arrival. He called Ned immediately and they decided to come to the lab that very evening to begin learning the manufacturing process. When we told Dathene she was going to get to work late after all because both men would be joining her to watch and learn, Marjie and I struggled to not laugh at the horrified expression on her face as she digested the news. We had told her several times this was how it was going to be; now she'd finally understood that when we said something, we actually meant it.

But even though it was difficult to get her going in the right direction (and would always remain so), Dathene did an outstanding job with the manufacturing process. She sterilized everything, even the new jars, and was meticulous in filling every jar to the brim. She said it was because each customer deserved a full measure in return for her money. And, she literally blessed each jar after it was filled, sometimes to the chagrin of Ned and Stan when they were in a hurry.

In the middle of the afternoon we got our first phone call requesting sample products to try. It was Martha Weddle. She quickly told me she wasn't making any promises that she would come with us, because Mary Kay had said she would get a large number of my people if she stayed with her. But she went on to say she did want to try our products. Sticking to my word that I would not overtly try to get them to come with me, I simply explained the products would be ready for her to pick up by the end of the week. Then I reassured her again that there would be no pressure from us to decide in our favor.

By 5:00 p.m. Marjie and I stood at Nina's desk, waiting for Stan and Ned to arrive so we could head for home. Dathene had already started warming up the ingredients that would be used in making the products and the smell of lavender oil permeated the whole building. The scent was clean and fresh, pleasing to the senses in every way. Our door was open to the hallway and we heard someone downstairs say, "Where is that wonderful scent coming from?" We looked at each other and smiled. It always feels good when someone else agrees with you.

Our manual would be far more detailed than Mary Kay's first one had been. It would address all aspects of the business, including product information, booking and holding clinics, and of course detailed information on our marketing plan. Specific commissions were listed for recruiting new consultants, directors (after qualification), plus the 2 percent for the third tier, which started the fight in the first place. Nina had finished typing most of the manual already and I told her how impressed I was with her work.

She answered, "I'm impressed, too, with your marketing plan. Is it really possible to make the kind of money you say here?"

Marjie and I replied at the same time, "Absolutely." By simply typing the manual, she'd seen the potential, and right then and there, she decided to become our very first new recruit. This occurrence ended our first day on a high note and the three of us left the office together.

It was after 10:00 by the time Ned got home from working in the lab. But instead of being exhausted, as I'd expected, he was so hyped he couldn't stop talking. The kids were asleep, so we turned off the TV and discussed the happenings of the day. After we'd reviewed the numerous events, I looked at him and said, "And, Ned, all that happened in just our first day of business." Little did we suspect that it was how it would be every day from then on.

By the end of the week, we began to get daily requests for samples of our products from our Mary Kay customers, as well as consultants interested in selling. Most were local, but some came from the letters we'd sent to out-of-town people (my sales organization and Marjie's) with details about our leaving Mary Kay. Each day we sent out more samples than the day before. And we began to have a glimmer of hope that new recruits would soon follow. When they found that the products were truly better than Mary Kay's, it could be the deciding factor to join us.

After we sent samples of the products to Anna Kendall and her people in Houston and they tried them, Anna called and wanted us to come to Houston the following week, the last week in April. Marjie decided that would be a good time because by then we should have everything labeled for them to see. The labels were expected to be ready in the next few days, which would be perfect timing. The possibility of Anna's entire unit selling our products in Houston was exciting, and our enthusiasm reached a whole new level.

After Nina decided to join us as a consultant, she wanted to get started as soon as possible. She already had a possible new recruit, Barbara Stubblefield. She and Barbara had been friends for some time and the minute Nina told her about the marketing plan, she was interested. Barbara and her husband, Dave, were moving to Cheyenne, Wyoming, soon and she wanted to finish her training before leaving.

Although we were not scheduled to have our glamour products in house until the middle of May, we were already packing demo kits, as items became available. The literature was ready, and I was in the process of making a new tape (similar to the one of mine that Mary Kay put in her demo kits). Our literature, however, was much different from Mary Kay's. In our manual, instead of using her fictional hide tanner's story, we used real names and dates. This included the hide tanner's name, J. W. Heath, and the fact that Beauticontrol had been marketed constantly since 1933.

But we had something even more powerful. Included in the demo kit, was a picture of J. W. Heath, his wife, and all of their children. In the picture, Mr. Heath's hands were in plain view and looked like hands of a much younger man, thanks to his own cream. It was the perfect testimonial that this was indeed a true story. In addition, his wife was seated beside him in the picture, but looked far more like his mother, although some people commented that having all of those kids could have been the reason for part of that difference in their appearance.

While things were moving along as scheduled, one of our most difficult challenges was to remember to call our presentations "clinics," instead of shows, as Mary Kay did. But we felt it was worth the effort, because it would suggest a more professional approach, and we were trying to differentiate ourselves from her as much as possible.

Since Nina wanted to begin selling right away, we had to place an ad for a new secretary in the Dallas Morning News to run over a weekend. On Monday our phone began ringing. We suspected the good response was because the ad said the job was for a cosmetic company, which was more glamorous than the usual ads. We hired Josie, a young woman whose husband was in dental school. Although Josie wasn't as seasoned as Nina, she did an adequate job, but we understood it would take her a while to learn the business. And until she did, Marjie or I had to be in the office at all times.

When I met Barbara Stubblefield, I was impressed immediately. She was a tall, attractive brunette with an outgoing personality. I recognized her as another "giant mug" immediately and was excited. Since I was in charge of sales, and there was no one else available to fill in, I had to hold the clinics and all other training sessions for Nina and Barbara. It was a makeshift training program, but we had to start somewhere—and soon. Both of them were to later become key people in the company.

Nina moved to west Texas and developed the area around Lubbock. And Barbara, after moving to Wyoming, was instrumental in ultimately developing the whole West Coast. So we were expanding already.

The labels arrived on schedule, and they were beautiful, even more so than we'd imagined. We were anxious to apply them to the jars, but we had to wait until the activity in the office slowed down. It was late afternoon before we could get started, and we quickly organized the products on the table in the lab along with the proper labels for each product. The Super Night Cream contained ammoniated mercury and because of that, the FDA required it to have a second label on the back of the jar. We knew it was important that all products were labeled correctly, which meant it would be tedious work.

Since we'd never done anything like this, we simply followed the instructions the supplier gave us. Using a damp cloth, we wetted the back of the label and carefully centered the "crown" on each jar before pressing it into place. As we'd expected, it was time-consuming and by the time we finished it was late. As we stood back and viewed the striking effect of the gold labels on the white jars, we were elated. It was far more elegant than Mary Kay's pink version. In high spirits, Marjie quipped, "Richard said we had no idea what we were getting into, but this is only a 'piece of cake.' Maybe Stan was right, and the worst is over and the best has begun." I hoped so, too, but I didn't say anything, because it would be almost too good to be true.

The next morning we headed straight for the lab to admire our work all over again. The jars were exactly where we'd left them, but unfortunately, the labels had curled up on the table beside the jars that they had fallen off. Marjie and I looked at each other in silence while we tried to fully comprehend the situation. Sighing, I finally said, "If this is a piece of cake, I can't imagine what a whole cake looks like."

It turned out that the company that made the labels had put the wrong kind of glue on the back. Rather than making all new labels, they brought us glue that worked. Now more work. We had to brush it on each label by hand, but before we could do that, we had to thoroughly clean each jar. However, this experience was not wasted. From that point on, we tested every new item before we spent hours of our time. And I thought of another of my mother's favorite sayings, "A stitch in time saves nine."

Martha picked up samples of the product, and after trying them called immediately to say they were far better than Mary Kay's. And, because of that she was very interested in joining us. Yet Mary Kay was still dangling incentives in front of her to stay with Mary Kay's company, so she was still undecided about what to do.

Again I assured her I understood. However, I did mention that Juanita Grable, one of Martha's recruits from Fort Worth, had called and was coming out to pick up products to try and to hear about our marketing plan. Juanita had several recruits under her who were interested as well. I knew this information would show Martha that there was a possibility that some of her people would be coming with us, regardless of her decision. Because Martha and I were open with each other in this way, I felt we would stay friends regardless of what she decided to do.

Marjie and I went to Houston as scheduled to meet with Anna and her people. Anna had a unique charisma, and her people followed right behind her. Once they'd tried and loved our product, the decision was made to join us. All that was left to do was for Anna to say when and every single person in Anna's unit came with her to our company. Since Anna had been Mary Kay's personal secretary and was very close with her, I wondered if she would take all of them leaving as a personal affront. I hoped she would remember that Anna was also Marjie's sister-in-law and not give her a hard time about her decision.

Anna volunteered to write new songs for us to sing at our first large meeting. It was to be held the first weekend of June at the Blanton Towers, not far from our offices. We decided to use the tune to "This Ol' House" for our theme song, and we couldn't wait to see how Anna rewrote the words for us. As we prepared to leave Houston for our drive home, we told the group how special it was for them to be charter members as the first new unit in the company. We had already announced that any director that came from Mary Kay with her people would not be required to go through another qualification, but instead would begin their tenure with us as directors.

As we drove, Marjie and I talked about how exciting it would be to have the whole Houston area almost to ourselves. Even though Mary Kay's daughter, Marilyn, lived there and was considered a consultant, she wasn't very active and shouldn't be a problem for Anna's group.

It was about a five-hour drive from Houston to Dallas, but we were energized from the results of the meeting and talked non-stop as we drove.

We fantasized about all the other trips we would take in the years ahead and how large our company would become, even though we'd begun with nothing. The outcome would prove to be even greater than the fantasy. Caught up in the moment, I turned to her and said, "You know Marjie, if you would just learn to carry a tune, we could save Anna the trouble and create that new song for us right now." And, as it would be for years to come, we bantered and laughed as we drove home through the dark night.

Business picked up steam much faster than we'd expected. Someone came up with the idea of calling all our Mary Kay customers and offering them samples of our new products. Once they tried it, they bought it. Since we were independent contractors, they were our customers and were free to buy from whomever they chose. In addition to buying products, they booked clinics to be held as soon as our glamour items arrived. We'd already decided to have new "looks" for each season, and the customers were literally standing in line to be among the first for the new experience.

When our glamour products didn't arrive as promised, Marjie called Kolmar to check. The guy she'd talked with originally hemmed and hawed with excuses until Marjie asked to speak with his manager. Although the man was reluctant, he finally admitted that somehow our order had been cancelled. "By whom?" Marjie demanded, almost yelling into the phone. The man went on to explain that he didn't have the name, but the call had come from Dallas. I was standing there when she hung up the phone, and we said simultaneously, "Richard."

Panicked, we began to toss ideas back and forth about what we could do about the situation. Suddenly Marjie said, "I just read an article about one of the founders of Kolmar in Women's Wear Daily. He's a great believer in the free enterprise system, and I'm going to call him and tell him what's happened."

That takes a lot of guts, I thought, but all I said to her was "Do it, right now." I sat in her office and listened to their conversation. She told him about reading the article, and explained that our use of the free enterprise system had been sabotaged. After she told him the whole story between Mary Kay and us, she made a passionate plea for his help in correcting the injustice of a large company trying to destroy a small one. She was still shaking from the emotion she'd put into the plea when she got off the phone.

I said sincerely, "If an award were to be given for the most passionate plea ever made, you'd win hands down."

She answered, "I got a little carried away, but it worked. He said he'd take care of it."

And he did. In just a little over a week, the merchandise was in our warehouse and ready to go. The products were perfect in every respect, and coordinated well with the skin care. How could we display them effectively? Suddenly, I remembered the cut crystal trays we'd seen at market. We rushed over during the noon hour and found one we loved: A large oval that everything would fit perfectly on. And as we were leaving we spotted a bud vase for a single fresh flower; just the touch we needed for completing our display.

As soon as we were back in the office, we assembled the products and set the tray on the small table between the two chairs in the reception area. The result was even more spectacular than we'd imagined. The sun coming through the window behind the desk danced across the crystal, creating little prisms of color. "And just wait," Marjie said, "until we add the flower."

Sometimes a seemingly unimportant thing happens that later plays a major role in life. One morning when I arrived at the office at 9:00 a.m. a tall, slim middle-aged woman was waiting for me. I noticed immediately that she was wearing magnificent jewelry that was obviously expensive. She introduced herself as Nell Davis and added that she had been a lifelong friend of Ova Spoonemore, Dathene's mother. I vaguely remembered Dathene mentioning her on our trip to Tyler.

After we were seated in my office, I said to Nell, "I assume you've also known Dathene a long time, too."

She laughed and said, "Yes, I have, and that's why I'm here. For you to succeed in a way this product deserves, there are some things you need to know about Dathene." She went on to tell me about her disregard of regular working hours and her addiction to "junk shopping." I told her quickly that we'd already learned that about her. "Good," she answered, "but you also need to be prepared that with five children there will always be a crisis with Dathene. I try to help with that, but I still thought you should know what you are in for."

Then Nell added, in a stern voice, "But those things did not entitle Mary Kay to beat her out of her inheritance. Her mother would turn over in her grave if she knew what Mary Kay has done. She thought Mary Kay was her friend." I listened without comment; Nell and I agreed completely on this major point. She stayed a little while longer just to visit, but she was to remain my friend for life. As I walked out with her, I invited her to our first official workshop, and she promised she would be there.

The following Monday, when Dathene walked in and announced that over the weekend when she was out junk shopping, she'd purchased a tent that would seat 5,000 people, leaving us all dumbfounded. When I could finally speak, I asked her, "Dathene, you mean you spent money you need for your children on a huge tent?"

Hearing the tone in my voice, she said defensively. "Well, you never know when I might need it." Many years later, after Dathene had retired, I visited her in Mena, Arkansas. She still had the tent. From that point on, when Nell tried to tell me something about Dathene, I paid closer attention. But even though she'd tried to warn me, I would have to see the many sides of

Dathene for myself before I could really understand what Nell was trying to say.

The end of the month was quickly approaching, as well as our workshop, and I had just about given up on Martha Weddle joining us. Then late one afternoon I got a frantic phone call from her. "Jackie," Martha said, "I've got to see you immediately." I had promised Marie I would be home early but I could tell something was urgent so I said, "Come on over, but be careful: I can tell you're upset."

"Upset is not the right word to explain it," she said and added, "but I'll be there soon," and hung up the phone. I filled Marjie in on the call and asked her to stay also.

I could hear Martha running up the stairs to our offices. When she lunged into the reception area, her face was bright red and her hair disheveled, I thought, This is serious. "What is it, Martha? Are you okay?"

"No, I'm not okay, just wait until you hear what happened." We settled down in my office and waited for her to catch her breath. As Marjie and I listened, hanging on to every word, she filled us in.

First of all, Martha admitted that she'd pretty much decided to stay with Mary Kay. She said it seemed so much easier than to take a chance on whether or not her people would join her if she came with us. Also Mary Kay was still promising that a large group from my unit would go into hers. Marjie and I just listened without commenting. Then she took a deep breath and said that Mary Kay had called her personally just before noon and asked her to come to the office right then, that she had something extremely urgent to discuss with her.

When she arrived, all the other directors were waiting for her. They took her into the meeting room and grilled her for three hours, accusing her of being a spy for us. Martha looked at Marjie and me with tears in her eyes and continued. "I tried to assure them that their accusations weren't true, but I could tell they didn't believe a word I said, and they finally asked me to go out and wait in the hall. They were going to vote as to whether or not I would be allowed to stay with Mary Kay. It was the most humiliating thing I have ever experienced in my life."

She wiped her tears away with her sleeve. "Finally, one of them came out to get me and took me inside to face the 'jury.' By a narrow margin they'd voted to allow me to stay. I finally came to my senses and told them, 'Thanks, but no, thanks. I can now see I've had my horse hitched to the wrong wagon.'"

When she finished Marjie and I clapped and cheered before giving her a big hug to welcome her into our company. Because of that treatment, Martha joined us with much greater zeal than we ever thought possible. She brought most of her own people with her, including Juanita Grable and her recruits, and then set out to recruit as many others as possible, without regard to whether they were currently with Mary Kay. She'd always been zealous in her pursuit of success, but now she was more like a tiger out for the kill.

As Marjie and I left the office for home I said, "Do you realize that we just got a 100 percent increase in directors for our new company? And we haven't even been in business for a full month."

"Oh, yeah," she answered, "I got it and I like it. Life is good."

In our excitement, it didn't occur to us that Mary Kay would not only refuse to accept this new development gracefully, but would retaliate with a vengeance we never dreamed possible.

CHAPTER EIGHTEEN

High Hopes

On the morning of June 1, Marjie and I arrived at our building at the same time and walked up to our offices together. As we entered the reception area, the transfixed look of horror on Josie's face stopped us in our tracks.

"What's the matter?" I asked, but Josie was unable to speak. She just pointed to the chair beside the table where a man in a business suit and a stern look on his face was sitting. He introduced himself as being with the FDA (Federal Drug Administration), and then explained that someone had called his office and insisted that they should take a look at our new manufacturing facilities.

Marjie and I looked at each other and without saying a word, knowing instantly who the "someone" was. I would probably have been terrified if I hadn't been so furious. I could hardly believe Richard had the gall to do such a thing, but I had learned from the years with Mary Kay not to show emotions; they could only do harm. I simply held out my hand and introduced myself as president of the company. He stood and shook my hand and said, as the stern look softened, "It's just routine, so please don't be nervous."

Before I took him into my office, I asked Marjie to tell Dathene that we would be in to see her later and sent a look that I hoped conveyed "prepare her for the visit." Thank God, for once Dathene was at work on time.

As soon as we were seated, I told him we knew they would visit us because it was part of their routine for new businesses, but didn't realize it would be so soon. He smiled a little sheepishly and admitted that the person who had called had demanded that they come immediately.

I assured him it was all right. "When it comes to competitors, good manners go out the window." He laughed, obviously glad that I wasn't going to chew him out for not giving us notice that he was coming. I explained that I was actually glad he was there, because I was new to the business and needed his help by telling me specifically what his department expected from us. He spent at least thirty minutes filling me in on information that I would need for years to come. Then we went into the lab to pick up labeled samples of all of our products for testing. Dathene was so nervous, she actually giggled. I considered pinching her to get her to stop, but finally she regained control and showed him all the products, obviously anxious to get this over with. I frowned at her impatience and took him through the lab calmly, showing him each area and explaining our method of sanitizing the mixing vats.

One-half hour later, he prepared to leave with the product samples and handed me his business card. "Call me any time you have a question," he said reassuringly, as he walked out the door. The minute he was down the stairs and out of sight, I breathed a sigh of relief. The FDA and the Internal Revenue Service were tied for first place on the list of people who make you nervous.

We settled into our lists of things that we had to accomplish before the coming weekend. We would be holding our first workshop at Blanton Towers—nice, but not too expensive. On Friday night, we would have our kick-off dinner for charter members and basically a celebration of our new venture. The whole event would be an exciting time for all of us, and we wanted it to be perfect. Marjie and I had already decided that our company should make a positive contribution to the lives of our people, and not just for sales purposes. No matter where they might go later on, we wanted them to feel they were better off because of their experience with us.

Saturday would be a full day of education, information, and inspiration. While it would be work, it would also be special because it would begin a new adventure in a direction we had never traveled before.

We had discussed at length the role each of us would play in the meeting. We were concerned about Dathene and certain that speaking in front of a group of people would be too hard for her. So we decided not to give her a structured speech but simply to let her mingle with the people at the Friday night dinner and during the breaks on Saturday, letting her get her feet wet before having to jump into the water to swim by making a full speech.

Dathene was our ace in the hole in our game with Mary Kay because she was the link to the creators of the formulas and she provided proof that the products had been on the market under the name Beauticontrol continuously since 1933. This longevity would lend credibility and respectability, and because of it, we felt certain that Mary Kay would look like the copycat she was. Our immediate challenge was to help Dathene get this information across in a way that was natural and comfortable for her.

We decided that Stan and Ned needed to be highly visible in their roles in the company, so husbands would feel welcome at our functions from the get-go. Yet, it was a company made up primarily of women for women, so we had to weigh the balance carefully.

Our preparations were going smoothly until mid-afternoon when Dathene came rushing into my office, her face drained of color. "Something terrible has happened," she said with tears streaming down her face.

"Is it a fire?" I asked, jumping up from my desk and running toward the door. I'd been afraid of one since learning the ingredients had to be heated, before manufacturing could begin.

"No, it's not a fire, it's worse than that."

"Tell me what it is—now!" I shouted. By this time, Marjie and Josie were gathered around.

"I put the wrong labels on the jars I gave to the man from the FDA," she croaked, hysterically.

We stood frozen in time while Marjie and I stared at her for what seemed like hours. Marjie spoke first, "Just what did you do exactly, Dathene?" she asked. Between sobs, Dathene told us she had put the warning label that was required for the back of the night cream on the wrong jar. The night cream contained ammoniated mercury and the FDA closely monitored all products with this ingredient. She was right; this was bad news and something the FDA could seriously reprimand us for not doing correctly. What could we do? Suddenly, I remembered that the man had given me his card, so I ran to my office to get it and dialed the number. He answered immediately and because I had no other recourse, I told him the exact truth. The jars weren't labeled correctly, and I needed to exchange them for the correct ones. Without hesitation, he said he was leaving for home, gave me his address, and asked me to meet him there with the new jars. No scolding, no nothing. Silently, I said "Thank you Lord for sending such a nice man." We had just dodged our first bullet but unfortunately, many more were waiting.

Dathene couldn't stop sobbing. Marjie and I put our arms around her and told her it was a mistake anyone could have made. But from now on, we would have to have safeguards to make sure nothing like that ever happened again (and it never did, because Marjie and I began checking such things ourselves).

As I left to make the exchange, I wondered if I would ever adjust to what seemed like constant stress. But then I shook myself and blocked out everything except the job at hand. Further preparations for the workshop would have to wait until tomorrow.

The next day, Marjie and I settled down to finishing the details for the meeting. In addition to the basics of the business, we wanted to add depth and fresh new material to the program. We would still sing, but now they would be our own songs, crow about all the good things already happening to us, and announce our contest for June, which would be the new craze, hair pieces (called wiglets at the time) instead of wigs.

But an important addition to the program would be a new source for obtaining bookings. As Mary Kay always preached, appointments were the lifelines of the business. Without appointments, there would be no sales.

As I'd held Mary Kay shows all over the area, women who were members of local clubs and organizations had invited me to speak at their meetings. In preparation, I'd spent a great deal of time thinking of content that would make a real difference to those in attendance. While I knew life consisted of three dimensions—spiritual, mental, and physical—and the first two were the important ones, I'd also made another huge discovery from dealing with hundreds of women. It was that once we felt good about our physical appearance, we could forget it entirely and concentrate on the two more important aspects of life. So it was actually better to confront the physical aspect first. Over the years, I've had thousands of testimonials to back up this premise.

Based on this concept, I wrote an outline for our people to use for club programs. The title was "Achieving your best total appearance." Even though it was short (thirty minutes), it contained specific information on how to analyze one's look and to create the best look for an individual lifestyle, both personal and business. And of course, it included the current trends in clothing, hairstyles, and cosmetics. At the end of the talk, everyone in attendance was offered a free facial and appointments were booked. In later years, I used this same idea and created programs for corporations and professional groups on an international basis. The main difference in those was they came with a price tag; they weren't free like the club programs.

By simply obtaining a list of women's clubs from the Chamber of Commerce and offering this free program to them on the importance of physical appearance, our consultants would have a valuable new resource. They would get new bookings for clinics as well as provide an excellent service for those in attendance. It was a win-win situation. In presenting this concept to others, it would also help our people improve their own self-confidence and self-esteem.

Presenting this new idea and introducing other speakers was to be my only speaking role in the workshop. As Mary Kay had done with us, I would focus on highlighting the people actually excelling in the business, by giving credit where credit was due.

Because we wanted our program to be fresh and exciting, we were adding another new session that would thereafter become a part of all major meetings. Betty Myers (the former modeling instructor who used to be in my unit at Mary Kay's) was going to teach the group modeling techniques, the same ones she had taught for John Robert Power's modeling agency. When someone had come to that agency aspiring to become a model, Betty taught them the tricks of the trade that were vital to becoming a success.

She had done a small segment at one of our sales meetings but nothing compared to this one. This would be the real thing. After Betty demonstrated the proper way to sit with back straight and knees together uncrossed, everyone in the room would follow suit, while Betty watched and corrected until it was done perfectly. In the same manner, she would cover the proper way to stand, showing each person how to align her body, enter and exit a car, and many other secrets, heretofore known only to models. We were all eagerly anticipating that part of the program because it would be fun as well as educational.

Suddenly Friday night was almost upon us. While the dinner would not be a formal occasion, it would be festive. There was much discussion about what everyone would wear. Ned and Stan were wearing dark suits, and Marjie and I decided to wear the outfits we'd bought for Mary Kay's wedding, that no one had seen because the groom disappeared. Everyone else appeared to be buying something new.

We expected about fifty people for dinner, mostly consultants, but also some husbands. There wouldn't be enough men to have a separate meeting for them this time, but Ned and Stan insisted that the husbands should still be treated as an important part of the group. So on the night of the dinner, the two of them stood at the door as people arrived, welcoming all of them and making a point of being especially attentive to the men. Juanita Grable's husband, Billy, was a skilled piano player and was to provide the music for both the dinner and the workshop the next day. We made certain he received special recognition for his services.

After everyone had arrived and we waited for the doors to open to the dinner room, I looked around at the elegantly dressed group. Martha Weddle stood out as the star of the show as she talked and laughed with Juanita Grable, who was her new star recruit on the horizon. Barbara Stubblefield and her husband, Dave, also added to the decor. Even though I'd known since I first met her that she had great potential, tonight I recognized it all over again. She had the looks, the drive, and the ambition to be a first-class leader, and I was excited about her upcoming move to Wyoming. As I watched her talk with Nina, I thought, If Nina doesn't do anything else with the business, she has made a major contribution by simply recruiting Barbara. But of course Nina excelled in the business herself by opening another new area in west Texas for us.

As the crowd talked and laughed, an electrical spark seemed to dance from person to person throughout the whole room. It was exhilarating to watch, and I said to myself, "We may not have quantity, but we certainly have the quality."

As they mingled, I took Dathene around and introduced her to new people. Marjie and I had helped her choose her outfit, and I had done her make-up. Tonight she looked wonderful and years younger than she had when Marjie and I first met her. She fit into the group perfectly, and I was overjoyed with the way everything was going. Yet it didn't seem real. As I was thinking this, Marjie walked up to me and said, "Can you believe that this is actually happening to us?"

She seemed to have read my mind. I answered, "No, I can't Marjie. It was just two and one-half years ago that I answered a newspaper ad and prayed that God would show me a way to change my life. And here's my answer," I said, waving my hand over the room. Then I added, "But the question is, what do we do now?"

Just then, the doors opened and a waiter beckoned for us to come in for dinner. Laughing, Marjie replied, "First, let's eat. We'll figure out the rest as we go along." And that pretty much became our game plan for the years ahead.

As we entered, Billy broke into a lively version of our new theme song, "This 'Ol House." Spontaneously, everyone began to clap and cheer more loudly than I had ever heard at Mary Kay's affairs. We all marched in time with the music as we went to our tables. Marjie and I looked at each other and smiled. It looked as if we'd brought the magic with us.

We'd already determined that we would begin every gathering with a prayer, and giving it became Ned's permanent job. Since the first time I heard him pray, I was always moved by the way he totally blocked out everything else and talked personally with God. Tonight, as he began by thanking God for this opportunity, Billy began to play The Lord's Prayer softly in the background. Lowering his voice, Ned continued with a fervent plea, "Help us, O Lord, with the monumental tasks we are facing, not only in building the company, but also with keeping our hearts pure because we truly want you to remain first in our lives." Taking a moment to control his emotions, he then ended with, "and we'll remember to always give you the glory and the praise."

I don't think I've ever experienced a more spiritual atmosphere than I did that night. I was so touched I could barely hold back the tears. And when his prayer was over, I noticed I wasn't the only one wiping my eyes. Many people came up to me the next day and said that his prayer set the pace for the entire meeting. In the future, it led us to have a strong Christian speaker, like Bill Glass, known for his prison ministry, at the very beginning of every event.

While I don't remember anything about the food we ate that evening, I will never forget the feeling that something that had been destined from the beginning was taking place. And suddenly I was filled with high hopes for what lay ahead.

After the meal was over, it was obvious that no one was ready to leave. We continued to cling together like a close family, excited about just being together. When someone finally said, "If we don't leave, we can't come back," we started to go. I stood at the door and passed out the certificates that had been exclusively designed for the charter members of Beauticontrol.

They were dated June, 1966, marking the foundation for a company that would one day produce more than one hundred million dollars a year in cosmetic sales, while improving the lives and earning potential for women worldwide.

At 8:00 a.m. sharp the next morning, everyone was in the meeting room, except for Dathene. Marjie, Stan, Ned, and I sat together near the podium so we could take turns introducing each other. Ned began with a very short prayer, simply asking God to bless the events of the day and everyone in attendance. As he presented me, I realized we hadn't discussed what he would say, which made me a little uneasy. He began with describing his role in the company, working in the lab and designing more efficient systems for production. He admitted that at this stage, he was just a glorified janitor, but he was well rewarded for his efforts. Then he raised his voice a few octaves and said, loud and clear, "I get to sleep with the president." Ned had an unusual sense of humor. At first, there was stunned silence, and I was horrified beyond anything I'd ever experienced. Then people laughed so loud that it seemed to shake the room. I was certain that much of it was because of the look on my face, so I did the only thing I could do—I laughed with them. Then they stood, cheered, and laughed some more. From that point, Ned became a favorite speaker at all events, and he never failed to entertain the crowd, usually at my expense.

Still laughing, Stan came to the podium and announced, "I won't even try to top that." Then he introduced Marjie and ended with, "So here Ned and I are, just where our wives want us: working for them," which drew equal laughter and applause from the crowd.

We had just established the roles the four of us would play for years to come, roles of camaraderie and solidarity, but fun loving at the same time.

Marjie and I took the podium together to present Martha and Anna, our first two directors. I presented Martha by lavishing her with praise for her sales and recruiting accomplishments; and then I promised that at the close of the day she would tell why she left Mary Kay and joined us.

Marjie recognized Anna as having a unit already with a strong hold in Houston; every single member had come with her to Beauticontrol. Of course, Marjie also crowed about the fact that Anna was her sister-in-law. Then she revealed the real reason we were so excited to have the two of them with us. It was because they could both carry a tune. And when she went on to say that Anna had rewritten the words for the songs we were about to sing, there was resounding applause of appreciation from the audience.

At this point Billy began playing "This Ol' House" on the piano, and Anna stepped forward to teach everyone the new words. It was much longer than Mary Kay's theme song had been, but because it told our story and was so motivational, no one cared. The main line in the song was "We are out to lead the nation in the beauty world today," and when that line was sung, the volume escalated to a whole new level.

We picked up momentum with each verse and by the time we'd finished, we were gasping for breath, from the pace and the laughter. Marjie leaned over and said to me, "The 'Mary Kay Enthusiasm Song' will never top that."

I stepped up to the podium and asked, "Would everyone that could use more bookings please raise your hands?" At a glance it appeared that everyone in the room did so. I then presented a complete mock performance of the club program. As I prepared to close my talk, Barbara Stubblefield raised her hand and said, "Is it okay to ask questions?" Because she was to be in a new area, she was vitally interested in this idea for getting appointments. The discussion that followed was so beneficial that from that day forward, we broke into small groups so individuals could have specific problems addressed.

Marjie followed with a talk entitled "Being a good listener is the secret to becoming a first rate sales person." This was a time when the majority of the population considered sales people to be "fast talkers," which was not a complimentary term, and made her topic especially apropos. While she used all kinds of illustrations to get her points across, in a nutshell her message was simply "Listen intently to what people say they want. Then show them what you are offering will help them get it. And a sale will be made, no matter what you are selling." I could tell her talk was being well received by the way the audience took notes. As I listened I realized for the first time that Marjie's job with us was primarily taking care of things nobody else wanted to do and she received very little praise or recognition for it. As she was finishing up, I joined her at the podium and said to the audience, "Marjie's job at the office is to take care of all the details that have to be done, but for which she gets very little praise or recognition. Yet, listening to her today, you can see her depth of knowledge and her contribution to our success. So now, let's show her we do appreciate her contribution." The entire audience rose instantly and gave her a standing ovation. Looking at the glow on Marjie's face, I regretted the praise was so long overdue.

After each speaker, Anna led the group in another new song, making sure the audience was alert and ready for the next part on the program. Then Marjie presented Martha, with more glowing praise, as the next speaker. Even though the accomplishments of Martha and Anna were repeated several times, it didn't seem to matter. Apparently, we never tire of hearing good words about ourselves.

Martha's approach to everything she did was dramatic, and her presentation of a mock clinic was no exception. As we watched her stunning performance, we sat, spellbound afraid to blink our eyes for fear of missing something. It wasn't just her words, but also the animation in the way she shared her secrets. She confided that she made each hostess her partner in business. And it was the hostess' job to book, sell, and recruit for her outside the actual clinic, which accounted for much of Martha's high performance. She rewarded each hostess with extra products and lavish praise. As I watched, I smiled and thought to myself, She's a quick study. She observed Mary Kay at work and used her technique.

During the glamour part of the clinic, Martha taught them the new look we'd designed for summer: blue eye shadow was out and a more natural look was in. She also pointed out that the huge bouffant hairstyles were out, but it would take a long time to convince women of that. Martha showed the hairpiece that we were giving as the monthly sales prize and announced she was also giving one to her own hostess with the highest sales for the month. I heard a gasp from the audience as they latched onto the idea and wrote it down. Using the same ploy, they could easily double their monthly production.

After she was finished, Martha promised to share the story at the close of the day, as to why she left Mary Kay and came with us. She left the podium amidst enthusiastic applause, and excited chatter continued about her performance even as we went for lunch.

At the beginning of the afternoon session, Anna again led us in an invigorating rendition of our new theme song. By the time we finished, everyone was again wide-awake and ready for more. Dathene had finally shown up (just in time for lunch), and I was thankful that we hadn't expected her to speak. In all the years we spent with her, we never really knew what to expect from Dathene. She gave the word 'unpredictable' a whole new meaning. Marjie and I had discussed this quality in her at length, and at one point Marjie said she thought that was why Mary Kay hadn't included Dathene in her business. I responded that we could never kick her out, and we would have to learn to deal with her as she was. Ned and Stan left after lunch, so for the rest of the day, Marjie and I were on our own.

Betty was first on the program for the afternoon. It worked out great because she kept all of us moving about and fully awake as we participated in each part of her modeling instruction. After each activity, she had us perform it in unison, much like a drill team. And not even waiting for the end, we applauded her instructions. We walked correctly, sat correctly, and stood still with our bodies perfectly aligned.

Presenting Anna was my most challenging job of the day because she had it all, and I hardly knew how to do her justice. She was always upbeat, appeared happy, a good listener, and complimentary to the person she was with. I could see why she had become Mary Kay's friend and confidant. When I mentioned to the audience that her topic was going to be "How to build a unit from the ground up when you don't know anyone in an area," I could hear the crowd scrambling for writing materials. What could be more important than this?

Not knowing anyone in Houston, Anna told everyone she met (at the cleaners, grocery store etc.) that she was looking for sales people for a fabulous new cosmetic line. She extolled the moneymaking potential, but her clincher was offering "a ground-floor opportunity." People on the lowest level would ultimately earn money on all future sales. This point is what booked clinics and got new recruits.

It had been a great day. The information was new and fresh and everyone was excited to get back to work. Even the fact that Jan and Idell, (the two directors I'd most counted on) hadn't left Mary Kay to come with me, didn't bother me so much anymore. The applause at the end of Anna's talk brought me back into reality and I returned to the podium.

We had planned to finish the day with impromptu discussions as well as Martha's story. But as I started to announce this, two men entered from the back of the room, rushed down the aisle and stopped in front of me. "ARE YOU JACKIE BROWN?" one of them bellowed. Although I don't remember answering, I must have because he handed me a thick legal document and announced just as loudly as before, "YOU HAVE BEEN SERVED."

The announcement was met with perfect stillness in the room, as if any movement could bring the roof down upon us.

Having been a legal secretary, I recognized the document he handed me. However, I had never been on the receiving end before. I don't know how long I looked at it before comprehending that Mary Kay was suing me for a million dollars. It felt like I was caught in a dream where strange and unreal things happen. A thought floated idly through my head: Does Mary Kay think that's how much I cost her by leaving?

When I came out of my stupor, I looked down at the front row where Marjie, Anna, and Martha were sitting. There was a look of stark terror frozen on their faces. Seeing it, a ball of fear landed in my stomach and raced through my entire being as I became fully cognizant of what was happening. Struggling for control, I suddenly seemed to hear Mary Kay's voice repeating something she'd said to me in the beginning, "The only cure for fear is faith."

Seconds had passed, even though it felt like hours. I picked up the document and held it up for the crowd to see. "This is a document based on fear. Fear that we will take all of Mary Kay's sales people and fear that we will try to pass Beauticontrol products off as hers. Basically, it's like Goliath trying to scare David out of a fight. But we know how that story ended, and I believe it will be the same for us." My own words actually filled me with assurance that our faith would prevail. At this point, I dropped all pretense of being nice to Mary Kay and proceeded to confide to the crowd that our basic reason for joining Beauticontrol was to help right the wrong that she had done to Dathene.

On pure impulse, I asked Dathene to come to the podium. As she stood there, white as a sheet, I explained to the audience that I wanted Dathene to share the story of what happened on a cold night in March when Marjie and I made the trip to Tyler. "There's no reason to be nervous, Dathene," I told her. "Just use your own words and tell it how you remember it happening."

I stayed beside her because her face was still so white; I was worried she might faint. And looking at Marjie, I was afraid she would, too. The look on her face asked, "What in the world are you doing?" I knew she was concerned because of Dathene's unpredictability but I had to take the chance.

Nervously Dathene began. "I'm not like Jackie and Marjie. I'm no speaker, so I hope you will bear with me." Applause erupted immediately at her simple humility. Once that happened, Dathene became calmer. She began by explaining how desperate her situation had been at the time Stan first contacted her (not even knowing where her next meal would come from), and since then had been praying that God would send help so she could take care of her five children. When Marjie and I came, from the minute she saw us, she knew that we would be that help. As she spoke humbly and sincerely, she began to cry, and so did the audience, with Marjie and me crying hardest of all.

She explained the whole connection with Mary Kay as she had to us. She apologized for being so dumb and not realizing that Mary Kay planned to take everything—her entire inheritance of the formulas, her family history, and even the company (Beauticontrol) for the measly $500 she had been paid. "And now she's still trying to get it all, with a lawsuit, and it's all my fault," she wailed.

In an instant, Martha was beside her, yelling, "She'll have to go through me first." Suddenly the whole group encircled her saying, "and me, and me," until every single one of us had joined the circle, even Nell Davis, who was attending the event as simply a visitor.

As we finally began to settle down, Martha shared her experience of how Mary Kay, and the directors, had humiliated her by accusing her of being a liar and a spy. Hearing all of it strengthened our resolve to stand up and fight. Calmer now, we took another look at the lawsuit. Stan and Marjie, Ned and I, Dathene, and Martha were being named all in one suit. Anna and Fred were being sued separately in another, no doubt because Mary Kay was especially angry with Anna since she had been her personal secretary and confidant.

Emotionally drained, we closed the day by forming a circle, locking arms, and forming a chain that was almost impossible to break through. Then Martha and Anna led us in a hymn that put it all in the right perspective: "He's got the Whole World in His Hands."

On the surface, it appeared that the lawsuit would be the straw that broke the camel's back. Instead, it became the glue that held our little band together as we fought the battle with Goliath. Stan and Ned demanded all the details of what had happened the minute they returned. But Marjie and I, spent from emotion, just shook our heads and said it would have to wait. We set up a time to meet the next day, Sunday, to go over the lawsuit together.

The minute we walked in our front door, I went straight upstairs and got Shannon out of her crib. I rocked and sang to her until she fell asleep, which gave me a great sense of comfort and release from the turmoil. Next I went into Sharon's room and found she was also almost asleep. But she snuggled close and said, "Stay with me for a while." When I could tell from her breathing that she was asleep, I slipped out of her room and into our bed where Ned was waiting with open arms. That routine became the one that helped me survive the years ahead. Every night I wrapped my family tightly around me and held onto the promise of the song, "He's Got the Whole World in His Hands."

CHAPTER NINETEEN

The Fight Is On

Sunday was ordinarily "fun day" for our family, but there was nothing ordinary about today. Just yesterday we had been handed a lawsuit filed by Mary Kay, trying to collect one million dollars from us. While my earnings with her company did make me feel rich, the million-dollar level wasn't even in my dreams. Even though Ned and I had vowed to hold on to faith, the dark cloud of yesterday continued to hover over us. Even Sharon and Shannon seemed subdued, although they couldn't possibly grasp the consequences of what was going on. Normally, when Shannon woke up, she pulled herself upright in bed and shook it until Ned answered her call. Today, when Ned went in to check on her, she was sitting quietly, waiting.

We hadn't discussed the lawsuit in front of Sharon, not wanting her to worry. But today as we headed to church, I handed Shannon into the back seat, and I said to Ned, "The church has been our strength and our refuge all these years, and now it looks like that may change. Do you think we will have to look for another church? The tension in ours could be unbearable for us in the months ahead." Many Mary Kay consultants went to this church, as did Mary Kay's attorney.

Frowning, Ned replied, "If Ralph Baker has his way, it will be. Mary Kay knew he was the most powerful deacon in our church, and that's why she chose him as her attorney. It's just another one of her ploys to intimidate us."

Children grasp more than we think, and Sharon knew something was very wrong. But now she moved up in the back seat until she was looking over our shoulders and asked, "Why would we have to move to another church? Isn't God still there in ours?"

Ned and I just looked at each other for several moments. Then I answered, "Of course He is sweetheart, and thank you for reminding us."

Still looking me in the eye, Ned mouthed the words. "Out of the mouths of babes."

There was a Mary Kay consultant in my Sunday school class, and even after I left the company, she had remained friendly. But today she seemed cool and aloof. Since the lawsuit had just been served to us yesterday, I shook off the impression and vowed I would save the paranoia until later on. I had a strong feeling that the climate in our church would get much colder before it ever became warm again.

After church, as always, we felt better. Dr. Criswell, our pastor, had preached on the power of discouragement. He pointed out it was Satan's favorite weapon for disrupting faith. And again, Ned and I looked at each other and smiled. The message seemed to be specifically aimed at us.

As we drove up to our office to meet Marjie and Stan, we noticed that Sheryl was with them. We decided quickly to have our meeting over lunch at Howard Johnson, and Sharon invited Sheryl to ride with us to the restaurant. As we listened to them talk and giggle in the back seat, our mood lightened. It reminded me of how much easier it is to wait out a storm with friends, than to endure it alone.

We sat the girls at a separate table, which they much preferred. By now, Sharon could take almost as good care of Shannon as we could, and Shannon adored her big sister. After lunch, we pulled out the document and went over it thoroughly. Just as we'd thought, it was based on fear that we would take her customers and her sales people. Yet nothing that was listed showed that we would actually be a threat to her company. Dumbfounded, I said, "In all my years as a legal secretary I have never before seen a lawsuit based just on fear. I didn't even know it was possible."

"It's a scare tactic," Stan said. "She's hoping to scare us and her people as well, so they won't leave and come with us."

Instantly, I realized his analysis was probably true. Unfortunately, I also knew it could work. People were scared to death of the courtroom. It seemed like the next step was a prison cell. After a lengthy discussion, we agreed that the lawsuit had no real merit, and the most dangerous thing about it was the expense. Even before the suit was served, our expenses had been much higher than we'd ever anticipated, and our operating capital was already far too low. Judging from the thickness of the document, I knew every supposition would have to be addressed and that would require big money. Mary Kay's tactics seemed to be that if she couldn't scare us away, then she would simply drain us dry. Idly I wondered why Dick Kelly, of World Gift, didn't do this to her. He had the actual evidence for a strong case but chose not to use it. And then I thought, I guess SHE doesn't believe in the Golden Rule, because that would require her to do the same for us.

After we finished reviewing the lawsuit, we agreed that we had to consult a lawyer the very next day, so we could see what our options were. Having decided on a course of action, we gathered up the kids and left for our respective homes.

Monday morning I called the law firm that we had used for reincorporating the company. Of the two young courtroom attorneys, I spoke with one, Brad Corrigan, about our case. I liked the sound of his voice immediately. It was calm and reassuring, and even as we talked I relaxed a little. After taking in the seriousness of the suit, he rearranged his schedule so that he and his associate, Fred Lohmeyeer, could meet with us that same afternoon.

As Marjie and I walked into their offices in downtown Dallas and I looked around their waiting area, I became a little nervous. The décor looked just as expensive as the firm I had worked for, and I knew how high their services were. Marjie had the same look of concern and nudged me to make sure I noticed. Her look said, "Let's keep this meeting as short as possible." When the lawyers came to the waiting area, smiled, shook our hands, and told us to call them Brad and Fred, I breathed a little easier. They seemed to be about our age and would be easy to work with. Brad was average height and build, with light brown hair and eyes that were kind and understanding. Fred had darker hair and a thinner build, as well as a livelier demeanor. There was nothing intimidating about either of them, and Marjie and I looked at each other and nodded. Even though the expense would be significant, at least our time with them would be amiable.

For the next three hours they perused the document word for word. Occasionally they asked questions about whether there was any truth to what Mary Kay was claiming, and of course we vehemently denied it and told them the real story. But mostly Marjie and I just listened to their comments to each other and waited for them to finish and give us their opinion. We had brought copies of Mary Kay's marketing plan that had been written down by several different people during Richard's presentations; we also brought the various contracts that Dathene had with Mary Kay and World Gift. They were proof that Mary Kay had not bought exclusive rights to anything.

Finally, after looking at all of it, Brad spoke, "My first thought about the situation is that I would much rather represent your case than theirs. Ralph Baker has his work cut out for him."

While Marjie didn't show much reaction to his statement, I felt as if a ten-pound weight had been lifted. I could tell Brad had made an important distinction between the two cases and a ray of hope dawned as he continued. He added that he would have to look at it more closely, but at this point it seemed I had grounds to sue Mary Kay for breach of contract, even though it was verbal and not written. And Dathene had grounds to sue her for obtaining the formulas by fraudulent means. Those words of encouragement warmed my heart, and from that point on I thought of Brad Corrigan as a friend and not just a business associate. Then he continued, "I'm sure Fred will agree with me that there is something you must do immediately." As we waited expectantly, Fred answered, "File the counter suit as soon as possible." I looked at Marjie, as dollar signs danced in my head.

Everything was moving so fast, and filing a counter suit would at least double the expense of the whole thing. I had thought we would have a little more time to increase our sales. We were barely scraping by as it was.

"Is that absolutely necessary?" Marjie asked. "That's going to be even more expensive. And as a new company this is devastating to us."

Again Brad was the one to answer. "We understand that, and we will work out something you can live with, but a good offense is the best defense, and that is what a counter suit would do in this game Mary Kay is playing. Actually, it is what you have to do in order to compensate for her having more money to spend and one of the most powerful lawyers in Dallas."

The resolved look on Marjie's face sent me her opinion: "I guess we gotta do what we gotta do."

Then in a final statement, Brad held up the contracts of Dathene's and said, "These are worth their weight in gold. I don't see how Ralph Baker is ever going to explain these away."

And I thought, *This man is smart. I think we've chosen the right lawyers.*

I had brought the company checkbook with us and before leaving their office, I wrote them a check as a retainer fee for representing us. It reduced our account balance to almost zero.

On our drive back to the office, we were high one minute about their appraisal of our case and down in the dumps the next over the expense. "It looks like we're going to have to dip into our grocery money," I said solemnly.

After a long pause, Marjie responded, "I thought we already had." I knew what she meant. We had used every extra cent we had for unexpected expenses. I had made certain that we put away enough money to pay Marie, but other than that we had almost depleted our resources. And I suspected the money situation was even tighter for Marjie and Stan.

As the four of us met that evening to discuss the day's events, Stan sized it up into a few words. "It looks like it's the counter suit or else we throw in the towel." At his remark our spines stiffened, because none of us were ready to throw in the towel.

The next morning as I dressed for work, I kept thinking about what Brad had said about a good offense. It was going to take time to get the counter suit ready, and we needed that offense now. Suddenly I remembered Rosalie McGinnis's article on Mary Kay. As soon as I got to the office, I called her on the phone. After I explained that Mary Kay had said that Rosalie had goofed when she said Mary Kay was related to the hide tanner, I had her full attention. Exasperated, she answered, "That's exactly what Mary Kay said, and I have my notes to prove it." Then I told her about our new association with Beauticontrol and Mary Kay's lawsuit against us. I added that we needed her help to clear it all up for our customers by telling them the real story. She agreed to come out that afternoon to meet Dathene and to take a look at the documents. I suspected that the main reason she agreed to this was because of Mary Kay's negative comments, and hearing our story might give her the chance to even the score. Whatever her reason, I was relieved. I wanted the simple truth in print, so that we could hand it to our customers to read for themselves.

On first sight I liked Rosalie McGinnis. I recognized her Arkansas accent as we introduced ourselves and told her I was from that state as well. She brightened up immediately, and we spent a few minutes discussing people we knew that were also from there. One of them was Jim Wright, who was on the editorial staff at the Dallas Morning News and was even from the same town as Rosalie. When I told her Jim and I had worked together at Sun Oil Company so she could check out my credibility, she warmed up to the idea of doing a story on us.

She called the newspaper and asked them to send a photographer as soon as possible. While we were waiting, Marjie, Rosalie, Dathene and I talked, and when Dathene revealed that she was from Mena, Arkansas, it suddenly felt like "old home week." I thought, *We should probably call the hogs, like they do at Arkansas football games.* As I watched all this unfolding around me I knew it was no coincidence and silently said a little prayer: *Thank you Lord for knowing we needed Your help. We're like a little family here.*

By the time we had filled Rosalie in on the whole story and had given her copies of all the documents, including the hide tanner's picture with his family, the photographer had arrived. We moved into the lab for pictures of Marjie, Dathene and me around the filling machine while Dathene filled product into containers. I was glad Rosalie chose this photo, because it would show we did our own manufacturing, which Mary Kay did not. After the photographer left, Rosalie informed us the article would appear in the Dallas Morning News in the next few days; she would call us about the exact date.

Marjie replied, "Good, because we may buy up every copy in town."

"That would be just fine," Rosalie said, laughing as she walked out the door. Her article wasn't just a good one; it was GREAT. It was written with fervor and rang with sincerity and truth. She told the whole story, pointing out that the actual granddaughter of the hide tanner and a couple of women formerly with another cosmetic company were restructuring Beauticontrol, Inc., in order to obtain greater success.

We called all of our local sales people, and they rushed out and bought up the newspapers. From that point on, whenever a customer asked about our connection with Mary Kay, all we had to do was hand her a copy of the article; there was no need to discuss the situation at all. With Dathene's family story in print for the whole world to read, it raised a huge question in the reader's mind about the authenticity of Mary Kay's exclusive claim to the formulas. And it put us into an offensive position, which was what we were going for in the first place, rather than having to defend ourselves from the claims in Mary Kay's lawsuit against us.

I don't think even General Motors could have come up with a better strategy than this one. The newspaper story made the lawsuit that Mary Kay had intended to destroy us actually work in our favor in competing for customers. Our consultants now had it easy; when any question arose about Mary Kay, they simply passed out the article, which explained the situation perfectly. The article also sparked the interest of Mary Kay customers and, after trying Beauticontrol, they bought it instead of Mary Kay. Our products sold as fast as we could make them, and many times we had to work in production into the night to keep up with sales. All the work fell on our shoulders because we didn't have a dime to spend on extra help. But we didn't mind the work. It was a small price to pay for the wonderful turn of events. I had an overwhelming feeling that Rosalie McGinnis had been the "Knight on a White Horse" who had charged in to save us, and I kept in touch with her for a very long time.

Marjie, Stan, Ned, and I discussed how we wished we could have seen Mary Kay's face when she realized what was happening. Unfortunately, we would soon learn that whenever we won a skirmish, a major battle followed. But even though this victory was brief, it was a good time for us. Not only were we selling products and getting a large number of new consultants locally, but we had also begun to recruit outside the area. I recruited my good friend, Melba Bowerman (my maid-of-honor when I married Ned), from Texarkana, who in turn recruited her sister, Johnnie, and her sister-in-law, Jean Rochelle, from Dallas. They jumped into the business with both feet, and Johnnie won the mink stole we were giving away in a current contest.

Jean saw our business as the way to enrich her life. Her husband traveled, so she was alone at home with her four young daughters much of the time. The article helped her get her business going, and she became a regular visitor at the office when she picked up products. I could tell she was beginning to feel her life was improving because of her association with us. Marjie and I were pleased, since this was how we'd discussed the way we wanted our people to feel.

And thanks to Martha Weddle, there were also new recruits from Chattanooga, Tennessee. Martha recruited her long-time friend, Crystal Lee, who then recruited others, and on it went. However, the vast majority of our sales were still in the Dallas-Fort Worth area. This was partially because, as a new director, Juanita Grable had recruited many new local consultants. Juanita put long hours of work into her job and she had begun to show up as the number one unit in our weekly newsletter. Although

Juanita didn't limit her efforts to her own area, because she lived in Fort Worth, the majority of her people were from the Dallas-Fort Worth area. Which, of course, increased sales and excitement throughout the area. All of this activity meant that so far, we were keeping our heads above water financially, and the counter suit hadn't even been filed yet.

There was no doubt that Mary Kay was feeling the heat from the article. We had even begun to get calls from some of her consultants. They seemed to finally realize that there was another side to the story Mary Kay was telling. One morning as Marjie and I were discussing our good luck, and enjoying every minute of it, Marjie asked, "How do you think Mary Kay is going to combat the problems the article is causing her? I can't figure out how she could possibly turn it around in a way that would help her. Can you?"

I'd been thinking about the same thing. And now I replied, "No, I don't see a way for her to do that, but one thing I am certain of: she will retaliate. We need to prepare ourselves to expect the unexpected."

Marjie looked at me thoughtfully and answered, "Let's not worry about it right now. Even though we aren't out of the woods yet with our money problems, things are definitely looking up. Let's enjoy it while we can. The next thing we have to worry about is the court hearing that's coming up. Until then, let's relish our little victory as long as possible." It was an exciting time for us, but I had a strong premonition that Mary Kay's next move would change that.

As I sat staring into space with my thoughts, Josie knocked on my office door and said, "Brad Corrigan's on the line and wants to speak with you."

As soon as I said "Hello," Brad announced, "Well, it's done. The counter suit has been filed and Mary Kay has been served. So I guess we can say 'The fight is on.' I expect the date for the hearing to be set in the next few days."

He went on to explain that there were clerical charges for filing the suit and for having Mary Kay served. Then he asked in the nicest way possible if we could send a check for that, but nothing more for the firm at this time. Although it made me shudder to know we had to lay out more money so soon, I assured him I would put the check in the mail that day. By the time I hung up the phone, Marjie was standing at the door.

She had heard enough to know what he'd said. "Let's celebrate," she cried. "I would have given anything to have seen Mary Kay's face when she was handed the document. I hope it shocked her good, after the way she served ours to us."

"At least she knows we are not going to roll over and play dead," I answered enthusiastically.

"Let's get Dathene and celebrate at lunch."

Later that evening, Stan and Ned were just as enthusiastic as we were over the news, and we agreed we had scored some major points in the game.

A few days later, Brad called again to say the court hearing had been set for July. In the meantime all the parties named in the lawsuit would have to be deposed. He explained that was a good thing because he needed to know what Mary Kay and Richard would say once they were under oath at the actual trial.

When we informed our salespeople that the counter lawsuit had been filed, again our sales and recruiting accelerated. All of us believed we were in the right and the counter suit backed up that belief. Spirits were at an all-time high, and we were reaping the benefits, financially.

Near the time the hearing was to take place, we had a strange call from an attorney in Houston. The caller informed me that he had clients who were interested in possibly purchasing Beauticontrol, Inc., and he wanted to set up a meeting with us. To say I was shocked out of my shoes would be an understatement. Instantly I could think of only one person in the entire world that would even consider buying a new, struggling company like ours. But I decided to play along. "What kind of an offer are we talking about?" I asked, as though I was seriously considering the idea. "And, I need to know who the party is that's interested."

After a long hesitation, he dodged my question by answering, "I think you would consider the amount of the offer more than generous, but at this point it's premature to discuss the name of the party. They wish to remain anonymous at this time. Can we set up a time to meet?"

Smiling, I thought, *I'll bet she does want to remain anonymous*. Then I informed him that I would have to discuss the matter with my partners, and we set a time for him to call me back in a couple of days. I laughed to myself as I realized just how scared Mary Kay must be to pull this. I didn't even consider telling Marjie about the content of the call until Ned and Stan joined us. When I repeated the conversation word for word, all of us laughed until we were breathless.

Stan spoke first: "Mary Kay must be desperate. I do wish we could know what we would have to agree to IF we took an offer from her to buy the company. I'll bet we would all have to move to Siberia or maybe even outer space. Do you think she actually believed we would fall for this act? If so, she must think we are really stupid."

"So, what else is new?" Ned offered, and we laughed some more.

Of course we declined the attorney's offer. But later we would look back on the event with the realization that it was Mary Kay's final attempt at a peaceful solution to her problem. Up to this point, the whole affair had been hurtful and demoralizing, which was bad enough. But if we'd had the faintest idea that Mary Kay's strategy would now turn dark and dangerous, we would have probably taken her offer to buy us out and run away from the whole affair as fast as we could.

CHAPTER TWENTY

Clashes in the Courtroom

In the 162nd Judicial District Court, Dallas, July 1966, I came as close as I ever had to Judgment Day on earth. Judge Dee Brown Walker presided over the hearing that would decide whether Mary Kay Cosmetics could force Beauticontrol to cease and desist doing business. If the judge ruled against us, we would have to shut our doors almost before they ever opened. My knees were banging against each other out of pure nerves.

The depositions for both parties had already been taken, and this was the first time since then that Marjie and I had seen Mary Kay face to face. As a legal secretary, I was familiar with court proceedings, but I had never before been on this side of the legal system. From what I knew of dealing with lawyers and judges, the fact that we were in the right and Mary Kay was wrong, meant almost nothing. Sometimes it all boiled down to insubstantial matters like what kind of mood the judge was in, which lawyer held the biggest bag of tricks, or whether or not one side simply presented their case more articulately than the other. The only comfort I had in our fight of David (us) against Goliath (Mary Kay) was that this was not a one-sided attack. We had filed our counter suit, which meant that it was our day in court as well.

All eight defendants walked in together, and we took our seats on the left side of the courtroom. Mary Kay, Richard, and Dalene, along with their attorneys, sat on the other side. Our collective myopic gaze remained stubbornly pasted in opposite directions. Once again, Marjie and I had dressed to the nines, including the hats. We wanted to look like players, even if we didn't feel like ones. These were the days when, to be stylish, everything in a woman's outfit had to match, so I dressed with skillful simplicity in a pink tailored suit with a pink sheer blouse and matching pink shoes. It did not escape my recollection that pink was Mary Kay's signature color. Looking back, I have to admit to indulging in a little spite of my own.

When the judge entered, everyone rose, and the proceedings were called to order. The plaintiffs presented their case first by calling Mary Kay herself to the stand. I was nearly suffocating with tension waiting to hear what she had to say about us. Suddenly, I knew we needed to prepare ourselves. I punched Marjie and leaned over and whispered, "Get ready; you are about to see the performance of a lifetime."

Yet I was totally unprepared for the mean-spirited attack that Mary Kay delivered. I had never before heard such words come out of her mouth. For the two hours that she sat there, her message was virtually the same. "When Jackie Brown met me she was a lowly secretary with no future. I gave her everything. She made more money that she ever dreamed of and how did she repay me?" she paused to catch her breath and then continued with new vengeance, "She lied, stole my ideas, and then tried to take away my entire company."

I flinched at the unfairness of the vicious attack while the fourteen-hour days I had spent building her company flashed through my mind. So this is the real Mary Kay, I thought, trying to regain my composure.

Then suddenly her demeanor changed again. She lowered her eyes and continued in a voice weighed down with self-pity, "You could say she tried to cripple her own fairy godmother." I didn't know whether to vomit or to jump to my feet and yell "Objection!" Instead I just laughed softly as the realization hit me that at least this was a step up from being compared to Judas Iscariot.

One of the first points she tried to make was that her manual, which was the blueprint for the shows her salespeople held for customers, was a finished product and a work of art when I joined the company. It was her contention that I had now stolen the content of that manual—information that she, herself, had developed—and was using it to build my own company. In effect, she claimed that besides the formulas, the customers, and the salespeople, this was one more thing I had stolen from her. Also, she was claiming that I was lying about the position of national sales director and the additional 2 percent that was to be paid for reaching that level. Her eyes closed and her chin fell to her chest in evidence of the betrayal she felt.

Only the hard rule of silence in the courtroom could keep my mouth from flying open in protestation of the picture she was presenting. I grabbed a sheet of paper and wrote a note to Brad Corrigan in huge letters: "Do something!"

He continued to look straight ahead paying careful attention to every word that Mary Kay said. After a few minutes he quietly picked up a pencil and wrote back, "Hold on, we'll get our turn." I knew that he had the actual first manual that consisted of less than ten pages as well as the new one that mostly contained material that I had perfected. He also had a tape of one of my actual shows that Mary Kay gave to all new recruits to use as a prototype. I knew this was proof that she was not telling the truth, but I did not see how I could sit still and listen to her much longer. So I did what I always do when I realize that I am powerless to handle a situation. I said a prayer. I asked God to take away the agitation and to give me peace. I also asked Him to be with Brad as his turn came for cross-examination.

It worked. A calm feeling came over me, and I sat without reacting while Mary Kay ranted about what a wretched, evil person I was. It was like I wasn't even there, but was listening to it all from a faraway place.

As her testimony continued, I had my first clue that Mary Kay was not there to play a game; she was going for a kill. Richard and Dalene were eventually called to the stand to back up everything Mary Kay said. As Mary Kay stepped down from the witness stand I tried to look her in the eye, but she turned her head. "How could this be?" I wondered, "The woman that had spent almost three years convincing me that I had everything I needed to be a success, was now declaring to the world that I wasn't even fit to live." As I saw myself through her eyes I felt sick to my very soul.

When our lawyer, Brad Corrigan, cross-examined, he launched his attack by asking immediately about the all-important 2 percent tier of the marketing plan, which had been promised and then withdrawn. Once again, she claimed that the whole idea existed only in the realm of my imagination. To prove her point, Mary Kay challenged us to point to the 2 percent tier anywhere in their material in the written word. The fact was that she and Richard had only announced it and had never written it down, so we could not meet the challenge.

In his unassuming, quiet manner, Brad nodded at Mary Kay's statement. Then after a pause he said, "Mrs. Ash, you just stated that you taught Jackie everything she knew, so are you saying that she believed what you told her even in matters that were not written down?"

Mary Kay hesitated and then answered, "Yes."

"So from the very beginning of her association with your company even before there was a real manual, you guided her in how to advance in the company?" Without waiting for a response he continued. "You advised her to work hard and recruit as many people as possible so that she could qualify for one of the top spots?"

This time he waited until she answered a weak yes and asked her to repeat it clearly for the record. "Even though Jackie had a difficult pregnancy, did you advise her that if she slowed down, she would probably lose the top spot to Dalene?"

The look on Mary Kay's face indicated that this was not going quite as she anticipated. However, she finally said yes to the statement. Next, Brad held up a thick computer printout of the sales for my unit just prior to my leaving the company. "This document shows hundreds of people and thousands of dollars in sales credited to Jackie Brown's work efforts. I want you to clarify for the court, did you give this business to Jackie, or did she complete all work requirements in order to receive compensation?"

After shuffling around in her chair for a while she finally admitted it was compensation for work performed. "Just one more thing on this point Mrs. Ash. Did you encourage your sales people to take notes diligently at all the meetings? In fact, isn't one of your famous quotes 'The faintest ink is better than the most retentive memory'?"

With a look of relief on her face, Mary Kay answered, "Yes, that is mine. I also like to say that you can always tell the graduate students from the undergraduates because when the professor comes in to class the undergraduates say 'good morning' and the graduates write it down." At this she laughed softly, safely back into her role as queen of the manor.

Brad reached down onto the table behind him and picked up a stack of papers. "Mrs. Ash, each one of these sheets contains notes taken by a different consultant while observing Richard drawing your marketing plan on a blackboard. As you can see, all of them contain the third tier, the controversial 2 percent. What is your explanation?"

Keeping her eyes lowered, Mary Kay muttered, "I don't know." The entire matter was so significant that later, the judge said, "I'm calling this the Case of the Two Percent." It signaled to me that he grasped the crux of why I had to leave the company.

Mr. Corrigan went on to cover other matters. In his possession were the various documents that Mary Kay had signed throughout the years, most of which came from Dathene. One by one, he read off the last names she had signed the papers with, which clearly indicated which man she had been married to at the time. He also slipped in two other married names that Dathene had contributed. As she sat majestically on the stand, her hands folded primly in her lap, he addressed her: "Mary Kay Rogers, Mary Kay Louis, Mary Kay Eckman, Mary Kay Weaver, Mary Kay Miller, Mary Kay Hollenbeck, and Mary Kay Ash. Are these all the same person?"

Her lawyer jumped out of his seat so fast I thought he had been goosed from behind. "Objection! Objection! This is immaterial, Your Honor."

"To the contrary," Mr. Corrigan answered. "We must establish whether the same person signed all of these contracts."

The judge answered, "I'll allow it," and effectively ordered Mary Kay to admit to the marriage rumors she had tried for so many years to squelch. I watched as her face hardened and her eyes flashed daggers at our attorney. I didn't know if anyone else could spot it, but the look deep inside her eyes was poisonous. This line of questioning had caught her completely off guard. The personal life she had fought so hard to keep hidden was being trotted out in its full regalia for all to see. It left her looking as exposed as a deer in headlights. She shot her lawyer another look to see if he was going to protect her from this humiliation, but there was nothing he could do. In retrospect, I believe it was at that moment that Mary Kay became truly infuriated and decided to pull out all the stops. She had always convinced herself and others that she was pure, immaculate, and above the fray. Nothing could touch her. She had managed to steer clear of previous threats of scandal, but here she was being treated like any ordinary mortal. It was something she was not used to, and it was more than she could tolerate.

Mary Kay had to admit that over the course of time, when she signed the various contracts, she was married to the man whose name she signed, and that she had married Weaver twice. She went on to claim that for the $500 Mary Kay was paying her, Dathene agreed to hand over everything—the story of the hide tanner, the family name, and the formulas. At this point Brad Corrigan interrupted her and in his least threatening voice said, "Excuse me for interrupting you, Mary Kay, but are you saying that Dathene sold you all rights to the hide tanner's story as part of this contract?" holding up the contract she had signed with Dathene.

"That's correct," Mary Kay answered.

Brad continued, "Why then is it not mentioned as part of the contract?" Without letting her recover from the realization of the mess she was in, he added, "And why have your attorneys contacted all of Dathene's sisters in an effort to buy the right to the hide tanner's story from them if, in fact, she already sold it to you?"

Stunned, Mary Kay mumbled an answer to his question.

"Would you repeat that please? I couldn't hear you."

When Brad restated the question, Mary Kay, losing her cool, almost shouted, "I said, that was just for insurance!"

Marjie and I exchanged a look that said, "What do you know, she's human after all."

Brad then gently led her back into her recitation of what she claimed to be buying for the $500. Taking a deep breath, Mary Kay repeated that Dathene agreed to do nothing with Beauticontrol from that point on except to sell it to friends and neighbors. Beauticontrol could go on making products on an extremely small scale, but it would never compete with the about-to-be-formed Mary Kay Cosmetics. Dathene was prohibited from ever telling anyone that her company had any connection whatsoever with Mary Kay's company. When she was finished, Mr. Corrigan paused to collect his thoughts, then said deliberately, "So what you're telling me is that you were only going to allow Dathene to sell a little bit of Beauticontrol products, but not ever enough to make a decent living for her family. In other words, for the amount of $500, she was vowing to spend the rest of her life in poverty."

Mary Kay wavered, then answered, "That's right, as far as Beauticontrol business is concerned. But she could always do hair if she wanted." The courtroom lapsed into a stunned silence. It was like Marie Antoinette saying, "Let them eat cake."

Then Brad said, "Just one more thing about that, Mary Kay. If Dathene was to be limited in her sales of Beauticontrol, why didn't you have it written into the contract?"

Mary Kay mumbled an answer and Judge Walker ordered, "Speak up please."

"I said I didn't think it was necessary," she answered loudly, obviously realizing she'd backed herself into a corner.

Corrigan then handed her a piece of paper, which he identified as a test page that was given to all new recruits. On it were questions about the history of the company that salespeople were required to know the answers to. He directed her to read a question, which asked what the original name of the company was that made the products she was selling. The answer: Beauticontrol.

297

"So," Mr. Corrigan said, "you were out there broadcasting to everyone that it was Beauticontrol that owned the original products which you took over, but you were not allowing Dathene to claim any connection to Mary Kay Cosmetics. You restricted her so much she couldn't answer yes or no. What did you expect the woman to do?"

Her silent stare lasted a second before she answered, "I have no idea."

After more questions that left the witness without suitable answers, Mr. Corrigan took out the contract that Dick Kelly of World Gift had signed with Ova Spoonmore, Dathene's mother, years before—the one that ostensibly showed that he had bought the rights to the hide tanner's formulas. Corrigan then brought out the contract Mary Kay had had Dathene sign. The wording of the two contracts was virtually identical. Only the names of the parties were different. "So," Corrigan said, "the wording of these contracts is almost exactly the same, and yet you are saying that you own everything of everything. If you have all the rights to the formulas, and Dick Kelly has all the rights to precisely the same formulas, what are we to do here? What, then, did Dick Kelly buy?"

"I have no idea."

"Did World Gift sue you when you started your company with the same formulas they had already bought?"

Her facade cracked a little. "No."

"Why not?"

"Objection! Calls for speculation."

The judge overruled. Corrigan said to his witness, "Well, if you can put Beauticontrol out of business, then it stands to reason that World Gift should be able to put you out of business. Is that not so? Would you agree that if this contract with Dathene gives you total rights to the original formulas, and World Gift has an almost identical contract that predates yours, they had the rights first? Isn't that correct?"

"Objection!" Baker was so rattled this time that he didn't even give a reason.

Brad then said, "I withdraw my question."

Mr. Corrigan didn't need an answer. His point had been made. He had dismantled her entire case and made her arguments look as empty as they were.

The atmosphere in the courtroom was so cold we could have killed hogs. Even at the breaks, only the attorneys spoke to each other. None of us made any pretense of being hospitable or decent. I looked over at Dathene and could tell that she was upset over Mary Kay's testimony. She had told me that she'd always liked and admired Mary Kay. She said the fact that they both had been married several times gave them a common bond. Because she considered Mary Kay a friend, she'd helped her make the curtains for her new office when she opened her company.

Suddenly, I felt an overwhelming surge of sympathy for Dathene. Somehow the whole affair was over her head. She didn't understand why Mary Kay would say ugly things about her. Watching her, I realized for the first time that this childlike vulnerability that Dathene had was the major reason that I left Mary Kay and joined Beauticontrol.

I knew, intuitively, that Dathene did not see the contradiction in her story of how Mary Kay ended up with the formulas. Her demeanor was that of a lost child hoping that someone would come forward to help her. Apparently, that someone was meant to be me. I was now her advocate in the war that raged around us.

It was inevitable that Dathene would be called to the stand. I never thought she was the strongest link in the chain, but until she took the stand, I didn't realize how weak of a witness she would be. By this time she felt so stupid for letting Mary Kay get hold of her grandfather's formulas in exchange for a "bowl of porridge," that she was obsessed with finding an adequate explanation for her actions.

On the witness stand, Dathene repeated over and over in her sweet but long-suffering voice that Mary Kay had tricked her out of her rightful inheritance and that she had stolen the formulas from World Gift. Dathene's posture remained defensive simply because she had to find a way to justify selling out for a mere $500. No matter what angle they questioned her from, however, no one could ever get her to say that she had handed over the formulas. In fact, she vehemently maintained that Mary Kay already had the formulas.

She stated emphatically that the only reason she had signed the contract was so Mary Kay wouldn't get sued for taking the formulas from World Gift. She said, "That's what Mary Kay asked me to do, and that's what I did." She further asserted that when she accepted the check, she never for a moment believed she was handing over anything real or anything of value. Nor was she making a commitment about the future of Beauticontrol. Her words rang true to me. I quickly wrote a note to Brad, "Does she sound believable?" Without showing any expression on his face, his note back to me said simply, "Yes."

The whole time she was testifying, I sat there and nodded silently to her as reassurance that even if no one else in the courtroom understood what she was saying, I did. I knew better than anyone how convincing Mary Kay could be. I wasn't sure how much damage, if any, was done while Dathene was being questioned, but I knew for certain that she talked too much. My experience in the law firms taught me that in court, short answers are always a better strategy. The more you say the more the other side can use against you. I breathed a sigh of relief when sweet, naive Dathene finally stepped down and returned to her seat.

When I took the stand, Mr. Baker wasted no time. He looked at me as one would at any lower life form and approached the bench. Without warning, he bellowed into my face, "You are a liar and a thief, and you are trying to steal this woman's company!"

His pronouncement was so vicious that every single person in the courtroom gasped. I almost fell out of my chair. As false as the words were, they cut to the bone. The fact that Baker was a well-known and respected Christian and a deacon in the church made his statement doubly painful. This was a man I used to esteem, and when I first heard he was to be Mary Kay's attorney, I was pleased. I thought he would behave honorably. Instead, he turned into a piranha in the courtroom.

Something inside me began to retreat. Since there was no truth at all to what he had said, I cannot explain why, but I was overwhelmed with a feeling of guilt and wished I had a hole to crawl into. Nothing brings guilt out in me faster than a direct attack on my integrity. I thought he had buried me, and from the look on his face it was clear that he thought so, too. But in a flash of inspiration I realized, *This is just about money and the fear of losing it! That's it. That's all it is.* In that moment of silence I found new confidence and courage because his words had nothing whatever to do with my character. I recovered quickly from Baker's blow and drew myself up to my full five feet of height with dignity. I looked him straight in the eye and with a ring of total authority I said, "I know what you're trying to do. You are trying to make me look like a criminal, but that doesn't make what you are saying true. I also know that you're afraid that I'm going to take Mary Kay's company, and that's what this is really all about."

Mr. Baker was a big man, but my simple retort seemed to surprise him and shrink him down a little. He was attempting to portray Mary Kay as standing on high moral ground with this lawsuit, fighting for what was right. But it was beginning to look as if she had no ground to stand on at all, and the only banner she was really waving was her right to make money on something she had never owned in the first place. As I watched Mr. Baker carefully, I thought he looked like a balloon whose air kept slowly escaping.

His tone changed suddenly, and from that day on he lost his power to intimidate me. I did, however, make one important decision. I decided to never again wear pink when going into battle. Red would be a more appropriate color.

The day dragged on until, by the end, we were all exhausted. My lawyers made only two other points that were significant. One was that, for all Mary Kay's claims that all the things she had done to start her company were original, the fact was she had borrowed heavily in every area from both Dick Kelly and Mary Crowley. Almost everything she had or did was actually borrowed from somebody else. The second point was about the salespeople's right to leave the company. Mary Kay had always been extremely careful to preserve the independent contractor status of all her salespeople. If she hadn't, she would have had to pay them benefits.

In court, however, Mary Kay took the opposite view, claiming that she owned all of us, that we had no right to leave her or to go anywhere else. I knew my lawyer would shred her testimony, and he did, but all I could think when she was talking was, *What these people really want is for us to be dead.* Everything they had said throughout the day was so aggressive and contentious that their only purpose could be to destroy not only everyone else's opinion of us, but also our own opinion of ourselves.

One event alone saved the dreary, punishing day, and that occurred after the hearing. Now that it was over, I at least had some breathing room to concentrate on the pressing problems of beginning a new company. The primary of these was money because, quite simply, there wasn't nearly enough of it. Marjie and I were racking our brains trying to figure out how we were going to buy groceries for the next few weeks. As I was walking out the door, Martha Weddle stopped me. "Could you wait just a minute? I have something to give you."

She handed Marjie and me the applications for four new recruits along with a cashier's check for one thousand dollars in new orders for products. I stood there in suspended animation holding the check. Marjie and I just looked at each other for several moments without saying a word. A thousand dollars at that time was like winning the lottery. Without saying a thing out loud, we both knew what the other one was thinking: God is watching over us.

Several days later the judge handed down his temporary ruling: Beauticontrol was free, for the moment, to continue doing business, but neither side was allowed to take away the other's customers or salespeople, nor to make any claims against them. In other words, we were to leave each other alone.

Two other points that he ruled on worked in our favor. One was that Mary Kay could no longer use real names when relating the hide tanner's story, which included the names Beauticontrol, Ova Spoonmore, and John Wesley Heath, the hide tanner. This took a significant bite out of the believability of the story for her. Two, she could not go on using the before-and-after photographs taken by Ova Spoonemore, Dathene's mother, which she had borrowed years ago and never returned. Taken years earlier, these pictures showed the remarkable results of women who had first used the products and then looked visibly younger afterwards.

Mary Kay was prohibited from using either the names or the photographs, but we were not, which ultimately proved to be a huge benefit to us because later we built our entire live television campaign around these two items. And, as a little side perk, he instructed Mary Kay to discontinue using my tape of a show, which she had been putting in her demo kits.

Naively, I thought the judge's ruling meant there was a cease-fire. In reality, the hearing was only the first shot that launched the rest of the war. A war that was so horrible I could never have imagined what it would include.

CHAPTER TWENTY-ONE

Dirty Deeds

That war, it turned out, was to be conducted largely on my home turf. Ralph Baker was one of the most esteemed lawyers in all of Dallas. When Mary Kay had gone looking for a hired gun, she had employed the best she could find. But Mr. Baker was a far bigger part of my life than just being my opponent's lawyer. Our families attended the same church. He and Ned were both deacons in that church, and Ralph Baker was chairman of the deacons. As such, he was well respected, and he carried a great deal of influence in our community. It did not take us long to realize that, with all the influence he carried, he was discussing this case and our supposed culpability with the other churchgoers. One day after church a couple that we played bridge with was leaving the building as we were. "Hey," I said spontaneously. "We're going to the Circle Grill for lunch; why don't you join us?" To our dismay the husband mumbled some excuse and, avoiding eye contact, they hurried out of the building.

"That figures," Ned said as we continued out of the church.

"What do you mean?" I asked, dumbfounded.

"I saw them talking to Ralph Baker earlier," Ned replied.

"If that's supposed to be the best example of Christian behavior that our church has to offer, we're in trouble," I said. Church had always been the place Ned and I went to for spiritual renewal. It was a respite against the world with all its cares, and the place where, on Sunday morning, we would gain strength to face the rest of the week. During this tumultuous period, renewal and strength were what we needed most. And yet suddenly, far from being an environment that offered a hiatus from our problems, it became the source of the most pain. As Sharon had reminded me, God was still there in that church, but I was no longer sure that He was still in some of the people in it.

After the hearing, every Sunday when we came out of services, we would see and hear the buzz all around us. Sometimes friends and acquaintances confronted us directly about the case, but often there was just a distinct chill in the air when people who used to be friendly would no longer speak.

For many people in a community like ours, personal life revolves around the church. It is not only the spiritual center of their lives, but also the social center. On Sunday nights, Ned and I both worked in the Training Union, a class that tutored young people in the ways of the church: how to use the Bible, how to participate in church activities, how to pray in public, and so on. We were involved with these kids and their parents in many areas of their lives. We took them ice skating, had parties for them in our home, and many times picked them up from their homes and took them to activities. One evening we picked up Brad first. He crawled into the back seat without a word, which was really unusual for a ten-year-old. "Are you okay, Brad?" I asked.

"I guess," he answered, "but could I ask you a question?"

"Of course," Ned and I answered together.

"Well, my mom said you had stolen something and had to go to court. Is that true?"

Ned explained the situation to him as simply as he could, but Brad was not quite the same after that. That night when we were getting ready for bed, Ned said, "We're going to have to start telling our side of the story, you know."

"I hate to stoop to that level," I answered, yet knowing it would probably come to that. There were others who had taught along with us who now would barely say hello. My friend, Joann, was in my Sunday school class and also happened to sell Mary Kay products. When I went to class one Sunday, Joann had transferred into another class. No doubt she took literally the court ruling that we were not to be in contact with any of Mary Kay's people. The awkwardness of this behavior kept the problem in front of me constantly.

From church, the word spread everywhere. There was no place in our lives that was not touched by the controversy. Everyone was calling everyone else and began asking us about the case. We had to keep explaining to them, until we were tired of hearing ourselves repeat the details, what was really going on and what was at stake. Defending yourself is a hard thing. No matter how innocent you are, if you have to defend that innocence enough times to enough people, you can begin to sound guilty.

With the rumors Ralph Baker was spreading in our fairly large congregation—18,000 people in all—there seemed to be no end to the number of people who wanted to hear our side of the story so they could figure out whose side to be on. The church was full of my customers, so of course they had a personal need to know the truth, but for many, it was just the gossip of the day.

People we thought were friends turned against us and that, for me, was the most painful aspect of this battle. It was ripping out the very center of our lives. Mary Kay had once been a member of that congregation. People had known her. People cared who was lying and who was telling the truth. I knew that I was not a liar, but the experience of not being believed by people I had trusted deeply was like salt in a gaping wound.

When the church atmosphere became so tense it did not provide the revival of spirit I needed to get through the next week, I had to find a new way to cope with the problem. In thinking about it, I remembered how I felt when I visited my former in-laws, the C. D. Franks, who still lived in the small town in Arkansas. When driving up to their house, I could usually smell food cooking, which seemed to provide a sense of comfort. Then, the minute I walked in the door, a feeling of love overwhelmed me and within a few minutes, I began to relax. I came to think of it as the house that love built. So when I was literally at my wits end, I began to visit them on a regular basis and I continued this practice as long as they lived.

The most contentious people of all during this time were the Mary Kay consultants from my group who stayed with her company. They drew a line in the sand and defended it. They told everyone they could what rogues we were and how we had betrayed Mary Kay. Whenever I thought the flames had died down to coals, they went out and fanned them back into flames again, instigating fights everywhere they turned. There was just no way to stop people from talking.

It was at this point that I decided to contact Mary Crowley. Mary was also a member of our church, and a personal friend of Ralph Baker. At one time her brother had been married to Mary Kay. Actually he had been married to her twice. Mary was president of Home Interiors, a large direct-sales company that sold decorations for the home. I was trying desperately to figure out in my own mind just who Mary Kay really was, and Mary Crowley seemed my best source of information. I knew that she and Mary Kay had their own conflicts, but I didn't know what their current relationship was. I was so apprehensive about whether or not she would even talk with me that my fingers kept slipping, causing me to have to redial the telephone several times. Finally, she answered the phone. "Mary," I said, "I would like to speak with you confidentially about a matter. It's something I would rather not discuss over the telephone. Could you spare a few minutes to meet with me?"

She hesitated but finally laughed and said, "This is intriguing. When would you like to come over?"

I went to her office the next day. Even though I knew a lot about her, I had not actually met her before. And I knew that she knew a lot about me from Mary Kay and Ralph Baker. I sat out in the waiting room and listened to her talking to someone on the telephone in her office. She was saying, "I don't care that you were not the one telling the tale, you listened and that is just as bad. You are OUT of the company. You knew the rules and refused to abide by them. I hope you learned your lesson." I couldn't believe my ears. She had just kicked out a top sales producer because she had listened to negative gossip. She didn't pass the buck to someone like Richard, as Mary Kay did. She handled it herself.

Completely unruffled by this incident, she came to the door and asked me to come into her office. I had to step over piles of

307

paperwork on the floor in order to get to a chair in front of her desk. "Now, what is this about?" she asked bluntly. I took a deep breath and jumped in. I told her what I knew about her and her company. I explained that when Mary Kay sent me to California on a recruiting mission that I didn't know it was her people I was trying to recruit. At this she just smiled and nodded.

Finally, I blurted out what I had come to ask. "Actually, Mary, what I really want to know is if you think Mary Kay is really a Christian or is this all just an act?" Mary just sat looking at me for what seemed like an hour. The only sound penetrating the silence was that of several clocks ticking. No doubt these clocks were part of her line. Just as I decided she wasn't going to respond, she answered. "I'm sure you know that I have known Mary Kay for many years. We have been friends, business associates, and sometimes—even family. I think that Mary Kay's heart is in the right place. I believe the problem with her is that when she prays, she can't wait for God to handle her request. She just has to take things into her own hands. I have seen this trait cause her unbelievable hardships, yet she continues to operate in this way."

We talked for a little while longer, and then I thought about what she had said all the way home. I decided that she had just explained Mary Kay. In spite of her talk to me about how faith overcomes fear, out of fear of losing her company Mary Kay had jumped in and set this entire horrendous conflict in motion. Even after realizing this truth, I still had one belief that I never said to anyone out loud. I was convinced that Mary Kay was destined to be a major player in the cosmetic business. Of course, I was hoping that Beauticontrol would be as well.

Weeks went by. In spite of everything, our little company was holding its own, and business was growing regardless of the controversy. Ned and I had each other and our two wonderful children, and Marjie and I depended on each other daily to keep our spirits up.

Late one evening after being out all day recruiting with one of our consultants, I was driving home alone. It was almost midnight, and I was on a lonely road in an undeveloped section of

Dallas. A steady rain had begun to fall, making me wish I were safely home in bed. All I could see through my headlights were an empty road, scrub grass, and a faint outline of a few deserted buildings. Suddenly, my car began to shake and I had to wrench it to a complete stop. It was a creepy part of town to be stuck in, and when I turned the engine off, the silence was spooky. The only sound was the patter of the rain hitting the top of my car. I shivered and thought, Ned always said something like this could happen.

When I glanced into my rearview mirror, I saw another pair of headlights pull up right behind me. I hadn't noticed the car there before so I was startled. The man got out of his car and approached my door. My heart raced as I rolled down the window a crack. The doors were locked, but I couldn't go anywhere even if I had to. This was many years before the cell phone was invented, so there was literally only one thing left for me to do—pray.

The man seemed friendly enough. "You've got a flat," he said, paying no attention to the rain soaking through his clothing. "If you have a spare tire, I'll change it for you." His smile was kind, and I couldn't help feeling relieved that he was there. He must have seen the fear in my eyes, for he said reassuringly, "You won't even have to get out of the car. Just give me the key, and I'll do the rest."

Feeling foolish, I pushed the key through the crack in the window. He changed the tire in a few minutes and was back at the window handing me my car keys. I was so grateful to him that I asked for his name and address so I could send his wife some of our products. He was soaked to the skin by this time, and he quickly reached into his pocket and took out his business card. He wrote his home number on the back and gave it to me. Inside the car, I turned the light on so I could read it, but before I could turn it over, the words on the front grabbed my attention. They read: The Dale Simpson Detective Agency.

"You're following me!" I shrieked.

He was shocked to realize the mistake he'd just made. Leaving the telltale card in my wet, shaking hand, he rushed back to his car and drove away before I could even get mine started. All the way home, I was tormented by a sense of foreboding. I didn't know how long he had been following me, but I was certain that his agency would not stop just because I had discovered them. Mary Kay was so tight with her money that adding the expense of a private detective was a serious step for her. This meant that everything was escalating to a whole new level of adversity. Before, the lawyers seemed to be doing the fighting for all of us while the players stayed out of the fray. People in the community were talking, and that was hurtful, but it wasn't threatening. I had never before experienced anything like this, and I knew I was out of my league.

That night when I arrived home, I told Ned what had happened. We stood in our living room looking at each other. "How did we get here?" we asked. Neither of us could answer. All we were trying to do was start a little company and provide a living for our family. We had never thought of ourselves as being in the big time. It wasn't as if this was General Motors going up against Ford.

At work, I discussed the incident with a few people besides Marjie, but I didn't announce it to the whole world. It had a sobering effect on everyone who heard it. Up until now, there had been a certain element of fun, even in the midst of the controversy. Who was going to outsell whom? Which company would people think had the best product? We thought there just wasn't enough money involved to take it too seriously. It had seemed more like a competition, and even after the hearing I hoped the acrimony would die down and matters would be settled in a civilized way. But hiring a private detective was an indication of just how seriously Mary Kay continued to take the problem of "us" being in business against "them."

It was striking a real chord of fear and resentment, and I couldn't help remembering the expression on her face in the courtroom when she was forced to reveal how many times she had been married. We had dared to expose her private life and to take what she considered to be hers. The blow we struck by separating from her was deep, and she thought she was fighting for her life. In a flash of comprehension, I knew that Mary Crowley had no idea just how dangerous Mary Kay could be.

And yet in the days that followed, our apprehension died down gradually. Our company was making steady progress. People loved the products and new recruits were coming out of the woodwork. Our recruit in Tennessee was showing signs of being a top producer, and Barbara Stubblefield, in Wyoming, continued to produce like a storm front moving in; nobody could stop her. Even in our own backyard, Juanita Grable continued to extend the business into other areas, which ultimately resulted in recruiting Kathy Ray from Detroit, who began selling Beauticontrol there. With all the business at hand, we were able momentarily to put Mary Kay and Dale Simpson's detectives out of our minds.

Marjie and I were thrilled with all the new recruits. I had always known that since I had brought all those women to Mary Kay, I could do the same for my own company, but actually seeing it happen before my eyes at times caused a dizzying rush of feeling to sweep over me. Between the tension of potential success and the tension of the ongoing battle with Mary Kay, Marjie and I ended up leaning on each other for support. Each of us brought different qualities to the playing field, something we counted on to meet all the challenges of starting a new organization.

I was the ambitious one. It was in my nature to be a go-getter. Success was like a health tonic to me; the more it came to me, the more energized I was to keep succeeding. Marjie was the steadfast one, who knew how to tame random chaos into at least organized chaos. She needed me for motivation and encouragement, and I needed her for organization and day-to-day dependability. We had manufacturers to communicate with, sales material to design, orders to fill, salespeople to enlist and train, a newsletter to put out, stock to keep track of, customers to satisfy, bills to pay, and an office to run. Sometimes I thought lines of exhaustion were beginning to appear in our faces. Marjie was excellent at keeping track of routine details and making sure that no task fell between the cracks. In short, I was still the "girl with the golden words," and Marjie was the steady hand that kept the ship from sinking every time life punched a little hole in it.

In addition, we relied on each other for a great deal of emotional support. Because of the long workdays, we spent more time with each other than we did with our husbands. We became each other's mainstay, propping up sagging spirits whenever it was needed.

With all that was going on, I was still determined to stay true to my promise to myself and to God to cherish my precious miracle child, who the doctors thought would never live. I made a point of remaining at home part of the morning to be with Shannon while Marjie went into the office early to get the business of the day going. In turn, I stayed on later at night so she could go home and be with Stan, Sheryl, and Stan's mother, Anita, who still lived with them.

Sometimes I had to travel around the country holding meetings for the company. Many times whenever I was preparing for such a trip, both of my children would cry. Sharon, who was twelve years old at the time, was aware of the court case and was continually worried about Ned and me. On one evening, as I was preparing to leave for Detroit the next morning, Sharon came in and sat with me as I packed. She was quiet for a little while and then blurted out, "Mom, do you really have to go?"

"I need to, sweetheart, because it will help our sales, and it will only be for a few days," I replied. She let it go and soon returned to her room. I woke in the middle of the night, hearing her crying hysterically. I rushed to her room and wrapped my arms tightly around her. "You've had a bad dream; everything is okay," I said as I rocked her gently.

"Don't go, Mom, don't go" she sobbed. "I dreamed your plane crashed and you were killed." I knew instinctively that this was one time I had to do what she asked. I called Marjie, and she went on the trip for me. Whenever there was something I just couldn't do, Marjie was there to pinch hit. She was that kind of person.

One afternoon, she and I were calling on suppliers. As we finished with the last one, I noticed that we weren't far from my house, and I felt a momentary need to stop by and see Shannon. Something about holding my baby close always brought me enormous comfort and strength. Fifteen minutes later Marjie and I were approaching my front door. Re Re (Shannon's translation for Marie), was on the porch with the door open before I even had my key out. The expression on her face told me immediately that she was agitated.

"What's wrong?" I asked, instantly sensing danger.

She motioned toward the den, where a man was standing next to the telephone. Shannon was jabbering away in baby talk as she toddled around at his feet. He was nondescript and not particularly threatening to look at. The only thing extraordinary about him was the fact that I had never seen him before in my life, and he was in my den holding my telephone in his hand. What was even more peculiar, was that he had unscrewed the mouthpiece.

"Who is that Marie?" I asked. "What is he doing here?"

"He said he needed to use the phone." In those days of lower crime and higher neighborliness, people did let strangers in to use the phone. "But," Marie said, "when he picked up the receiver, he said something was wrong with it, and he had to fix it."

He's installing a listening device, I thought as I sized up the situation. He paused to look at me, his glance sweeping over me like a searchlight. I bolted across the room and jerked the phone from his hand. Fury traveled through my body, yet my voice sounded calm as I heard myself say, "You have ten seconds to get out of here or I'm calling the police."

He didn't take five. He dashed to the door and was gone. The controversy had permeated our church, our business, and our life with friends and neighbors. Now it was in my home. After all Mary Kay had said to me over the years about the sanctity of faith and the family, my disappointment in her was profound. How could she stoop to this? I had thought all along that fear was causing her to act out of character since the lawsuit had begun. And now I had to admit that I was simply kidding myself.

The very impression of seeing my helpless daughter at the feet of a strange man sent a cold tremor up my spine. Up until then, the only people who had been threatened were Ned and me. That was scary enough, but as adults we could take care of ourselves. Now my children were involved, and that represented a seismic change that was totally unacceptable to me. An explosion of anger raged through me and filled my voice. "I am not sitting still for this! They are not going to run me out of town."

If they were trying to scare me, it worked, but not the way they wanted it to. Far from paralyzing my efforts, this incident only galvanized me to work harder and to move full steam ahead in the fight with Mary Kay.

The four of us, as well as everyone else named in the lawsuit, were beginning to get the picture: there was no safe place. If an outsider could work his way into my home in the middle of the day and stand within a few feet of my baby girl, where was I to hide? We all felt very breakable, like thin glass.

We spent a great deal of time discussing the extreme measures Mary Kay was taking to put us out of business. The very intensity of her fervor didn't make sense to us. From month to month, we were having a hard time scraping up a stack of quarters to pay the office rent. Why couldn't she just leave us alone and let us struggle through the basics of building our modest little company?

I remembered again Mary Crowley's assessment of Mary Kay, which in turn triggered the memory of the story of Jacob and Esau. Rebekah had to take matters into her own hands. She could not leave it up to God, and the problems that resulted lasted for generations. It appeared now that Mary Kay was headed in the same direction.

Over the years, I came to learn that this was not uncommon in the cosmetics industry. Where this much money, power, and glory were to be gained, there were no measures that were considered too extreme to use in order to win.

As the days passed after the telephone incident, amazingly we were once again able to fall back into the routine of life. We occupied virtually the entire second floor of our building; only one small office across from Marjie's and my offices wasn't ours, and the owner said it was being used for storage. Since Marjie came in earlier, I sometimes worked into the night alone, and Ned and Stan were occasionally there also taking care of their end of the business. One evening, we heard movement in the unused office. "If that's a rat," Ned said, "it sure is a big one," and then we all forgot about it.

In the next few days, we began to notice a man slipping in and out of that office. If he was trying to escape our notice, he could hardly have done a worse job. Walking with a hat drawn down over his forehead and his collar pulled up so that we couldn't see his face, he looked like an ad for rent-a-cop. Whenever he came in or out, he actually tiptoed. There was a sullen, caged look to him that did anything but make him invisible. I don't think we wanted to admit to ourselves what was happening, so for as long as we could, we did our best to ignore him.

As a born optimist, every time something happened I could not help thinking that it was just an isolated incident. In spite of my fears that the harassment would go on and on, my true belief was, "Things will get better," because that was my theme song. All my life I had held that attitude. Perhaps I inherited it from my family or perhaps it came from my religious beliefs, but many a time my eternal optimism had gotten me through rough spots in life. And so I hoped it would do the same for me during this trying period. Looking back I am thankful that I didn't have a clue how bad it was going to get before it got better.

One day, the man knocked something over in the spare office space, and we heard the noise. We could ignore the man's presence no longer. That evening, when I knew the office should be empty because the cleaning people were already gone, there was a light under the door. I was alone. As I watched a shadow pass behind the door, I felt my scalp prickle. As quickly as I could, I gathered my things and left the building.

The next morning, I talked to Marjie, and together, we confronted the building's owner. He finally admitted that "they" had offered him a lot of rent money for just that tiny little office. How could he turn them down? When we asked who "they" were, he didn't seem to have an exact answer. Finally, we tracked down the truth: the Dale Simpson Detective Agency had rented the room and placed a man in there to watch our every move.

We were not about to pick up and move out of our offices. For one thing, we had enough on our hands. For another, we had no intention of being run out of town. And for a third, it wouldn't do us any good. Wherever we went, they would hound us there, too. So we kept on working where we were, but we put continuous pressure on the owner of the building to get rid of the stranger. Soon after that, the man was not spotted again. The detective agency probably had not needed much convincing; now that we knew who the man was, he was certainly not going to find out very much. Ultimately, it was just one more incident to let us know that we couldn't relax. Each time we began to breathe a little easier, the battering ram would strike again.

Ned and I discussed the incidents many times and tried to comfort each other. The one thing we both naively assumed was that the worst was now over. "After all," I said to Ned, "what else could they possibly do?"

Because I almost always had to work late, Re Re was the one to have dinner ready when Ned came home, and he would eat with the girls. When Re Re first came to work with us, she made it clear that she was not a "fancy cook," but that she could manage basic cooking. And we loved her basic food, especially her beans and rice.

One evening I was able to leave the office early. "Surprise," I called as I walked through the door of our home.

"Mommy," Sharon and Shannon yelled, running to meet me. Seeing the joy on their faces because I was home brought a lump to my throat. Sharon said, "Oh, Mom, I'm so glad you're home; there's something we have to do tonight."

"Okay. Sharon," I answered as I leaned over to pick up Shannon, who was holding her hands up and waiting patiently. "But first, what's for dinner?" I asked, looking at Ned. He was standing a little apart from the group, quietly watching the exchange. He chuckled as he said, "Now that may be the real surprise. I haven't looked yet." As always, he came to me and hugged me tight, massaging my shoulders. Love and gratitude welled up in my throat again as the four of us clung together.

"Well, let's find out what our feast will be," I said, already moving toward the stove where a large covered pot was waiting. Ned beat me to it and lifted the lid. He stared into the pot in silence.

"Well, what is it?" I asked. "You won't believe this, but would you like to try to guess?" he said laughing. At that, we pushed him out of the way and looked down into the pot. There sat four large green avocados, boiled and waiting to be our dinner. We laughed until tears ran down our faces. We made a pact that Re Re would never know of our reaction. Ned ran up the street for Goff's hamburgers, which we consumed with a side dish of laughter for another hour. This is still one of our favorite family stories to share whenever we get together. We all agreed, however, that we should have tasted them. They could have been delicious.

Later, Ned, Sharon, Shannon and I settled in for one of our favorite pastimes—just enjoying each other's company. After dinner, we cleaned up the kitchen together and talked about the day's events. For the first time in a long while, our house felt like a safe and normal home.

Before joining Mary Kay Cosmetics, I had always made dresses for Sharon. With the petticoats, satin belts, and matching hair decorations, she was one of the best-dressed girls in school and in church. I had started a dress for her months before, and it was still unfinished. This was the project that she wanted to finish tonight. It was brown plaid with an empire waist. I cannot honestly say that I was in love with that dress, but as I watched Sharon pirouette around in front of the mirror admiring herself and telling me how perfect it was, I was filled with contentment. It took so little to make her happy. Ned, who most people considered to be quiet and reserved, was at his best in this setting. He said in his finest teasing voice, "What's so important, Sharon, that you have to have this dress by tomorrow? You aren't trying to impress Mark Crouch, are you?"

"Oh, Dad, that's not it at all," she replied testily, "It's just that I wanted something new to wear for our home room party tomorrow." Ned and I exchanged glances over her head that silently agreed, "She wants to impress him alright."

As I finished the detail on Sharon's dress, he played cards with her. They went through three games that night: Old Maid, Go Fish, and Crazy Eight. While I listened to them laugh and argue whenever the other person scored a point, I tried, as I had come to do often, to wrap the feeling safely around me and store it away. I would bring it out and hold it close to me whenever fear crept in again. That time was to be sooner than I thought.

Sharon's bedroom was in the front of the house with her window facing the street. I had much of the say in the decorating for the rest of the room, but the large closet with double doors was her private domain. She hung her favorite pictures and homecoming corsages everywhere, and she had a large make-up mirror hung at head level. She had just begun to wear a little make-up at this point, and the one thing she wouldn't go anywhere without was her eyeliner. From the time Shannon had learned to walk, Sharon had her trained. In the morning when Sharon woke up, she would yell, "Now, Shannon" into the other room. My little toddler would then jump up and fetch a glass of water for my budding teenager to use for her cake eyeliner. Every day when this happened I thought, *She's trained like a flea.*

That night, I watched my eldest daughter take off her eyeliner with cream and get ready for bed. From the very beginning of starting Beauticontrol, Ned and I had let both Sharon and Shannon stay up until we were all ready to call it a night. Our lives were so erratic; this was the only way we could ensure spending time with them.

Our little ritual remained the same. We put Shannon to bed first, and after kisses from everyone and prayers, which included a blessing for the dog, Sniffles No. 2, we added "Good night, sleep tight, don't let the bedbugs bite." It didn't matter that all over America, other parents were probably repeating the same old saying to their children. For me it was deeply personal. Sharon was too old for the baby stuff, yet every night she still mouthed the words to me, "I wouldn't let you go for a dollar." This evening was like any other, and it was with a sense of peace that Ned and I went to our room.

We had our own ritual before going to sleep. After a relaxing shower, I pulled out a long gown that I knew Ned particularly liked. He used to buy me ultra short "baby doll" pajamas as gifts, but with the children always present he had switched styles. I have always liked the idea of looking as glamorous as possible when going to bed. Ned saw me more at this time than any other, and I wanted him to carry that image of me with him. After we adjusted our pillows and turned on the radio to a station that played soft music, I handed Ned the product that he liked best. It was the creamy body lotion that he thought had the most sensuous smell of any. I positioned one foot so that he could apply the body lotion and begin the massage. No matter how tired I was, this ritual always relaxed me and renewed my spirit. We looked at each other and smiled. God was in His heaven, and all was right with the world.

The first sharp sound of shattering glass is what penetrated my deep sleep, and it was followed by Sharon's piercing screams. Ned and I bounded into her bedroom where we were faced with a scene I hope never to see again. My twelve-year-old was glued to the headboard sucking in huge gulps of air as if she were drowning in her own breath. All around her on the bed and floor were fragments of glass, and in the midst of them on the floor was a beer bottle, virtually intact. Her pillow was littered with glass shards, which moments before must have been inches from her face. I stood there frozen in the moment, unable to move. Instead of taking action, I looked at the bottle and thought, *Isn't that strange, the beer bottle sailed through the window and shattered it, but the bottle didn't break.* I just stood there in a daze and vaguely wondered how that happened.

Ned stood beside me in the same state. Within a few minutes I was able to let in the whole spectrum, and as I did so, adrenaline crashed through my body in sickening waves.

"You don't think . . ." Ned began.

"I absolutely do think!" I yelled. A new fury had taken over my entire being.

"But how could they have known where to throw the bottle?"

"Don't you remember that Richard and Mary Kay were at our house that time? Richard went through the entire house. He knows exactly where everything is."

"Yes, but how could the bottle have been thrown precisely enough to avoid hitting Sharon's head?"

"Ned," I answered with deadly calm, "they weren't trying to miss her head."

I dusted the glass shards off the bed the best I could and tried to comfort my trembling daughter. It was with a sick relief that I examined her and found that she was unharmed. Cradling her head against my chest, I looked up at Ned. "You and Stan were actually right about Richard. He isn't as smart as the rest of us thought he was. If he were, he NEVER would have put our children at risk!"

"We can't prove this, so I guess there's no point in calling the police," Ned said.

I agreed the police would probably just say it was done by a bunch of teenagers. But then, with more fury than I had ever felt in my life, I said, "I'm through with being on the defensive! This is the final blow! If they want war, then they've got it."

Far from flattening my will, this one act galvanized me into action in a way I had never known before. It triggered an almost superhuman sense of purpose that I would make Beauticontrol a major competitor to Mary Kay Cosmetics, or I would die trying. Years later when I looked back on this incident, I had an epiphany. I realized that violence of any kind sealed the end of a relationship for me.

From then on, I experienced an explosion of strength that was contagious. Among all of us who were in on the ground floor of this faltering little company, there was a huge new surge of determination. Ironically, I thought of something I had learned from Mary Kay: "Once you make a definite and resolute commitment, life colludes to help you succeed. People and events you never dreamed of seem to pop up everywhere and conspire to help you achieve your goal."

And so it was with us. I decided that come hell or high water, Beauticontrol would survive. Before, we had kept ourselves busy putting out fires, defending ourselves against our attackers. Now the tables had turned. We kept an active account of every single incident in which Mary Kay or her people violated the injunction. Every time a report came in that Mary Kay or her people were saying that we stole, cheated, or lied, we turned it over to our lawyers and they took legal action. Ignoring the expense, we fought fire with fire. While it didn't stop the talk, it definitely made it harder for Mary Kay's company.

In a way this also made it more difficult for our people on the front lines: our salespeople who were the most active in the community. In addition to bearing the brunt of the rumors, we now had them relating every little detail to us, including time, place, and person. We found out later that poor Jean Rochelle had to deal with these incidences several times a day, and it was taking its toll on her.

We were also busy on other fronts. We told anyone who would listen—friends, relatives, customers, potential recruits, and business acquaintances—every dirty deed they heaped upon us. After the deed was related, the person would usually say, "Well, do you think Mary Kay is behind this?"

We answered simply, "What do you think?" and left it at that. We were confident enough to let people form their own opinions.

And it worked. For the longest time, many people had been sitting on the fence, but not anymore. With the spreading of information of how far Mary Kay and her people were taking this, the tide of public opinion was beginning to turn in our favor. Little by little, we could sense that people saw this as a fight between David and Goliath, and there was no question as to which one was the hulking giant. We were the underdog, and suddenly, people were rooting for us. Public opinion, we were fully aware, was important. It was about time that we learned to use it in the fight of our life.

People everywhere love a good scandal, and everyone who was a part of this one got their two cents in whenever they could. I can honestly say that during this period, there wasn't a dull moment.

And yet, as we stepped up the pressure, it caused another backlash, for Mary Kay's side felt compelled to accelerate their campaign as well. They brought out the big guns and launched a stronger attack. A horrible event awaited us, and we didn't even see it coming.

CHAPTER TWENTY-TWO

The Ultimate Tragedy

When we changed our method of dealing with Mary Kay from trying to avoid conflict to jumping into the middle of it, public opinion began to shift quickly in our favor. I told every person in our company about each dirty deed Mary Kay pulled, and they spread the story far and wide. Mary Kay had finally gone too far. It didn't matter who in her company actually ordered the beer bottle to be thrown through the window, ultimately the buck stopped with her. No one seemed to approve of a tactic involving innocent children in a fight between two companies, as we were certain she had done.

As a direct result of this new approach, our sales and recruiting continued to grow exponentially. And because of this turn of events, Martha Weddle, who was still smarting from her humiliation by Mary Kay, became bolder in her recruiting approach. Even though we had a temporary injunction against contacting Mary Kay's consultants, which Marjie and I strictly honored, Martha decided to call one of her recruits who was still with Mary Kay. The young woman also happened to be the daughter of Gordon McLendon, the owner of multiple radio stations in the Dallas area. When she realized it was Martha calling, she secretly taped their entire conversation and immediately turned it over to Mary Kay. And of course Mary Kay hauled us back into court because of Martha's violation of the temporary injunction.

But we didn't accept this action lying down. Nell Davis had reported to us that a Mary Kay consultant was telling Nell's acquaintances that Jackie Brown had stolen the formulas from Mary Kay. And some of the people told were willing to testify in court on our behalf. Since spreading such rumors was also forbidden in the injunction, we quickly served Mary Kay for violating it as well. The judge slapped both of our hands and reminded us that the injunction was to be adhered to exactly as stated.

As for Martha, who had come out with both guns blazing in her search for new recruits, she simply put both guns back into her holster—at least for a while. Although there were several more trips back to court before the temporary injunction was made permanent, we soon realized it was a waste of time and money to risk violating it. Instead, we had to work smarter, and we constantly sought new and creative ways to outfox Mary Kay. While the fight added extra pressure that took away time we could have spent growing our own company faster, everyone soon learned to cope with the constant need to explain the whole mess. Everyone that is, except Jean Rochelle.

Jean had somehow gotten into a hotbed of bickering with Mary Kay consultants. They called her constantly, telling her that by being with our company she was associating with liars and thieves. Almost daily, Jean was in my office or on the phone with me, crying about the harassment. I explained over and over to her that we had already been to court over this, and we'd found it was better to simply avoid confrontations whenever possible. I assured her that everything would be okay in the end, but my words had no effect.

Jean seemed to be in a constant state of hysteria. One day when she was in my office going over all of this again, I told her I was deeply concerned about her and nothing was worth this kind of frustration. Then I went on to say in spite of the fact she had done so well with us, it might not be the job for her.

"But this job was supposed to save me from the life I had," she cried. "It was to give me something to feel good about. Instead it's done just the opposite."

As soon as she left, Marjie came into my office. She had overheard most of the conversation and as a counselor was deeply concerned. "There's something more going on with her besides her problems with us," she said. "I didn't like the sound of it."

"I know, Marjie. I just hate that we are a part of it at all. Every area of her life seems to be stressful. I've heard it's not the mountain that gets you, but the grain of sand in your shoe, and I think that's it with Jean. All the little things have stacked up against her."

"No, I don't think that's what it is," Marjie insisted. "I think she may be mentally unstable. She really needs to seek professional help."

I told her that was a good idea and asked her to talk with Jean about it at the next opportunity. Marjie agreed and said she would think of someone Jean could call.

Marjie never had the chance to give her the advice.

The very next day, on my way to work, I was listening to the radio. Suddenly, I heard a man's deep voice proclaim. "Some years ago, there was a man whose business was tanning hides. As he turned stiff, ugly hide into soft pieces of leather, like gloves, he wondered, 'If you can do that with old stiff hides, why can't you do the same with human skin?' From this original discovery, evolved Mary Kay Cosmetics."

I was so stunned by the commercial I almost hit another car before I could regain control. I pulled off the road as quickly as I could and changed radio stations. This was all I could take. But the same announcement was playing there too. And then, I tried another and yet another. The commercial was being blitzed over every one of Gordon McLendon's radio stations. It was cleverly worded so that it barely escaped the terms of the injunction, told as if it was simply a fictional story and not as the actual history of the product. I was so shaken that the rest of the drive to the office was a blur.

Marjie was waiting for me when I drove up, and I knew immediately she'd heard the commercial, too. "What are we going to do now?" she asked in the most depressed tone I had ever heard from her. "The phone is ringing off the wall, and Jean Rochelle has already called twice."

Knowing how devastating this would be to Jean, I said a silent prayer, "Please Lord, help her cope with this until we can find a way to help too." By the time I made it to my office, she was on the phone again, crying hysterically. While I couldn't really understand all she was saying, I did make out a few words between sobs, "I just can't do this anymore."

Before I had a chance to respond, she hung up the phone. A horrible feeling came over me that Jean was in a dangerous state of mind. But then I shook it off, telling myself I was over-reacting.

Marjie and I stared at each other for several minutes, in shock over the new development. I told her that we had to do what we had always done: not to show fear. We'd call Brad and get his advice, but we had to remember that the worse thing we could do was panic. Marjie nodded, and for the rest of the day we talked with consultants.

Then we set up a meeting to discuss how we would deal with the matter. We decided to use the same game plan we'd been using. When our customers asked how on earth Mary Kay could use our story this way, our reply would be: "Was the commercial worded like a fictional story, or did it use names and facts?" And, when they admitted there were no facts, we suggested they call Mary Kay's company and ask if it was a true story; if so, what was the name of the hide tanner. We never found out how many of them took our advice, but the suggestion seemed to settle their concern, and the number of questions declined.

Weary from discussing what effect Mary Kay's new advertising blitz might have on us, Ned and I went to bed early. Sometime after midnight, the ringing of the phone woke us starkly. It was Melba Bowerman. Jean Rochelle, her sister-in-law, had committed suicide by putting a gun into her mouth and pulling the trigger. I was so stunned from the news that I couldn't think straight. The only other thing I remember about the conversation was that Melba said she would call me later with information about the funeral.

Ned had heard it all and was watching me anxiously as I hung up the phone. Without saying a word, he got out of bed and went downstairs to make coffee. There would be no more sleep that night. He came back with two steaming cups, and we propped ourselves up in bed and drank it in silence; each of us trying to make sense out of what had happened.

I don't know how much time passed before Ned finally asked, "This is the worst thing that could possibly have happened. Do you think we can survive it?"

Even though I had thought that Jean was in a dangerous state of mind, I had never expected this, and the shock left me speechless. I felt like I had sunk into a deep, dark hole, and I had to fight my way to the surface before I could answer him. "I don't know how we can."

I didn't call Marjie until the next morning. I wanted her to have one last night of peaceful sleep. After I related the sparse information I had been given, we decided to wait until we got to work to discuss it further.

But once we were seated in my office later in the morning, there seemed to be nothing we could say to make it any better. So we sat in silence until finally Marjie said, "The feud with Mary Kay has gone WAY too far."

Still in shock, I had to wind myself up in order to respond, "Yes, it has, and it's got to stop." She didn't reply and for the rest of the day we went through the motions of doing business as usual as best we could.

Suicide is toxic and practically unbearable, because of the tragedy and also the guilt that we all felt. Surely, we could have done something to prevent it.

Melba finally called to say the funeral would be in four days and gave us the location. She explained that because it was a suicide, all kinds of tests had to be run, and that's why it would take so long to put her to rest. Marjie and I decided to go together, and for the next four days we tried to block out the horror from our minds.

I was struck by the strangeness of my own reaction. I had always shed tears at the drop of a hat. But now when a flood of tears would have helped to wash away the pain, none came. How could this be? It was the ultimate tragedy and might prove to be the kind of pain that nothing could ease.

We were in a daze while waiting for the funeral, until something happened to shock us back into reality. When Dathene walked in for the first time after the tragedy, she stopped in the reception and said, "Why is it so quiet in here? It feels like somebody just died." I walked quickly to my office, leaving Marjie to explain it all. I just couldn't handle it. Marjie also took most of the calls from our people asking for details. She explained as simply and briefly as possible about Jean's problems. But they were just empty words because there weren't any words that could make sense of the tragedy.

After the funeral service was over, Marjie and I were silent again as we drove back to our offices. There are times when there's nothing you can say. Finally I did come up with one comment: "I will never forget the sight or the sounds of those little girls crying for their mother." And I never have. Marjie nodded in agreement and I continued. "I've been thinking about it, and I know what we have to do to ease the constant conflict with Mary Kay."

Surprised, Marjie stepped on the brakes, turned to me, and asked, "What's that?"

"We have to get out of Dodge," I said firmly and then continued. "Our problems are so intense because we are all in the same area. I think if we grow faster outside this area, it will reduce the tension tremendously.

I could tell Marjie was biting her tongue to prevent reacting too harshly. "Since we barely have enough money to survive here from week to week, how do you plan to get enough together to develop outside areas?" she asked, struggling not to raise her voice. I opened my mouth to answer, but she continued, "I guess you're going to say God will show us the way."

I knew she was being facetious, but I answered seriously. "If our company is meant to survive, He will show us the way." I suppose she just didn't have an answer to that one, so we drove the rest of the way without further discussion.

After the kids were asleep that night and we were getting ready for bed, I asked Ned not to turn on the TV because I wanted to talk about something. Because of their work, Ned and Stan didn't attend the funeral, and now Ned looked at me with understanding and said, "I know the funeral must have been awful." I assured him that it was and added, "But I want to talk about something else." Always a man of few words, he just waited for me to begin. I related what I had told Marjie, that we had to develop our business outside the area. I also told him as plainly as I knew how that I would no longer pursue money at all costs, because this cost was far too high, and I felt that's what we'd done. Because of it, four children would live the rest of their lives without their mother, and there was not enough money in the world to justify that.

As Ned continued to listen, I told him I wanted to go to Texarkana to hold a meeting with the few sales people we had there. After the meeting, I would go on to the Franks' house and spend the night with them. I'd been thinking about the wonderful sense of peace I always felt in their home, and I desperately needed to feel that now. Without a word, Ned simply nodded and took my hand as he'd done so many times before. We continued to sit in the darkness, lost in our own thoughts.

I drove to Texarkana for my meeting on a Friday afternoon. The group was small but surprisingly enthusiastic, in view of the fact they knew all about the tragedy. Their sales had been good so they had a lot to "crow" about. By the time I left the meeting I was already feeling better. I continued the short drive to the Franks' house. I could smell chicken frying as I turned onto their street, and a sense of comfort seeped into my whole being. As I walked through the door into Mrs. Franks' waiting arms, the love and peace that seemed to always fill their house filled me as well. I breathed a sigh of intense relief and silently prayed, "Thank you, Lord, for these people and this place." Even though the visit was short, it was exactly what I needed.

I began my trip back with new determination to build our company outside the Dallas area. Because most of our business was concentrated in Dallas it seemed almost ridiculous to believe we could drop our endeavors there and move into the unknown. This meant that ultimately we would be almost giving up the Dallas area to Mary Kay. I realized it sounded impossible when I said it out loud, but I knew we would find a way to do just that.

Only a few weeks later, we had to make another trip to the courthouse. I don't even remember which one of us was the culprit for violating the injunction, but during the hearing, I got the opportunity to tell Judge Walker about the tragedy. When I said Jean Rochelle had shot herself over the conflict with Mary Kay, Judge Walker leaned over the bench and cried, "Dead?" Everyone in the courtroom sat motionless, and even Mary Kay looked shocked and concerned. Apparently, she hadn't heard about the tragedy. The message was plain to everyone present: the cost of this conflict had become far too high. Thinking back, I believe that this was the turning point for all of us. From this point on, we all seemed to try harder to keep the peace.

I thought constantly about how we could build new areas where we didn't have many sales people, and cheaply at that. We had tried newspaper ads, and while we had calls, something was missing. We weren't reaching the kind of people we now had that were doing so well. These included Anna Kendall in Houston, Juanita Grable in Fort Worth, Barbara Stubblefield in Cheyenne, Wyoming, and Nina Harris in west Texas. These people had already qualified as directors and were steadily growing. My goal was to help them grow faster and to recruit others just like them. Martha Weddle was still the only director in Dallas proper at the time, and she was also building outside the area.

In addition to these five groups, people outside the area, who had been in Marjie's unit, and mine, were considered to be part of the office unit. So the entire company at this point consisted of six units.

After racking my brain until it hurt, I came up with the idea of holding a special meeting myself in each of the four outside areas once a month. The meeting would have to be so exciting that everyone would want to participate. Three of the areas were within driving distance. The only area I would have to fly to was Wyoming. All of this meant the idea would be cheap, which was a major requirement.

I finally came up with a plan. I could buy a $50 gift for $25 at the wholesale market. And at that time, 1966, it would be top-of-the-line merchandise. Since I would be starting in November, I chose Christmas items as the prizes for the first month of the contest. The winners could choose between an angel centerpiece, made of crystal, that held two tall candles or an elegant china dessert set, hand-painted with green holly and red berries.

There would be a recruiting contest in each area, and the winner of the prize would be the consultant who had recruited the most new people for the month. Directors would not participate since they would benefit from the increased sales. I talked Marjie into doing the same for Martha's unit and for the office unit, which would be done through the mail. We had already reached the stage that when the president or the vice president came to a meeting, it created added excitement, much as it had when Mary Kay had done the same. It all boiled down to the fact that when an executive of the company presented the winner with an elegant prize, accompanied by lavish praise, it was extra special.

While I wanted to build outside areas, we certainly could not afford to abruptly begin to ignore our local sales people because they were still our bread and butter. For a while we had to have the income from the sales in the Dallas area to pay for developing others. If the contest produced only two new recruits from each group, we would pick up twelve brand new people. And their first orders of $500 retail would produce about $6,000 in new retail sales. Because they would be primarily outside Dallas, the new people would be totally free of the Mary Kay mess. Their initial orders would more than justify the expense of the prizes for the contest.

It worked. The competitive spirit took hold and instead of just the twelve new people I was hoping for, we got sixteen. Of course, the prizes were elegantly wrapped and presented at the meetings with great fanfare. And there had been no haggling with Mary Kay people for the entire month. Even in Dallas, excitement centered on the contest. The successes from it whetted my appetite. I found myself thinking non-stop about how we could do it on a much larger scale and in areas where we didn't have any current consultants. But Christmas was upon us, and I knew it would be January before we could pursue the matter further.

Ned decided we needed to make a quick trip to visit his mother in Florida. He hadn't been there since his father died, and the family had not even seen Shannon yet. Even though it was long, it was a fun trip. We sang Christmas carols and played "bird on a wire." When we spotted a bird and yelled out bird on a wire, Shannon laughed and clapped her hands. We got so involved in the game, the eighteen-hour trip seemed to fly by.

Of course I took all of our cosmetic supplies and recruiting materials, just in case someone would be interested. As I'd hoped, Ned's two sisters, Betty Millergren and Mary Louise Smith, were. So in addition to having a great family time, we came home with two more new recruits—the first ones in the state of Florida.

Not to be outdone, when Marjie went to New Mexico, she recruited her mother. Another new state to be added our credit. We decided that when the time came for meetings in those areas, we would switch so it would be business rather than just family. Marjie would hold Florida meetings, and I would hold the ones in New Mexico.

We had the company Christmas party in our home, and we invited the entire local group of consultants and their families. And because Josie was still our only office employee, we invited her and her husband as well. Although it wasn't nearly as lavish as the ones we had at the country club the years before, it was even more fun. After a traditional Christmas meal, we gathered around the fireplace and told stories about Christmases past. Martha Weddle and some of the others had beautiful singing voices and entertained us with their favorite songs. For a little while the sadness from Jean Rochelle's death was forgotten, and hope began to grow anew in our hearts; it was the perfect gift for us all.

Dathene stayed behind until the others had gone and presented Marjie and me with small Christmas presents. She continued this practice for all the years to follow. Dathene earned a good salary, but her addiction to junk shopping kept her constantly strapped for cash. Still, she found a way to buy us small gifts. Because we knew she didn't have an extra dime to her name, we were deeply touched.

Soon after the first of the New Year, we got a call from Betty Millergren in Florida. One of her new customers had told her the local TV station had a show where people could promote their products, and it only cost $35. It consisted of a five-minute interview that looked like a regular show and not a commercial, and during that time you could say anything you wanted about your business. As Marjie and I discussed the huge potential of being on a television show, Marjie commented, "You know, Jackie, this just might be our answer for developing our business in outside areas."

I simply nodded, but there was no "might" about it. The minute I heard about it, I was as certain as I'd ever been in my life that God had just answered our prayers about how we could build our business outside Dallas.

As we'd agreed, Marjie would go to Florida to do the show and hold a meeting with Ned's sisters and with all the new recruits we hoped to get as well. We spent hours defining exactly what the five-minute show would consist of. Our beautiful set of cosmetics, on the cut-crystal tray, would be displayed in front of Marjie as she talked. The person doing the interview would ask her questions in the sequence we gave her.

First, Marjie would tell how the formulas were discovered—the hide tanner's story. Then, while showing the before-and-after pictures on the screen, she would talk about the problem each woman had and how our products had corrected it for her. She closed the interview by saying that anyone who called the telephone number on the screen, which belonged to an answering service, would receive a free facial with our remarkable products. Then she would add that we would also be interviewing for a few new consultants in the area to represent this exciting line.

Even before she finished the interview, the answering service was swamped with calls. Dozens of women booked clinics for facials, and many were also interested in becoming consultants. When Marjie called to tell me this, she was so excited she could hardly talk. We had just found our way we to develop the whole United States. It stemmed from this local TV show in Panama City, Florida, that cost only $35. This show became the prototype for ones that would later be held nationwide.

All television shows were done live at this time. Therefore, there was no room for error, and of course it was stressful. As it turned out, Marjie didn't enjoy it, although she continued to do it when necessary. I soon became the regular one on the program. I had done so many Mary Kay shows, I had learned to block out everything except the message I was there to impart. This was, of course, to sell the product and recruit new people. There was no time or energy spent on what people thought of me. Years later, I used this experience from appearing live on air when I sold cosmetics on QVC.

From extensive research, we learned that almost every television station in the entire country had a similar program available. The price for five minutes of time ranged from $35 to $50.

Because of the court order that enjoined Mary Kay from using the before-and-after pictures, as well as actual names of the people who developed the products, at last we didn't have to worry about Mary Kay competing with us in this fantastic new way of advertising. Sometimes miracles come in huge packages.

We first went to areas to do these shows where we already had sales people that could help handle the business, such as Lubbock and Houston, as well as New Mexico. With practice, the response increased, and we were on our way.

The experience with Jean Rochelle was always in the back of our minds, but it no longer totally consumed us. Periodically, the memory would pop up again, vividly. Just recently, my friend Melba told me that Jean's girls had contacted her asking for information that would revive memories of their mother. They wanted something of her to hold on to.

Although it had been over forty years since the tragedy, the grief and guilt returned, and felt new and raw all over again. But through the years when things like this happened, I learned to turn to the serenity prayer: "Lord grant me the serenity to accept the things I cannot change, the courage to change the things I can, and the wisdom to know the difference."

CHAPTER TWENTY-THREE

New Horizons

Television shows were the answer; they let us increase our business outside Dallas. Once we realized that, our company grew so fast, we had to pinch ourselves sometimes to see if we were dreaming. Although the travel meant extra work, there was less stress because the new areas we advertised in weren't embedded with Mary Kay consultants, which meant we didn't have to deal with constant questions about Mary Kay.

Our sales now brought in enough money that we didn't have to hold our breath from week to week to see if we were still in business. But the lawsuit remained in full force and was a constant expense, which meant we still didn't get to draw salaries. I tried not to think about how much money this venture was costing me and hoped it would someday be worth the sacrifice.

Even though the tension between our sales people and Mary Kay's had lessened because of our concentration on outside areas, she seemed determined to keep the lawsuit active. We felt it was her way of holding onto her people so they wouldn't come over to our side. As far as I know, none of our people ever left to go with her. It was three and one-half years before the temporary injunction became permanent. The permanent injunction simply made the temporary one final. Mary Kay could not use any of the facts about the actual history of Beauticontrol and could only tell the hide tanner's story as a fictional one. In addition, we had to leave each other's sales people alone. If the injunction was violated, we would still have to go back to court; but we would not otherwise have the constant ongoing legal expense.

The only reason Mary Kay agreed to the permanent resolution, even then, was probably because she wanted to go public with her stock, and she would have to list in the prospectus the fact we were suing her. Potential investors would demand full revelation of the circumstances, so Mary Kay finally decided she'd rather settle than fight that battle. But that didn't dissolve the tension and conflict between the two companies. Even today, both companies still have to try to explain the connection between them.

We quickly outgrew our offices. We had no space for new employees or for increasing the manufacturing area. As Stan conducted his insurance business around town, he looked for a place to fit our needs. He found that there were new buildings being constructed in the Great Southwest Industrial Park in Arlington, which was about fifteen miles from our present location and near the original Six Flags Over Texas Amusement Park. We decided on the location even though it would be a longer commute for Ned and me. The price was right, and we were elated that we could design the space exactly as we needed for offices and for manufacturing.

The building was near Six Flags Inn, which had wonderful meeting facilities for large groups and excellent food. The front of our building would be stone, in earth tones of gray, tan, and brown, and one entire side would be glass. Marjie and I would have garden areas just outside our offices. We could enjoy the flowers, the sunshine, and the rain, instead of being shut away in a dark space.

After we made a decision to go forward with the plan, Stan decided that since we had to hire someone anyway, he would quit the insurance business and take over the job of running the office and the lab, which meant that Marjie could help more with sales. Of course he would have to take a cut in pay, but they decided they could handle it, hoping that before long all of us could be properly remunerated for our efforts. Stan would join us full time after we moved into the new building. Ned was not happy that Stan would be full time in the company and he would not, but there no way he could also join us at this time. He couldn't take a cut in pay because we had to have his full salary so that we could keep Marie to look after Shannon.

He was doing well in his job, so for the time being he had to stay put.

About this same time we made another decision that was to be important to our future. We joined the Direct Sales Association (DSA). It was made up of the most respected companies in the nation who marketed their products through direct sales: companies like Avon, Tupperware, Home Interiors, Stanley Home Products, and of course Mary Kay. It wasn't an easy thing to do. We had to fill out extensive forms and provide references to prove our business practices were ethical.

As far as we knew, everything we did was on the up and up. But we were still nervous until we officially heard we'd been accepted. The DSA held their meetings at the best locations, and expenses incurred from attending them were tax deductible. Stan suggested that Ned and I attend the first one; he and Marjie would go later. I suspected this was to appease Ned's feelings over his joining the company first. The meeting Ned and I chose to attend was to be held in Boca Raton, Florida. We couldn't help fantasizing about running into Richard and Mary Kay there, but that was months away, and now we had to concentrate on our business.

Time passed quickly as Marjie and I continued to build outside areas. With each show, results improved, and we decided to try it in a larger city—Denver. We had to book the television time several months in advance, which gave us time to move and settle into our new office before we launched the campaign. Stan would have to hold down the office, because this venture would take both Marjie and me to handle it.

Recently, Mary Kay had created the Gold Goblet Club, which was for the consultants that purchased at least $1,000 wholesale during one month. The goblet was just gold plated, but as with most contests, it added excitement and increased sales. And it gave prestige to the ones who belonged. Special functions, such as luncheons, were held for them at meetings, which was another way of recognizing them as special. Everyone wanted that kind of attention.

We kicked the idea up a notch by creating The Diamond Deb Club. The first time our people purchased $1,000 wholesale during a month, they received a 14-karat gold ring. Each month thereafter when they met this challenge, they received a diamond to add to it. At the time, gold was $30 an ounce compared to over $1,300 an ounce today. Later, when Mary Kay began her Pink Cadillac program, we began a gold one. Both programs required reaching and maintaining a definite amount of sales to keep the leased Cadillac free of charge. If they fell below the quota, they had to pay the lease payment for that month.

Finally, competition between our two companies wasn't so destructive. While it was still a game of one-upmanship, at least it was no longer threatening and much less stressful than it had been before.

Once the rock was in place on the front of our new building, we had to make a decision on the kind of sign we wanted there. Because our products were packaged so elegantly, I insisted that our sign should reflect that image and have a shiny, real gold finish. The others thought we should have a plain black metal sign, mostly because of the expense.

It was a major battle, but I had always visualized the name Beauti-Control Cosmetics, written in script like our labels, in large, sparkling, gold letters on the front of the building. So I exercised my rights as CEO and said we were doing this my way. To get the effect I wanted, the sign had to be made of black metal and coated with 14-karat gold. Gold was cheap at the time, but even the sign company was concerned over the added expense, especially because they had never done one like it before. I still insisted that was what I wanted, because our image was at stake. I instructed them to call me the minute the sign had been mounted, because I wanted to be the first one to see it.

It was about 10:00 a.m. when the man called and said it was in place. Before I could ask how it looked, he hung up. Without even mentioning it to Marjie, I drove to Arlington as fast as I could, anticipating the spectacular sight that would greet me.

I rushed to the front of the building, which faced west, and glanced up, expecting to see the flashing gold sign I had envisioned. It wasn't there. I checked quickly to make sure I was at the right building and returned to the front to check again. This time I looked more closely at the area where the sign should be. Sure enough, the words were there, but barely visible. Horrified, I thought, *This can't be real.* I was already picturing the looks on everyone else's face when they saw it. The problem was that the gold of the sign had blended into the earth tones of the rock, so it was practically invisible.

I failed to mention to Marjie that I'd already been out to see the sign. It took me until after lunch just to tell her about it. Stan met us at the building at 5:00 that afternoon. I tried desperately to think of something to say that might justify the horrible mistake, but nothing came. I braced myself for their reaction and was shocked to see Stan grinning from ear to ear. The afternoon sun was hitting the sign, causing a burst of gold to brilliantly flash the words 'Beauti-Control Cosmetics' in a way that could be seen for miles.

Unfortunately, it was the only time of day that it could be seen at all, and even then it lasted for only about ten minutes before disappearing again into the earth tones of rock. I was forced to tell them the whole story, after which they could barely control their anger. They had tried to tell me, but I wouldn't listen. Marjie and I drove back to the office in total silence, and as I got out of the car, she called out, "I can't wait to see how God gets you out of this one."

I didn't even have the nerve to ask Him for such a miracle. I did pray fervently for a way to make up for my expensive mistake, but life took care of it for me. A few weeks later, as we began moving into the building, I was astonished at what I saw. I blinked and looked again. For some reason, the gold coating on the sign had shattered into thousands of tiny pieces, almost as if it had decided to destroy itself. The sign company took full responsibility, melted the gold off, and returned some of our money. Then they replaced it with the plain black sign that everyone else had wanted in the first place. The new sign was readable at all hours of the day. Marjie asked me a dozen times, "How did you manage that?" I just smiled and never admitted that I was more surprised than anyone.

We moved into our new building before our first seminar. We decided we needed some extra money in order to furnish it properly, so Marjie and I made the rounds to the banks. This was the era when loans to women were almost unheard of, and we weren't surprised when we were turned down over and over. Again, Stan pulled a rabbit out of a hat. He had a friend who was a vice president of a bank. And because he had known Stan for a long time, he loaned us $5,000 with only Stan's word that it would be repaid within six months, and it was. This was the only money we ever borrowed for the company. As Mary Kay had done, we accepted only cash, money orders, or cashier's checks in payment for merchandise purchased by our sales people. Therefore, we could accurately predict our profit margin. There were no bad checks to deal with. As business increased, our cash reserve grew rapidly.

For the new reception area, Marjie wanted touches of the same Mexican theme as she'd used in her own office, and she wanted pink as an accent color. Still opposed to copying Mary Kay in any way, I suggested she use a much deeper pink than Mary Kay's. When the area was finished, the dark green curved couch and the pink and green accent pillows looked great. Because I let her have her way in the decorations, I felt a little better about the sign fiasco.

We soon had the building in good shape. Marjie and I visited antique shops where we purchased a round table for our kitchen area, and on impulse we also bought a high-back chair that had beautiful, intricate carving. It looked like a throne. When we finished painting it gold, we covered it with glitter and upholstered it in rich, red velvet. It was a throne, and it would be used for our Queen of Sales in all the seminars to follow. As always though, we spent money sparingly. Even years later, when Mary Kay had an actual throne built for her seminars, we continued to use our homemade version and still maintained our motto: "We're not the biggest, but we are the best."

Ned went to work on the lab. He glassed in the entire manufacturing area so people could observe the products being made without entering the sterile environment. Everything was painted stark white, adding to the impression of purity, and employees wore blue uniforms, as well as hairnets for sanitation purposes. As we looked at the finished results, I was certain that Johnson and Johnson could not be prouder of their facilities than we were of ours. We couldn't wait for our sales people to see it.

Everything about our first seminar was magical. People came from all over—Wyoming, Colorado, Tennessee, Georgia, New Mexico, Arkansas, Florida, and of course, Texas. Several of those present are still with Beauticontrol today, including Betty Smith and Betty Bennett. On Friday, the first day of the seminar, everything was similar to Mary Kay's. The time was filled with songs, speeches, applause, and laughter. Everyone was giddy with excitement, mostly because we all recognized how far we'd come in just one year.

Dathene was scheduled to give her first real talk in front of the crowd. Marjie and I had discussed at length about how important her speech would be and decided we'd better write it for her. We hoped that by having notes in front of her, it would reduce her nervousness. And in all honesty, we also hoped that it would keep her from going on again about how Mary Kay had cheated her. Things had settled down between the two companies, and we wanted to keep it that way.

On Friday, Dathene went to the podium to give her talk amidst rousing applause. Her story had gotten around, and people were sympathetic to her plight. She began by picking up the pages of her speech and showing it to the audience. She giggled and said, "Jackie and Marjie wrote this speech for me, and I guess I'll have to give it, but if you will come to my room later, I'll give you the real scoop on everything." The whole room rocked with laughter, and we learned a valuable lesson. Dathene was simply who she was, and we might as well stop trying to change her.

Right after the seminar, something wonderful happened for Dathene. She met a man named Joe Territo at a dance, and only a few months later they were married. Joe was a nice, down-to-earth man, and he adored Dathene. Like Mary Kay and Mel, Joe and Dathene remained married for the rest of Joe's life.

Most of those attending the first seminar brought their families along, including us, and from that point on Beauticontrol became a family business, with everyone participating. There were songs, skits, square dancing, and a myriad of other types of entertainment at "fun night" (always on Friday) over the years. At this first one, Shannon, now two, Sharon, and Sheryl were in the middle of everything, and Sheryl carried the crown for our Queen of Sales on awards night. In the years that followed, Shannon took over that job and continued it for the rest of our years with Beauticontrol.

The two days of the first seminar used the same format as Mary Kay's. But at future seminars, we did full productions. The information, inspiration, and education were still there but were incorporated into something similar to a Broadway production, which added an element of entertainment to the mix. The second year the theme was "Alice in the Wonderful World of Beauticontrol." I wrote the script and worked into it all of the business basics throughout the two days.

Anna wrote the theme song, which I still think is one of the best tunes I've ever heard. Ned designed the program and backdrops, and all of us worked like slaves to put it together. After this one, all our seminars were grand and a labor of love; plus, we had more fun doing them than anyone could imagine.

Awards night was always a formal affair, with long gowns for women and tuxedoes for men. Even Shannon had a long dress, as did Sheryl and Sharon. Marjie and I picked up beautiful gowns for very little money by buying samples, which cost even less than wholesale, at the Apparel Mart. Mine cost $10, but it looked elegant and expensive.

The banquet room, where we'd have dinner and present awards, also had a theatrical stage, which was equipped with professional lighting and draped with a metallic gold curtain for the background. We hung a massive array of glittered gold stars on string from the ceiling and placed the throne in the middle. Although it strained our budget, we hired a live band to provide music for dinner and the coronation ceremonies. As Ned, Stan, Marjie, and I surveyed the finished work, Stan asked: "In comparing our first seminar setting with the one Mary Kay had in her warehouse, what do you think?"

With no modesty at all we answered, "We win—hands down."

Not surprising to anyone, Martha Weddle was our first Queen of Sales. Marjie presented her with a bouquet of roses, and I crowned her with a glittering tiara and presented her with a luxurious fur coat. While the band played a rousing fanfare, the crowd cheered and clapped as Martha enjoyed every single minute. Furs were the rage of the time, ranging from coats, stoles, boas, and accessories, like fur hats and muffs. All the top producers received some type of fur. And as Mary Kay had done, we chose each prize to fit the individual receiving it.

In addition, each winner received a small 14-karat gold pin, shaped like the crown on our label, with a diamond in the center. Marjie and I were green with envy over the fur coats and vowed that one day we would have one as well. Juanita Grable was the queen at the second seminar; and she was also the first winner of the gold Cadillac.

After the seminar, the time for the DSA meeting drew near. Ned and I began looking forward to the trip. Marie was staying with the children, and we were excited about taking a short break from our hectic lifestyle. Even though we would attend the business sessions, we had every intention of spending time in the sun too, just relaxing. One of the first couples we met at the meeting was Saul and Laura Skoler. Saul was president of Tri-Chem, a New Jersey company that sold liquid embroidery on the party plan. Tri-Chem was a much larger company than ours, with its stock traded on the stock exchange. Saul was a Harvard graduate and obviously an astute businessman. But he and Laura were also warm and fun to be with. He was interested in the cosmetic business and asked all kinds of questions, especially about profit margins.

He told me about a Young Presidents Club within the DSA. Apparently, I was eligible to join. It wasn't hard; the only real requirement was that you had to be less than forty years of age, and I was way below that. Being a part of that club turned out to be extremely beneficial. It opened a lot of doors for publicity and for meeting people I would otherwise never have met. From then on, we looked forward to seeing Saul and Laura at meetings. We did see Richard from a distance at the first DSA meeting before we left to return home, but there was no sign of Mary Kay.

Back at home, next on our agenda was the television campaign in Denver. We had discovered that the best time of day for interviews was during the noon hour. The main viewers were stay-at-home housewives, and this is when they watched. Tentatively, we booked three consecutive shows on the Star Yelland Show, which reportedly had a great following of women viewers.

Snow was virtually uncommon where I lived, but it was a typical sight in Denver in the winter, where I had already been for several meetings. The plane pitched and rocked as we landed, and we realized it wasn't simply snow that greeted us, but a major blizzard. Marjie looked at me. "What do you think this kind of weather will do to our response to the ad?"

"We'll just have to wait and see," I answered. "But I think it will make or break us."

Surprisingly, it made us. We were more successful than we ever dreamed. Because everyone was snowed in, all kinds of people were watching television that ordinarily wouldn't have been. Fortunately, out of some kind of inexplicable foresight, we had hired an answering service that was capable of taking a large volume of calls. We had also bought huge flip charts filled with enormous sheets of paper to write down all the information about the callers, no matter how many there were. We were staying in a cheap hotel, but it was in the center of town and near the TV station. Everywhere we looked people were falling down from the ice on the streets, and I couldn't risk that, so even though the station was a short distance away, I had to take a cab to it.

Star Yelland seemed nice and was obviously good at his job. I quickly went through the questions I wanted him to ask, and the director signaled that we needed to take our places. Star was so smooth, it seemed as if we were simply having an enthusiastic conversation about some exciting new products and we were letting the public in on it. As soon as we were off the air, his assistant came up and said people couldn't get through to the answering service listed on the screen because it was so jammed with calls, so the station had started taking names as well.

From that one segment we had over 400 calls from people who wanted the facials. Barbara Stubblefield and her consultants were used to the weather, so their cars were equipped for it. Like an army of dedicated troops, they went out in mass to keep the appointments. Several of their consultants bunked in our room when the appointments ended too late to go home. Amazingly, we recruited over forty new consultants—almost as many as we started the company with—during that trip. And we had to cancel the other two shows because we simply couldn't handle any more appointments. From this we learned that the worse the weather, the better the response. We also learned that about 10 percent of the total callers would become consultants.

Of course, this set Barbara up in style. But she also grasped the fact that everything comes at a price. With a perplexed look on her face she said, "I'm going to have the money alright, but I won't have time to spend it." Weary from the long hours of work, and very little rest, we literally laughed until we hurt. Before Marjie and I left for the airport the next day to head home, our group went out to the home of one of the consultants who had quite a few snowmobiles. We played in the snow for two hours—the perfect way to end a perfect trip.

Our families always met us at the airport on our return home from trips. And nothing will ever erase the picture in my mind of Ned, Sharon, and Shannon standing at the gate, waiting for me as I stepped off the plane. It was okay to go, but it was far better to come home.

Not long after this trip, I set up a TV appearance in Jackson, Mississippi. I would do this one by myself, because it was a much smaller area. We had a few consultants there, but nothing like the group in Colorado. JoAnne Case, who lived in the small town of Purvis, had just been recruited, but then left to cope on her own. I had spoken with her on the phone several times, and she seemed to have the desire to succeed, but desperately needed training. I set up only one show in Jackson. Even though it was much smaller than Denver, it was surrounded with rural areas, which responded very well to our ads.

Too incredible to be a coincidence, Hurricane Camille hit the area a few days before my TV show. With Denver fresh on my mind, I decided to go on with the show anyway. And when JoAnne breezed into our meeting prior to the show, I took one look at her and knew I'd made the right choice. She was the epitome of a "Southern belle," with good looks and lots of charm. And there was no doubt her ambition could be rated as a giant mug. I asked her what she wanted to get out of our business, and she looked at me a long time before answering, "The truth is I've never been outside this immediate area in my entire life. When I see planes flying over my house, I want to know about the places they're going. I think you're my ticket." She was so serious that I was certain she would succeed more than she could imagine. Ultimately, she visited almost every country in the world.

The results of this TV show were similar to Denver's. Everyone was indoors because of the hurricane, so the phone rang off the wall with people requesting facials. From all the clinics that were booked, there were over twenty new recruits. The new giant mugs in the area included Shirley Gilder from Hattiesburg, Mississippi, and Jean Magee, who lived in one of the rural areas.

But Shirley had the greatest fear of speaking in front of people that I had ever seen. The first time she won a major contest and had to speak in front of the group, I could actually hear her knees knocking. We've laughed about it many times. It took her years to take control of that fear, yet she went on to achieve the highest level of sales management in Beauticontrol, and is still there today.

Although Jean and JoAnne didn't stay permanently with Beauticontrol, they were both super successful directors. Before long, JoAnne was giving Barbara Stubblefield and all the other top producers a run for their money. Kathy Ray had become a strong director in Detroit, Michigan, causing the competition between the North and the South to begin all over again.

In addition to being business associates, we all became good friends, visiting each other's homes and traveling together. From hearing it discussed constantly, our children knew almost as much about the business as we did and were proud to watch their mothers when they were crowned like royalty and presented with elegant prizes. This experience let them see first-hand that women could achieve high success, which meant they could too.

After our second year in business, Ned joined us full time, and we all began drawing salaries—finally! Sharon was in junior high by this time and had been elected cheerleader; practice was immediately after school. Because she had the responsibility of taking care of Shannon during this time, it created a problem. To solve it, the cheerleading sponsor made Shannon the mascot, and I made her a uniform to match the ones the cheerleaders wore. She performed with them at all the games, and we wouldn't have missed a game for anything. Shannon, dressed in her uniform, also began to do a cheer of her own creation in our living room. Waving her arms and jumping around she chanted, "Beat Mary Kay, beat Mary Kay." We loved it, but we were glad it was just for us and not for the whole crowd at the football games.

After Ned joined us, it was good to have all four present for discussions and seemed much easier to reach decisions. But a few months after Ned made the move, I noticed a change in him. We would appear to reach a decision at work, but once we got home, Ned would suddenly disagree. Then he insisted I go back the next day and tell Marjie and Stan I was changing it to whatever Ned wanted. This reminded me of what he used to do with Mary Kay, and it made me uneasy. I tried to get him to speak up and say what he wanted in the meetings, rather than carry on with all this subterfuge, but he refused. He was unclear about his reasons, but he was adamant about doing it this way. Rather than fighting with him, I continued to do as he asked. I hoped that Stan and Marjie didn't realize what he was doing;

but knowing how astute Stan was about such things I suspected he did. Other than this one unnerving development, everything continued to improve.

Later, after we'd started the Cadillac program, I personally got a white El Dorado with a gold leather top as a company car. The seats were covered with genuine ostrich skin and were by far the most sumptuous and tasteful I had ever seen. Stan and Marjie chose a Buick. These splurges, which we had worked hard to earn, made us feel we were finally on our way to making our dreams come true.

Now that Ned and Stan were both holding down the office, Marjie and I began to take on the TV work in areas where we had no consultants. It was usually a two-week trip and I hated leaving Sharon and Shannon for such long periods. But I consoled myself with the fact it wouldn't be forever. We chose North Carolina as a new state to develop, and we set up television appearances in Greensboro and Winston-Salem. It took two days to drive there, so we stopped for the night in Nashville, Tennessee. Always looking for new adventures, we gave ourselves the treat of attending the Grand Ol' Opry, which was a "must" for Southerners.

It was autumn and as we drove through the Smokey Mountains in my El Dorado, the view was breathtaking. The leaves were vibrant shades of orange and gold; the gold ones looked like shiny coins hanging on the trees. By the time we reached Greensboro, we felt as if we'd been on vacation for several days, and were prepped to get to work.

The pace of doing television, holding clinics, and recruiting and training consultants was long and hard. However, the sheer success of the venture was extremely satisfying. We decided to take our time returning home so we would be rested when we reconnected with our families. We indulged ourselves by stopping to browse at antique shops and dawdled at roadside stands for cheese and apple cider. It was a great way to unwind before returning to business as usual the minute we got home.

In preparing for our third seminar, when we bought furs for contest winners, Marjie and I got ones for ourselves this time.

Marjie's was a full-length ranch mink, perfect with her blonde hair. Remembering Mary Kay in her full-length leopard, I chose a similar one with a ranch mink collar, and rows of mink at the bottom. Since my choice cost much less than Marjie's, I also allowed myself a matching ranch mink hat plus something I had always dreamed about owning—a ranch mink muff. It was one more way we rewarded ourselves for jobs well done.

Childhood goes quickly. In what seemed like a blink of an eye, Sharon was turning into a lovely young woman. Even though she didn't actually date until after her sixteenth birthday, suddenly we seemed to have a constant string of boys at our house (and Shannon seemed to think they were all there to see her). Soon, two of them stood out as the most frequent visitors: Mark Crouch, who was dark and handsome, and Brad Lowe, with blonde curly hair and big blue eyes. Brad had perfect manners, and both my daughters adored him. On Sharon's fourteenth birthday, Brad gave her a "promise ring," a 14-karat gold ring set with a small diamond. At the time it meant it was a sign of more serious things to come. Ned thought she was far too young and was so upset over the gift, I thought we were going to have to scrape him off the ceiling. But he needn't had worried. Sharon insisted on wearing the ring all the time, but because it was too large, when she was baking a cake one day, it fell off into the batter without her knowledge and was lost forever. Undaunted, Brad kept his promise and showed up again in Sharon's life years later. And Mark Crouch remained her good friend for life.

By the time our fourth seminar rolled around, we had grown so much we decided to have the event in one of the new elegant hotels in downtown Dallas. Each year we felt we had to dress more lavishly than the last. Buying everything wholesale at the Apparel Mart had become a matter of routine for us. For this affair, Marjie bought a full-length pink and white brocade gown with a coat to match. The collar and cuffs on the coat were trimmed with white mink. My gown was made of cream-colored shadow print taffeta with a matching coat that had a hood that was edged with ranch mink. Of course I planned to carry my mink muff as an accessory. Ned and Stan dressed to the nines also. They actually bought their own tuxedoes for evening, as well as new suits for the daytime events.

One new addition this year was that our program included renowned national speakers, among which was a former Miss America. Not surprisingly, she was a favorite among our group.

Because we had always been on a strict budget and bought only necessities, being able to add a few luxuries was exhilarating and made the hard work we'd put in seem worth the effort. But sometimes I looked at how fast my children were growing and wished I could stop the clock and relish each moment with them to the fullest. Not earning money for so long was now easily forgotten. But sacrificing time with my children was the real price I'd had to pay for the success we'd achieved.

We began the New Year of 1971 being more successful than we'd ever thought possible. With the lawsuit settled, our bank accounts were impressive. And our salaries provided us with a good lifestyle. However, Marjie and I still wanted dream homes and hoped that would be our next reward.

A meeting of the Young Presidents Club was scheduled for late March in New York City. I was going, and I talked Margie into making the trip with me; New York was about the last place we hadn't explored together. But even with all of the excitement about the trip, I noticed Marjie sometimes seemed distracted. Finally, I asked her what was going on. After a long hesitation, she said that Stan had become moody lately, and it was beginning to bother her.

Suddenly, I realized that he did seem different. Stan was a "man's man." He was gregarious and confident, and men seemed to be instantly drawn to him. Even the salesmen that called on us did everything they could to please him. He was regularly invited to lunch at the nearby Great Southwest Golf Club. But lately Stan had begun to refuse their invitations. I knew this was one of the signs that caused Marjie to be concerned. Yet, I simply told her that people all have their ups and downs, and we were probably being overly dramatic about it; we shouldn't go looking for problems where there weren't any. She wasn't convinced, but gave a sigh of resignation anyway and let it go.

That evening, I asked Ned if he had noticed anything different in Stan's behavior. He hesitated, and it seemed as if he wanted to say something, but he just shrugged his shoulders and said, "Not really."

A shiver ran down my spine; intuitively I knew that something was wrong. I was, however, unwilling to accept the possibility that it was anything serious. This was partly probably because I genuinely cared for them both and didn't want there to be. So I shrugged it off as well and returned to thinking about our dream trip to New York City.

CHAPTER TWENTY-FOUR

The Price of Spring

"New York" was written in huge letters on my calendar on the day we were to leave, and I could barely contain my excitement. One of the world's greatest and most renowned cities, it was the epitome of glamour. In the six years since I had taken my first plane trip to California for Mary Kay, I had visited almost every major city in the country; this was my Mount Everest. And now, I was finally going!

Ned did not have the same reaction. The minute I told him I would be attending the Young Presidents' meeting there, he turned absolutely frantic. He said the people were rude, the crime rate was high, and it was dangerous for everyone. He was especially afraid for me as a woman alone. I pointed out, logically, that I would hardly be alone; Marjie would be with me. But he rolled his eyes as if that was too ridiculous to answer. Unfortunately, his fears planted the bug. Instead of being just excited, I began noticing New York crime stories in the news.

In thinking about why Ned was so overprotective of me, as well as our whole family, I decided it was because he was twenty-nine years old when we married. He loved being a family man, and I think he was afraid something would happen to ruin it.

Marjie, on the other hand, wasn't concerned at all about the crime rate. Her focus was whether she was fashionable enough. Her fingernails, she insisted, were stubby when they should have been long and brightly polished. She was so obsessed by this that she constantly looked for a solution and enlisted me to research the entire range of nail products. Nevertheless, she couldn't find anything that would help. This eventually led to research for a product of our own.

One morning she stopped at my office door and announced, "I've found the solution." My face went blank, so she explained that she'd found a set of false fingernails to glue on and paint any color she wanted.

"Really?" I asked, "Will they actually stay on your nails all day, no matter what you do?"

Now she was hesitant. "Well," she answered, "I'm not sure about that yet. I'm still experimenting. But I am going to wear them to New York and test them out."

I smiled to myself over our different concerns. I was worried about crime, and Marjie was obsessed with her nails; and she considered her problem far more serious than mine.

We would be in New York only three days, but we took enough bags to stay a month. Included were the sumptuous gowns we'd bought for our last seminar, because we were going to the Starlight Room, atop the Waldorf-Astoria Hotel, on our last night there. In fact, the main reason for going was the opportunity to wear our finery. Carol Lawrence was the scheduled entertainment, which made it even more exciting.

It was about 2:00 p.m. when Ned and I reached Love Field and found Marjie and Stan already there. This was a time when airliners were being hijacked on a regular basis, so everyone was required to arrive early for security purposes. Of course this made Ned even more nervous about the trip. After we'd checked our bags and arrived at our gate, Stan quickly told Marjie goodbye and left. He had barely spoken to us and I looked at Ned, hoping for an answer, but he simply shrugged his shoulders. As Ned kissed me goodbye he whispered again to be careful and to beware of strange men. Marjie and I looked at each other and smiled. Now, we could concentrate on the trip.

Our plane was a 747, and it was the first time for both of us to ride on one. After we were seated and spent several minutes of looking around, Marjie said, "I thought we were scheduled to take off as soon as everyone was onboard." As soon as the words came out of her mouth, two policemen walked down the aisle, looking at each passenger carefully. They stopped a few rows behind us, where a shabbily dressed man was sitting. After talking with him a few minutes and checking his boarding pass, they ushered him off the plane. Remembering the recent hijackings, I was mortified. I didn't want anything to interfere with this trip. I whispered to Marjie, "What's going on?"

Marjie stopped a stewardess and asked. She hesitated but finally answered, "The man had signed his name as A. Bomb on the check-in list. We're pretty sure it's just a practical joke, but of course we can't be too careful." He had three bags, and the delay was going through them as well. I told Marjie that I thought we should call Ned and Stan, and see what they thought we should do. I couldn't be the one to make the call, because I knew Ned would insist I get off the plane, so Marjie did it.

When she returned she was laughing so hard she could hardly talk. "He said to be sure and get out some extra life insurance before we take off." I thought the comment showed lack of concern, but it was more like the Stan I knew so perhaps everything was okay with him, after all. After another thirty minutes, we finally took off. I took out my book; Marjie began gluing on her false fingernails, then polished them a bright pink. She stopped the next stewardess that came down the aisle and asked, "Did they find the man's three bags?"

After hesitating again, she answered ominously, "They found only two of them."

By this time we were about thirty thousand feet in the air and we could either laugh or cry over this news. We chose to laugh, although I did say a silent prayer for our safety and vowed that this was one story Ned would never hear. About three hours later as we were beginning our descent, the pilot came on the air and said that New York was having a freak snowstorm, even though it was technically spring and our landing might be a little rough. "What else can go wrong?" I asked Marjie. "We haven't even gotten to where Ned said we would face the greatest danger." But the excitement wasn't over. It had actually just begun.

As we stood outside Kennedy Airport in the freezing sleet and snow with our mountain of luggage, the cabs flew by us, filled with passengers. Fortunately, we were wearing our fur coats, and I drew mine closely around me. Marjie stepped up to the curb and announced with determination, "I'm going to get us a cab." As a stretch limousine with a passenger inside approached us, Marjie stepped off the curb and waived frantically. Tires squealed as the driver stopped in front of us. The man in the back seat rolled down his window and said, "May we drop you off somewhere?" I frowned at Marjie and shook my head no, but she was already accepting the offer and the driver was loading our bags. Amazed at her accomplishment I thought, I guess sometimes that blonde hair is worth all the trouble.

The man introduced himself as Hans Berger (I remember from associating it with hamburger), and he explained that he'd just arrived from Geneva, Switzerland. He was an investment banker, in the states to meet with clients who were interested in taking their stock public. Marjie filled him in on our cosmetic business and Mr. Berger seemed intrigued. He invited us to meet him the following evening for a drink at Delmonico's, the famous New York bar, to discuss our business further. As a signal for her to refuse, I punched her sharply, but she accepted anyway.

The limo driver dropped us off at the Savoy Hotel, just across the street from the Waldorf-Astoria. Mr. Berger refused our money to help with the cab fare and said he would see us at 7:00 p.m. the next evening. The Savoy was a far cry from the posh Waldorf, but it was also far less expensive. It was supposed to be a safe, clean place to stay, even though Ned said there was no such thing in New York City. Our room was so small there was barely room for our two beds. But we didn't plan to spend much time there, so we didn't care. But when I noticed there were three bolts on the door, I wondered if Ned was right about the safe part.

We soon realized that New York never sleeps. By the time we were settled in our room, it was almost 10:00 p.m., yet the crowd on the street seemed oblivious to the time. Too keyed up to think about going to bed, we decided to check out what was happening downstairs. After I got my coat out of the closet and turned to go, Marjie was nowhere in sight. When I called her name, a muffled voice came from the floor near her bed. Her false nails had fallen off and she was trying to retrieve them. I sighed because I was afraid this would be a major activity for the rest of the trip.

The Young Presidents Club meeting and luncheon was to be at noon the next day at a famous hotel near Central Park, which Ned had warned was the most dangerous area of all. There were snow banks everywhere, but the weather didn't cool my enthusiasm. Saul Skoler was saving me a seat at his table, since it was my first meeting with the group. My main concern was leaving Marjie by herself, but she assured me she was looking forward to shopping alone.

Saul was waiting for me at the door, and I was amazed at the crowd already there. There were reporters from most of the major magazines, as well as other invited guests. As soon as we were seated at our table, Saul began asking me questions, as he had done at the DSA meeting, about the profitability of the cosmetic business. I explained it was a great business for one reason: if women had to choose between buying food or cosmetics, they would choose cosmetics every time. Saul laughed and said I was probably right. But now I was curious about his interest, so I asked him point-blank if he was thinking of adding cosmetics to his line of products.

He replied, cautiously, that he wasn't interested in just any cosmetic, but he might be interested in ours if we ever decided we wanted a partnership of some kind. Stunned, I didn't know how to respond, so I said jokingly, "Well, I don't think we are right at this moment, but never say never."

A reporter from Glamour magazine sat on the other side of me, and I turned to visit with her. She, too, showed curiosity about the cosmetic business and asked a lot of questions, particularly about direct sales. A couple of months later, she quoted me on something I said to her, along with quotes from Lady Byrd Johnson and other famous women. I had never been so flattered.

That evening Marjie and I decided to walk to Delmonico's to meet Mr. Berger. We were told it was only four blocks, and it would be faster to walk than get a cab. What we weren't told was that each New York block was about a mile long, so we were late. Mr. Berger already had a drink in front of him and seemed a little impatient. We both ordered cola, much to the waitress's and to Mr. Burger's, surprise. I began the conversation by asking him what he would like to know about the cosmetic business. He admitted that he had heard about Mary Kay's success in going public with her stock, and that was primarily why he wanted to hear more about our business.

After several minutes, something brushed against my leg under the table. I lifted the tablecloth and there was Marjie, on the floor looking for her false nails. I laughed and the waitress, who had just arrived with our colas, laughed too. Soon everyone else in the room was laughing hysterically. Everyone, that is, except Mr. Berger. Placing his napkin on the table, he excused himself (we assumed to go to the little boy's room). Fifteen minutes later, when he still hadn't returned I asked the waitress if she'd seen him. She said he had left, and added that he'd paid for his drink; then she handed us the bill for our colas.

Marjie and I laughed all the way back to the Savoy. Apparently, we were not the kind of clients that Mr. Berger liked to work with. We decided if there was no other excitement on this trip, it had already been worth it all. We also knew beyond a doubt that Marjie and her false nails had left an unforgettable impression, especially on Mr. Berger.

For the next two days we shopped at Tiffany's, visited the Statue of Liberty, and attended a Broadway matinee of Hello Dolly. Through it all, Marjie continued her quest to keep the false nails in place.

Our last night in the city came much too soon, and as we dressed for the most elegant affair of all, Marjie again began pressing on her false nails. Thinking quickly about how to ask, I said, "Marjie, would you do me a big favor?"

"Sure, what is it?"

Taking a deep breath I answered, "Would you please leave the nails behind, just for this evening."

After a brief hesitation, she laughed before she answered, "You're afraid I'll cause another scene at the most elite club in New York, aren't you?" I nodded sheepishly, and she graciously removed the nails.

Marjie looked magnificent in her pink brocade gown and matching coat trimmed with white mink. And glancing in the mirror at myself with my hand in my mink muff, I thought, *I don't look too bad myself.* As we walked out of the Savoy to the Waldorf, the streets were still icy and my feet slipped, but Marjie grabbed my shoulder so I didn't fall. A policeman was watching it all and commented, "Don't fall; it causes too much paper work." In response I thought Ned was right about the attitude here, but wrong about the danger; we hadn't even been pinched.

Marjie and I looked at each other and smiled as we walked into the swanky hotel. She knew what I'd been thinking: I have never witnessed anything as grand as this. The orchestra was playing as we entered the Starlight Room, and the maitre d' met us at the door. Stunning in his tuxedo, he looked every bit as impressive as the guests did. He escorted us to our table, handed us the menus, bowed, and left us to choose our dinner. Marjie gasped as she opened the menu, leaned over, and whispered, "The prices are not even listed."

After I caught my breath I answered, "Let's read the entrees and choose what looks like the least expensive." We ruled out steak, lobster, and pheasant under glass, and finally settled on Cornish hen. As the orchestra played, and people danced in their luxurious clothes, I watched Marjie's expression. She was perfectly at ease in the setting, as if she'd been a part of it her whole life. Even though I had experienced grandeur in the last few years, it wasn't anything compared to this. I now felt I was on the outside looking in, like that girl from a poor dirt farm in Arkansas trying to fit in where she didn't belong.

Instantly, I shrugged off the negative feelings and vowed never to let such thoughts enter my thinking again. And years later, even when I had dinner at the White House, none did.

Carol Lawrence was the perfect entertainment for the evening. Her singing and dancing were far superior to anything we had ever seen before. Time flew by and when our waiter handed us our check, Marjie grabbed it and gasped. "It's $35.00 for each of us. You'd think for that price the waiters would have danced with us." (Today the cost would be at least $350 per person).

I laughed and thought, Maybe she isn't as at home with such opulence as I'd imagined.

The next morning we rose early and packed our things before going downstairs for breakfast. I wrapped my mink muff in the pillowcase I'd brought it in and placed it on top of my clothes in my bag. As we started to leave the room, the phone rang. It was Stan; Marjie motioned for me to go on and mouthed the words, I'll see you in a minute.

Thirty minutes later she finally joined me. "What's wrong?" I asked, apprehensively.

"I guess I might as well tell you. Stan and Ned had a major disagreement while we've been gone." A feeling of dread washed over me, but I realized I wasn't really surprised. I had sensed something was brewing, but I wouldn't let myself think about it.

"How bad is it?" I asked, not wanting to hear the answer.

"I'm afraid it's pretty bad," Marjie admitted. Then she added, "It's been going on for a while, but I kept hoping it would improve."

Reality settled in my stomach like a ball of lead, and I knew we were going to have to face a mountain we might not be able to climb. Our appetites gone, Marjie and I paid for just coffee and went upstairs to get our bags.

The flight home was opposite from the one coming. There was very little activity in the cabin, and we both quietly read our books. As we stepped off the plane and saw the long faces of Ned and Stan, we braced ourselves and made no attempt to act normal. Without a word, we picked up our baggage and went our separate ways. As soon as we were in the car I asked about the problem, but Ned suggested we wait until we were home to discuss it, and even then not in front of the kids. I knew that meant it was really serious. I shivered with the old premonition that a rabbit had run across my grave.

As Sharon and Shannon greeted us, the mood lightened, and I gave them the little gifts I had promised; both were tee shirts with a big red apple on the front. As we settled in front of the fire, with Shannon on my lap and Sharon huddled next to me, they told me about their activities while I was gone, and I told them about mine. I also promised that one day we would go as a family. Even though Ned didn't participate, I was comforted just being with my family. Whatever the problem was, we would handle it together.

After the girls were asleep, I opened my bag to put away my clothes. The pillowcase, with my gorgeous mink muff inside, was gone.

"Oh, no!" I yelled, and Ned came running from the bathroom. Through my tears, I managed to tell him that my muff had been stolen. He had been right about the crime in New York after all. He sat down on the floor beside me and tried to calm me down, but to no avail. I loved that muff.

The next morning Ned and I were again discussing the fact that everything seemed to have a price. Shannon, now a precocious five-year-old, asked me what that meant, and I explained about losing my muff. She seemed to understand how much it had meant to me and quickly changed the subject to something she thought far more interesting. The cardinals were building a nest in our yellow jasmine, and Shannon had been watching the process. The eggs had begun to hatch, and she was enamored with the tiny birds. Again, my spirits were lifted by the sweet innocence of my child; I left for work feeling ready to face whatever awaited me. We had been careful about discussing the problem about the office, and Ned said I would know it all soon enough.

As soon as I arrived, I went straight to Stan's office. I knew I had to confront the problem head-on. I sat down in a chair in front of his desk and when he looked up, I asked, "Can we talk about this?"

After a long silence, he said, "We could, but I don't think it would do any good. Our partnership isn't working out. Ned and I don't seem to be able to stick to a boundary, and we keep getting involved with each other's responsibilities."

I listened carefully but made no comment. I needed to also hear what Ned had to say on the subject. Next, I went to Ned's office in the lab and told him I needed to hear what he thought the problem was and I needed to know right now. He had put me off at home, using the children as an excuse. But I knew it was because he realized I would be extremely upset over it all. Finally, he said that he felt he was stuck with the hard work in the lab and Stan got to do all the fun part, like talking to salesmen and being taken to lunch.

I knew Ned's view was not a fair assessment. Stan played a vital role in the business. He was so good at keeping up with inventory control that we never had back orders, which could ruin our business. In addition, he ran the office and still helped out in the lab when necessary. In spite of what they said, I felt the core of the problem was that Ned thought Stan's role was more important than his.

I remembered how hard Ned had pushed for control of the stock. And suddenly, it was clear that he had been right. This was the kind of problem that could be resolved only with that kind of authority. A CEO could decide on the kind of sign to use, but this kind of a decision was a whole different ballgame. It all boiled down to which of them was more important in the chain of command. The only way I knew to determine that was by a majority vote of the stockholders, and we were split 50/50.

All afternoon I tried to think of a resolution, but finally gave up and went back to Stan's office. I said, "Stan, will you promise me that you will think this through before doing anything rash?" He looked me in the eye and nodded. But I knew that from the look on his face he'd already decided. I'd have to wait and see what that decision was.

I didn't have long to wait. That evening, just as we sat down to dinner, the doorbell rang. When Ned opened it, a man in uniform said, "I have a document to be delivered to Jackie and Ned Brown, and I will need both signatures to show acceptance. I was standing beside Ned and asked the messenger, "Who is it from?"

"Stan and Marjie Slaten," he replied, glancing at the envelope.

My heart sunk. We signed for the document and took it directly to the kitchen table. It was the Buy or Sell Agreement we'd set up in the beginning. It was to be used as a way to dissolve the partnership in the event one of us wanted out of it. By serving us with this document, they were giving us the right to choose whether to buy their stock or to sell ours to them. It was to reveal what they were willing to pay for it, if we decided to sell to them. Or, if we decided to buy, then we could buy at the same price. I could hear my own heart beating in my chest as I tried to comprehend what they were offering. But Ned had already figured it out.

Agitated he said, "They aren't even offering enough to cover what you earned in two years at Mary Kay. We have five years invested in this company, so we have to come up with a way to buy them out, since we get to choose. And, the agreement states they have to accept the same price they offered us."

Suddenly I realized Marjie had to have known Stan was considering this move, and I was deeply hurt that she hadn't even given me a hint so I could prepare myself. But I also realized that Stan probably told her not to mention it. And of course, she had to honor his wishes. Years later, when we finally discussed it, she admitted this was exactly what had happened. And she'd felt as badly as I had for not being able to tell me.

As it all soaked in, I felt like a ton of bricks had been dropped on my head, yet I managed to say, "I don't know Ned. I can't stand the thought of having to handle the whole thing without Marjie. I don't get to spend nearly enough time with the kids as it is. And, if we used our cash reserve in the company to buy them out, then we would be back to barely making ends meet."

He said he understood, but his mouth was set in a firm line, and I knew he was going to insist on buying them out anyway. He checked the document again and said we had to tell them whether we wanted to buy or sell within three weeks.

By this time, my head felt as though it might burst, so I told Ned we had to wait until morning to discuss it further. Even though it had been spring for a while, the next morning actually felt like it. The birds were singing and the sun was shining, which lifted my spirits considerably. As I had waited for sleep to come the night before, I remembered Saul saying he would be interested in our business if we ever decided to bring in partners.

But I decided not to mention this to Ned until I had a chance to think it through.

That morning, as we prepared to walk out the door for work, Shannon mentioned again the cute baby birds in the cardinal's nest. She checked on them at least twice a day, and I cautioned her to be careful because the mother and daddy birds might not understand and think she was trying to harm them. "I would never do that," she said, alarmed, and added, "I don't want anything bad to ever happen to our baby birds."

"None of us do," I assured her as I kissed her goodbye.

We decided to ride to work together that day, and on the way Ned said, "The exterminators are coming late this afternoon. Remind me to get us home before they arrive. With all the trauma, I may forget." I promised I would.

The day was filled with tension. We didn't want to upset the employees, so we pretended as best we could that everything was normal. But anyone could see it wasn't. The worst part for me was ignoring Marjie. I couldn't cover the hurt I felt, and I knew she could read it on my face. The banter and laughter we'd shared for five years had been replaced with stone cold silence. I knew we had to resolve the situation soon, before it affected the entire company.

When I looked at my watch in the afternoon, it was already 4:00 p.m. I rushed into Ned's office and reminded him the exterminators were coming and we had to hurry to make it on time. They were scheduled for 5:00, so we thought we had time. But the traffic was heavy and by the time we reached our house, they had come and gone. Instead of waiting for instructions on where to spray, they had sprayed everything. When we walked in the door, Shannon was crying hysterically and saying something about the baby birds. We walked out back to where the nest was and saw the mother and daddy birds circling the area and screaming in pain. Ned checked the nest and found the tiny chicks dead from the exterminator's chemicals.

We all cried from the horror of the event and from the guilt we felt from not protecting the little creatures. Shannon, of course, cried the hardest and longest of all. But finally she looked up at us and asked through her tears, in her precocious way, "Is it the price of spring, Mommy? Is it?"

I wrapped my arms around her and said, "I guess it is, sweetheart; I guess it is."

The stress of it all was getting to be too much, and I decided that bringing in a partner could be the answer. I finally told Ned about Saul's interest in the company, and a look of relief transformed his face. "That's the answer," he cried. "Let's call him right now." After I pointed out that it was after 7:00 p.m. in New Jersey, we decided to wait until the next morning.

Saul was surprised yet delighted to hear from me so soon. I explained what had happened with the Slatens, and he immediately said he would like to send his team of experts (accountants, sales executives, etc.) to look over our books. If all of the reports were satisfactory, then he would make both the Slatens and us an offer to purchase stock. This meant that we would not be able to actually finalize anything until the very end of the three weeks allotted in the Buy or Sell Agreement.

Stan said they were using an attorney from another law firm to represent them, so I set up a meeting with Brad Corrigan. He agreed to represent Ned and me and cautioned me to be careful in dealing with high-powered New York attorneys. Next, I had to tell Marjie and Stan about what we were considering. Stan hit the ceiling, saying that was not what the Buy or Sell Agreement was meant to allow. I think his reaction was due to the fact that he was so sure we would sell them our stock that it hadn't occurred to him that we might take a different approach.

But our attorney explained that what we were doing had not been disallowed, so it would fit within the guidelines of the agreement. Then I suggested that Stan check it out with his own attorney before we talked about it further. I also mentioned it would take the full three weeks he allowed us to make a final decision.

For a few years, we had held our May workshop in Denver. Barbara Stubblefield had developed the whole western area by this time and was a great help in engineering the meetings. Because it would take three weeks before we knew what would happen with the company, Marjie and I would both have to attend the workshop and act as if nothing unusual was happening. I wasn't sure that either of us was that good of an actress.

We were so close-knit, that if our sales people knew one couple would be leaving, it would cause a distraction almost as bad as the one with Mary Kay. As a result our sales would go downhill. The only good thing about the situation was that we all realized our first priority was protecting the stability of the company, since at this stage we didn't know definitely who would end up the owners.

At the same time this was happening, we had a family crisis so serious it made the one with the company pale in comparison. Sharon, now seventeen and a junior in high school, began having episodes where she blacked out for a few seconds at a time. She never knew when one would hit her. Remembering her dad's brain tumor, I took her to her regular doctor immediately. After some tests of his own, he sent her to a neurosurgeon for a spinal tap and brain X-rays. While I tried to assure Sharon it was just precautionary, I couldn't even take a deep breath because of my severe apprehension.

The tests were a terrible experience, especially the spinal tap, and Sharon had to lie in bed for days without raising her head. The results wouldn't be available for almost a week, and I had to go on to Denver for the workshop before they were ready. Leaving for that trip was one of the hardest things I ever had to do, even though I knew Marie would take perfect care of my children in my absence. Ned couldn't hide the fact that he wished I didn't have to go.

For the first time, Marjie and I took separate flights to Denver. I boarded the plane, sick at heart and feeling more alone than I had felt in my whole life. As always, I turned to the scriptures I had stored in my heart, such as "Lift up thine eyes unto the hills, from whence cometh thy help." I repeated it over and over to myself and by the time I reached Denver, I began to look up in faith, instead of down in fear.

Marjie and I had also booked separate rooms at the hotel. Usually, when Ned and Stan weren't traveling with us, we shared a room to save on expense. Amazingly, no one seemed to notice anything unusual about our actions. The workshop went off without a hitch, and the enthusiasm seemed to be even greater than ever. The area was expanding rapidly; the momentum had taken over, and it seemed that nothing could stop it.

As the workshop was coming to a close, Marjie came up to me and whispered she had something to tell me. While Barbara was speaking, we slipped into the hall and I waited expectantly. "Sharon's doctor called, and they put the call through to my room by mistake. Before I could explain I wasn't you, he told me the tests revealed that Sharon has a lesion in her brain, and you need to make another appointment with him as soon as you get home."

Suddenly the coping mechanism I'd had when I was expecting Shannon returned; Marjie's voice seemed to be coming from far away. I heard the words but it all appeared to be happening to someone else. Because it didn't seem real, I didn't have to think about what it could mean.

On the flight home, I was finally able to face Sharon's condition more rationally. I reminded myself of how hopeless it looked for Shannon to be healthy because of the blood problem; yet she was. From that experience I knew that Sharon could be fine now as well. My next thought was that Marjie would not be there to help me through whatever I had to face, as she'd been with Shannon, and the ache in my heart returned.

But my faith had strengthened, and Sharon and I held onto it until we saw the doctor again. Marjie had said they had found a lesion so I immediately asked what that was. The doctor admitted it was what they called something when they didn't know exactly what it was. In Sharon's case, they decided to keep a close check on it to see if it grew. And thank God, it didn't. For a time they did put her on a medication to prevent the blackouts, but after a while she was able to stop that.

All of this reminded us of what is truly important in life, and we settled into dealing with the company situation in a calmer manner. Saul called me to report that his team had found that everything about our company was in top-notch shape. He was ready to make an offer, and he was coming to Dallas to do it in person.

Saul knew Stan was unhappy that we had contacted him, so he decided to resolve the deal with him first. His offer to Stan and Marjie was more than twice what they were offering us in the Buy or Sell Agreement. In addition, he offered them a five-year contract for a non-compete agreement, which would provide them with a healthy yearly income for the duration. After Saul had explained all this to us, I told Ned I would have snapped up such an offer in a minute, and I wasn't surprised when the Slatens did the same.

His offer to us was just as generous. There would be a lump sum up front, which was far greater than Stan's total offer. It would only cover a portion of our stock, but would give them controlling interest. At the end of our five-year contract, they would purchase the remaining stock. In addition, there would be an incentive plan, where we got a yearly bonus based on an increase in sales. And at the end of our five-year contract, the final buy-out would be computed on the total increase in sales from the time of the purchase. Although Saul first talked about a partnership with the arrangement he offered, Tri-Chem would end up owning the company. While it wasn't everything we would have liked, it was the best solution we had available.

There was no going away party for the Slatens. They were simply there one day and gone the next. We announced their leaving in our newsletter, and for a year thereafter I continued having to explain it in person to our sales people all over the country. We had been as close as any family, and all of us had to adjust to their absence. I felt it was much harder on me than any-one else. One day when Ned was boasting about how well we had come out on the deal, I stopped him cold. "You may think it was free and easy, but it came at a high price for me."

Surprised, he asked, "How is that?"

"It cost me one of the best friends I've ever had," I answered while choking back the tears. While a day didn't go by that I didn't think of them, there was no news about where they were or what they were doing. They seemed to have simply vanished.

Several months later, I heard from Anna that they had moved to Guadalajara, Mexico, where they remained for two years before returning to New Mexico, their home state.

In search of our dream homes, Marjie and I had looked at almost every house for sale in the Dallas-Fort Worth area, ranging from quaint old cottages to mansions in Highland Park. Now, to console myself I started looking at houses again, and this time in North Dallas. As before, I took Sharon with me. We fell in love with one place located off Preston Road. It was ordinary on the outside, but magnificent on the inside, with 4,000 square feet of space and four and one-half bathrooms, plus a guesthouse, with another bath. And the house was built so that all rooms opened onto an Olympic-size swimming pool.

The rear of the property backed up to Clint Murchison's estate, which had a private helicopter pad. At the time Mr. Murchison was listed as one of the wealthiest people in the nation. During the time we lived there, Shannon was a Brownie Scout and sold him cookies every year. Each time he had to borrow money from the maid to pay Shannon.

After we first discovered the house and railroaded Ned into looking at it, we bought it on the spot and moved into it within a month. Sharon was now a senior in high school and had only one year there before going away to college. But Shannon made life-long friends during her six years in the neighborhood. When my mother first visited us there, she kept counting the bathrooms as if she'd made a mistake on the number.

If I thought I had traveled a lot before, now that Marjie was gone, it was ten times as much. I had to stay in constant touch with the sales people, both to motivate them and to reassure them that all was well with the company. We had been working on a new compact design for our Day Radiance make-up foundation. Even before the Slatens left, we had done the required testing to make sure the product and compact were compatible. Now it was finally being shipped to our salespeople.

In a meeting at Chattanooga, Tennessee, I pulled out a new compact filled with product to show the group, and when I opened it, it broke into a dozen pieces in my hand. I was horrified and called Ned immediately. I told him to call both the manufacturer and the product supplier and tell them what happened. This was the kind of thing that could ruin us, and fast at that. You don't show products that fall apart.

The minute I got back to work I went into Ned's office, which was formerly Stan's, and asked if he had taken care of the problem with the Day Radiance. He said he had tried, but the manufacturer of the compact and the product supplier simply blamed each other; neither would accept responsibility for the problem. Then he informed me I would have to handle the problem myself because I had more authority as the CEO of the company.

I got the warehouse crew together, and we checked the huge inventory of the product we had just received from Kolmar, who had filled the container with the product. All of it was defective. Each compact we opened broke apart in our hands, just as the first one had done. Then Ned and I went into his office and checked the invoices for the shipments. We had been billed over $100,000 for totally useless merchandise.

My first call was to Kolmar, the manufacturer of the actual product. He read me the positive results of tests they had run and said the problem had to be from a change made in the composition of the compact after those tests were made.

My next call was to Eugene Paul, president of Motor City Plastics in Detroit. I started by explaining nicely what a catastrophe this was for us. He answered by blaming Kolmar again, and I interrupted and told him they had proof of compatibility. When they had filled the compact used for testing with their product, it was okay at that time. So the problem had to be that the composition of the compact had been changed after that test.

When he started again to argue the point, I had had enough. I raised my voice and said, "STOP RIGHT THERE. We're going to settle this once and for all. I'll be on the next plane that leaves Dallas for Detroit. You meet me at the airport; you will recognize me: I'll be the little short woman with a giant baseball bat in my hand."

"Don't come—don't come," he pleaded. "I'll call Kolmar and we'll work this out."

And they did. This story circulated throughout the industry, and everyone seemed to think it was hilarious, but I wasn't kidding. I was going to go to Detroit, as I'd promised. I just wasn't sure exactly where I would get the baseball bat to take with me.

This incident caused me to think that Ned was not ever going to handle such matters. Soon thereafter, when the salespeople started calling about back orders, I knew he wasn't going to keep up with purchasing either. After the Slatens left, Ned had become the vice president of the company. Apparently, he was taking his new role as an executive to heart, and chose not to handle mundane tasks any longer. Ultimately we hired a chemist for the lab, a purchasing agent, and an office manager to fill the void from Stan's leaving.

Ned took care of the things that Stan had done that had seemed important, such as talking with salesmen and meeting with bankers. As our cash reserves grew, banks began courting us for our business, which included taking Ned to lunch on a regular basis. And to help Ned's self-esteem even more, he and I were paid equal salaries.

For a year I handled sales alone. While we did continue to grow, I felt that I had to have help in order to make the company grow faster. I talked with Saul, and he offered to lend us a young man, Dick Heath, from Tri-Chem to help in sales occasionally. Dick reminded me of Richard Rogers when he was in front of a crowd. He revved up the audience with the marketing plan and sent them racing out the door to work harder. Whenever he joined me after a television presentation, our percentage of recruits from the shows increased dramatically. But the main reason Dick worked out so well was because he fit into our philosophy of working hard but having fun at the same time.

Brad Corrigan, our attorney since the lawsuit with Mary Kay, handled our contract with Tri-Chem. He stated specifically that I was to retain full power as CEO of the company. This turned out to be important because Saul and Tri-Chem were interested primarily in the bottom line, as many people had warned they would be. The idea we'd had in the beginning of enriching the lives of our people was often ignored, so I had to fight for it.

And even though it wasn't easy, we continued with the idea of including families in the business.

Instead of just rewarding the salespeople for meeting their goals, we began including the office staff. As we reached new sales goals, we took the entire staff and their families on periodic trips to dude ranches and at Christmas time to the best restaurants in Dallas. By rewarding them as well as the salespeople when sales increased, they worked even harder to help make that increase happen.

While we still had to deal with explaining our connection to Mary Kay, it was far less than in the beginning. However, the competitive spirit was still there, and even after Mary Kay went public with her stock and was much bigger than we were, we still maintained we were the best. Occasionally, consultants from her company would ask to join us. Sometimes I wondered if they were sent to spy on us, and I later learned that she always had an informant reporting on our every move. I didn't waste time wondering why. I decided that she just couldn't stand not knowing what was going on with us.

Each year as we continued to grow nationwide, we added better incentives, such as trips to exotic places. The first was to Hawaii, and the last one that Ned and I went on was to Paris, France. Included in this one were Dick Heath and his new wife Jinger (who would later take up the torch and carry Beauticontrol's success to even higher ground). As a special treat for Dathene, we also took her along. It was a trip of a lifetime. We arrived in Paris late Christmas day. The streets were lined with trees covered with lights. For most of us it was our first time there, and of course, none of us spoke the language. After sightseeing all day, we congregated in someone's room at night and talked and laughed into the wee hours of the morning.

On New Year's Eve, we took a side trip by train to Geneva, Switzerland. We drank hot chocolate and ate tiny ham sandwiches in small cafes and browsed through the shops as Christmas music filled the air. The next morning when we were all on the train to return to Paris, Dathene was nowhere to be found. I was frantic. We tried to ask for help in locating her, but the residents just shook their heads, indicating they didn't understand what we were saying. So we finally had to leave without her.

The next morning Dathene came dragging in to our hotel in Paris. She had been junk shopping and didn't make it to the train on time. She was distraught because they had put her in a sleeper car with a strange man for the ride back to Paris. Of course we never let her live this down, and every time I saw her over the years, I reminded her again.

The years raced by and before we knew it, it was 1976. Our contract was up with Tri-Chem. The company had grown consistently, and although the final payoff for our stock did not make us wealthy, it did provide some security. Saul offered me another five-year contract to stay on as president, with generous benefits. But they did not offer one to Ned. It was tempting, but deep inside I knew that if I stayed and Ned didn't, there would no longer be harmony in our home. And my family was still second on my list of priorities.

Sharon was out of college and was getting married in June to Brad Lowe, the boy who had given her the promise ring in junior high. Brad had shown up again during their college years and this time came to stay. Because it was a bicentennial year, their wedding colors would be red, white, and blue. We had already had an arched steel bridge constructed to go over the pool. Brad's attendants were members of his college football team, so the bridge had to be strong to hold them all for photographs.

The upcoming wedding meant I would have plenty to keep me busy, if I left Beauticontrol. Besides, in the back of my mind, I was still thinking of returning to college. I was only forty-two, and now that Sharon was out of college, Ned couldn't use the old argument that I couldn't go because I had to support her, as he'd always done before.

Ned insisted that I had to be the one to decide whether to stay or to go from Beauticontrol. I decided it was time to go, but the thought of leaving people that felt like my own family was almost more than I could bear.

My last act as president of the company was to fly the entire office staff and their families to San Antonio for a weekend.

Because it offered activities like horseback-riding and gondola rides, it was a perfect place for families to have a good time. For the last time, we played and laughed together, and at the end we cried together. I still cherish the silver, engraved serving tray they gave us at the end of our trip.

On my last day with the company, I sat in my office and my thoughts turned again to the cold, snowy day in 1963 when I answered a newspaper ad placed by a new company called Mary Kay Cosmetics. I'd been looking for a way to change my life, and that was exactly what I got. From what might seem like an impossible dream to many, I went from being what Mary Kay had called a lowly secretary to president of a company. And even though we started that company from nothing, it had thrived and was now a strong contender in the marketplace.

The years had contained joy and heartbreak, loyalty and betrayal, heady success, depressing failure, and even tragedy. But out of it all, two companies survived that have probably done more than any other to enhance the lives of women worldwide. It was a bumpy trip, but I wouldn't have missed the ride for anything. As Ned would say, "To God be the glory for it all."

CHAPTER TWENTY-FIVE

Full Circle

Marjie was absent from my life for almost twenty years. It was as if the Slatens had dropped into the Grand Canyon. But in the early nineties I heard Stan had terminal cancer. I immediately contacted some of the people from the old Beauti-control days, and most of us wrote letters and made phone calls, telling the Slatens how much we thought of them, hoping to offer what support we could. Finally, the deep freeze that had developed between us, beginning in 1971, began to melt. After Stan's death, Marjie and I reconnected.

From Mexico, they had moved back to New Mexico, their home state, and Marjie went back to counseling in the school system there. When she came to Dallas to visit Anna, we got together and simply picked up where we'd left off.

We decided to take one more trip together. Flying to Vienna, Austria, we rented a car and drove through Austria, Italy, and Switzerland, bantering and laughing just like the old days. Marjie still insisted on doing the driving and, as always, would not use maps. She maintained, just as she had since our early days together, that her great sense of direction was all she needed. Of course, this meant we were lost much of the time, especially in cities like Florence, Italy. Once, when we couldn't find a bed and breakfast where we had reservations, instead of arguing as we did in the old days, I suggested we hire a cab to guide us there. By the trip's end, we had repeated this so many times that I mentioned jokingly that she hadn't changed a bit. I could still read her expressions, and I noticed she considered this statement criticism.

375

After almost three weeks on the road, we arrived in Geneva, Switzerland, to board our flight home. In spite of both of our idiosyncrasies, it had been a wonderful trip. We had visited quaint old Swiss villages in the Alps and seen the artwork of the masters. But as we checked in the rental car and I was getting the last bag out of the trunk, Marjie slammed the lid shut. It hit the back of my head and blood spurted everywhere. The car agency wanted to call an ambulance, but I refused. I had to get home because I had an upcoming appearance scheduled on QVC. And I knew the airline would not let me on the plane if they were aware of such an injury, so we bandaged it as best we could. Marjie apologized all the way home and kept assuring me it was an accident. Of course I knew it was, but I couldn't help enjoying her guilt a little and let her rave on.

From that point on, without Stan's admonitions not to speak to each other, we stayed in touch, often by phone. Soon after the turn of the century, she phoned me with the news that she had developed a lung disease called pulmonary fibrosis. The Mayo Clinic confirmed the diagnosis. She had previously begun a renovation on her old family home in Tinnie, New Mexico, and she vowed she would live to finish it. As we should all do anyway, she now lived one day at a time. I never heard her say, "Why me?" She particularly cherished each day she had with her daughter and grandchildren.

We talked on the phone almost daily; even though she never admitted it, she seemed weaker each time we had a conversation. One day the call I had been dreading came. Her voice was barely audible as she asked if I could come to see her. When I told her I was on my way, she promised she would hold on until I arrived.

Tinnie, New Mexico, was a hard place to get to. I had to take a plane from Dallas to Lubbock, rent a car, and then drive to her house. It was late afternoon when I finally arrived. She had finished fixing up her parents' house after all, and it was wonderful.

She lay in a huge four-poster bed, and at first glance she looked the same. Her hair was still a perfect shade of blonde with no dark roots, and her skin was smooth and free of wrinkles. But when she moved the covers slightly, I could tell her body had shriveled so much it now appeared to be that of a small child. I tried with all my might not to let the horror I felt show on my face.

But other than the way she looked, Marjie was the same. Except her faith had grown amazingly stronger. She told me immediately that she wasn't afraid to die, and I could tell it was true. She also said it hurt her to talk, so she would listen while I talked. I couldn't resist saying, "Well, that will be a first." She laughed, in spite of the look of physical pain on her face.

For two days I tried to do the things for her I knew she liked. I cooked chicken and dumplings and combed the area for pink flowers. When they were nowhere to be found I bought three dozen white roses and put them in one of her mother's antique crystal vases. I could tell she liked them and didn't seem to mind that they weren't pink.

She knew I planned to write a book about our early experiences and asked me to tell her every detail about it. After I finished, she croaked, "I wish I could be here to read it." While I tried to not be emotional in her presence, when I went to my room I cried far into the night.

Finally, it was time to leave for home. After I loaded the car I went to her room for our final good-bye. As I sat down beside her bed, I said, "I do have a question, and I want you to tell me the truth about it."

"What is it?" she asked in surprise.

"When we were in Switzerland, did you slam that trunk lid on my head on purpose?"

Horrified, she answered, "Of course not," but when she saw I was smiling, we had our last good laugh together. And then it became serious. She managed to whisper, "Thank you for coming; I can go now." I pushed back a lock of hair that had fallen onto her face and said that I knew she was ready and that Stan was anxiously awaiting her arrival. She nodded and added one last thing. "I'll look for a house for you in heaven. I know what you like."

And I answered, "As long as it's next door to you, it will be fine."

She closed her eyes as I tiptoed out of the room. I barely remember the drive back to Lubbock. When I turned in the rental car I was surprised to find that it was wet from rain. I hadn't noticed the weather. I had been lost in a world of precious memories.

As I opened the door to my retirement home that was filled with peace and contentment, the telephone was ringing. I wasn't surprised to hear the message. At almost the same time I was opening my door, Marjie was opening the door to hers in heaven. And hers was filled with eternal love.

CHAPTER TWENTY-SIX

Mary Kay

In the mid-nineties, Texas Monthly magazine printed a story about the beginning years of Mary Kay Cosmetics that rehashed the competition with Beauticontrol. I had heard that Mary Kay was having health problems, and on impulse I called her assistant and asked for an appointment to see her. Within minutes, she called back and said Mary Kay would like to see me as soon as possible and we set a time for the meeting.

Mary Kay's executive offices were located off the North Dallas Tollway. I drove there in my gold Lexus SC 300 and glanced around the parking area to see if I could spot her personal Cadillac. When I didn't see anything resembling it, I realized she probably had a private parking garage. The tall, curved office building appeared to be made of rose-colored marble and suited Mary Kay perfectly.

The entire bottom floor appeared to be the reception area. I told the receptionist who I was and she made a quick call; someone would be there for me in a few minutes. While I waited, I asked her if Mary Kay still drove a Cadillac. She looked at me as if I were a mental case and replied, "Oh no, Mary Kay has a chauffeured limousine."

I barely managed not to laugh and thought, Of course she does. What was I thinking?

Suddenly someone tapped me on the shoulder, and I turned to find a well dressed, perfectly made up woman standing beside me. She introduced herself and told me how much she liked my white wool suit and gold accessories. She was a National Director with Mary Kay and said I looked like I should be one, too. I wanted so badly to tell her I was supposed to have been the first one the company ever had, but instead I just thanked her for the compliment as Mary Kay's secretary arrived to take me to her office.

Mary Kay's office literally took up the whole top floor of the building. There were built-in curio cabinets along the walls, and they were filled with gifts that had been given to Mary Kay through the years. Of course, the whole room was decorated in various shades of pink. My mind flashed back to the small, low-key area in Exchange Park where I had first met Mary Kay. Literally speaking, she had traveled a long way from there.

At first, it was a little awkward. I couldn't stop looking at Mary Kay. She had always appeared perfectly groomed, but now her appearance was on a much higher level. I was no spring chicken myself at the time, and I knew she was about twenty years older, yet she still looked great. Her teal colored suit was obviously haute couture and appeared to be straight from Paris. However, I had learned a great deal about applying make-up, and now I fully realized that her face had no contrast. Her wig was still platinum and her skin pale ivory. I caught myself wishing I could do her make-up so she could see how much better she would look. Then I almost laughed at the absurd thought.

She seemed much smaller than I remembered, and I wondered if it was because she had always appeared larger than life to me. She hugged me and told me she was glad to see me. To break the ice, I told her someone tried to recruit me in the reception area. We laughed at that, and as we sat down on one of her sofas, she began her rhetorical speech that sounded like a tape recording about how she built her company. I just looked her in the eye and listened. When she seemed to remember who I was, she stopped abruptly and said, "Tell me about you."

I then explained that the reason I wanted to see her was to tell her that in my opinion she had done more to advance the economic status of women than any other person had in the twentieth century. I could tell she was touched, and from that point on, she was much more like the Mary Kay I remembered and loved. We talked for hours about the early years and how we had to do everything ourselves. We both remembered the exact food we had cooked for the first seminar and the excitement we felt as the company began to grow.

Then her tone changed. She told me about her daughter dying and how terribly she missed her. She also said Richard had left the company. It looked as if no one in the family was interested in working there, although she still had hopes that one day her grandson would be. I could feel her loneliness, and as she talked I couldn't help thinking, *This is a woman who is trapped in her ivory tower.*

Again, she changed the subject and said, "Can I ask you a question?"

"Of course, anything," I answered.

She paused a few seconds and said, "If you had it to do all over again, would you answer my newspaper ad?"

Without hesitation I said, "In a heartbeat, Mary Kay. You showed me a way to accomplish my goals in life." I wanted to ask her if she had it to do over would she simply leave the 2 percent in the marketing plan as they had promised, especially since they ended up putting it back in anyway. But then I realized I didn't even need an answer. I had already decided that if they had, then Beauticontrol would probably have never had a chance and the great wrong that has been done to Dathene's family by taking away their family history would never have been made right.

All at once I realized that I had probably stayed too long and got up to leave. I had brought along the Texas Monthly magazine that contained the recent story with her picture on the front. I asked her to autograph it for me. "I hate that picture and the story about the rivalry between our companies as well."

Then out of the blue she asked me an unusual question. Dick and Jinger Heath headed up Beauticontrol at that time, and Mary Kay asked me if I thought they would be willing to end the conflict between the two companies. After a few seconds of hesitation, remembering how terrible it had been to try to constantly explain the story between the two, I told her I thought they would be happy to let it go and suggested she talk with Dick about it.

Even as I spoke, it occurred to me that she was probably hoping I would do that for her.

The irony of it all was that both companies had dropped the hide tanner's story and changed the formulas of the products, as well as their marketing plans. Yet just as in the story of Jacob and Esau, the conflict between the two companies continues.

Instead of autographing the magazine, she gave me a copy of her new book and autographed it. As I started to walk out the door she gave me a real hug and told me to stop by the "Wall of Fame" on the first floor. She wanted me to see my pictures displayed there. When I looked at her questioningly, she said, "You are an important part of our history."

As I walked toward my car, I glanced up at the top floor. The curtains were drawn back from the window, and I knew Mary Kay was watching. With a heavy heart, I waved to her as tears began to fall. Somehow I knew we had just said good-bye forever.

In thinking about Mary Kay's question about what I would do over, I wished I had said, "If I could do just one thing over, I would try much harder to put God first, family second, and career third." And I wondered if Mary Kay would do the same.

Epilogue

At the beginning of the Centennial, the year 2000, both Beauticontrol and Mary Kay Cosmetics were successful by any standards. Beauticontrol sales were reported to be approximately 100 million dollars a year, and Mary Kay's approximately a billion. Soon after that, Mary Kay's name was reported to be one of the ten best-known names in the entire world. So again, as in the story of Jacob and Esau, God blessed them both; but Mary Kay, like Jacob, was given the Promised Land.

Skip Hollandsworth, the editor of Texas Monthly magazine, said to me, "Beauticontrol got its millions and Mary Kay got her billions. What do you get?"

I answered, "The best of all; I get to tell the story."

Dalene Brewer, Helen McVoy, and Idell Moffett are among those that stayed with Mary Kay and became national directors. Kathy Ray and Shirley Gilder are still with Beauicontrol in top sales management positions. Marjie and Stan's daughter, Sheryl, and her family live in New Mexico.

Many of the people in this story, as Dr. Criswell would put it, are "absent in the body, but present with the Lord," including Mary Kay and Mel Ash, Mary Crowley, Dathene Territo, Stan and Marjie Slaten, Ned Brown, JoAnne Case, Marie (Re Re) Johnson, Ralph Baker, and Nell Davis.

Shannon graduated college with a business degree. She inherited her dad's creative abilities and today designs Web sites. She and her husband live in the Dallas area.

Sharon graduated college with a degree in Elementary Education and still teaches in a middle school in the Dallas area. She has two daughters, Lindsay and Lacy, and twin grandsons, Cade and Colby. She also has two granddaughters, Mattylin, who is our little princess, and Emmylin Pearl. Emmylin was born

June 17, 2010, and named after her Great-Great-Grandmother, Emma Pearl Franks.

And, as for me, I did go back to college after I left Beauticontrol, but only for one semester, because there was to be another company in my future and it would be my very own. I was president of it for thirty years.

In the late 1990s when I finally retired, I was determined to finish my college degree. At this time there were new reports claiming that many of our brain cells die as we age, and that would affect our learning capability. So, with fear and trembling, I enrolled at Texas A&M at Texarkana anyway. I graduated in 2000 with a huge group of young people, who apparently had all of their brain cells still intact.

But then something miraculous happened. I received notification that I had been named to the National Dean's List, which is made up of the top 1 percent of all college students in the nation. I hadn't even known such a list existed, and now I was on it.

My college diploma is front and center on my wall of memorabilia. But the book containing the names and photos of all the people on the National Dean's List is on my coffee table. I keep it there as a reminder that it may take awhile, but God does grant us the desires of our heart.

It is worth mentioning that the reports of brain cells dying were later challenged. Instead, scientists now say that as long as we keep our brains active, the cells remain active as well.

The pot of gold at the end of the rainbow has managed to elude me. But I am rich—in my faith, my family, and my friends.

I am fully aware that I was just a tiny spark that helped to get both Mary Kay and Beauticontrol started, so they could go on to benefit women worldwide. But I take great comfort in the well-known proverb that says, "It is better to light one small candle than to curse the darkness."

LaVergne, TN USA
25 January 2011
213980LV00005B/4/P